THE PENGUIN POETS

THE PENGUIN BOOK OF SPANISH VERSE

J. M. Cohen, born in London in 1903 and a Cambridge graduate, was the translator of many volumes for the Penguin Classics, including versions of Cervantes, Rabelais and Montaigne. For some years he assisted E. V. Rieu in editing the Penguin Classics. He collected the three books of *Comic and Curious Verse* and anthologies of Latin American and Cuban writing. With his son Mark Cohen he also edited the *Penguin Dictionary of Quotations* and the two editions of its companion *Dictionary of Modern Quotations*. He frequently visited Spain and made several visits to Mexico, Cuba and other Spanish American countries.

J. M. Cohen died in 1989. *The Times*' obituary described him as 'one of the last great English men of letters', while the *Independent* wrote that 'his influence will be felt for generations to come'.

THE PENGUIN BOOK OF

SPANISH VERSE

INTRODUCED AND EDITED BY

J. M. COHEN

WITH PLAIN PROSE TRANSLATIONS OF EACH POEM

PENGUIN BOOKS

PENGUIN BOOKS

Published by the Penguin Group
Penguin Books Ltd, 27 Wrights Lane, London W8 5TZ, England
Penguin Books USA Inc., 375 Hudson Street, New York, New York 10014, USA
Penguin Books Australia Ltd, Ringwood, Victoria, Australia
Penguin Books Canada Ltd, 10 Alcorn Avenue, Toronto, Ontario, Canada M4V 3B2
Penguin Books (NZ) Ltd, 182-190 Wairau Road, Auckland 10, New Zealand

Penguin Books Ltd, Registered Offices: Harmondsworth, Middlesex, England

First published 1956
Second edition 1960
Third edition 1988
7 9 10 8

Filmset in Linotron 202 Garamond

Printed and bound in Great Britain by
BPC Wheatons Ltd
A member of
The British Printing Company Ltd

TO MY GRANDDAUGHTER
EMMA,
THIS THIRD EDITION

TABLE OF CONTENTS

*

PART TWO: MODERN TIMES

which he invented his own mythology of angels, to the strict realism of the Civil War. During his exile, he wrote plays, film-scripts and radio plays, and remained a fervent, if eccentric, Communist. In the 60s he moved from Argentina to Italy, and after Franco's death returned to Spain, where he has been politically active but has written little poetry.

LUIS CERNUDA (1904–1962). Born in Seville, he underwent various influences from English, German and French poets before leaving Spain after the Civil War. He spent some years at Glasgow University as a reader and some of his poems of this period are markedly English in tone. After the War he left for Mexico, where after a brief period of happiness he took his own life, leaving a posthumous volume from which the last two poems are taken.

MANUEL ALTOLAGUIRRE (1904–1959), a scrupulous and evocative poet, who wrote little and who left Spain after the Civil War. He was an expert typographer.

JUAN GIL-ALBERT (*b.* 1906), he left Spain after the Civil War but returned and lives in Valencia. He has published a

ACKNOWLEDGEMENTS

OVER the translations of these additional poems I have had great help from Ann Frost, who checked my first versions and discussed with me most carefully emendations and improvements, and, once more, Mavora Forward transformed my tangled text into a clean typescript. This third edition owes much to them both.

INTRODUCTION

NO body of lyrical poetry is so seriously underestimated by British readers as the Spanish. For the majority, Spain is the country of a single prose masterpiece, *Don Quixote*, and of a dramatic literature much praised at home, which has, however, never been successfully translated, let alone presented on the British stage; Lope de Vega, Tirso de Molina, Pedro Calderón de la Barca, are no more than names to those who have not read them in the original. So, indeed, are the Spanish lyrical poets, though with the added disadvantage that here Spain has not the reputation of France or Italy. Nevertheless, during her two grand periods she was certainly the equal, and possibly the superior, of either in this field. These two great flowerings of Spanish poetry, to which this anthology is devoted, lasted, the first for upwards of two centuries, from the beginning of the fifteenth to half-way through the seventeenth, and the second for some fifty years, from the 1880s to the defeat of the Spanish Republic in the Civil War.

The beginnings of Spanish poetry are only gradually emerging from obscurity with the discovery of refrains, written in Arabic or Hebrew characters and tacked on to Arabic or Hebrew poems from the Moorish emirates. From these small evidences some scholars have endeavoured to prove that there was a continuous tradition of poetry, sung as an accompaniment to dancing, extending from late Roman times – when Spanish dancing girls were famous – right through to such pieces as the Marqués de Santillana's *villancico* for his three daughters, a fifteenth-century poem which finds a place in this book. Certainly there is a continuous tendency towards elaboration, and a characteristic choice of imagery in the Spanish poets of Andalusia throughout the ages, which unites them with their Arabic-writing, if not with their Latin-speaking ancestors; there are forms also – the *villancico* with its refrain is one – that are common to the whole Western Mediterranean, Moslem and

Christian alike. The reader of much Spanish poetry will constantly be reminded that the Straits of Gibraltar are narrow, and will find it easy too, even when he comes to the twentieth century, to distinguish between the firm European outline of the Northerner's images and the shimmering extravagances of the Southerner. Africa and Europe fight for the Spanish poet's loyalty; the contrast, even in recent days, between the Biscayan dourness of Unamuno and the kaleidoscopic changes of mood and colour of Juan Ramón Jiménez the Andalusian, between the metaphysical strictness of the Madrileño Pedro Salinas and the complex grandeur of Vicente Aleixandre, the Sevillian, is one of the features that make modern Spanish poetry so colourful and so various. It is the poetry of at least two conflicting Spains; for the old cleavage between the lush Moorish emirates and the barren Christian kingdoms is, in literature at least, still a living reality.

The kingdoms of the north produced their earliest poetry under the influences of France and of the little Atlantic kingdom of Galicia, in the north-west, whose language was, and still remains, closer to Portuguese than to Spanish. The *Poema del Cid*, from which this book contains a few dramatic sections, is an epic of the twelfth century, telling of a hero of the border wars, who was only recently dead when the poem was written. It is in the convention of the *Chanson de Roland*, though it has a certain Spanish realism about it that its French models lack. Spain's first poet to leave us his name, Gonzalo de Berceo, the author of some pleasing tales of the saints, is also patently writing in the French manner, though with a peasant plainness that is all his own. The lyrical poets of the fourteenth century, on the other hand, model themselves closely on the style, and sometimes on the actual language of the Galicians, whose songs were a last offshoot of the Troubadour tradition, carried along the pilgrim road to Galicia's shrine, the tomb of St James at Compostella, after the destruction of Provençal civilization in the Albigensian wars.[1]

Whereas the first lyrics of Spain's great period were Galician in inspiration, the *romances*, or ballads, of the early fifteenth century were rooted in the tradition of the northern epics, whose metres and

[1] These poems belong more properly in a Portuguese anthology than here. There is a good and cheap selection of them, with translations into Castilian facing each poem – the *Florilegio del Cancionero Vaticano* – made by the Argentine poet Francisco Luis Bernárdez, and published by Losada of Buenos Aires.

assonances they follow. Many of them recount incidents from epics which have not survived; some tell of the Cid and his exploits; others of the Seven Princes of Lara; and the first two in this book belong to the cycle of Roderick the Goth, the eighth-century king through whose sin – so the legend ran – the Moors were first brought into Spain. Many of the *romances*, however, dealt with more recent incidents, either from the border wars with the kingdom of Granada, or out of contemporary novels, which told of Charlemagne, of Arthur, Tristram, and Lancelot, and which, as we know from *Don Quixote*, had entirely captured the public imagination in the fifteenth century. These *romances*, most of which survive in several versions, were much collected in the sixteenth century. They will bear comparison with our own Northern ballads, with which they are roughly contemporary, in everything but their air of mystery. Many of the Spanish ballads tell tales of magic, but seldom with the suggestive overtones of our own 'King Estmere'. Doña Alda's dream, or the young princess whose hair covered a whole oak-tree are poetic figments, but in no way mysterious. Yet there are among the *romances* pieces that possess a fortuitous haze of the supernatural which they owe to their very fragmentariness, beginning as they do in the middle of a story – which must have been known to their original audience – and trailing away with the incident only half narrated. The 'Romance del Prisionero' and 'Conde Arnaldos' are poems of this kind.

The fourteenth and fifteenth centuries yield several other treasures, amongst them that astounding miscellany, *El libro de buen amor*, the Spanish counterpart to the *Canterbury Tales* in its creation of characters, though in other ways it is far more like the total assembly of a minstrel's repertory, narrative, song, satire, and rough allegory all nicely strung together on a thread of the imaginative autobiography of a worldly and amorous priest. Other considerable figures of this time are Juan de Mena, the author of a long didactic poem *El laberinto de la fortuna*, which attempts to follow Italian models, and from which it is impossible to make a fitting anthology extract, and the Marqués de Santillana, who also endeavoured to naturalize the Italian style. But he collected some of the old song-books from Galicia as well, and it is by a mere handful of perfect lyrics written in the old forms that his name survives. With him the great epoch of Spanish poetry begins, to be continued by Jorge Manrique, whose verses in memory of his father, with their solemn and soberly northern celebration of death and its victories, is one of the lyrical masterpieces of all time, comparable to the best of Dunbar or Villon, who were the contemporaries of this master of a single poem.

The successful introduction of Italian themes and measures by Boscán and his greater friend Garcilaso de la Vega, early in the sixteenth century, carried Spanish poetry to new heights. The impact of the Petrarchan style, as Garcilaso found it practised in the Italy of his day, was this time immediate; it is as if our own earliest Renaissance poet, Sir Thomas Wyatt, had possessed the power and musical mastery of Edmund Spenser. Spain's first poet in this tradition was also her greatest. Nevertheless, there was in Spain no such abrupt break with medieval themes or forms as there was in England or in France. For a while a group of poets, of whom Cristóbal de Castillejo was the chief, resisted these Italianate innovations. Moreover, the popularity of the *romances* and *villancicos* was such that seventeenth-century poets continued to write them, though sometimes in very sophisticated forms.

If one looks for a parallel to Garcilaso's First Eclogue, one may think of Spenser's 'Prothalamion' – for its first refrain is similarly haunting – or of 'Il Penseroso'; that is the measure of this young Spanish soldier who, by a miracle, found in the Platonic convention a medium to fit his life experience. For the recurrent theme of this Italian poetry, in its last and most musical phase, was the loss of love, and Garcilaso's mind was scarred by his failure to win a Portuguese lady-in-waiting, Doña Isabel Freire, a loss which drove him to banishment, to rashness, and to an early death on an insignificant battlefield.

With Fernando de Herrera, these Renaissance forms take on a garish glitter; what had been gold is now brass; and echoes of Biblical language reinforce the pastoral and latinized vocabulary of Garcilaso. Herrera plangently celebrates Spain's new-won greatness under Charles V and Philip II. Echoes from the Book of Kings stress the Spaniards' role as the new *chosen people.* For modern readers, however, it is not this Sevillian 'state poet', but two monks from the north, the first philosophical, the second mystical, that make Spain's *siglo de oro* a golden age of lyrical poetry. Luis de León modelled himself on Horace and Virgil, both of whom he translated; San Juan de la Cruz transformed Garcilaso's imagery *a lo divino* – into metaphysical terms – the soul longed for her Master as the shepherd for his mistress – and this with some reminiscences of *The Song of Songs*, whence this metaphor had originally derived. Both these poets convey an exalted experience in language absolutely fitted to it, Luis de León's severe, as suited his lower vision and his longing for rest and release, Juan de la Cruz's more plastic, lyrical, and ecstatic, in keeping with the rare height to which his soul ascended. One may compare Luis de León to the Milton of the 'Nativity Ode', but for Juan de la Cruz we have no parallel. It is as if the insight of Vaughan's rarest moments were hymned by the Shelley of the 'Ode to the Skylark'.

In the final quarter of the sixteenth century Spanish poetry proliferated; the age of gold – and of brass – was succeeded by an epoch of highly chiselled silver. Horatian directness and restraint, Andalusian subtlety, exercises in elaborate Italian styles from the school of Granada, lyrics like snatches of folk-song, lapidary sonnets, snarling satire, pieties and indelicacies alike twisted into the form of punning nursery rhymes, sophisticated *romances*, fables in which ancient legends were incrusted with the semi-precious stones of modern allusion; all these, together with solemn moralizings at the expense of a corrupt court and a decaying nation, made up what was essentially a court poetry of immense accomplishment.

The greatest creators in this age of magnificent decadence were the dramatists Lope de Vega and Calderón, and the poets Luis de Góngora and Francisco Quevedo. Lope, both as dramatist and poet, represented moderation, and a logical development from the Renaissance tradition; his sacred sonnets, perhaps his supreme achievement among a great deal of lyrical poetry, have been treasured among the masterpieces ever since his own day; and his songs, only recently gathered from his tremendous output of plays, seem to-day, as they must have seemed then, masterpieces as unforced as folk-songs. There is much about them to remind one of Shakespeare's songs. Góngora and Quevedo, however, were poets so much of their own age that, like Donne or Crashaw, they fell into neglect after their deaths, and were not adequately revalued until some twenty-five years ago. Tricks of antithesis and parallelism, a narrow and conventionalized range of imagery and a highly latinized vocabulary, interspersed with deliberately cultivated cant-phrases, a Ciceronian syntax, and an elaborate use of sustained metaphors and conceits: all these distinguish their poetry from that of any other age or country. Góngorism, once a term of abuse, has now come simply to denote this elaborate technique, depending on metaphors often at one remove, by which, for example, a feather or a drop of wax, as in Trillo y Figueroa's sonnet in this book, inevitably refer to Icarus's false wings and his fall into the ocean, mention of which – the middle term – is omitted by the poet. While Góngora's name is associated with this form of writing, Quevedo's is connected rather with that other feature of Baroque complexity, the conceit. But the *cultismo* of Góngora and the *conceptismo* of Quevedo – the Latinism and the elaborate metaphor – are not opposites; they can often be found together in the same poem.

While Góngora and Quevedo carried the grand style of Herrera to consummate extremes, many other types of poetry were being written in Spain. Elaborate Andalusian craftsmanship did not exclusively sway the fashion. The brothers Argensola, men of Aragon who owed a strong debt to Luis de León, and through him to Horace, and the restrained and classical Francisco de Medrano, a Horation also, strove by example, and sometimes by abusive attacks, to hold their country's poetry back from too fatal a plunge into the morass of the *culto* style. There were, indeed, many Malherbes to set the example, though some of them at times committed the very sins they preached against. But there came no Boileau to codify the classical rules and establish an approved vocabulary, and no Roi Soleil to impose Augustan order on the declining civilization of Spain. The age of Góngora abounded in magnificent writing; it ended in exhaustion.

Spanish poetry of the late seventeenth century and of the eighteenth is not very interesting, and that of the early nineteenth contains nothing that was not done better in France, in Britain, or in Italy. I have therefore devoted the limited space of my single volume to Spain's great periods only, and jumped from the lesser contemporaries of Calderón to the mid-nineteenth century and to the poetry of a man and a woman each of whom distilled a melancholy that was individual and uncompromising, and that is still to-day strangely moving. Gustavo Adolfo Bécquer and Rosalía Castro were the first poets in the Spain of last century to write out of passionate and painful experience. Bécquer, a Sevillian, wrote of thwarted love, of the pains of living on with a memory, and of death as a consummation and a release. He used no romantic rhetoric and substituted assonance for rhyme; he did not permit his words to take on poetic associations, but used them roughly, somewhat in the manner of Thomas Hardy. He did not allow himself more than a single mood, and here he recalls the Heine of the poems written from his 'mattress-grave'.

Rosalía Castro was a Galician who wrote chiefly in her native dialect. Her poems portray a landscape of rocks and wide river estuaries, of barren hills and empty skies, in keeping with her moods. But she translated more of her native province into her poetry than its landscapes; she used its folk-songs as her models, and so linked modern Spanish poetry up once more with the traditional Galician forms that had nourished it in the fourteenth and fifteenth centuries. The old song-books were unknown to her. They had never been printed, and the manuscripts were lying forgotten on library shelves. But by returning to the songs of the villagers, she pointed a way for later poets, and after her no considerable Spanish figure followed the road of urban romanticism. In contrast to that of other countries, modern Spanish poetry has remained organically at one with a tradition, the medieval or seventeenth-century shape of which can readily be detected beneath its contemporary dress.

The next generation of Spanish poets, however, those of the nineties, were disciples of the French parnassians and symbolists; and their chief, Rubén Darío, a Central American by birth and a cosmopolitan, was far from valuing the traditional qualities of the literature to which his vigour brought new life. He envisaged, in fact, not a development of what was specifically Spanish, but a broadening of what he thought of as modernism, which was to be the international style of all the Spanish-speaking republics. Already poetry was being written in Mexico and Colombia, in Peru and Cuba, poetry less Spanish and more French in form even than Darío's. Soon independent literatures were to spring up in all the South American states.

The immediate reaction to this growing internationalism, and to Spain's defeat in the war of '98 with the U.S.A., was a rebirth of Spanish traditionalism. Antonio Machado's poetry is the poetry of Castile, a harsh country which suited his intellectual stoicism as well as the rocks and mists and skies of Galicia had responded to Rosalía Castro's melancholy. At the same time Juan Ramón Jiménez revived the shimmering poetry of Andalusia, which had been dormant since the age of Góngora; and hand in hand with this revival of poetry went a revival of scholarship. The old poets were re-discovered and re-edited, and Góngora – although not all his contemporaries – was once more in currency by the twenties of the present century. The poets of that decade were various, but on the whole closer to the Andalusian style than to the northern. García Lorca, the most assured of them, wrote of gipsies and bullfighters, of death and of maidens, of the Civil Guard and the images in the churches as figures in a kind of Baroque frieze of his own composition. His imagery is often tinsel imagery, as that of José de Valdivielso, for instance, had been in the seventeenth century, but the music of his words and his link with tradition made his 'Romancero gitano' into a popular poetry, beloved by the soldiers in the Civil War. It is in fact, however, as artificial as the *romances* of Góngora, which enjoyed their hour of popularity too, and it is probably by his grand elegy on the death of his friend the bullfighter Sánchez Mejías that Lorca's name will eventually survive.

Of Lorca's contemporaries Rafael Alberti, a more intellectual poet, accepted the influences of Góngora and of surrealism, and advanced to create his own world, peopled by angels half peasant, half platonic idea. Now, from exile, he writes with delicate detail of the Spanish past and the cruder Argentinian present. He seems in his last work to be feeling out towards a new myth of the American shore and its rivers.

Jorge Guillén, a slightly older poet, translated Valéry, and learnt from him and from Juan Ramón Jiménez to write of mists and sudden flashes, the poetry of the isolated moment of vision. Pedro Salinas, on the other hand, inhabited a more abstract and misty country, in which the poet seemed to confront himself as a stranger.

The murder of Lorca by Franco sympathizers and the outbreak of the Civil War put an end to this second period of Spain's poetic greatness. Spanish America, which had once more come to look on the motherland as a leader, looked hastily in other directions. By the end of that war all Spain's principal poets were dead or silenced, in prison or in exile; the metropolis of Spanish poetry was now Mexico; its chief publishers were in Buenos Aires.

A revival in Mexican poetry had begun with the revolution of 1917. For the first time poets – and painters – turned to their own country with its own tradition, part Castilian and Moorish, part Aztec. Mexico's first considerable poet, Enrique González Martínez, a purist and an enemy to Darío's rhetoric, stood a little aside from the new tendencies; and it was Ramón López Velarde who first wrote of the Mexico of the coloured man, a theme from which such later poets as Octavio Paz partially departed to follow and absorb French – but not Spanish – influences. In Peru César Vallejo wrote of the villages in a similar manner to Velarde's, but with a political indignation that grew so violent as to drive him into exile in Europe, where he lost his character of a native poet, and wrote shrilly in a cosmopolitan style. In Cuba Nicolás Guillén composed Negro poetry, also radical in tone, in which he seems only fortuitously to have made use of the Spanish language. In Argentina, Ricardo Molinari, without political bias, wrote as an exile from a Europe that he had known long ago as a guest, in language deeply influenced by the Spanish seventeenth century.

It is hard to say what has happened to the Spanish tradition in the last fifteen years. In Spain much poetry is being written, a great deal of it on religious subjects and all of it of a somewhat minor purity, while in Spanish America nothing new seems to be emerging. There, as elsewhere, the best comes from men of fifty or over; and there, too, the accent is on criticism rather than on creation. Indeed, the conflicting polemics of the friends and foes of the Chilean poet Pablo Neruda seem to be shouting down such native talents as find their way into print in the periodicals. Neruda has set out to write the poetry of South America, to make himself its Whitman. In some sections of his gigantic *Canto general* he succeeds in conveying not only a faithful portrait of his rain-soaked country with its surrealist lichens, its worked out mines, and its scarred rocks, but something of its history. At times he calls to life the Araucanian tribesmen and the Spanish adventurers who conquered them; at other times, however, he is content to shout Communist slogans at Chile's oppressors, and to paint martyrs' haloes of rhetoric around its heroes' left-turned heads. He is, nevertheless, at his best, one of the most important and the most powerful poets writing to-day, one who has absorbed all the European influences, which rather dangerously circulate in the South American capitals, and gone forward to genuine creation.

The prose translations on each facing page aim at no literary merit; they are intended purely as aids to the reading of the Spanish. In printing the original poems I have adhered to the practice of semi-modernized spelling followed by Dámaso Alonso in his anthology of medieval poetry, *Poesía de la Edad Media*, for everything up to the Renaissance; after that I have used completely modern spelling except for a few words which seem usually to be printed in their seventeenth-century forms (*escuro* for *oscuro*, *agora* for *ahora*). In certain modern poems also, I have followed the poet's orthography where it differs from the common convention.

I have, on the whole, refrained from cutting poems, but have ventured to give extracts from the *Poema del Cid* and *El libro de buen amor*, which will, I hope, read well, even in isolation.

In one or two poems of the late seventeenth century, there are passages where I am not sure that I have caught the meaning. Some of these uncertainties probably arise from corrupt texts; the minor Gongorists have not yet, for the most part, been properly edited. Others may merely be due to my failure to catch the point of some word-play or contrived ambiguity. This seems to me no good reason for omitting a fine poem, the music and imagery of which will carry a reader over such slight difficulties as arise in the reading of Baroque poetry in any language.

This book owes a great deal to friends, first to Ricardo Molinari, to whom it is dedicated, for guidance in selections, and for much conversation and correspondence on the subject of poetry; also to Rafael Alberti for several conversations in Buenos Aires. Among English friends, I am grateful to Professor J. B. Trend and to Professor E. M. Wilson for answering my questions on various points of interpretation, to J. L. Gili for getting me some necessary books, to H. L. Livermore and the Hispanic Council for the use of their library, and to Señor Xavier de Salas and the Instituto de España for similar favours, also to Miss Helen Matthew for reading and checking my typescript, and setting me right in a number of places, and to Mrs Tatyana Schmoller for a final and most thorough proof-reading.

J.M.C.

London, October 1954

INTRODUCTION TO THE SECOND EDITION

IN the five years since the completion of this anthology I have grown increasingly aware of my failure properly to appreciate the new poetry which was beginning to be written in Spain at the time when I was making my choices. Moreover, in the interval yet more new poets have emerged who deserve representation. A poetry of resistance, for the most part not overtly political, has begun to call for freedom of speech and belief, and for an end of the repression and intellectual stagnation of the dictatorship. A parallel can be drawn with the renaissance of French poetry under the German occupation, and of Italian in the last years of Mussolini. I have therefore added a final section in which the best of the new poets appear, and have included in it two recent pieces by the spiritual godfather of the new movement, Vicente Aleixandre, to whom I did not do justice in my first edition. I have added nothing new from Spanish America, having found nothing of the first importance in these last years.

In revising this book, and setting right quite a few errors in translation, I have taken advantage of the many points made by scholars and critics in reviewing the first edition. But I owe a particular debt to Professor E. M. Wilson and Mrs Helen Grant, who performed the more than friendly service of checking a number of the most difficult poems and commenting on my versions of them. In almost every case I have adopted their suggestions, and I now hope that the book is reasonably free from inaccuracies both of text and translation.

J.M.C.

London, September 1959

INTRODUCTION TO THE THIRD EDITION

THE second edition of this anthology in 1959 included half a dozen young poets of the post-war era. But the book's chief accent was on the Spanish Americans. Now, however, twenty-five years later, it has been possible to present a fair body of poetry from the intellectual opposition of the last Franco years and a number of poets of the democratic revival. Older poets who have returned to Spain are represented by their recent poetry, and the great survivor of the Lorca generation, the Nobel Prize winner Vicente Aleixandre and the long-exiled Jorge Guillén are given more space, the former for one earlier poem, which should have appeared in 1959, and four short pieces from the work of his magnificent old age. For the rest, the poets first included in 1959 now receive more space and a number of new names appear, including Juan Gil-Albert, whose work I had not seen in 1959. Luis Cernuda also, who died in exile, has two poems here from his posthumous collection.

But in 1986 it is possible to celebrate a new era in Spanish Poetry, which is now more closely related to the European tradition than were the poets of the 20s. Several of those who appear have spent some years abroad in teaching posts in British, American or German universities. One sees the impact of the British Romantics on Rodriguez, Brines and Sahagun, of a wide reading from Cavafy to the great Peruvian poet César Vallejo on Valente, and of the Pound and Eliot tradition on the poets of the 70s. The rhetorical weaknesses of much 20th-century Spanish poetry are yielding to a greater conciseness combined at times with a hermetism characteristic of contemporaries in the U.S.A. and Western Europe.

To make room for some fifty new poems, almost all written since 1959, the Spanish American poets of the second edition have been excluded, though with one exception. This is Rubén Darío, who, though a Central American, appears in most Spanish anthologies, since his place in the Spanish tradition is too strong for him to be passed over. Three-quarters of a century ago he was the one modern Spanish poet widely read in Spain and well known abroad. Without him the chain of Spanish poets would lack a vital link.

For help and advice with my selection I am grateful to Helen Grant of Cambridge; the late Vicente Aleixandre and Carlos Bousoño in Madrid; D. J. Lyon of Bristol; and Antonio Masoliver, who, at the publishers' request, before I began work on this third edition, prepared a list of proposed exclusions and additions. In a dozen cases I find myself in agreement with him, but more often, while respecting his point of view, I make different choices of both poets and poems. But two anthologists could hardly be in complete agreement.

J.M.C.

Pangbourne, January 1986

PART ONE

TO THE END OF THE SEVENTEENTH CENTURY

The Cid's Farewell to his Wife and Daughters, whom he Leaves under the Protection of the Monastery of Cardeña

WHEN the prayer was done, and they had finished the Mass, they came out of the church and made ready to ride away. The Cid went to Doña Jimena and embraced her, and Doña Jimena then kissed the Cid's hand. Her eyes were so full of tears that she knew not how to stop. He turned to the daughters and gazed (hard) at them:

'I entrust you to God, and to the holy Abbot: now we leave one another. God knows when we meet again.' His eyes were so full of tears that you never saw the like, and thus they leave one another, as the nail leaves the flesh.

My Cid with his vassals was ready to ride away. He turns his head as he goes, to see if they all are coming. Minaya Álvar Fáñez spoke with great joy: 'Cid, where is your courage? Lucky the hour your mother bore you! Enough of this. Let us go on our way. All our troubles will turn to joy yet; God, who gave us our souls, will will us counsel . . .'

Then they slackened their reins and began to ride off; the time is coming close when they must leave the kingdom.

The Last Night that the Cid Sleeps in Castile. An Angel Consoles the Exile

MY Cid lay down to sleep as soon as it was night; so soundly did he sleep that he had a sweet dream. The angel Gabriel came to him in a vision: 'Ride on, my Cid the good (and) Mighty-in-battle, (said he) for never did any warrior ride out in so lucky an hour; so long as you live everything will go well with you.' When the Cid awoke, he made the sign of the cross over his face.

del CANTAR DE MÍO CID

Adiós del Cid a su mujer e hijas, confiadas al monasterio de Cardeña

LA oración fecha, · la missa acabada la han,
salieron de la eglesia, · ya quieren cavalgar.
El Cid a doña Ximena · ívala abraçar;
doña Ximena al Cid la manol' va besar,
llorando de los ojos, · que non sabe qué se far.
E él a las ijas · tornólas a catar:

«A Dios vos acomiendo · e al Padre spiritual;
agora nos partimos; · ¡Dios sabe el ajuntar!»
Llorando de los ojos, · que non vidiestes atal,
assís parten unos d'otros · commo la uña de la carne.

Mío Cid con los sos vassallos · penssó de cavalgar,
a todos esperando, · la cabeça tornando va.
A tan grand sabor · fabló Minaya Álbar Fáñez:
«Cid, ¿dó son vuestros esfuerços? · en buena ora nasquiestes de madre;
pensemos de ir nuestra vía, · esto sea de vagar.
Aun todos estos duelos · en gozo se tornarán;
Dios que nos dio las almas, · consejo nos dará . . .»

Soltaron las riendas, · pienssan de andar;
çerca viene el plazo · por el reino quitar.

Última noche que el Cid duerme en Castilla. Un ángel consuela al desterrado

I se echava mío Cid · después que fue çenado,
un sueñol' priso dulçe · ¡tan bien se adurmió!
El ángel Gabriel · a él vino en sueño:
«Cavalgad, Cid · el buen Campeador,
ca nunqua en tan buen punto · cavalgó varón;
mientra que visquiéredes · bien se fará lo to.»
Cuando despertó el Cid, la cara se sanctigó.

The Cid Camps on the Frontier of Castile

HE made the sign (of the cross) over his face, then commended himself to God; he was very pleased with the dream that he had dreamed. Next day, in the morning, they began to ride away; this is the last day granted him (by the King), one day remained and no more.

The Cid, who is Besieged in Alcocer, Comes Out to Battle with his Besiegers. Pedro Bermúdez Strikes the first Blows

THEY threw open the gates and rushed outside; when the Moorish sentinels saw them they turned back to the camp. What a bustle there is among the Moors! They all began to arm; beneath the clatter of their drums the earth seems about to crack. You would have seen the Moors arming, and hastily falling into line. On the Moorish side there are two principal banners, and the common pennons, who could count them? The Moorish battle formations are already moving forward to engage with my Cid and his men.

'Keep your ground, my men (says he), here in this place. Let no one break ranks (to attack) until I command him to.' That man Pedro Bermúdez could not endure this: he holds the banner in his hand, and begins to spur (his horse). 'May the Lord come to your help (he cries), loyal Cid the Mighty-in-battle! I am going to plant your banner in their main line of battle. You men whose duty it is, I shall see how you rush to defend it!' Said the Mighty-in-battle: 'Do not do that, for mercy's sake!' Pedro Bermúdez answered: 'I will not hold back for anything in the world!' He spurred his steed forward and rode into their main ranks. The Moors meet him in battle, to gain the standard. They deal him great blows, but they cannot throw him down. Said the Mighty-in-battle: 'Defend him, for mercy's sake!'

El Cid acampa en la frontera de Castilla

SINAVA la cara, · a Dios se fo acomendar,
mucho era pagado · del sueño que sonada ha.
Otro día mañana · pienssan de cavalgar;
es' día ha de plazo, · sepades que non más.

El Cid, cercado en Alcocer, sale a luchar con sus sitiadores.
Pedro Bermúdez hiere los primeros golpes

ABRIERON las puertas, · fuera un salto dan;
viéronlo las arrobdas de los moros, · al almofalla se van
tornar;
¡Qué priessa va en los moros! · e tornáronse a armar;
ante roído de atamores · la tierra querié quebrar;
veriedes armarse moros, · apriessa entrar en az.
De parte de los moros · dos señas ha cabdales,
e los pendones mezclados, · ¿quí los podrié contar?
Las azes de los moros · yas' mueven adelant,
por a mío Cid e a los sos · a manos los tomar.
«Quedas seed, mesnadas, · aquí en este logar,
non derranche ninguno · fata que yo lo mande».
Aquel Pero Vermúez · non lo pudo endurar,
la seña tiene en mano, · compeço de espolonar:
«¡El Criador vos vala, · Cid Campeador leal!
Vo meter la vuestra seña · en aquella mayor az;
los que el debdo avedes · veremos commo la acorrades»
Dixo el Campeador: «¡Non sea, por caridad!»
Respuso Pero Vermúez: «¡Non rastará por ál!»
Espolonó el cavallo · e metiól' en el mayor az.
Moros le reciben · por la seña ganar,
danle grandes colpes, · mas nol' pueden falssar.
Dixo el Campeador: «¡Valelde, por caridad!»

The Cid's Men Attack, to Rescue Pedro Bermúdez

THEY grasp their shields in front of their chests. They couch their lances, each one with its pennant round it; and they bent their heads over their saddle-bows, and went (out) to attack them with stout hearts.

In a loud voice he cried, who was born in a lucky hour: 'Strike at them, my knights, for the Creator's sake! I am Ruy Díaz, the Cid of Vivar, the Mighty-in-battle!'

They all fall on the ranks where Pedro Bermúdez is. They are three hundred lances, and each one has a pennon; each one kills a Moor, each with a single blow; and as they turn back as many more are (struck) dead.

They Destroy the Enemy Ranks

YOU would have seen so many lances lowered and raised, so many shields pierced and torn, so many coats of mail cut and broken, so many white pennons that came out red with blood, so many fine steeds going on without their riders. The Moors call on Mahomet, and the Christians on Saint James.

There fell on the field, in a very small space, quite one thousand three hundred dead Moors.

The Virgin's Lament

(The Jews, sent by Pilate, go to guard the tomb of Christ. The watchmen's song.)

THEY returned to the tomb, clad in coats of mail, uttering many foul insults, and singing (impromptu) songs that were not worth a farthing (lit. not worth three figs), (and) playing musical instruments: zithers, small harps, and three-stringed rebecks.

Los del Cid acometen para socorrer a Pedro Bermúdez

EMBRAÇAN los escudos · delant los coraçones,
abaxan las lanças, · abueltas de los pendones,
enclinaron las caras · de suso de los arzones,
ívanlos ferir · de fuertes coraçones.

A grandes vozes llama · el que en buen ora nasco:
«¡Feridlos, cavalleros, · por amor del Criador!
¡Yo só Ruy Díaz, de Bivar · el Cid Compeador!»

Todos fieren en el az · do está Pero Vermúez.
Trezientas lanças son, · todos tienen pendones;
seños moros mataron, · todos de seños colpes;
a la tornada que fazen · otros tantos muertos son.

Destrozan las haces enemigas

VERIEDES tantas lanças · premer e alçar,
tanta adágara · foradar e passar,
tanta loriga · falssar e desmanchar,
tantos pendones blancos · salir vermejos en sangre,
tantos buenos cavallos · sin sos dueños andar.
Los moros llaman Mafómat · e los cristianos sancti Yagüe.

Cayén por el campo · en un poco de logar
moros muertos · mill e trezientos ya.

GONZALO DE BERCEO

Duelo de la Virgen

(Van los judíos, enviados por Pilatos, a guardar el sepulchro de Cristo. Canción de vela.)

TORNARON al sepulchro vestidos de lorigas,
diciendo de sus bocas muchas sucias nemigas,
controbando cantares que no valían tres figas,
tocando instrumentos, cedras, rotas e gigas.

The rascals were singing rhymed songs, which were bitter and most cruel to His mother: 'Oh band of Jews, let us keep watch, let us take good care. If we do not, they will make a scoff and a mockery of us.'

Song

MIND, watch out! Mind, watch out! Mind, watch out!

Watch, Oh band of Jews – Mind, watch out! – so that they do not steal the Son of God from you. Mind, watch out!

For they will try to steal him from you – Mind, watch out! – Andrew and Peter and John. Mind, watch out!

You will not get enough peace – Mind, watch out! – to come out from beneath the stone. Mind, watch out!

They are all (such) mangy thieves – Mind, watch out! – that they are watching through the latch. Mind, watch out!

That talkative tongue of yours – Mind, watch out! – has got you into trouble. Mind, watch out!

They are a higgledy-piggledy lot – Mind, watch out! – (a) mixed (collection of) strays. Mind, watch out!

Cantaban los trufanes unas controvaduras
que eran a su Madre amargas e muy duras:
«Aljama, nos velemos, andemos en corduras,
si non, farán de nos escarnio e gahurras.»

Cántica

¡Eya velar, eya velar, eya velar!

VELAT aljama de los judíos
¡eya velar!
que non vos furten el Fijo de Dios.
¡Eya velar!

Ca furtárvoslo querrán
¡eya velar!
Andrés e Peidro et Johan.
¡Eya velar!

Non sabedes tanto descanto,
¡eya velar!
que salgades de so el canto.
¡Eya velar!

Todos son ladronciellos,
¡eya velar!
que assechan por los pestiellos.
¡Eya velar!

Vuestra lengua tan palabrera,
¡eya velar!
havos dado mala çarrera.
¡Eya velar!

Todos son omnes plegadizos,
¡eya velar!
rioaduchos mescladizos.
¡Eya velar!

Your careless tongue – Mind, watch out! – has brought you to a bad end. Mind, watch out!

You do not know enough tricks – Mind, watch out! – to get out of prison. Mind, watch out!

You have not got enough sense – Mind, watch out! – to get out by the end of this year. Mind, watch out!

Thomas and Matthew – Mind, watch out! – are very anxious to steal him. Mind, watch out!

The disciple sold him – Mind, watch out! – the Master could not understand it. Mind, watch out!

Don Philip, Simon, and Judas – Mind, watch out! – are looking for help to steal him. Mind, watch out!

If they want to do the job – Mind, watch out! – now is the day to turn up. Mind, watch out!

Mind, watch out! Mind, watch out! Mind, watch out!

As they joked and made their lying boasts (saying) most unseemly things and great villainies, the King of Heaven was grieved by all the nonsense they spoke about Christ and his company.

Vuestra lengua sin recabdo,
 ¡eya velar!
por malcabo vos ha echado.
 ¡Eya velar!

Non sabedes tanto de engaño,
 ¡eya velar!
que salgades de la prisión.
 ¡Eya velar!

Non sabedes tanta razón,
 ¡eya velar!
que salgades ende este año.
 ¡Eya velar!

Tomaseio e Matheo,
 ¡eya velar!
de furtarlo han gran deseo.
 ¡Eya velar!

El discípulo lo vendió,
 ¡eya velar!
el Maestro non lo entendió.
 ¡Eya velar!

Don Philipo, Simón e Judas,
 ¡eya velar!
por furtar buscan ayudas,
 ¡Eya velar!

Si lo quieren acometer,
 ¡eya velar!
¡oy es día de parescer!
 ¡Eya velar!
¡Eya velar, eya velar, eya velar!

Mientre ellos triscaban, dicían sus truferías,
cosas muy desapuestas, grandes alevosías,
pesó al Rey del cielo de tan grandes follías
cuomo decían de Cristo e de sus compañías.

Don Melón Entrusts his Suit to an old Procuress

I SOUGHT out Dame Trot-the-convents, as Cupid told me to. Of all the mistresses (of the trade) I had picked the best. Thanks to God and my good fortune, which was my guide, I struck the shop of a good broker!

I found an old woman such as I needed, a cunning one, a mistress (of the art) and a very knowledgeable (dame); the lady Venus could not have done as much for Pamphilus as that woman did to please me.

She was an old pedlar of the kind who sell jewels; they lay the noose, they dig the traps. There are no such Troy-wreckers as those old procuresses; they deal the finishing blow. Listen, if you have ears.

She said that the lady was an old acquaintance of hers. I said to her: 'For God's sake, friend, look out for storms.' She said: 'Since she has been married, be sure she'll have no compunction. For there is no pack-mule that won't take panniers.'

In face of Doña Endrina's resistance, Trot-the-convents marshals good arguments to convince her

MY broken-down old crow began her incantations: 'When your late husband, God rest his soul, sat in this doorway, he overshadowed the houses and shed light on the whole street. But a house with no man in it doesn't count for much.

'So there you are, my girl, a marriageable widow, alone and companionless, like the turtle-dove. I think that is why you are sallow and thin. For where there is nothing but women, there's never a lack of wrangling.

'God has (always) blest the house where the good man rules. There is always feasting, joy, and pleasure there. That is why I should like such a bridegroom for you. You would see the improvement before many days had passed.'

JUAN RUIZ, ARCIPRESTE DE HITA
del *LIBRO DE BUEN AMOR*

Encomienda don Melón sus amores a una vieja tercera

BUSQUÉ Trotaconventos cual me mandó el amor.
De todas las maestras escogí la mejor.
¡Dios e la ventura que me fue guiador!:
acerté en la tienda del sabio corredor.

Fallé una vieja cual avía menester,
artera e maestra e de mucho saber;
doña Venus por Pánfilo non pudo más fazer
de cuanto fizo aquésta por me fazer plazer.

Era vieja buhona destas que venden joyas;
éstas echan el laço, éstas cavan las foyas.
Non hay tales maestras como estas viejas troyas;
éstas dan la maçada: si has orejas, oyas. . . .

Dixome que esta dueña era bien su conoscienta.
Yol' dixe: «Por Dios, amiga, guardatvos de sobervienta.»
Ella diz': «Pues fue casada, creed que no se arrepienta,
que non hay mula de alvarda que la troxa non consienta» . . .

Vista la firmeza de doña Endrina, Trotaconventos la va convenciendo con buenas razones

COMENÇÓ su escanto la vieja coitral:
«Cuando el que buen siglo aya seía en este portal,
daba sombra a las casas e reluzié la cal';
mas do non mora ome, la case poca val.

Así estades, fija, biuda e mancebilla,
sola e sin compañero como la tortolilla:
deso creo que estades amariella e magrilla,
que do son todas mugeres nunca mengua renzilla.

Dios bendixo la casa do el buen ome cría,
siempre han gasajado, plazer e alegría;
por ende tal mancebillo para vos lo querría,
ante de muchos días veriedes la mejoría.»

The lady replied to her, saying: 'It would not be right for me to marry for a year. It isn't becoming in a widow to marry until the mourning that she wears is a year old: for that obligation goes with mourning.

'If I were to marry earlier, I should get a bad name (and) I should lose the legacy that has been left me, (and) I should not be as much respected by my second husband, and I should be in a position that I could not bear for long.'

'Girl,' said the old woman, 'the year is up already. Take this suitor for your husband and your bridegroom. Let us go to him, let us talk to him, and let us keep it secret. Your fates have brought you good fortune indeed.

'What good do you get from wearing (that) black cloth, and walking about so bashfully and as such a laughing-stock? Lady, give up your grief, and celebrate the year's end; the swallow has never offered better advice this twelvemonth.

'Coarse cloth for a bad master, rough brown for a bad husband, is the proper clothing for gentlemen and ladies; but they should wear it little and not make too much display of it. Much pleasure and little grief is every man's desire.'

Doña Endrina replied: 'Enough, I should not dare to do what you say, or what he may want. Recite no more of this litany to me now. Do not press me so hard out of hand, on the first day!'

Of the Characteristics of Small Ladies

I SHOULD like to cut my preaching short for you, since I have done well with short sermons, short ladies, and short arguments. For what is small and well-put sticks in the heart.

People laugh at a great talker, and a great laugher is a madman; in a short woman there is great love not small; there are very tall ladies whom I would not take (in exchange) for short ones; but if a man takes short ones for tall ones, he does not regret the exchange.

Respondióle la dueña, diz': «Non me estaría bien
casar ante del año, que a biuda non convien'
fasta que pase el año de los lutos que tien'
casarse; ca el luto con esta carga vien'.

Si yo ante casase, sería enfamada,
perdería la manda que a mí es mandada,
del segundo marido non sería tan onrada,
ternie que non podría sofrir grand temporada.»

«Fija», dixo la vieja, «el año ya es pasado;
tomad aqueste marido por ome e por velado;
andémoslo, fablémoslo, tengámoslo celado:
¡hado bueno que vos tienen vuestras fadas fadado!

¿Qué provecho vos tien' vestir este negro paño,
andar envergonçada e con mucho sosaño?
Señora, dexat duelo e fazet el cabo d'año:
nunca la golondrina mejor consejó ogaño.

Xergas por mal señor, burel por mal marido,
a cavalleros e a dueñas es provecho vestido;
mas dévenlo traer poco e fazer chico roído:
grand plazer e chico duelo es de todo ome querido.»

Respondió doña Endrina: ¡«Dexat, non osaría
fazer lo que me dezides, nin lo que el querría,
non me digas agora más desa ledanía,
¡non me afinques tanto luego el primero día!»

Des las propriedades que las dueñas chicas han

QUIERO vos abreviar la predicación,
que siempre me pagué de pequeño sermón,
e de dueña pequeña et de breve razón,
ca lo poco e bien dicho finca en el corazón.

Del que mucho fabla ríen, quien mucho ríe es loco;
es en la dueña chica amor grande e non poco;
dueñas hay muy grandes que por chicas non troco,
e las chicas por las grandes, non se arrepiente del troco.

Cupid asked me to speak well of the short ones, and to speak of their noble qualities; I should like to recount them now. I would say of short ladies that you take them in jest: they are cold as the snow, and they burn like fire.

They are cold outside, (but) burning when in love; in bed they are comfortable, jovial, cheerful, and gay: in the house they are sensible, happy, peaceful, and virtuous. You will discover much more. So pay good attention to it.

In a small zircon (precious stone) great value lies, in very little sugar resides great sweetness, in a small woman lies very great love. Few words are enough for a man with a good head.

The seed of the good sweet-pepper is small, but it is more comforting and warming than the nutmeg; it is the same with a small woman: if she grants (you) complete love, there is no pleasure in the world that is not to be found in her.

As there is great colour in a small rose, great price and value in a little gold, as in a little balsam there lies a very fine scent, so in a small woman there lies very great love.

As a small ruby has great goodness, colour, virtue, value, and noble clarity, so a small woman has great beauty, loveliness, grace, love, and loyalty.

The lark is small and the nightingale is small, but they sing much more sweetly than any larger bird; because a woman is small she is not the worse for it; with affection she is sweeter than sugar or (any) flower.

The parrot and the oriole are very small birds, but both of them are sweet singers. A gifted, lovely, and prized singer; even so is a small woman in love.

De las chicas que bien diga, el amor me fizo ruego,
que diga de sus noblezas; yo quiero las dezir luego:
dirévos de dueñas chicas, que lo avredes por juego:
son frías como la nieve, e arden como el fuego.

Son frías de fuera, con el amor ardientes:
en la cama solaz, trebejo, plazenteras, rientes:
en casa cuerdas, donosas, sosegadas, bien fazientes.
Mucho ál falleredes, bien parad í mientes.

En pequeña girgonça yaze grand resplandor,
en açúcar muy poco yaze mucho dulçor,
en la dueña pequeña yaze muy grand amor,
pocas palabras cumplen al buen entendedor.

Es pequeño el grano de la buena pemienta,
pero más que la nuez conorta e calienta;
así dueña pequeña, si todo amor consienta,
non ha plazer en el mundo que en ella non sienta.

Como en chica rosa está mucho color,
en oro muy poco grand precio e gran valor,
como en poco blasmo yaze grand buen olor,
ansí en chica dueña yaze muy grand amor.

Como robí pequeño tiene mucha bondat,
color, virtud e precio e noble claridad,
ansí dueña pequeña tiene mucha beldat,
fermosura, donaire, amor e lealtad.

Chica es la calandria e chico el ruiseñor,
pero más dulce cantan que otra ave mayor;
la muger, por ser chica, por eso non es pior;
con doñeo es más dulce que açúcar nin flor.

Son aves pequeñuelas papagayo e orior,
pero cualquier dellas es dulce gritador;
adonada, fermosa, preciada cantador:
bien atal es la dueña pequeña con amor.

With a little woman there is nothing to compare; she is a paradise upon earth and a comfort, a solace and a joy, a pleasure and a blessing; she is better in the testing than at first meeting.

I have always liked a small woman better than a big or a bigger one. It is not imprudent to fly from a great evil; of evils take the least, says the sage (Aristotle): therefore the smallest of women is the best.

The Archpriest's (Unfortunate) Treatment by his Messenger Ferrán García

MY eyes will not look on the light, because I have lost (Mistress) Cross, Mistress Cross who was my cross, the baker's wife; I took for my sweetheart, I took a footpath for the main road, like an Andalusian.

Thinking that I should get her, I asked 'Pincher' García to arrange the business and be my negotiator and guide.

He said that he would gladly oblige me, and became Mistress Cross's favourite. He gave me the husk to chew, (while) he ate the sweetest bread.

He promised her, on my instructions, some good wheat I had, and the sharp, tricksy traitor gave her a rabbit (himself).

God damn such a ready and unreliable messenger! May God never prosper a rabbiter* who does his hunting like that!

* This word has indelicate associations. Indeed the whole poem is full of double-entendres, which are not difficult to pick up. It is described as a *trova cazurra*, a type of coarse poem sung by common minstrels.

De la muger pequeña non hay comparación,
terrenal paraíso es e consolacíon,
solaz et alegría, placer et bendición:
mejor es en la prueva que en la salutación.

Siempre quis' muger chica más que grande nin mayor,
non es desaguisado del grand mal ser foidor;
del mal tomar lo menos, dízelo el sabidor:
por ende de las mugeres la mejor es la menor.

De lo que conteció al Arcipreste con Ferrán García, su mensajero

MIS ojos no verán luz,
pues perdido he a Cruz.

Cruz cruzada, panadera,
tomé por entendedera,
tomé senda por carrera
como un andaluz.

Cuidando que la habría,
dixiélo a Ferrand García
que trujés' la pleitesía,
y fuése pleités y duz.

Dixome quel' placía de grado,
e fizose de Cruz privado,
a mi dió rumiar salvado,
el comió el pan más duz.

Prometiól', por mi consejo,
trigo que tenía añejo,
e presentol' un conejo
el traidor falso marfuz.

¡Diós confonda mensajero
tan presto e tan ligero!
¡Non medre Dios conejero,
que la caça ansí aduz.

Song to the Virgin Mary

LADY, since I have known your help, my hope is in you, and I promise to be a pilgrim to your house in Guadalupe.

You have always been a most sweet medicine to the unhappy, and have come very promptly to those who put themselves under your protection. Therefore in my troubles and in my most harsh imprisonment, my first desire has been to visit your image.

Lady, since I have known your help, my hope is in you, and I promise to be a pilgrim to your house in Guadalupe.

Still and unfailingly I call on you in my troubles, Lady, oh my sweet advocate; and therefore my heart adores you, since in this great sadness I have had ease and true comfort for my cares.

Lady, since I have known your help, my hope is in you, and I promise to be a pilgrim in your house in Guadalupe.

You who are the star that guards those astray, calm my grief, and get me pardon for my sins, and let them be forgotten on your account, and lift me to that height where pleasure is complete.

Lady, since I have known your help, my hope is in you, and I promise to be a pilgrim to your house in Guadalupe.

PEDRO LÓPEZ DE AYALA

Cantar a la Virgen María

SEÑORA, por cuanto supe
tus acorros, en ti spero,
e a tu casa en Guadalupe
prometo de ser romero.

Tú muy dulce melesina fueste siempre a cuitados,
e acorriste muy aína a los tus encomendados:
por ende en mis cuidados e mi prisión tan dura
vesitar la tu figura fue mi talante primero.

Señora, por cuanto supe
tus acorros, en ti spero,
e a tu casa en Guadalupe
prometo de ser romero.

En mis cuitas todavía siempre te llamo, Señora,
o dulce abogada mía, e por ende te adora
el mi coraçón agora, en esta muy grand tristura,
por el cuido haber folgura e conorte verdadero.

Señora, por cuanto supe
tus acorros, en ti spero,
e a tu casa en Guadalupe
prometo de ser romero.

Tú, que eres la estrella que guardas a los errados,
amansa mi querella, e perdón de mis pecados
tú me gana, e olvidados sean por la tu mesura,
e me lieva aquel altura do es el plazer entero.

Señora, por cuanto supe
tus acorros, en ti spero,
e a tu casa en Guadalupe
prometo de ser romero.

Round-song

THAT tree that is stirring its leaves has taken fancy to something.

The fine-looking tree looks as if it is going to burst into flower; it has taken a fancy to something.

That tree that is so good to see looks as if it is going to burst into flower. It has taken a fancy to something.

It looks as if it is going to give us flowers. They are already showing. Come out and see them. It has taken a fancy to something.

It looks as if it is going to flower. They are already showing. Come out and see them. It has taken a fancy to something.

They are already showing; come out and see them. Call out the ladies to cut the fruit. It has taken a fancy to something.

Love's Farewell

AS I was going through a strange meadow, sad (and) very pensive, I heard a frightening shout, a shrill voice in great anger. 'Mountain', this voice was saying, 'now may God be good to you, for I care no more for Spain.'

DIEGO HURTADO DE MENDOZA

Cosante

A AQUEL árbol que mueve la foxa
algo se le antoxa.

Aquel árbol del bel mirar
face de maniera flores quiere dar:
algo se le antoxa.

Aquel árbol del bel veyer
face de maniera quiere florecer:
algo se le antoxa.

Face de maniera flores quiere dar:
ya se demuestra; salidlas mirar:
algo se le antoxa.

Face de maniera quiere florecer:
ya se demuestra; salidlas a ver:
algo se le antoxa.

Ya se demuestra; salidlas mirar.
Vengan las damas las fructas cortar:
algo se le antoxa.

GARCI FERNÁNDEZ DE JERENA

Despedida del amor

POR una floresta estraña,
yendo triste muy pensoso
oí un grito pavoroso,
boz aguda con gran saña:
«Montaña»
iba esta boz diziendo,
«ora a Deus te encomiendo
que non curo más de España.»

I was alarmed by the voice and looked in great fear, and saw that it was Love, crying out in his grief. He was making his great plaint of his own accord, (and) I heard him say: 'I see high glory brought low.'

When I saw that he was complaining, to find out his grievance, I asked a girl who was walking through the thicket. The girl replied without pleasure: 'I am pleased to tell you why Love was so sad.

'You must know, friend, that Love lives in dishonour, and now he is leaving Castile; and never so long as you live will you know where he has made his home. You will have cause to complain of a woman who was much praised.'

For Love of a Moorish Girl

WHOEVER falls in love with a pretty girl must expect pardon if she is a Moor.

De la boz fui espantado
e miré con grand pavor,
e vi que era el Amor
que se chamava cuitado.
De grado
o seu grand planto fazía,
segund entendí dezía:
«Alto prez veo abajado».

Desque vi que se quexava,
por saber de su querella
pregunté a una donzella
que por la floresta andava;
falava
la donzella sin plazer:
«Plázeme de vos dezer
por qué Amor tan triste estava:

«amigo, saber devedes
que Amor vive en manzela,
e se va ja de Castela
e nunca mientra bivedes
sabredes
dónde faze su morada;
por una que foy loada
de quexa porfazaredes.»

~

ALFONSO ÁLVAREZ DE VILLASANDINO

A los amores de una mora

QUIEN de linda se enamora,
atender deve perdón
en casso que sea mora.

Love and chance sent me to see a most charming creature of Hagar's race; anyone who spoke the pure truth might well say that she has not a shepherdess's figure.

I saw a lovely (and) most delicate rose planted in an orchard, kept under a secret key by Ishmael's stock. Although this is a serious matter, with all my heart I take her for my mistress.

The bold Mahomet ordained that she should be so, of noble and perfect beauty, with white crystalline breasts, and what is covered by her smock must most certainly be of polished alabaster.

He gave her so much beauty that I cannot tell of it; all who gaze on her face love to serve her. In elegance and gentleness she beats all those of her race, (in the place) where she lives.

I know no man, however cautious, who could look on her splendour and not be conquered in a moment by love of her. To receive such a gift, I would put my sinful soul in peril.

El amor e la ventura
me fizieron ir mirar
muy graciosa criatura
de linaje de Aguar;
quien fablare verdat pura,
bien puede dezir que non
tiene talle de pastora.

Linda rosa muy suave
vi plantada en un vergel,
puesta so secreta llave
de la linea de Ysmael:
maguer sea cossa grave,
con todo mi coraçón
la rescibo por senõra.

Mahomad el atrevido
ordenó que fuese tal,
de asseo noble, complido,
alvos pechos de cristal:
de alabasto muy broñido
devié ser con grant razón
lo que cubre su alcandora.

Diole tanta fermosura
que lo non puedo dezir;
cuantos miran su figura
todos la aman servir.
Con lindeza e apostura
vence a todos cuantos son
de alcuña, donde mora.

Non sé ombre tan guardado
que viese su resplandor,
que non fuesse conquistado
en un punto de su amor.
Por aver tal gasajado
yo pornía en condición
la mi alma pecadora.

In Love and Praise of a Lady

BELOVED face, take pity on me. For I live in sadness, desiring you.

That beauty of yours has captivated me, and on account of this (mis)fortune to my heart, sadness divides us at all seasons; which is why your image so saddens me.

All my care is for your praise, for I cannot forget the times that are past. It would be fair of you to remember me, for I always served you willingly and loyally.

Every day I am sad and joyless. If only one day I could see you, I should take comfort from the sight of you. Thus I should recover the good that I have lost.

As I was arguing in this manner, the birds were flying (past); (and) beside some grass I found myself sadly grieving. Then, at that moment, I remembered a gentle lady whom my sighing heart adores night and day.

Por amor e loores de una señora

VISSO enamoroso,
duélete de mí,
pues vivo pensoso
desseando a ti.

La tua fermosura
me puso en prisión;
por la cual ventura
del mi coraçón
nos' parte tristura
en toda sazón:
por én' tu figura
me entristece assí.

Todo el mi cuidado
es en te loar,
quel tiempo passado
non posso olvidar:
farás aguissado
de mí te membrar,
pues siempre de grado
leal te serví.

Estoy cada día
triste sin plazer;
si tan sólo un día
te pudiesse ver,
yo confortar me ía
con tu parescer:
por én' cobraría
el bien que perdí.

Razonando en tal figura
las aves fueron bolando;
yo aprés de una verdura
me fallé triste cuidando:
e luego en aquella ora
me membró gentil señora
a quien noche e día adora
mi coraçón sospirando.

Statement on the Vanities of this World

IN God's name, gentlemen, let us remove the veil that so confuses and blinds our sight; let us look at death, who conquers the world, throwing high and low to the ground. Let our groans pierce the heavens, each one demanding of God pardon for those transgressions which he committed at all ages, as an old man, a young man, and a boy.

For it is not life that we live, since, as we live, cruel and elusive death comes (ever) nearer; and when we think we are living, then we die. We are quite certain where we were born, but we are not certain where we shall die. We have no certainty of life for an hour; we come in tears, we go in tears.

What has become of the emperors, popes and kings, great prelates, dukes and counts, famous knights, the rich, the strong and the learned, and of all those who loyally served their loves, fighting their battles in every place, and of those who invented sciences and arts, doctors, poets, and troubadours?

(Of) fathers and sons, brothers, relations, friends, and women friends, whom we greatly love, with whom we ate, drank, and sported, many graceful and beautiful creatures, ladies, maidens, and valiant young men who are enjoying their youth under the earth, and other gentlemen whom we saw here present (only) a few days ago?

FERRANT SÁNCHEZ CALAVERA

Dezir de las vanidades del mundo

POR Dios, señores, quitemos el velo
que turba e ciega así nuestra vista;
miremos la muerte qu' el mundo conquista
lançando lo alto e baxo por suelo.
Los nuestros gemidos traspasen el cielo
a Dios demandando cada uno perdón
de aquellas ofensas que en toda sazón
le fizo el viejo, mancebo, mozuelo.

Ca non es vida la que bevimos,
pues que biviendo se viene llegando
la muerte cruel, esquiva; e cuando
penssamos bevir, estonce morimos.
Somos bien ciertos dónde nascimos;
mas non somos ciertos a dónde morremos.
Certidumbre de vida un ora non avemos;
con llanto venimos, con llanto nos imos.

¿Qué se fizieron los emperadores,
papas e reyes, grandes perlados,
duques e condes, cavalleros famados,
los ricos, los fuertes e los sabidores,
e cuantos servieron lealmente amores
faziendo sus armas en todas las partes,
e los que fallaron ciencias e artes,
doctores, poetas y los trobadores?

¿Padres e fijos, hermanos, parientes,
amigos, amigas, que mucho amamos,
con quien comimos, bevimos, folgamos,
muchas garridas e fermosas gentes,
dueñas, doncellas, mancebos valientes
que logran so tierra las sus mancebías,
e otros señores que ha pocos días
que nosotros vimos aquí estar presentes?

(Of) the Duke of Cabra and the admiral and other very great men of Castile, also Ruy Díaz, whose death left such a mark on the people that his great fame for prowess and absolute goodness has resounded even into the East, and his noble bearing and gentle appearance are a light indeed in this great court?

(Of) all those who have here been named, some have become ashes and nothing; others are bones with the flesh stripped off, and have been scattered in the ditches; others are already dismembered, heads without bodies, without feet, and without hands; others the worms are beginning to eat; others have only just been buried.

So where are the empires and where the powers, kingdoms, revenues, and lordships? Where do pride and fame and valour go? Where go the exploits and where the achievements? Where go the sciences and learning, where the masters of poetry? Where the rhymers of great accomplishment? Where the singers and where the players of instruments?

Where go the treasures, vassals, and servants? Where go the jewels and precious stones? Where go the pearls and costly apartments, where the civet and perfumed waters? Where go the cloth of gold, and shining chains, where go the necklaces, the garters, where go the marten skins, grey and sable, where the timbrels that resound as they go?

¿El duque de Cabra e el almirante
e otros muy grandes asaz de Castilla,
agora Ruy Díez, que puso manzilla
su muerte a los gentes en tal estante
que la su grant fama fasta en Levante
sonava en proeza a en toda bondat,
que en esta grant corte luzié por verdat
su noble meneo e gentil semblante?

Todos aquestos que aquí son nombrados,
los unos son fechos ceniza e nada;
los otros son huesos, la carne quitada
e son derramados por los fonsados;
los otros están ya descoyuntados,
cabeças sin cuerpos, sin pies e sin manos;
los otros comiençan comer los gusanos;
los otros acaban de ser enterrados.

Pues ¿dó los imperios e dó los poderes.
reinos, rentas e los señoríos,
a dó los orgullos, las famas e bríos,
a dó las empressas, a dó los traheres?
¿A dó las cïencias, a dó los saberes,
a dó los maestros de la poetría;
a dó los rimares de grant maestría,
a dó los cantares, a dó los tañeres?

¿A dó los thesoros, vasallos, servientes,
a dó los firmalles, piedras precïosas;
a dó el aljófar, posadas costosas,
a dó el algalia e aguas olientes?
¿A dó paños de oro, cadenas luzientes,
a dó los collares, las jarreteras,
a dó peñas grisses, a dó peñas veras,
a dó las sonajas que van retinientes?

Where go the feasts, suppers, and luncheons? Where go the jousts and where the tourneys? Where go new dresses and strange demeanours? Where go the arts of the dancers, where the food and the provisions? Where goes generosity and where goes waste? Where goes laughter and where goes pleasure? Where go the minstrels and the actors?

In my belief, beyond a doubt the time that the prophet Isaiah, the son of Amos, told us of is up. He said that all order would cease, and that desolation would come on account of (the world's) corruption, and that good men would be glad to die and that they would be wept for at their doors, and that the towns would fall into destruction.

It is this death with great tribulation that Jeremiah, a prophet full of anger (spoke of), his eyes weeping with repentance and great abundance of tears, showing his sins and his most grievous error. Any man who reads this chapter carefully will clearly see that, without any doubt, this is the time.

Therefore it would be sensible to adorn (our) impoverished souls with virtues, and to cast away those honours gained by the body, since we are certain that we have to lose them. Whoever cares to take this advice will have no fear of ever dying, but will pass from death to live a life eternal which will never fail.

¿A dó los combites, cenas e ayantares,
a dó las justas, a dó los torneos,
a dó nuevos trajes, estraños meneos,
a dó las artes de los dançadores,
a dó los comeres, a dó los manjares,
a dó la franqueza, a dó el espender,
a dó los rissos, a dó el plazer,
a dó menestriles, a dó los juglares?

Segunt yo creo sin fallecimiento,
complido es el tiempo que dixo a nos
el profeta Yssayas, fijo de Amos:
dis que cessaría todo ordenamiento
e vernie por fedor podrimiento,
e los omes gentiles de grado morríen,
e a sus puertas que los lloraríen,
e sería lo poblado en destruimiento.

Esta tal muerte con grant tribulança
Geremías, profeta lleno de enojos,
con repentimiento llorando sus ojos
e de muchas lágrimas grant abondança,
mostrando sus faltas e muy grant errança.
Quien este escripto muy bien leerá
en este capítulo bien claro verá
que este es el tiempo sin otra dubdança.

Por ende buen sesso era guarnesçer
de virtudes las almas que están despojadas,
tirar estas honras del cuerpo juntadas,
pues somos ciertos que se han de perder.
Quien este consejo quisiere fazer
non avrá miedo jamás de morir,
mas traspasará de muerte a bevir
vida por siempre sin le fallesçer.

An End of his Praise to the Saints

AS Boniface did with the pantheon of all the saints, celebrating a feast for them all in one day and a small space, so I here, although not done, conclude my praise of you, sweetest sirs, with this brief encomium.

'Who honours you honours me; he despises me who despises you': that is a saying of the King whom the heavens adore. Flowers with which all blessed paradise is in love, give continuous praise to the most holy Lady!

Bloom, precious flowers; smell sweet again, most sacred lilies; sing your sweet songs, larks and nightingales, martyrs and confessors and virgins, with the birds whose gentlest songs are always offering praise to God.

Gleaming stars, make this dark world clear and luminous with your lovely virtues; clear and living sparks lit from the divine fire, pray with outstretched hands to the flower of maidens.

FERNÁN PÉREZ DE GUZMÁN

Fin de loores de santos

COMO fizo Bonifacio
del panteón todos santos,
faziendo fiesta de tantos
en un día e poco espacio,
yo aquí, aunque no sacio,
fago fin a los loores
de vos, muy dulces señores,
con este breve laudacio.

«Quien a vos, a mí onora;
a mí esperne quien a vos»,
son estas palabras dos
del rey a quien el cielo adora.
¡Flores de quien se enamora
todo el santo paraíso,
dad loor non interciso
a la muy santa Señora!

Floresced, preciosas flores,
reholed, lirios muy santos,
suenen vuestros dulces cantos,
calandrias e ruiseñores;
mártires e confesores,
e vírgines con las aves,
cuyos cantos muy suaves
siempre dan a Dios loores.

Resplandescientes estrellas,
fazed claro e luminoso
este mundo tenebroso,
con vuestras virtudes bellas;
claras a bivas centellas
del divino fuego ancesas,
orad con manos estesas
a la flor de las donzellas.

In Praise of Santa Clara the Virgin

CLARA (shining) in name and works and virtue, moon of Assisi and daughter of Ortulana, model and salvation of holy women, among widows sole and supreme:

Principle of exalted goodness, and persevering youth, and fountain from which humble poverty springs, and bolt driven home, most worthy sister of the seraphic sun.

You triumph, virgin, triumphant in your triumph and precious palm of victory. So no one strays who takes refuge with you, and counts you among the ruling number of the saints, o holy and beloved saint. Therefore, pray for me now, blessed Clara.

Carol to Three of his Daughters

IN a charming meadow of dainty flowers and roses, I saw three lovely ladies who were in search of love. With quick goodwill I went to greet them. One of them began to sing this very chaste song: 'They are waiting for me: such guards never did I see'.

To see the beauty of these three charming ladies, I covered myself with the branches and got down on the grass.

IÑIGO LÓPEZ DE MENDOZA, MARQUÉS DE SANTILLANA

En loor de Sancta Clara, virgen

CLARA por nombre, por obra e virtude
luna de Assís, e fija de Ortulana,
de sanctas doñas enxemplo e salud,
entre las viudas una e soberana:

principio de alto bien, e juventud
perseverante, e fuente de do mana
pobreça humilde, e closo alamud,
del seráphico sol muy dina hermana.

Tú, virgen, triumphas del triumpho, triunphante
e glorïoso premio de la palma:
assí non yerra quien de ti se ampara

e te cuenta del cuento dominante
de los sanctos, o sancta sacra e alma;
pues hora ora pro me, beata Clara.

Villancico a unas tres fijas suyas

POR una gentil floresta
de lindas flores e rosas,
vide tres damas fermosas
que de amores han recuesta.

Yo, con voluntad muy presta,
me llegué a conoscellas;
començó la una de ellas
esta canción tan honesta:

«Aguardan a mí:
nunca tales guardas vi».

Por mirar su fermosura
destas tres gentiles damas,
yo cobríme de las ramas,
metíme so la verdura.

The second began to sigh most sadly, and with most chaste restraint to sing this song: 'The girl who is in love, how shall she sleep alone?'

So as not to disturb them, I did not care to go nearer. Said the third with a pleasing face to those who had sung in such harmony: 'Since you two, exalted ladies, have sung, it is right that I should sing: Let the wretch be punished; may God avenge me on him.'

After they had sung, these ladies I am speaking of, I emerged sadly, like a shelterless man. They said: 'Friend, it is not you we are seeking. But sing since we have sung': 'The girl passed sighing, but not for me, as I knew too well.'

Hill-song of La Finojosa

I SAW on the border no girl so lovely as a cow-girl of La Finojosa.

La otra con grand tristura
començó de sospirar
e dezir este cantar
con muy honesta mesura:

«La niña que amores ha,
sola ¿cómo dormirá?»

Por non les fazer turbança
non quise ir más adelante.
A las que con ordenança
cantavan tan consonante,

la otra con buen semblante
dixo: «Señoras de estado,
pues las dos avéis cantado,
a mí conviene que cante»:

«Dejadlo al villano pene;
véngueme Dios delle».

Desque ya hovieron cantado
estas señoras que digo,
yo salí desconsolado,
como home sin abrigo.

Ellas dixeron: «Amigo,
non sois vos el que buscamos
mas cantad, pues que cantamos:»

«Sospirando iva la niña
e non por mí,
que yo bien se lo entendí.»

Serranilla de la Finojosa

MOÇA tan fermosa
non vi en la frontera,
como una vaquera
de la Finojosa.

As I was making my way from Calatreveño to Santa María, overcome by sleep, I lost my way on the rough ground, where I saw the cow-girl of La Finojosa.

In a green meadow of roses and flowers, guarding her herds with the other cow-herds, I saw her, so charming that you would scarcely believe that she was a cow-girl of La Finojosa.

I do not believe that the roses of spring would have seemed so lovely or anything like it – to make a long story short – if I had known beforehand of that cow-girl of La Finojosa.

I would not look too much at her beauty, so as not to lose my liberty. But I said: 'Lady' – in order to find out who she was – 'where is the cow-girl of La Finojosa?'

Faziendo la vía
del Calatreveño
a Sancta María,
vencido del sueño,
por tierra fragosa
perdí la carrera,
do vi la vaquera
de la Finojosa.

En un verde prado
de rosas e flores,
guardando ganado
con otros pastores,
la vi tan graciosa
que apenas creyera
que fuesse vaquera
de la Finojosa.

Non creo las rosas
de la primavera
sean tan fermosas
nin de tal manera
(fablando sin glosa),
si antes sopiera
de aquella vaquera
de la Finojosa.

Non tanto mirara
su mucha beldad
porque me dexara
en mi libertad.
Mas dixe: «Donosa»
(por saber quién era),
«¿dónde es la vaquera
de la Finojosa?»

With something like a laugh, she said: 'You're welcome, for now I quite understand what you are asking. (But) she doesn't want, and she doesn't expect, to love – this cow-girl of La Finojosa.'

Hill-song of Bores

A GIRL from Bores, down by La Lama, made me in love.

I thought that love had forgotten me, as one who had long since ceased to have those pains that burn lovers worse than a flame.

But I saw that beauty, so lovely to look at, with a pleasant face as fresh as a rose, and with such a complexion as I have never seen, gentlemen, in a lady or in any woman.

I said to her therefore: 'Lady, now your beauty shall indeed spread beyond these uplands, for it deserves the fame of great praise.'

Bien como riendo,
dixo: «Bien vengades;
que ya bien entiendo
lo que demandades:
non es deseosa
de amar, nin lo espera
aquessa vaquera
de la Finojosa.»

Serranilla de Bores

MOÇUELA de Bores,
allá do la Lama,
púsome en amores.

Cuidé que olvidado
amor me tenía
como quien se avía
grand tiempo dexado
de tales dolores,
que más que la llama
queman amadores.

Mas vi la fermosa
de buen continente,
la cara plaziente,
fresca como rosa,
de tales colores
cual nunca vi dama
nin otra, señores.

Por lo cual: «Señora»
(le dixe), «en verdad
la vuestra beldad
saldrá desde agora
dentre estos alcores,
pues meresce fama
de grandes loores.»

She said: 'Knight, go away. Let the cow-girl cross to the hill. For two peasants of Frama are wooing me, both of them cow-herds.'

'Lady, I will be a cow-herd if you wish. You may command me as your servant. (The sound of) lowing will be a greater pleasure to me than to hear the nightingales.'

So we concluded our suit, having committed no wrong, and came to an agreement. And the flowers around Espinama were our accomplices.

Dixo: «Caballero,
tiradvos afuera:
dexad la vaquera
pasar al otero;
ca dos labradores
me piden de Frama,
entrambos pastores.»

«Señora, pastor
seré si queredes:
mandarme podedes,
como a servidor:
mayores dulçores
será a mí la brama
que oír ruiseñores.»

Así concluimos
el nuestro processo
sin fazer excesso,
e nos avenimos.
E fueron las flores
de cabe Espinama
los encobridores.

Verses on the Death of his Father

LET the sleeping soul arouse its senses and awake, to contemplate how life passes, how death approaches so silently; how quickly pleasure goes, and how once remembered (on waking) it gives pain, (and) how, as we see it, any time in the past was better.

For if we see the present, how it has gone and is over in a flash, (and) if we judge wisely, we will count the future as already past. Let no one at all deceive himself by thinking that what he is expecting will last longer than what he has seen. For everything will pass in the same way.

Our lives are the rivers that flow out into the sea, which is death. There lordships go straight to their ends, to be consumed. There the great rivers, and there the others, of middling size and smaller, are equal when they arrive: those who live by their hands and the rich.

JORGE MANRIQUE

Coplas por la muerte de su padre

RECUERDE el alma dormida,
abive el seso y despierte,
contemplando
cómo se passa la vida,
cómo se viene la muerte
tan callando;
cuán presto se va el plazer,
cómo después de acordado
da dolor,
cómo a nuestro parescer,
cualquiera tiempo passado
fue mejor.

Pues si vemos lo presente
cómo en un punto se es ido
y acabado,
si juzgamos sabiamente,
daremos lo no venido
por passado.
No se engañe nadie, no,
pensando que ha de durar
lo que espera
más que duró lo que vio,
pues que todo ha de passar
por tal manera.

Nuestras vidas son los ríos
que van a dar en la mar
que es el morir:
allí van los señoríos
derechos a se acabar
y consumir;
allí los ríos caudales;
allí los otros, medianos
y más chicos,
allegados son iguales,
los que biven por sus manos
y los ricos.

I omit the invocations of the famous poets and orators; I do not care for their fictions, for they smell of secret drugs. I commend myself only to Him, I truly invoke only Him, whose divinity the world did not know when He lived in this world.

This world is the road to the other, which is a dwelling-place without sorrow; but one needs to have good judgement to make that journey without going astray. We set out when we are born, we travel as long as we live, and we arrive at the moment when we perish; so it is that when we die we rest.

This world would be good if we made the good use of it that we ought; for, according to our faith, its purpose is that we may gain that other (world) to which we look forward. And, in order to raise us to heaven, even that Son of God came down to be born here among us, and to live on this earth, where He died.

Dexo las invocaciones
de los famosos poetas
y oradores;
no curo de sus ficciones,
que traen yervas secretas
sus sabores.
Aquel solo me encomiendo,
aquel solo invoco yo
de verdad,
que en este mundo biviendo,
el mundo no conosció
su deidad.

Este mundo es el camino
para el otro, que es morada
sin pesar;
mas cumple tener buen tino
para andar esta jornada
sin errar.
Partimos cuando nascemos,
andamos mientre bivimos,
y llegamos
al tiempo que fenescemos;
assí que cuando morimos
descansamos.

Este mundo bueno fue
si bien usássemos dél
como devemos,
porque, según nuestra fe,
es para ganar aquel
que atendemos.
Y aun aquel fijo de Dios
para sobirnos al cielo
descendió
a nascer acá entre nos,
y a bivir en este suelo
do murió.

If it were in our power to make a lovely face flesh again, as it is to make the soul in its glory angelical, what lively efforts should we make every hour, and how quick we should be to restore the slave, while allowing the mistress to decay!

See how little the things we go after and pursue are worth, for in this treacherous world even before we die we lose them. Some of them are decayed by age; others by disasters that occur; others, on account of their quality, when they are in their highest state fall away.

Tell me, how does beauty, a charming freshness and complexion, the pink and white (of the cheeks) end up when old age approaches? The tricks and agility and physical strength of youth all turn to heaviness when one comes to the suburbs of senility.

Si fuesse en nuestro poder
tornar la cara fermosa
corporal,
como podemos fazer
el ánima gloriosa
angelical,
¡qué diligencia tan biva
toviéramos toda hora,
y tan presta,
en componer la cativa,
dexándonos la señora
descompuesta!

Ved de cuan poco valor
son las cosas tras que andamos
y corremos,
que, en este mundo traidor,
aun primero que muramos
las perdemos:
dellas desfaze la edad,
dellas casos desastrados
que acaescen,
dellas, por su calidad,
en los más altos estados
desfallescen.

Dezidme, la fermosura,
la gentil frescura y tez
de la cara,
la color y la blancura,
cuando viene la vejez,
¿Cuál se para?
Las mañas y ligereza
ya la fuerça corporal
de joventud,
todo se torna graveza
cuando llega al arraval
de senectud.

For by how many roads and in how many ways is the exalted greatness of Gothic blood, (great) lineage, and the nobility, so swollen with pride, destroyed in this life! Some through small worth – and how low and abject is their reputation! – and others through poverty, keep themselves alive by (performing) unseemly offices.

Who doubts that estates and riches suddenly leave us? We expect no constancy from them, since they belong to a lady who changes. These are Fortune's favours, which she spins on her rapid wheel, for she cannot be of one mind or remain stable, or dwell on one thing.

But I tell you that they may stay with their possessor, and remain with him to the grave. In this way they will not deceive us, for life passes quickly as a dream. And the pleasures in which we delight here are temporal, and the torments there, which we expect on account of them, are eternal.

Pues la sangre de los godos,
y el linage, y la nobleza
    tan crescida,
¡por cuántos vías y modos
se sume su grand alteza
    en esta vida!
Unos, por poco valer,
¡por cuán baxos y abatidos
    que los tienen!
y otros por no tener,
con oficios no devidos
    se mantienen.

Los estados y riqueza,
que nos dexan a deshora,
    ¿quién lo duda?
No les pidamos firmeza,
pues que son de una señora
    que se muda;
que bienes son de Fortuna
que rebuelve con su rueda
    presurosa,
la cual no puede ser una,
ni estar estable ni queda
    en una cosa.

Pero digo que acompañen
y lleguen hasta la huessa
    con su dueño:
por esso no nos engañen,
pues se va la vida apriessa
    como sueño.
Y los deleites de acá
son, en que los deleitamos,
    temporales,
y los tormentos de allá
que por ellos esperamos,
    eternales.

The pleasures and sweetnesses of this toilsome life that we lead, what are they but fleeting? And is not death the snare into which we fall? Without a thought for our hurts, we rush headlong and do not stop; and when we see the deceit and want to turn back, there is no time.

Those mighty kings that we see in the writings of the past, by sad and lamentable accidents their good fortunes were reversed. So nothing is sure, for Death treats popes, emperors, and prelates even as she does poor cow-herds.

Let us leave the Trojans, since we have seen neither their disasters nor their glories; let us leave the Romans, although we hear and read their stories; let us not trouble to know about that past age and what became of it; let us come to affairs of yesterday, which are as thoroughly forgotten as the tale of Rome is.

Los plazeres y dulçores
desta vida trabajada
que tenemos,
¿qué son sino corredores,
y la muerte la celada
en que caemos?
No mirando nuestro daño,
corremos a rienda suelta
sin parar;
desque vemos el engaño
y queremos dar la buelta,
no hay lugar.

Essos reyes poderosos
que vemos por escrituras
ya passadas,
con casos tristes llorosos
fueron sus buenas venturas
trastornadas;
assí que no hay cosa fuerte,
que a papas y emperadores
y perlados
assí los trata la Muerte
como a los pobres pastores
de ganados.

Dexemos a los troyanos,
que sus males no los vimos,
ni sus glorias;
dexemos a los romanos,
aunque oímos y leímos
sus estorias;
no curemos de saber
lo de aquel siglo passado
qué fue dello;
vengamos a lo de ayer,
que tan bien es olvidado
como aquello.

What has become of the King Don Juan? The princes of Aragon, where are they? What has become of all those gallants? What has become of the many innovations they brought? The jousts and tourneys, ornaments, embroideries, and crests, were they only an imagination? What were they but the grass of the threshing-floors?

What has become of the ladies, of their head-dresses, their robes and their scents? What has become of the flames of the fires the lovers lit? What of all that playing, and of the harmonious music that they made? What has become of that dancing, and of the beautiful dresses that they wore?

Then that other, his heir Don Enrique, what power he attained! How smoothly, how flatteringly the world gave itself to him, with its pleasures! But you will see how hostile, how contrary, and how cruel it proved to him, having once been his friend, how short a time what it gave stayed with him.

¿Qué se fizo el rey Don Juan?
Los infantes de Aragón,
¿qué se fizieron?
¿Qué fue de tanto galán?
¿Qué fue de tanta invención
como truxieron?
Las justas y los torneos,
paramentos, bordaduras,
y cimeras,
¿fueron sino devaneos?
¿qué fueron sino verduras
de las eras?

¿Qué se fizieron las damas,
sus tocados, sus vestidos,
sus olores?
¿Qué se fizieron las llamas
de los fuegos encendidos
de amadores?
¿Qué se fizo aquel trobar,
las músicas acordadas
que tañían?
¿Qué se fizo aquel dançar,
aquellas ropas chapadas
que traían?

Pues el otro heredero,
don Enrique, ¡qué poderes
alcançava!
¡Cuán blando, cuán falaguero
el mundo con sus plazeres
se le dava!
Mas veréis cuán enemigo,
cuán contrario, cuán cruel
se le mostró,
aviéndole sido amigo,
cuán poco duró con él
lo que le dio.

The disproportionate gifts, the royal palaces full of gold, the vessels so resplendent, the *Henricuses* and *reals* (gold coins) of his treasure, the harnesses and the steeds of his people, and such rich finery, where shall we go to seek them? What were they but dew of the meadows?

Then his brother, the innocent, who called himself his successor in his lifetime, what an excellent Court he had, and how many a great lord followed him! But, since he was mortal, Death soon laid him on her anvil. Oh, divine justice, when the fire burnt hottest you threw on water!

Then that great constable, the (Grand) Master whom we knew as such a favourite, it is not fitting that we should say more of him than that we saw him beheaded. His countless treasures, his towns and villages, his command, what were they to him but tears? What were they to him but griefs when he left them?

Las dádivas desmedidas,
los edificios reales
llenos de oro,
las vaxillas tan febridas,
los enriques y reales
del tesoro,
los jaezes, los cavallos
de su gente, y atavíos
tan sobrados,
¿dónde iremos a buscallos?
¿qué fueron sino rocíos
de los prados?

Pues su hermano el inocente,
que en su vida sucessor
se llamó,
¡qué corte tan excelente
tuvo, y cuánto gran señor
le siguió!
Mas como fuesse mortal,
metiólo la Muerte luego
en su fragua.
¡O juizio divinal!:
cuando más ardía el fuego,
echaste agua.

Pues aquel gran condestable,
maestre que conoscimos
tan privado,
no cumple que dél se fable,
sino solo que lo vimos
degollado.
Sus infinitos tesoros,
sus villas y sus lugares,
su mandar,
¿qué le fueron sino lloros?
¿qué fuéronle sino pesares
al dexar?

Then the other two brothers, (Grand) Masters as prosperous as kings, who kept the great and the middling so obedient to their laws, what was that prosperity (of theirs) that rose so high and (was so) exalted, but a light that when burning brightest was put out?

All those splendid dukes, so many marquises and counts and warriors as we saw, all so mighty, tell me, Death, where have you hidden or removed them? And those famous deeds they did, in war and in peace, when you grow angry, cruel one, with your strength you fell them and destroy them.

The innumerable hosts, the pennons and standards and flags, the impregnable castles, the walls and bulwarks and barricades, the strong and deep ditch or any other refuge – of what use is it? If you come in fury, you pierce it right through with your arrow.

Pues los otros dos hermanos,
maestres tan prosperados
como reyes,
que a los grandes y medianos
truxieron tan sojuzgados
a sus leyes,
aquella prosperidad
que tan alta fue sobida
y ensalçada,
¿qué fue sino claridad
que estando más encendida
fue amatada?

Tantos duques excelentes,
tantos marqueses y condes,
y varones
como vimos tan potentes,
di, Muerte, ¿dó los escondes
y traspones?
Y las sus claras hazañas
que fizieron en las guerras
y en las pazes,
cuando tú, cruda, te ensañas,
con tu fuerça las atierras
y desfazes.

Las huestes innumerables,
los pendones y estandartes
y vanderas,
los castillos impunables,
los muros y baluartes
y barreras,
la cava honda chapada,
o cualquier otro reparo,
¿qué aprovecha?
que si tú vienes airada,
todo lo passas de claro
con tu flecha.

It would not be right for me to praise the great and famous deeds of that most renowned and valiant Grand Master Rodrigo Manrique, that protector of good men, beloved for his virtue by the people, for they (his deeds) were seen. Nor do I wish to magnify them, for the world knows what they were.

What a friend to his friends! What a master to his servants and kinsmen! What an enemy to his enemies! What a leader to the bold and valiant! What a sound brain to the wise! What a jester with the witty! What a mind! How kind to his subordinates, and to the bold and harmful a lion!

In good fortune an Octavian, a Julius Caesar in his conquests and battles, in virtue a (Scipio) Africanus, a Hannibal in his knowledge and labours, in goodness a Trajan, a Titus in liberality and joy, an Aurelian in (the strength of) his arm, a Marcus Atilius in keeping to his promised word.

Aquel de buenos abrigo
amado por virtuoso
de la gente,
el maestre don Rodrigo
Manrique, tanto famoso
y tan valiente,
sus grandes fechos y claros
no cumple que los alabe,
pues los vieron,
ni los quiero fazer caros,
pues el mundo todo sabe
cuáles fueron.

¡Qué amigo de sus amigos!
¡Qué señor para criados
y parientes!
¡Qué enemigo de enemigos!
¡Qué maestro de esforçados
y valientes!
¡Qué seso para discretos!
¡Qué gracia para donosos!
¡Qué razón!
¡Qué benigno a los subjetos,
y a los bravos y dañosos,
un león!

En ventura Octavïano,
Julio César en vencer
y batallar,
en la virtud Africano,
Aníbal en el saber
y trabajar,
en la bondad un Trajano,
Tito en liberalidad
con alegría,
en su braço Aurelïano,
Marco Atilio en la verdad
que prometía.

An Antonius Pius in clemency, a Marcus Aurelius for equanimity, a Hadrian for eloquence, a Theodosius for humility and good disposition, he was an Aurelius Alexandrus for discipline and strictness in war, a Constantine in his faith, a Camillus in his great love for his country.

He did not leave great treasures, nor win great riches or plate, but he made war on the Moors, capturing their fortresses and their towns, and in the fights that he won many Moors and (their) horses were killed. In this capacity he won the lands and vassals that were given to him.

And how in other times past did he fight for his honour and position? When he was left unprotected, he maintained himself with his brothers and his servants. After he had performed famous deeds in this said war that he waged, he made such honourable treaties that he received even more land than he held.

Antonio Pío en clemencia,
Marco Aurelio en igualdad
del semblante,
Adrïano en eloquencia,
Teodosio en umildad
y buen talante.
Aurelio Alexandre fue
en diciplina y rigor
de la guerra,
un Costantino en la fe,
Camilo en el gran amor
de su tierra.

No dexó grandes tesoros,
ni alcançó grandes riquezas
ni vaxillas,
mas fizo guerra a los moros,
ganando sus fortalezas
y sus villas;
y en las lides que venció,
muchos moros y cavallos
se perdieron,
y en este oficio ganó
las rentas y los vassallos
que le dieron.

Pues por su onra y estado,
en otros tiempos passados
¿cómo se huvo?
Quedando desamparado,
con hermanos y criados
se sustuvo.
Después que fechos famosos
fizo en esta dicha guerra
que fazía,
fizo tratos tan onrosos,
que le dieron aun más tierra
que tenía.

Now in his old age he recoloured those old scenes that he had painted in his youth by (the strength of) his arm, by means of yet more victories. Now, by his great mastery, by his merits and his well-spent old-age, he attained the dignity of the great knightly Order of the Sword.

And he found his towns and lands occupied by tyrants, but by sieges and wars and the strength of his hand he recovered them. And whether our rightful king was well served by the deeds he did, let him of Portugal say, and those who were on his side in Castile, when he departed.

After having staked his life so often on behalf of the right, after having so well served the crown of his true king, after so many exploits that no fixed number would be enough (to count them), Death came to knock at his door in his town of Ocaña.

Estas sus viejas estorias,
que con su braço pintó
en joventud,
con otras nuevas victorias
agora las renovó
en senectud.
Por su grand abilidad,
por méritos y ancianía
bien gastada,
alcançó la dignidad
de la grand cavallería
del Espada.

Y sus villas y sus tierras,
ocupadas de tiranos
las falló,
mas por cercos y por guerras
y por fuerça de sus manos
las cobró.
Pues nuestro rey natural
si de las obras que obró
fue servido,
dígalo el de Portugal,
y en Castilla quien siguió
su partido.

Después de puesta la vida
tantas vezes por su ley
al tablero,
después de tan bien servida
la corona de su rey
verdadero,
después de tanta hazaña
a que no puede bastar
cuenta cierta,
en la su villa de Ocaña
vino la Muerte a llamar
a su puerta,

Saying: 'Good knight, leave this deceptive world and its flattery; let your steely heart display its famous courage in this adversity; and since in pursuit of fame you set so little store by life and health, let your virtue take strength to suffer this affront that calls you.

'Do not let the fearful battle that you expect make you bitter, for here you have left a second and longer life behind you, that is equally glorious. Although this life of honour is not eternal either, or true, it is better than the other and perishable (existence).

'Lasting life is not gained by worldly estates, nor with pleasant living in which lie the sins of hell. But the good monks gain it by prayers and tears, the famous knights by labours and hardships against the Moors.

diziendo: «Buen cavallero,
dexad el mundo engañoso
y su halago:
vuestro coraçón de azero
muestre su esfuerço famoso
en este trago;
y pues de vida y salud
fezistes tan poca cuenta
por la fama,
esfuércese la virtud
para sofrir esta afruenta
que vos llama.

«No se os faga tan amarga
la batalla temerosa
que esperáis,
pues otra vida más larga
de fama tan gloriosa
acá dexáis.
Aunque esta vida de onor
tampoco no es eternal
ni verdadera,
mas con todo es muy mejor
que la otra temporal
perescedera.

«El bivir que es perdurable
no se gana con estados
mundanales,
ni con vida deleitable,
en que moran los pecados
infernales;
mas los buenos religiosos
gánanlo con oraciones
y con lloros,
los cavalleros famosos
con trabajos y aflicciones
contra moros.

'And since you, famous warrior, spilled so much pagan blood, you may expect the reward that you gained in this world with your hands; so with that assurance and with the complete faith that you have, depart with good hopes that you will gain that other, third life.'

'Let us not waste time now, (he answered) in this base life, like this. For my will is in agreement with the divine in everything: and I consent to my death with a joyful, clear and pure will, for it is madness that a man should wish to live when God wishes him to die.

'You who, on account of our wickedness, took servile shape and lowly name. You who united to Your divinity a thing so vile as man, You who suffered without resistance such great torments with Your body, not for my merits but only out of Your clemency, pardon me.'

«Y pues vos, claro varón
tanta sangre derramastes
de paganos,
esperad el galardón
que en este mundo ganastes
por las manos;
y con esta confïança,
y con la fe tan entera
que tenéis,
partid con buena esperança,
que esotra vida tercera
ganaréis.»

«No gastemos tiempo ya
en esta vida mezquina
por tal modo,
que mi voluntad está
conforme con la divina
para todo;
y consiento en mi morir
con voluntad plazentera
clara y pura,
que querer ombre bivir
cuando Dios quiere que muera
es locura.

«Tú, que por nuestra maldad
tomaste forma servil
y baxo nombre,
Tú, que a tu divinidad
juntaste cosa tan vil
como el ombre,
Tú, que tan grandes tormentos
sofriste sin resistencia
en tu persona,
no por mis merescimientos,
mas por tu sola clemencia
me perdona.»

So, with that understanding, and preserving his full mortal consciousness, surrounded by his wife, his sons, and brothers and servants, he gave his soul to Him who had given it to him, and may He place him in His glory in Heaven. Although his life has perished, his memory has left us sufficient consolation.

Lover's Lament

TEARS of my consolation, which have worked wonders and do so still, flow, flow without misgivings, and wet these cheeks as you are used to.

Soon, oh my desires and passions, you must bring me to my end, so I trust. Oh, plaint of Jeremiah, come now to compare yourself with mine!

Oh, souls in Purgatory, who are writhing in two thousand tortures, if my evil plight is known to you, you will clearly see that you are resting in glory.

Assí con tal entender,
todos sentidos umanos
conservados,
cercado de su muger,
de sus fijos y hermanos
y criados,
dio el alma a quien gela dio,
el cual la ponga en el cielo
en su gloria,
y aunque la vida murió,
nos dexó harto consuelo
su memoria.

GARCI SÁNCHEZ DE BADAJOZ

Lamentaciones de amores

LÁGRIMAS de mi consuelo,
que habéis hecho maravillas
y hacéis,
salid, salid sin recelo,
y regad estas mejillas
que soléis.

Ansias y pasiones mías,
presto me habéis de acabar,
yo lo fío;
¡oh planto de Hieremías,
vénte agora a cotejar
con el mío!

Ánimas de Purgatorio,
que en dos mil penas andáis
batallando,
si mi mal os es notorio,
bien veréis que estáis en gloria
descansando.

And you who lie in chains for eternal remembrance, when you know my troubles your tortures will seem to you a glory.

Babel, you that lament that famous tower of yours now desolate, when you know my feelings you will feel your own rage appeased.

Oh, fortune of the seas that wrecks so many vessels on which I do not travel, if you wish to grow calm come and see the ills that I suffer.

Oh, house of Jerusalem, you that were destroyed for your errors, come now, you also, and you will see what joy you have in life.

Constantinople, you who are, to your misfortune, alone and full of people, turn your face, and when you see what my soul suffers you will be able to rest.

Troy, you that were destroyed, you that were once the world's flower, rejoice in my sorrow, for now my plaint is reaching the very depths.

Y vosotras que quedáis
para perpetua memoria
en cadena,
cuando mis males sepáis,
pareceros ha que es gloria
vuestra pena.

Babilonia, que lamentas
la tu torre tan famosa
desolada,
cuando mis ansias sientas
sentirás la tua rabiosa
aconsolada.

¡Oh fortuna de la mar
que trastornas mil navíos
do no vengo,
si te quieres amansar,
vén a ver los males míos
que sostengo.

Casa de Hierusalén,
que fuiste por tus errores
destruida,
vén agora tú también
y verás con que te goces
en tu vida.

Constantinopla que estás
sola y llena de gente
a tu pesar,
vuelve tu cara y podrás,
viendo lo que mi alma siente,
descansar.

Troya, tú que te perdiste,
que solías ser la flor
en el mundo,
gózate conmigo triste,
que ya llega mi clamor
al profundo.

And you, swans who sing beside the reed-beds, close to the river, since you die of your song, consider if there is not reason for me to die of mine.

And you, phoenix who burn yourself and, as a victory, destroy yourself with your own wings, and after you have thus brought yourself to an end transform yourself into another, as a memorial, even so I, sad and miserable, dying for one from whom I hope for no reward, give myself a continual death and return as before to my passion.

Mérida, that once upon a time were the Rome of the Peninsula, look on me and you will see that there is a greater fire and worm in my entrails than in you.

Romance of Fortune's Warning and of Don Rodrigo's Defeat

THE winds were adverse and the moon was full, the fish uttered groans at that bad weather that arose when the good King Don Rodrigo slept with La Cava in a rich tent well garnished with gold.

Y vos, cisnes que cantáis
junto con la cañavera
en par del río,
pues con el canto os matáis,
mirad si es razón que muera
con el mío.

Y tú, fénix que te quemas
y con tus alas deshaces,
por victoria,
y, después que ansí te extremas,
otro de ti mismo haces
por memoria,

ansí yo triste, mezquino,
que muero por quien no espero
gualardón,
dome la muerte contino
y vuelvo como primero
a mi pasión.

Mérida, que en las Españas
otro tiempo fuiste Roma,
mira a mí,
y verás que en mis entrañas
hay mayor fuego y carcoma
que no en ti.

ANÓNIMO

Romance del aviso de la Fortuna y de la derrota de don Rodrigo

LOS vientos eran contrarios, · la luna estaba crecida,
los peces daban gemidos, · por el mal tiempo que hacía,
cuando el buen rey Don Rodrigo · junto a la Cava dormía
dentro de una rica tienda · do oro bien guarnecida.

Three hundred silver ropes held the tent up; inside were a hundred maidens, magnificiently dressed: fifty of them were playing instrucments in the rarest harmony; fifty of them were singing in the sweetest unison.

Then one maiden spoke, whose name was Fortune: 'If you are sleeping, King Don Rodrigo, wake up, I beg of you, and you will see your evil destiny, (and) your worse final end, and you will see your people dead and your main army broken, and your towns and cities destroyed in one day; your castles and fortresses ruled by another man. If you ask me who has done this, I will certainly tell you: (it is) the Count Don Julián, out of love for his daughter, because you dishonoured her and she was all he had, he has just sworn an oath which will cost you your life.'

He awoke in great distress on hearing that voice, and with a sad and doleful face replied in this way: 'Thank you, Fortune, for these tidings of yours.'

At this moment there arrived one who brought news that the Count Don Julián was ravaging his lands. Quickly he called for a horse and rode out to meet him; his opponents were so many that his courage was of no avail; captains and soldiers, all fled pell-mell.

Rodrigo leaves his lands and goes out of his country, the unfortunate man goes alone, taking no company. His horse could hardly move for weariness; it goes where it will, for he does not check its course. The King is so exhausted that he has lost all sensation; he is so dead from hunger and thirst that it is painful to see him. He was so red with blood that he looked like a live coal, the jewel-encrusted armour he wore was dented, the sword he carried was all so notched from the blows he had received, his helmet was so dented that it sank down on his head; he rode with his face swollen from the grief he suffered. He climbed to the top of a hill, the highest there was thereabouts; from there he gazes on his people and sees how defeated they look; from there he gazes on his banners and standards and sees them all so trodden underfoot that the earth covered them. He looks for his captains, but none of them appears; he looks at the field (all) stained with blood, which

Trecientas cuerdas de plata · que la tienda sostenían;
dentro había cien doncellas · vestidas a maravilla:
las cincuenta están tañendo · con muy extraña armonía;
las cincuenta están cantando · con muy dulce melodía.
Allí habló una doncella, · que Fortuna se decía:
«Si duermes, rey Don Rodrigo, · despierta por cortesía,
y verás tus malos hados, · tu peor postrimería,
y verás tus gentes muertas · y tu batalla rompida,
y tus villas y ciudades · destruidas en un día.
Tus castillos, fortalezas, · otro señor los regía.
Si me pides quién lo ha hecho, · yo muy bien te lo diría:
ese conde Don Julián · por amores de su hija;
porque se la deshonraste · y más d'ella no tenía,
juramento viene echando · que te ha de costar la vida.»
Despertó muy congojado · con aquella voz que oía;
con cara triste y penosa · d'esta suerte respondía:
«Mercedes a ti, Fortuna, · d'esta tu mensajería».
Estando en esto ha llegado · uno que nueva traía,
como el conde Don Julián · las tierras le destruía.
Apriesa pide el caballo · y al encuentro le salía;
los contrarios eran tantos · que esfuerzo no le valía;
que capitanes y gentes · huye el que más podía.
Rodrigo deja sus tierras · y del real se salía;
solo va el desventurado, · que no lleva compañía.
El caballo de cansado · ya mudar no se podía;
camina por donde quiere, · que ni le estorba la vía.
El rey va tan desmayado, · que sentido no tenía;
muerto va de sed y hambre, · que de velle era mancilla.
Iba tan tinto de sangre · que una brasa parecía;
las armas lleva abolladas, · que eran de gran pedrería;
la espada lleva hecha sierra · de los golpes de tenía;
el almete de abollado · en la cabeza le hundía;
la cara lleva hinchada · del trabajo que sufría.
Subióse encima de un cerro, · el más alto que allí había;
de allí mira su gente · cómo iba de vencida;
de allí mira sus banderas · y estandartes que tenía,
cómo están todos pisados · que la tierra los cubría.
Mira por los capitanes · que ninguno parescía;
mira el campo tinto en sangre, · al cual arroyos corría.

was running in streams. In his sadness at the sight of this, he felt great shame within him; with his eyes full of tears he spoke to this effect:

'Yesterday I was king of Spain, and now I am not king of a single town; yesterday I possessed towns and castles, today none; yesterday I had servants and people who waited on me, today I have not one battlement that I can say is mine. Unhappy was the hour, unhappy was the day in which I was born and inherited my very great domains, since I was to lose them all at once, in a single day! Oh, death, why do you not come and take this soul of mine from this wretched body, for it would thank you for it?'

Romance of the Penitence of King Rodrigo

AFTER the King Don Rodrigo had lost Spain he departed in despair, fleeing from his misfortune; the unhappy man travelled alone, he wanted no other company than that of the pain of death which was following after him. He went into the thickest wilderness he could find. He has met a shepherd who was driving his herd:

'Tell me, good man,' said he, 'what I want to ask – whether there is a monastery or any churchmen hereabouts.'

The shepherd replied promptly that he would seek one in vain, for in the whole of that barren land there was one hermitage, where there dwelt a hermit who lived a very holy life.

The King was glad of that, for he wished to end his life there, and begged the man to give him something to eat if he had anything, for the strength of his body had entirely failed him. The shepherd took out a bag in which he carried his bread, and gave him some of it, with some dried beef that he happened to have in with it; the bread was very black and tasted very bitter to the King; the tears started from his eyes, he could not hold them back, when he remembered the food he had eaten in his time.

After he had taken a rest he asked for the hermitage. The shepherd then pointed out to him a path by which he would not lose his way; the King gave him a chain and a ring which he was wearing; these were jewels of great value which the King treasured very highly.

Setting out on his way, just as the sun was setting he reached the hermitage in the very high hills.

El triste de ver aquesto, · gran mancilla en sí tenía;
llorando de los sus ojos, · d'esta manera decía:
«Ayer era rey de España, · y hoy no lo soy de una villa;
ayer villas y castillos, · hoy ninguno poseía;
ayer tenía criados · y gente que me servía,
hoy no tengo una almena · que pueda decir que es mía.
¡Desdichada fue la hora, · desdichado fue aquel día
en que nací y heredé · la tan grande señoría,
pues lo había de perder · todo junto y en un día!
¡Oh, muerte!, ¿por qué no vienes · y llevas esta alma mía,
de aqueste cuerpo mezquino, · pues se te agradecería?»

Romance de la Penitencia del rey Rodrigo

DESPUÉS que el rey don Rodrigo · a España perdido había
íbase desesperado · huyendo de su desdicha;
solo va el desventurado, · no quiere otra compañía
que la del mal de la Muerte · que en su seguimiento iba.
Métese por las montañas, las mas copesas que veía
Topado ha con un pastor · que su ganado traía;
díjole: «Dime, buen hombre, · lo que preguntar quería:
si hay por aquí monasterio · o gente de clerecía»,
El pastor respondió luego · que en balde lo buscaría,
porque en todo aquel desierto · sola una ermita había
donde estaba un ermitaño · que hacía muy santa vida.
El rey fue alegre desto · por allí acabar su vida;
pidió al hombre que le diese · de comer, si algo tenía,
que las fuerzas de su cuerpo · del todo desfallecían.
El pastor sacó un zurrón · en donde su pan traía;
dióle de él y de un tasajo · que acaso allí echado había;
el pan era muy moreno, · al rey muy mal le sabía;
las lágrimas se le salen, · detener no las podía,
acordándose en su tiempo · los manjares que comía.
Después que hobo descansado · por la ermita le pedía;
el pastor le enseñó luego · por donde no erraría;
el rey le dió una cadena · y un anillo que traía;
joyas son de gran valor · que el rey en mucho tenía.
Comenzando a caminar · ya cerca el sol se ponía,
a la ermita hubo llegado · en muy alta serranía.

He found the hermit, who was more than a hundred years old. 'I am the unhappy Rodrigo, who was once king, and who has lost his soul for sins of love (and) for whose black sins all Spain has been destroyed. I beg you, for God's sake, hermit, for God's sake and Saint Mary's, to hear me my confession, for it is my wish to die.'

The hermit was afraid and said in tears: 'As for confession, I will confess you; but absolve you I cannot.'

While they were thus talking, a voice from heaven was heard: 'Absolve him, confessor, absolve him on your life, and give him a penance in his own grave.'

What was revealed to him the King put into effect. He got into the grave, which was beside the hermitage; in it slept a serpent, most fearful to look upon; it coiled three times round in the tomb, and had seven heads.

'Pray for me, hermit, that I may make a good end to my life.' The hermit encouraged him and covered him with the tombstone. He prayed to God at his side all the hours of the day.

'How goes it with you, penitent, with your mighty companion?' 'He is biting me now, biting me now where I sinned most, right in the heart, the source of my great misfortune.'

The little bells of heaven rang out with sounds of joy; the bells of earth rang of their own accord; the penitent's soul rose into heaven.

Romance of Fajardo

THE King of the Moors was playing, playing at chess one day with that good man Fajardo, out of the love he felt for him. Fajardo staked Lorca, and the Moorish King Almeria; the King gave him check with his rook, and the standard-bearer took it. The Moor cried in a loud voice: 'The town of Lorca is mine.'

'Be silent, be silent, my lord King. Do not be so contentious, for even if you win it from me it would not yield to you. I have knights within (its walls) who will defend it from you.'

Then spoke the Moorish King. Indeed, you shall hear what he said. 'Let us play no more, Fajardo, and have no more contention, for so good a knight are you that all the world fears you.'

Encontróse al ermitaño · más de cien años tenía.
«El desdichado Rodrigo · yo soy, que rey ser solía,
el que por yerros de amor · tiene su alma perdida,
por cuyos negros pecados · toda España es destruida.
Por Dios te ruego, ermitaño, · por Dios y Santa María,
que me oigas en confesión · porque finar me quería.»
El ermitaño se espanta · y con lágrimas decía:
«Confesar, confesaréte, · absolverte no podía.»
Estando en estas razones · voz de los cielos se oía:
«Absuélvelo, confesor, · absuélvelo por tu vida
y dale la penitencia · en su sepultura misma.»
Según le fue revelado · por obra el rey lo ponía.
Metióse en la sepultura · que a par de la ermita había;
dentro duerme una culebra, · mirarla espanto ponía:
tres roscas daba a la tumba, · siete cabezas tenía.
«Ruega por mí el ermitaño · porque acabe bien mi vida.»
El ermitaño lo esfuerza, · con la losa lo cubría,
rogaba a Dios a su lado · todas las horas del día.
«¿Cómo te va, penitente, · con tu fuerte compañía?»
«Ya me come, ya me come, · por do más pecado había,
en derecho al corazón, · fuente de mi gran desdicha.»
Las campanicas del cielo · sones hacen de alegría:
las campanas de la tierra · ellas solas se tañían;
el alma del penitente · para los cielos subía.

Romance de Fajardo

JUGANDO estaba el rey moro · y aun a ajedrés un día,
con aquese buen Fajardo · con amor que le tenía.
Fajardo jugaba a Lorca, y el rey moro Almería;
jaque le dio con el roque, · el alférez le prendía.
A grandes voces dice el moro: «La villa de Lorca es mía».
«Calles, calles, señor Rey, · no toméis tal porfía,
que aunque me la ganases, ella no se te daría:
caballeros tengo dentro, · que te la defenderían.»
Allí hablara el rey moro, · bien oiréis lo que decía:
«No juguemos más, Fajardo, · ni tengamos más porfía,
que sois tan buen caballero, · que todo el mundo os temía.»

Romance of the Siege of Alora

ALORA, the besieged, you who are beside the river, the Governor besieged you on one Sunday morning. The field was well filled with foot-soldiers and cavalry; with his great artillery he had made a breach in your walls. You would have seen Moorish men and women all flying to the citadel; the women were carrying clothing, the men flour and grain, and the fifteen-year-old Mooresses were carrying fine gold, and the little Moorish boys were carrying raisins and figs. On top of the wall they had hung their flag. Between one battlement and another a young Moor had stayed, armed with a crossbow, and in it was an arrow. He cried out aloud, so that the people heard him: 'A truce, a truce, Governor; the citadel surrenders to you!'

The Governor lifts his vizor, to see who had spoken. He had aimed at his forehead, and it came out at the back of his head. Paul took him by the rein, little James by the hand – those two whom he had brought up in his house from childhood. They took him to the surgeons, to see if he could be cured. The first words he uttered were to tell them his will.

Romance of the Moorish King who lost Alhama

THE Moorish King was riding about, through the city of Granada, from the gate of Elvira to the gate of Vivarrambla. 'Alas for my Alhama!'

Letters had come to him that Alhama was captured. He threw the letters in the fire and killed the messenger. 'Alas for my Alhama!'

He got down from a mule and mounted a horse; he rode up the Zacatín to the Alhambra. 'Alas for my Alhama!'

The moment that he was inside the Alhambra he gave orders that his trumpets should be sounded, and his silver pipes. 'Alas for my Alhama!'

And that a call-to-arms should hastily be sounded on the war-drums, so that his Moors should hear it, the Moors of La Vega and of Granada. 'Alas for my Alhama!'

Romance de Alora, la bien cercada

ALORA, la bien cercada, · tú que estás en par del río,
cercóte el Adelantado · una mañana en domingo,
de peones y hombres de armas · el campo bien guarnecido;
con la gran artillería · hecho te había un portillo.
Viérades moros y moras · todos huir al castillo:
las moras llevaban ropa, · los moros harina y trigo,
y las moras de quince años · llevaban el oro fino,
y los moricos pequeños · llevaban la pasa y higo.
Por cima de la muralla · su pendón llevan tendido.
Entre almena y almena · quedádose había un morico
con una ballesta armada, · y en ella puesta un cuadrillo;
en altas voces decía, · que la gente lo había oído:
«¡Treguas, treguas, Adelantado, · por tuyo se da el castillo!»
Alza la visera arriba · para ver el que tal le dijo,
asestárale a la frente, · salídole ha al colodrillo.
Sacólo Pablo de rienda, y de mano Jacobillo,
estos dos que había criado · en su casa desde chicos.
Lleváronle a los maestros, · por ver si será guarido.
A las primeras palabras · el testamento les dijo.

Romance del rey moro que perdió Alhama

PASEÁBASE el rey moro · por la ciudad de Granada
desde la puerta de Elvira · hasta la de Vivarrambla.
«¡Ay de mi Alhama!»
Cartas le fueran venidas · que Alhama era ganada:
las cartas echó en el fuego · y al mensajero matara.
«¡Ay de mi Alhama!»
Descabalga de una mula · y en un caballo cabalga;
por el Zacatín arriba · subido se había al Alhambra.
«¡Ay de mi Alhama!»
Como en el Alhambra estuvo, · al mismo punto mandaba
que se toquen sus trompetas, · sus añafiles de plata.
«¡Ay de mi Alhama!»
Y que las cajas de guerra · apriesa toquen al arma,
porque lo oigan sus moros, · los de la Vega y Granada.
«¡Ay de mi Alhama!»

The Moors who heard the sound that calls to bloody war, one by one and two by two, formed up in a great host. 'Alas for my Alhama!'

Then there spoke an old Moor. This is how he spoke: 'What are you calling us for, King? What is this summons for?' 'Alas for my Alhama!'

'You must learn, my friends, a disastrous piece of news, that (certain) valiant Christians have captured Alhama from us.' 'Alas for my Alhama!'

Then there spoke an Alfaquí (a Moorish elder), with a long, hoary beard. 'That serves you right, my good King! That, my good King, has paid you out.' 'Alas for my Alhama!'

'You killed the Abencerrajes, who were the flower of Granada. You arrested the renegades of Córdoba, the famous.' 'Alas for my Alhama!'

'For that you deserve, King, a most severe punishment; (you deserve) to lose your life and your kingdom and here to lose Granada.' 'Alas for my Alhama!'

Romance of Durandarte

DURANDARTE lies dead at the foot of a great mountain, a stone for a pillow and beneath a green beech; all the birds of the mountain circle him for company, Montesinos bewailed him, who had been with him at his death, he has dug his grave in a rocky cavern; he was stripping him of his helmet, ungirding his sword, he was taking the armour from his chest, he was tearing out his heart to send it to Belerma, as Durandarte had asked him to. And when he had torn it out he put his face to Durandarte's, (and) weeping so bitterly, swooned a thousand times; and when he came to himself he spoke these words: 'Durandarte, Durandarte, may God pardon your soul and take me from this world so that I may go with you.'

Los moros que el son oyeron · que al sangriento Marte llama,
uno a uno y dos a dos · juntado se ha gran batalla.
«¡Ay de mi Alhama!»
Allí habló un moro viejo, · d'esta manera hablara:
«¿Para qué nos llamas, Rey, · para qué es esta llamada?»
«¡Ay de mi Alhama!»
«Habéis de saber, amigos, · una nueva desdichada:
que cristianos de braveza · ya nos han ganado Alhama.»
«¡Ay de mi Alhama!»
Allí habló un Alfaquí, · de barba crecida y cana:
«¡Bien se te emplea, buen Rey! · ¡Buen Rey, bien se te empleara!»
«¡Ay de mi Alhama!»
«Mataste los Abencerrajes, · que eran la flor de Granada;
cogiste los tornadizos · de Córdoba la nombrada.»
«¡Ay de mi Alhama!»
«Por eso mereces, Rey, · una pena muy doblada;
que te pierdas tú y el reino, · y aquí se pierde Granada.»
«¡Ay de mi Alhama!»

Romance de Durandarte

MUERTO queda Durandarte · al pie de un gran montaña,
un canto por cabecera, · debajo una verde haya,
todas las aves del monte · alrededor le acompañan,
llorábale Montesinos · que a su muerte se hallara,
hecha le tiene la fuesa · en una peñosa cava;
quitándole estaba el yelmo, · desciñéndole la espada,
desarmábale los pechos, · el corazón le sacaba,
para enviarlo a Belerma · como él se lo rogara,
y desque lo hubo sacado · su rostro al suyo juntaba,
tan agramente llorando · mil veces se desmayaba,
y desque volvió en sí · estas palabras hablaba:
«Durandarte, Durandarte, · Dios perdone la tu alma
y a mí saque deste mundo · para que contigo vaya.»

Romance of Doña Alda

IN Paris is Doña Alda, the bride of Don Roldán (Roland), three hundred ladies with her to keep her company; all wear the same dresses, all wear the same shoes, all eat at one table, all ate of the same bread, except for Doña Alda, who was the mistress. A hundred of them spun gold, a hundred of them weave fine silk, a hundred play instruments to entertain Doña Alda.

To the sound of the instruments Doña Alda has fallen asleep; she had dreamed a dream, a very grievous dream. She awoke in terror, and in very great terror uttered such loud cries that they were heard in the city. Then her maids spoke, indeed you shall hear what they said: 'What is it, my lady, who is it that hurt you?'

'I dreamed a dream, maidens, which has given me great grief: I saw myself on a mountain, in a deserted place, and over the highest mountains I saw a goshawk fly. After it came an eaglet that pressed him very close. The goshawk, in great distress, sheltered under my skirt; the eaglet, in great fury, was just dragging him out; it plucked his feathers with its claws and tore him with its beak.'

Then spoke her chief waiting-maid, indeed you shall hear what she said: 'That dream of yours, my lady, I shall know how to interpret it: the goshawk is your bridegroom, coming from over the sea; and the eaglet is yourself, whom he is going to marry, and that mountain is the church, where they will throw the marriage veil over you both.'

'If that is true, my waiting-maid, I shall know how to reward you.'

Next day, in the morning, letters were brought her from abroad; they came written inside in ink, but outside written in blood, (and said) that her Roldán had died in the chase of Roncesvalles.

Romance of Baldwin

THE moon is as bright as the sun at midday, when Baldwin comes out from the aqueduct (of Carmona) of Seville. He met a pretty Moorish girl, and seven years long Baldwin has had her as his mistress.

Romance de doña Alda

EN París está Doña Alda, · la esposa de Don Roldán,
trescientas damas con ella · para la acompañar:
todas visten un vestido, · todas calzan un calzar,
todas comen a una mesa, · todas comían de un pan,
si no era Doña Alda, · que era la mayoral.
Las ciento hilaban oro, · las ciento tejen cendal,
las ciento tañen instrumentos · para Doña Alda holgar.
Al son de los instrumentos · Doña Alda adormido ha:
ensoñado había un sueño · un sueño de gran pesar.
Recordó despavorida · y con un pavor muy grande,
los gritos daba tan grandes · que se oían en la ciudad.
Allí hablaron sus doncellas, · bien oiréis lo que dirán:
«¿Qué es aquesto, mi señora, · quién es el que os hizo mal?»
«Un sueño soñé, doncellas, · que me ha dado gran pesar:
que me veía en un monte · en un desierto lugar;
de so los montes muy altos · un azor vide volar,
tras del viene un aguililla · que lo ahinca muy mal.
El azor con gran cuita · metióse so mi brial;
el aguililla con grande ira · de allí lo iba a sacar:
con las uñas lo despluma, · con el pico lo deshace.»
Allí habló su camarera, · bien oiréis lo que dirá:
«Aquese sueño, señora, · bien os lo entiendo soltar:
el azor es vuestro esposo · que viene de allén la mar;
el águila sedes vos, · con la cual ha de casar,
y aquel monte es la iglesia · donde os han de velar.»

«Si así es, mi camarera, · bien te lo entiendo pagar.»
Otro día de mañana · cartas de fuera le traen;
tintas venían de dentro, · de fuera escritas con sangre,
que su Roldán era muerto · en la caza de Ronscesvalles.

Romance de Valdovinos

TAN claro hace la luna · como el sol a mediodía,
cuando sale Valdovinos · de los caños de Sevilla.
Por encuentro se lo hubo · una morica garrida,
y siete años la tuviera · Valdovinos por amiga.

When the seven years were up Baldwin heaved a sigh.

'Do you sigh, Baldwin, my best beloved friend? Either you are afraid of the Moors or you have fallen for a new mistress.'

'No, I have no fear of the Moors, nor even less have I a new mistress. But, you being a Moor and I a Christian, we are leading an evil life and, like flesh on Friday, my law forbids it.'

'For love of you, my Baldwin, I will turn Christian, if you will have me for your wife, or if not, let it be as your mistress.'

Romance of the Princely Avenger

BEHOLD, behold where comes the princely avenger, riding with short stirrups (in the Moorish style) on a swift steed, his cloak rolled over his arm, his colour changed, and in his right hand a cutting javelin. With the point of it you could cut out a harvest-bug. Seven times it was tempered in the blood of a dragon, and sharpened as many times, so that it might cut the better; the iron was smelted in France and the haft made in Aragon; he was trying its edge on the wings of his falcon. He was going to seek Don Cuadros, Don Cuadros the traitor, and there he found him beside the Emperor, holding the wand in his hand, for he was a chief justice.

Seven times the Prince reflected whether he should throw it or no, and when he had thought eight times he flung his javelin. Instead of hitting the said Don Cuadros, he hit the Emperor; he has pierced through his cloak and his coat, which was made of shot silk, and plunged it into the brick floor, more than four inches deep.

Then the King spoke to him, indeed you shall hear what he said: 'Why did you throw at me, Prince? Why do you throw at me, traitor?'

'May your Highness pardon me, but at you I did not throw; I threw at the traitor Cuadros, that false deceiver. For I had seven brothers, and he has spared none, none but me. Therefore in front of you, good King, I defy him.'

All take the part of Don Cuadros, and of the Prince only one maiden – the Emperor's daughter – who took them by the hand and led them to the field.

At the first encounter Cuadros fell to the ground. The Prince dismounted

Cumpliéndose sus siete años · Valdovinos que sospira:
«¿Sospiraste, Valdovinos, · amigo que yo más quería?
O vos habéis miedo a moros · o adamades otra amiga.»
«Que no tengo miedo a moros, · ni menos tengo otra amiga,
que vos mora y yo cristiano · hacemos la mala vida,
y como la carne en viernes, · que mi ley lo defendía.»
«Por tus amores, mi Valdovinos, · cristiana me tornaría
si quisieras por mujer, · si no sea por amiga.»

Romance del infante vengador

HELO, helo por do viene · el infante vengador,
caballero a la gineta · en un caballo corredor,
su manto revuelto al brazo, · demudada la color,
y en la su mano derecha · un venablo cortador.
Con la punta del venablo · sacarían un arador.
Siete veces fue templado · en la sangre de un dragón,
y otras tantas fue afilado · porque cortase mejor;
el hierro fue hecha en Francia, · y el asta en Aragón;
perfilándoselo iba · en las alas de su halcón.
Iba a buscar a Don Cuadros, · a Don Cuadros el traidor,
allá le fuera a hallar · junto al Emperador.
La vara tiene en la mano, · que era justicia mayor.
Siete veces lo pensaba, si lo tiraría o no,
y al cabo de los ocho · el venablo le arrojó.
Por dar al dicho Don Cuadros · dado ha al Emperador:
pasado le ha manto y sayo · que era de un tornasol,
por el suelo ladrillado · mas de un palmo le metió.
Allí le habló el Rey, · bien oiréis lo que habló:
«¿Por qué me tiraste, Infante? · ¿Por qué me tiras, traidor?»
«Perdóneme tu Alteza, · que no tiraba a ti, no;
tiraba al traidor de Cuadros; · ese falso engañador,
que siete hermanos tenía, · no a dejado, si a mí no;
por eso delante de ti, · buen Rey, le desafío yo.»
Todos fían a Don Cuadros, · y al Infante no fían, no,
si no fuera una doncella, · hija es del Emperador,
que los tomó por la mano, · y en el campo los metió.
A los primeros encuentros · Cuadros en tierra cayó.

and cut off his head, and put it on his lance and presented it to the good King. When the King saw it he married him to his daughter.

Romance of Julianesa

'FORWARD, dogs, forward! May the evil rabies kill you! On Thursday you kill the boar, and on Friday you eat the flesh. Alas, it is seven years today that I have been wandering in this valley. For my feet are unshod and my nails are oozing blood, I eat raw flesh and drink red blood. Sadly I am seeking Julianesa, the Emperor's daughter, for the Moors took her from me early on the morning of St John's day, while she was gathering roses and flowers in an orchard of her father's.'

Julianesa hears him as she lies in the Moor's arms; and the tears from her eyes fall on the Moor's face.

Romance of the Fair Melisenda

ALL the people were asleep who were under God's authority, but Melisenda, the Emperor's daughter, did not sleep for love of Count Airuelo would not let her rest. She leapt out of bed (naked) as her mother bore her, and put on a smock, for she could not find a skirt. She wandered about the palace where her ladies were; and with slaps for them all she began to cry: 'If you are asleep, my maidens, if you are asleep, wake up, and any of you that know about love, please give me some advice. Let those who do not know about love, keep this a secret for me: love for Count Airuelo will not let me rest.' Then spoke an old woman, an old woman of great age: 'Now is the time, my lady, to take your pleasures, for if you wait for old age, not a lad will want you. I learnt this when I was a girl and I cannot forget it, at the time when I was a servant in your father's house.' When Melisenda heard this she would not listen to more; she went to look for the Count at the palace where he was. She ran into young Hernando, one of her father's guards.

Apeárase el Infante, · la cabeza le cortó,
y tomárala en su lanza, · y al buen Rey la presentó.
De que aquesto vido el Rey · con su hija le casó.

Romance de Julianesa

«¡ARRIBA, canes, arriba! · ¡Que rabia mala os mate!
En jueves matáis el puerco · y en viernes coméis la carne.
¡Ay, que hoy hace los siete años · que ando por aqueste valle,
pues traigo los pies descalzos, · las uñas corriendo sangre,
pues como las carnes crudas · y bebo la roja sangre.
Buscando triste a Julianesa, · la hija del Emperante,
pues me l'han tomado moros mañanica de Sant Juane,
cogiendo rosas y flores en un vergel de su padre.»
Oídolo ha Julianesa · qu'en brazos del moro estáe;
las lágrimas de sus ojos · al moro dan en la faze.

Romance de la linda Melisenda

TODAS las gentes dormían · en las que Dios tiene parte,
mas no duerme Melisenda, · la hija del Emperante;
que amores del conde Airuelo · no la dejan reposar.
Salto diera de la cama · como la parió su madre,
vistiérase una alcandora · no hallando un brial;
vase para los palacios · donde sus damas están;
dando palmadas en ellas · las empezó de llamar:
«Si dormís, las mis doncellas, · si dormides, recordad;
las que sabedes de amores · consejo me queráis dar;
las que de amor non sabedes · tengádesme poridad:
amores del conde Airuelo · no me dejan reposar.»
Allí hablara una vieja, · vieja es de antigua edad:
«Agora es tiempo, señora, · de los placeres tomar,
que si esperáis a vejez · no vos querrá un rapaz.
Esto aprendí siendo niña, · y no lo puedo olvidar,
el tiempo que fui criada · en casa de vuestro padre.»
Desqu'esto oyó Melisenda · no quiso más escuchar,
íbase a buscar al Conde · a los palacios do está.
Topara con Hernandillo, · un alguacil de su padre.

'What is this, Melisenda? What can this be? Either you are lovesick, or you are going out of your mind!' 'No, I am not lovesick, nor have I any cause for grief, but when I was young I had an illness. I promised to say a Mass, there in St John Lateran. The ladies went by day, and now the maidens are going.' When Hernando heard this he stopped speaking; the Princess in her fury wanted to avenge herself on him. 'Lend me now, Hernando, lend me your dagger, for I am afraid of the street dogs!' He took the dagger by the point, and gave her the hilt; she dealt him such a stab that he fell to the ground dead. She went to the palace where the Count Airuelo was; she found the doors locked, and did not know how to get in; with a magic spell she opened them wide. At the noise Count Airuelo began to shout: 'Help, my knights; help me, and do not delay. I think it is my enemies who have come to kill me.' The discreet Melisenda began to speak to him: 'Do not be alarmed, sir, please do not take fright, for I am a Moorish girl, come from over the sea.' The Count recognized her as soon as he heard this. The Count went up to her and took her hands, and in the shade of a laurel they played the game of love.

Romance of the Palmer

THE Palmer left Mérida, that city of Mérida; his feet were unshod and his nails oozed blood. He wore a torn pilgrim's robe that was not worth a farthing. Under it he wore another – and that was worth a city! For no king or emperor could get one like it. He took the straight road for that (famous) city of Paris: he did not ask for an inn nor yet for a poor man's house, he asked for King Charles's palace, (he asked) where it was. A porter was at the door, and he began to speak: 'Tell me now, porter, where is King Charles?'

When the porter saw him he was very much astonished that so poor a pilgrim should ask for the King.

«¿Qu'es aquesto, Melisenda? · Esto que podía estar?
¡O vos tenéis mal de amores, · o vos queréis loca tornar!»
«Que no tengo mal de amores, · ni tengo por quien penar,
mas cuando yo era pequeña · tuve una enfermedad.
Prometí tener novenas · allá en San Juan de Letrán:
las dueñas iban de día, · doncellas agora van.»
Desque esto oyera Hernando · puso fin a su hablar;
la Infanta mal enojada · queriendo d'él se vengar:
«Prestásesme hora, Hernando, prestásesme tu puñal,
que miedo me tengo, miedo · de los perros de la calle.»
Tomó el puñal por la punta, · los cabos le fue a dar;
diérale tal puñalada · qu'en el suelo muerto cae.
Ibase para palacio · do el conde Airuelo está;
las puertas halló cerradas, · no sabe por do pasar;
con arte d'encantamento · las abrió de par en par.
Al estruendo el conde Airuelo · empezara de llamar:
«Socorred, mis caballeros, · socorred sin más tardar;
creo son mis enemigos, · que me vienen a matar.»
La Melisenda discreta · l'empezara de hablar:
«No te congojes, señor, · no quieras pavor tomar,
que yo soy una morica · venida de allende del mar.»
Desqu'esto oyera el Conde · luego conocido la ha;
fuése el Conde para ella, · las manos le fue a tomar,
y a la sombra de un laurel, · de Venus es su jugar.

Romance del Palmero

De Mérida sale el Palmero, · de Mérida, esa ciudade;
los pies llevaba descalzos, · las uñas corriendo sangre.
Una esclavina, trae rota, · que no valía un reale,
y debajo traía otra, · ¡bien valía una ciudad!
Que ni rey ni emperador · no alcanzaba otra tale.
Camino lleva derecho · de París, esa ciudade;
ni pregunta por mesón · ni menos por hospital;
pregunta por los palacios · del rey Carlos do estáe.
Un portero está a la puerta, · empezóle de hablare:
«Dijésesme tú, el portero, · el rey Carlos, ¿dónde estáe?»
El portero, que lo vido, · mucho maravillado se hae,
cómo un romero tan pobre · por el rey va a preguntare.

'Tell me where he is, sir, and do not be alarmed.'

'He is at Mass, Palmer, there in Saint John Lateran. An archbishop is saying the Mass and a cardinal is saying the offices.'

When the Palmer heard him he went to Saint John's; as he comes in through the door you shall see indeed what he does. He bowed to God in heaven and to Saint Mary his mother, he bowed to the archbishop, he bowed to the cardinal – because he was saying the Mass, not because he deserved it otherwise – he bowed to the Emperor and to his royal crown, he bowed to the twelve who eat bread at one table. He did not bow to Oliver, nor yet to Sir Roland, because they had a nephew who was in Moorish hands, and though they could do so, they had not gone to rescue him. When Oliver saw this, when Roland saw this, they both drew their swords and attacked the Palmer. The Palmer began to protect his body with his staff.

Then the King spoke, and indeed you shall hear what he said: 'Stop, stop, Oliver! Stop, stop, Sir Roland! Either this Palmer is mad or he comes of royal blood.'

He took him by the hand and began to speak to him: 'Tell me, Palmer, and do not deny me the truth, in what year and in what month did you pass the waters of the sea?'

'In the month of May, sir, I crossed them. For one day I was on the seashore in my father's garden, there to take my pleasure; the Moors took me prisoner and carried me over the sea. They went and presented me to the Princess of Sansueña, and when the Princess saw me she fell in love with me. I should like to tell you, King, the life that I led. I ate at her table and went to lie in her bed.'

Then the King spoke. Indeed you shall hear what he said: 'Captivity like that any man would accept. Tell me, Palmer, what if I were to go and capture her?'

'Do not go there, good King. Good King, do not go there, because Mérida is very strong and will defend itself well against you. It has three hundred castles, and they are a marvel to see, and the smallest of them all would put up a good defence against you.'

«Dígadesmelo, señor, · desto no tengáis pesar.»
«En misa estaba, Palmero, · allá en Sant Juan de Letráne:
que dice misa un arzobispo · y la oficia un cardenale.»
El Palmero que lo oyera · íbase para Sant Juane;
en entrando por la puerta · bien veréis lo que haráe.
Humillóse a Dios del cielo · y a Santa María su Madre,
humillóse al arzobispo · humillóse al cardenale
porque decía la misa, · no porque merescía máse;
humillóse el Emperador · y a su corona reale,
humillóse a los doce · que a una mesa comen pane.
No se humilla a Oliveros, · ni menos a Don Roldáne,
porque un sobrino que tienen · en poder de moros estáe,
y pudiendo lo hacer · no le van a rescatare.
Desque aquesto vío Oliveros, · desque aquesto vío Roldáne,
sacan ambos las espadas, · para el Palmero se vane.
El Palmero con su bordón · su cuerpo va a mampararе.
Allí hablara el buen Rey, · bien oiréis lo que diráe:
«Tate, tate, Oliveros, · tate, tate, Don Roldáne,
o este Palmero es loco, · o viene de sangre reale.»
Tomárale por la mano, · y empiézale de hablare:
«Dígasme tú, el Palmero, · no me niegues la verdade,
¿en qué año y en qué mes · pasaste tú aguas de la mare?»
«En el mes de mayo, señor, · yo las fuera a pasare.
Porque yo estaba un día · a orillas de la mare
en el huerto de mi padre · por haberme de holgare;
cativáronme los moros, · pasáronme allende el mare.
A la infanta de Sansueña · me fueron a presentare;
la Infanta desque me vido · de mí se fue a enamorare.
La vida que yo tenía, · Rey, quiérovosla contare.
En la su mesa comía, · y en su cama me iba a echare.»
Allí hablara el buen Rey, · bien oiréis lo que diráe:
«Tal catividad como ésa · quien quiera lo tomaráe:
dígasme tú, el Palmerico, · ¿si la iría yo a ganare?»
«No vades allá, el buen Rey, · buen Rey, no vades alláe,
porque Mérida es muy fuerte, · bien se vos defenderáe.
Trecientos castillos tiene, · que es cosa de los mirare,
que el menor de todos ellos · bien se os defenderáe.»

Then spoke Oliver, then spoke Sir Roland: 'The Palmer is lying, sir, lying, and not telling the truth, for in Mérida there are not a hundred castles, nor ninety, to my thinking, and those that are in Mérida have no one to defend them, for they have not a commander, nor even anyone to guard them.'

When the Palmer heard this he was moved by great sorrow. He raised his right hand and struck Roland a blow.

Then the King spoke in fury and great sorrow: 'Arrest him, my officers, and take him to be hanged.'

The officers have taken him to be punished, and even there at the foot of the gallows the Palmer began to speak. 'Ill will betide you, King Charles. God means to do you ill, for you have one only son, and you order him to be hanged.'

The Queen had heard this, and she stopped to look at him: 'Let him go, officers; please do him no harm. If he were my son, it would be impossible to conceal it, for on one side he will have a very large birthmark.'

Now they take him to the Queen, now they are going to take him: they strip him of one pilgrim's robe, which was not worth a farthing: now they strip off the other, which was worth a city. They have discovered the Prince, they have discovered the mark on him. They made such a rejoicing that no one could say how great.

Romance of Lancelot

THE King had three small sons, three small sons and no more; out of the anger he felt against them he has cursed them all. One was turned into a deer, one was turned into a dog, and one was turned into a Moor and crossed the waters of the sea.

Lancelot was riding, and jesting with the ladies, and one cried out: 'Sir Knight, stay (a moment). If the fate were mine, my destiny would be fulfilled, were I to marry you and you willingly to marry me, and were you to give me as a bride's portion that deer with the white foot.'

'I would give it to you, lady, with all my heart and gladly, if I knew in what land the deer was reared.'

Now Lancelot rides, now he rides and departs. In front of him he has his

Allí hablara Oliveros, · allí habló Don Roldáne:
«Miente, señor, el Palmero, · miente, y no dice verdade,
que en Mérida no hay cien castillos, · ni noventa a mi pensare,
y éstos que Mérida tiene · no tiene quien los defensare,
que ni tenían señor, · ni menos quien los guardare.»
Desque aquesto oyó el Palmero, · movido con gran pesare,
alzó su mano derecha, · dio un bofetón a Roldáne.
Allí hablara el Rey · con furia y con gran pesare:
«Tomalde, la mi justicia · y llevédeslo ahorcare.»
Tomádolo ha la justicia · para habello de justiciare;
y aun allá al pie de la horca · el Palmero fuera hablare:
«¡Oh, mal hubieses, rey Carlos! · Dios te quiera hacer male,
que un hijo solo que tienes · tú le mandas ahorcare».
Oídolo había la Reina, · ya se le paró a mirare:
«Dejédeslo, la justicia, · no le queráis hacer male,
que si él era mi hijo · encubrir no se podráe,
que en un lado ha de tener · un extremado lunare.»
Ya le llevan a la Reina, · ya se lo van a llevare;
desnúdanle una esclavina · que no valía un reale;
ya le desnudaban otra · que valía una ciudade;
halládole han al Infante, · halládole han la señale.
Alegrías se hicieron · no hay quien las pueda contare.

Romance de Lanzarote

TRES hijuelos había el Rey, · tres hijuelos, que no más;
por enojo que hubo de ellos · todos maldito los ha.
El uno se tornó ciervo · el otro se tornó can,
el otro se tornó moro, · pasó las aguas del mar.
Andábase Lanzarote, · entre las damas holgando,
grandes voces dio la una: · «Caballero, estad parado:
si fuese la mi ventura, · cumplido fuese mi hado
que yo casase con vos, · y vos conmigo de grado,
y me diésedes en arras · aquel ciervo del pie blanco.»
«Dároslo he yo, mi señora, · de corazón y de grado,
si supiese yo las tierras · donde el ciervo era criado.»
Ya cabalga Lanzarote, · ya cabalga y ya se vía,
delante de sí llevaba · los sabuesos por la traílla.

hounds on a leash. He had come to a hermitage in which a hermit lived.

'God save you, good man.'

'A good welcome to you. A huntsman you seem to me, by the dogs you have with you.'

'Tell me, hermit, you who lead a holy life, where are the haunts of that deer with a white foot?'

'Stay here, my son, until it is day, and I will tell you what I have seen and all that I know. Last night it passed by here, two hours before day, seven lions with it, and a lioness, that has had cubs. Seven counts were left dead and many knights. God preserve you for ever, my son, wherever you may go; but whoever sent you here did not wish to keep you alive. Oh, Dame Quintañones, may an evil fire burn you, for so many good knights have lost their lives for you!'

Romance of Sir Tristram

SIR Tristram has been wounded by an evil lance-thrust, which the King his uncle gave him with a poisoned lance. He dealt it him from a tower, for he dared not come near. He has the iron in his body, and the haft trembles without; Queen Iseult, his lovely mistress, goes to see him, swathed in black cloth which was called the (cloth of) mourning.

Seeing him in such an evil plight, the sorrowful lady said: 'May he who wounded you, Sir Tristram, suffer in agony. For there is no surgeon to be found skilled enough to cure your wounds.'

They put their mouths together like tame turtle-doves. The one weeps, the other weeps, they bathe the bed in tears. There grew a bush that was called the white lily; any woman who eats of it immediately feels herself pregnant. I did so, poor girl that I am, to my own misfortune.

Romance of a Moorish Girl

I WAS the Mooress Moraima, a Moorish girl fair to look upon; a Christian came to my door, poor wretch that I am, to deceive me. He spoke to me in Arabic, like someone who knows it well: 'Open the door to me, Mooress, if Allah is to keep you from harm.'

'How can I open to you, wretch that I am, since I do not know who you are?'

Llegado había a una ermita, · donde un ermitaño había:
«Dios te salve, el hombre bueno.» · «Buena sea tu venida;
cazador me parecéis · en los sabuesos que traía.»
«Dígasme tú, el ermitaño, · tú que haces santa vida,
ese ciervo de pie blanco · ¿dónde hace su manida?»
«Quedáisos aquí, mi hijo, · hasta que sea de día,
contaros he lo que vi, · y todo lo que sabía.
Por aquí pasó esta noche · dos horas ante del día,
siete leones con él · y una leona parida.
Siete condes deja muertos, · y mucha caballería.
Siempre Dios te guarde, hijo, · por do quier que fuer tu ida,
que quien acá te envió · no te quería dar la vida.
¡Ay dueña de Quintañones, · de mal fuego seas ardida,
que tanto buen caballero · por ti ha perdido la vida!»

Romance de Don Tristán

HERIDO está Don Tristán · de una mala lanzada,
diérasela el Rey su tío · con una lanza herbolada.
Diósela desde una torre, · que de cerca non osaba.
Que el hierro tiene en el cuerpo, · de fuera le tiembla el asta;
valo a ver la reina Iseo, · la su linda enamorada,
cubierta de un paño negro, · que de luto se llamaba.
Viéndole tan mal parado · dice así la triste dama:
«Quien te hirió, Don Tristán, · heridas tenga de rabia,
que no hallase maestro · que sopiese de sanallas.»
Júntanse boca con boca · como palomillas mansas,
llora el uno, llora el otro, · la cama bañan en agua;
allí nace un arboledo · que azucena se llamaba,
cualquier mujer que la come · luego se siente preñada.
¡Así hice yo, mezquina, · por la mi ventura mala!

Romance de una Morilla

YO m'era mora Moraima, · morilla d'un bel catar;
cristiano vino a mi puerta, · cuitada, por m'engañar.
Hablóme en algarabía, · como aquél que la bien sabe:
«Ábrasme las puertas, mora, · si Alá te guarde de mal.»
«Cómo t'abriré, mezquina, · que no sé quién tú serás!»

'I am the Moor Mazote, your own mother's brother, who has left a Christian lying dead; the constable is coming after me. If you do not open to me, my life, here you will see me killed.'

When I, poor wretch, heard this, I began to get up. I put on a rough cloak, not finding my silk skirt, and I went to the door, and flung it wide open.

Romance of the Garland

'THAT garland of roses, daughter, who gave it to you?' 'A knight gave it to me, who passed by my door; he took me by the hand and carried me to his castle; in a small dark gateway he took his pleasure with me; he laid me on a bed of roses, on which I had never been laid (before). He did something to me, I do not know what, so that now I am in love with him. I have got my shift, Mother, all stained with blood.'

'What a cruel outrage! My mind is all distraught. If you tell the truth, daughter, your honour is worth nothing. For people have spiteful tongues, and you will immediately be disgraced.'

'Be quiet, Mother, be quiet, be quiet, my beloved mother. For a good friend is better than to be unhappily married. Give me a good friend, Mother, a good cloak and a good skirt; a girl who gets a bad husband leads an unhappy life.'

'Daughter, since you would have it so and you are content, I am satisfied.'

Romance of the Fair Maid

'YOU are fair, my lady, fairer than the sun's ray. May I sleep this night, unarmed and free from fear? For it is seven years – yes, seven – since I took off my armour. My flesh is blacker than a burnt coal.'

'Sleep tonight, sir, sleep unarmed and without fear, for the Count has gone hunting to the mountains of León.'

'May his dogs die of rabies and the eagles kill his falcon, and may his chestnut steed drag him home from the forest.'

Just as they were talking, her husband came home: 'What are you doing, fair maiden, daughter of a treacherous father?'

'My lord, I am combing my hair, combing it in great sorrow, because you have left me on my own and gone away to the mountains.'

«Yo soy moro Mazote, hermano de la tu madre,
que un cristiano dejo muerto; · tras mí viene al alcaide,
si no me abres tú, mi vida, aquí me verás matar.»
Cuando esto oí, cuitada, · comencéme a levantar,
vistiérame un almejía, · no hallando mi brial,
fuérame para la puerta · y abríla de par en par.

Romance de la Guirnalda

«ESA guirnalda de rosas, · hija, ¿Quién te la endonara?»
«Donómela un caballero · que por mi puerta pasara;
tomárame por la mano, · a su casa me llevara,
en un portalico oscuro · conmigo se deleitara,
echóme en cama de rosas · en la cual nunca fui echada,
hízome – no sé qué hizo – · que d'él vengo enamorada;
traigo madre la camisa · de sangre toda manchada.»
«¡Oh sobresalto rabioso, · que mi ánima es turbada!
Si dices verdad, mi hija, · tu honra no vale nada:
que la gente es maldiciente, · luego serás deshonrada.»
«Calledes, madre, calledes, · calléis, madre muy amada,
que más vale un buen amigo · que no ser mal maridada.
Dame el buen amigo, madre, · buen mantillo y buena saya:
la que cobra mal marido · vive malaventurada.»
«Hija, pues queréis así, · tú contenta, yo pagada.»

Romance de blanca niña

BLANCA sois, señora mía, · más que el rayo del sol:
¿si la dormiré esta noche · desarmado y sin pavor?
Que siete años había, siete, · que no me desarmo, no.
Más negras tengo mis carnes · que un tiznado carbón.
«Dormilda, señor, dormilda, · desarmado sin temor,
que el Conde es ido a la caza · a los montes de León.»
«Rabia le mate los perros, · y águilas el su halcón,
y del monte hasta casa · a él arrastre el morón.»
Ellos en aquesto estando · su marido que llegó:
«¿Qué hacéis, la blanca niña, · hija de padre traidor?»
«Señor, peino mis cabellos, · péinolos con gran dolor
que me dejáis a mí sola · y a los montes os váis vos.»

'That answer, my girl, was treachery and nothing else. Whose is that horse that neighed down below?'

'My lord, it was my father's, and he has sent it to you.'

'Whose is that armour lying in the gallery?'

'My lord, it was my brother's, and he has sent it to you today.'

'Whose is that lance, which I can see from here?'

'Take it, Count, take it, and kill me with it yourself. For that death, good Count, I certainly deserve at your hands.'

Romance of the Young Princess

THE knight went out to hunt, to hunt as was his custom. He had tired his dogs, and he had lost his falcon. He leant against an oak, which was marvellously high. On a very high branch he saw a young princess sitting: the hair of her head covered the whole oak.

'Do not be alarmed, Knight. Do not be in so great a fright. I am the daughter of the good King and the Queen of Castille; seven fairies put a spell on me when I was in my nurse's arms, that I should wander seven years alone on this mountain. Now the seven years are up, or tomorrow morning they will be. I beg of you in God's name, Knight, take me in your company, if you will have me for your wife, or if not as your mistress.'

'Wait for me, lady, until tomorrow morning, and I shall go to my mother, to ask her advice.'

The girl gave him her answer, and this is what she said: 'Oh, woe betide the knight who leaves a girl alone!'

He goes to take advice, and she stays on the mountain. His mother advised him to take her for his mistress. When the knight came back he did not find her on the mountain; he saw her being led away with a very great escort. When the knight saw this he fell to the ground, and when he came to himself he said these words: 'A knight who loses so great a prize deserves a great punishment. I will be my own judge. I will be my own executioner. They shall cut off my hands and feet and drag me through the town.'

«Esa palabra, la niña, · no era sino traición:
¿cúyo es aquel caballo · que allá bajo relinchó?»
«Señor, era de mi padre, · y envióoslo para vos.»
«¿Cúyas son aquellas armas · que están en el corredor?»
«Señor, eran de mi hermano · y hoy os las envió».
«¿Cúya es aquella lanza · desde aquí la veo yo?»
«Tomalda, Conde, tomalda, · matadme con ella vos,
que aquesta muerte, buen Conde, · bien os la merezco yo.»

Romance de la Infantina

A CAZAR va el caballero, · a cazar como solía;
los perros lleva cansados, · el falcón perdido había,
arrimárase a un roble, · alto es a maravilla.
En una rama más alta · viera estar una infantina;
cabellos de su cabeza · todo el roble cobrían.
«No te espantes, caballero, · ni tengas tamaña grima,
fija soy yo del buen rey · y de la reina de Castilla:
siete fadas me fadaron · en brazos de una ama mía,
que andase los siete años, · sola en esta montiña.
Hoy se cumplían los siete años · o mañana en aquel día;
por Dios te ruego, caballero, · llévesme en tu compañía,
si quisieres por mujer, · si no, sea por amiga.»
«Esperéisme vos, señora, · hasta mañana aquel día,
iré yo tomar consejo · de una madre que tenía.»
La niña le respondiera, · y estas palabras decía:
«¡Oh mal haya el caballero · que sola deja la niña!»
El se va a tomar consejo, · y ella queda en la montiña.
Aconsejóle su madre · que la tomase por amiga.
Cuando volvió el caballero · no la hallara en la montiña;
vídola que la llevaban · con muy gran caballería.
El caballero desque la vido · en el suelo se caía;
desque en sí hubo tornado · estas palabras decía:
«Caballero que tal pierde, · muy gran pena merecía;
yo mesmo seré el alcalde, · yo me seré la justicia;
que le corten pies y manos · y lo arrastren por la villa.»

Romance of the Prisoner

FOR it was in May, in May, at the time of the great heat, at the time when lovers go to serve their loves. Only I, sad and wretched, lie in this prison, and I do not know when it is day, nor yet when it is night, except by a little bird which used to sing to me at dawn. A cross-bowman killed him for me, may God give him an ill reward!

Romance of Fonte-frida

COOL fountain, cool fountain, cool fountain of love, where all the little birds go to console themselves, except the turtle-dove who is widowed and sorrowing. By it there passed that traitor, the nightingale. The words that he spoke were full of treachery: 'If you would allow me, lady, I would be your servant.'

'Go away, enemy, evil, false deceiver. I do not perch on a green bough, nor in a meadow that is in flower, and if I find the water clear, I drank from it turbid. I do not want a husband, so that there may be no children. I want no pleasure with children, nor yet any consolation. Leave me, sad enemy, wicked, false, evil traitor, for I do not want to be your mistress, nor to marry you either.'

Romance of Constancy

MY ornaments are arms, my rest is in the fight, my bed it is the hard stones, my sleep perpetual watching. The fastnesses are dark, the roads yet to be trod, heaven with its inconstancy sees fit to work my hurt, as I wander from crag to crag along the edge of the sea, to see if my fortune may find a place to ease my pain. But for you, my lady, everything must be borne.

Romance del prisionero

QUE por mayo era, por mayo, · cuando los grandes calores,
cuando los enamorados · van servir a sus amores,
sino yo, triste, mezquino, · que yago en estas prisiones
que ni sé cuándo es de día · ni menos cuándo es de noche,
sino por una avecilla · que me cantaba al albor;
matómela un ballestero: · ¡déle Dios mal galardón!

Romance de Fonte-frida

FONTE frida, fonte frida, · fonte frida y con amor,
do todas las avecicas · van tomar consolación,
si no es la tortolica · qu'está viuda y con dolor.
Por allí fuera a pasar · el traidor del ruisenõr;
las palabras que le dice · llenas son de traición:
«Si tú quisieses, señora, · yo sería tu servidor».
«Vete d'ahí, enemigo, · malo, falso, engañador,
que ni poso en ramo verde, · ni en prado que tenga flor;
que si el agua hallo clara · turbia la bebía yo;
que no quiero haber marido · porque hijos no haya, no;
no quiero placer con ellos, · ni menos consolación.
¡Déjame, triste enemigo, · malo, falso, mal traidor,
que no quiero ser tu amiga · ni casar contigo, no!»

Romance de la Constancia

MIS arreos son las armas, · mi descanso es pelear,
mi cama las duras peñas, · mi dormir siempre velar.
Las manidas son escuras, · los caminos por usar,
el cielo con sus mudanzas · ha por bien de me dañar,
andando de sierra en sierra · por orillas de la mar,
por probar si mi ventura · hay lugar donde avadar.
Pero por vos, mi señora, · todo se ha de comportar.

Romance of the Fresh Rose

'FRESH rose, fresh rose, so graceful and loving, when I held you in my arms I did not know how to please you, and now that I would please you I cannot have you.'

'The fault was yours, friend. It was yours, not mine. You sent me a letter by your servant; and instead of delivering it, he told me another story, that you had married, friend, away in the land of León, that you had a beautiful wife and children as (fair as) a flower.'

'Whoever told you that, lady, did not tell you the truth, for I have never been in Castile, nor yonder in the land of León, except when I was small and knew nothing of love.'

Romance of Count Arnaldos

WHO could have had such fortune on the waters of the sea as had Count Arnaldos on St John's morning? With a falcon on his fist he was going out hunting when he saw a galley approaching, trying to make land. Its sails were of silk and its shrouds were of fine crêpe, and the sailor who commanded it came singing a song, which made the sea calm, and made the winds die down, which made the fish that swim in the deep rise to the surface, and the birds that fly past perch on the mast.

Then Count Arnaldos spoke. Indeed you shall hear what he said: 'I beg you in God's name, sailor, tell me now this song of yours.'

The sailor answered him, and this is the answer he gave: 'I only tell this song to those who come with me.'

Romance de rosa fresca

ROSA fresca, rosa fresca, · tan garrida y con amor,
cuando yo's tuve en mis brazos · no vos supe servir, no,
y agora que vos serviría · no vos puedo yo haber, no.
«Vuestra fue la culpa, amigo, · vuestra fué, que mía no;
enviástesme una carta · con un vuestro servidor,
y en lugar de recabdar, · él dijera otra razón:
qu'érades casado, amigo, · allá en tierras de León;
que tenéis mujer hermosa · y hijos como una flor.»
«Quien os lo dijo, señora, · no vos dijo verdad, non,
que yo nunca entré en Castilla, · ni allá en tierras de León,
sino cuando era pequeño · que no sabía d'amor.»

Romance del conde Arnaldos

¡QUIÉN hubiese tal ventura · sobre las aguas del mar,
como hubo el conde Arnaldos · la mañana de San Juan!
Con un falcón en la mano · la caza iba a cazar,
vio venir una galera · que a tierra quiere llegar.
Las velas traía de seda, · la ejarcia de un cendal,
marinero que la manda · diciendo viene un cantar
que la mar facía en calma, · los vientos hace amainar,
las peces que andan n'el hondo · arriba los hace andar,
las aves que andan volando · n'el mástel las faz' posar;
allí fabló el conde Arnaldos, · bien oiréis lo que dirá:
«Por Dios te ruego, marinero, · dígasme ora ese cantar.»
Respondióle el marinero, · tal respuesta le fue a dar:
«Yo no digo esta canción · sino a quien comigo va».

Ballad Sung by the Ninth Order (of Angels), which are the Seraphim

LET joy be shown on earth and happiness in limbo, let there be rejoicing in Heaven for Mary's delivery, let no sadness be found in any place on such a pleasant day, for today of a maiden the son of God was born, humbled to human flesh so that by this means there may be restored to those (heavenly) seats what was missing there.

How great is your power, love! Since your sweet persistence not only made him man, but sent him to death, let us say to the holy boy with soft melodies:

You are a child and have love. What will you do when you are bigger?

Since at your birth charity consumes you, who will suffer its heat when you are of a man's age?

You are a child, etc.

Its fire will be so strong that, with its importunate demand to save the blind world, it will give you the pains of death.

FRAY ÍÑIGO DE MENDOZA

Romance que cantó la novena orden, que son los seraphines

GOZO muestren en la tierra
y en el limbo alegría,
fiestas hagan en el cielo
por el parto de María;
no halle lugar tristeza
en tan plazentero día,
pues que hoy de una donzella
el hijo de Dios nascía
humillado en carne humana,
para que por esta vía
se repare en estas sillas
lo que en ellas fallescía.
¡O alta fuerça de amor!,
pues que tu dulce porfía
no sólo le hizo hombre,
mas a la muerte le embía,
digamos al sacro niño
con suave melodía:

Eres niño y has amor:
¿qué farás cuando mayor?

Pues que en tu natividad
te quema la caridad,
en tu varonil edad
¿quién sufrirá su calor?

Eres niño y has amor:
¿qué farás cuando mayor?

Será tan bivo su fuego,
que con importuno ruego,
por salvar el mundo ciego,
te dará mortal dolor.

You are a child, etc.

Its desire will burn so that you will wish to pay human nature for its apple with a malefactor's death.

You are a child, etc.

Oh most astounding love, since in this holy boy you must proclaim yourself so loud, let us sing in his praise:

You are a child, etc.

A MOUNTAIN bird was the heron, and of very high flight; there is no one who can take her.

My watchful thought has found out her nest. But the more she is followed the more she defends herself. I am content to follow her to enjoy the sight of her. There is no one who can take her.

Many others have followed her, thinking that they could take her, and the one who comes nearest is the one she most forgets. Service to her is sufficiently paid by the mere pleasure of desiring to look at her. There is no one who can take her.

Eres niño y has amor:
¿qué farás cuando mayor?

Arderá tanto su gana,
que por la natura humana
querrás pagar su mançana
con muerte de malhechor.

Eres niño y has amor:
¿qué farás cuando mayor?

¡O amor digno de espanto!,
pues que en este niño sancto
has de pregontarte tanto,
cantemos a su loor:

Eres niño y has amor:
¿qué farás cuando mayor?

JUAN DEL ENCINA

MONTESINA era la garça
y de muy alto volar:
no hay quien la pueda tomar.

Mi cuidoso pensamiento
ha seguido su guarida,
mas cuanto más es seguida
tiene más defendimiento;
de seguirla soy contento
por de su vista gozar:
no hay quien la pueda tomar.

Otros muchos la han seguido
pensando poder tomalla,
y a quien más cerca se halla
tiene más puesto en olvido;
harto paga lo servido
en sólo querer mirar:
no hay quien la pueda tomar.

I never saw such prettiness, nor a bird of such breeding. But to anyone who has hopes she shows great disdain. With her beauty she could easily take the whole world captive. There is no one who can take her.

The Little Flock

SUCH a good little flock, and in such a valley, is a pleasure to keep.

A flock from the mountains, and of such a breed, very quickly exhausts its bad pastures, but in good grass, and in this valley, it is a pleasure to keep.

Therefore I want to keep my herd, all about this meadow with its very good sheepfolds. With such fertile soil, and in this valley, it is a pleasure to keep.

It is very vigorous, and being always silent, does not go about baaing, nor is it tiresome. Far from it, it is restful in any valley; it is a pleasure to keep.

Nunca vi tanta lindeza
ni ave de tal criança,
mas a quien tiene esperança
muéstrale mucha esquiveza;
puede bien con su belleza
todo el mundo cativar:
no hay quien la pueda tomar.

El Ganadico

TAN buen ganadico,
y más en tal valle,
placer es guardalle.

Ganado d'altura,
y más de tal casta,
muy presto se gasta
su mala pastura;
y en buena verdura,
y más en tal valle,
placer es guardalle.

Ansí que yo quiero
guardar mi ganado,
por todo este prado
de muy buen apero:
con este tempero,
y más en tal valle
placer es guardalle.

Está muy vicioso
y siempre callando,
no anda balando
ni es enojoso;
antes da reposo
en cualquiera valle:
placer es guardalle.

It is necessary to watch a precious thing. For people, being covetous, try to steal it. A flock without fault, and in this valley, is a pleasure to keep.

If a shepherd encloses himself in a safe valley, I swear to you that the wolves do not make war on him. A mountain flock, brought down to such a valley, is a pleasure to keep.

I would gladly be a shepherd always, for this flock gives me such joy; and I have sworn an oath never to leave it but always to keep it.

THEY say that I must marry. I do not want a husband, no.

I prefer to live in security on this hill and at liberty, rather than take a chance whether I marry well or no. They say that I must marry. I do not want a husband, no.

Conviene guardalla
la cosa preciosa,
que en ser codiciosa
procuran hurtalla.
Ganado sin falla,
y más en tal valle,
placer es guardalle.

Pastor que se encierra
en valle seguro,
los lobos te juro
que no le dan guerra.
Ganado de sierra
traspuesto en tal valle
placer es guardalle.

Pastor de buen grado
yo siempre sería,
pues tanta alegría
me da este ganado;
y tengo jurado
de nunca dejalle,
mas siempre guardalle.

GIL VICENTE

DICEN que me case yo:
no quiero marido, no.

Más quiero vivir segura
n'esta sierra a mi soltura
que no estar en ventura
si casaré bien o no.
Dicen que me case yo:
no quiero marido, no.

Mother, I will not be married, so as not to have a weary life, and perhaps waste the grace God gave me. They say that I must marry. I do not want a husband, no.

There will not be and there is not a man born fit to be my husband, and since I know that I am the flower (of maidens) they say that I must marry. I do not want a husband, no.

THE girl is angry. Oh God, who would speak to her?

The girl goes over the hills, pasturing her flock, lovely as the flowers, angry as the sea. The girl is angry as the sea. Oh God, who would speak to her?

THE maiden is very charming. How lovely and beautiful she is!

Tell me, sailor, you who live in ships, if ship or sail or star is as lovely.

Tell me, knight, you who wear arms, if horse or arms or war is as lovely.

Tell me, young shepherd, you who keep your flock, if flock or valley or hill is as lovely.

Madre, no seré casada
por no ver vida cansada,
y quizá mal empleada
la gracia que Dios me dio.
Dicen que me case yo:
no quiero marido, no.

No será ni es nacido
tal para ser mi marido;
y pues que tengo sabido
que la flor yo me la só,
dicen que me case yo:
no quiero marido, no.

SAÑOSA está la niña.
¡Ay, Dios!, ¿quién le hablaría?

En la sierra anda la niña
su ganado a repastar,
hermosa como las flores,
sañosa como la mar.
Sañosa como la mar
está la niña.
¡Ay, Dios!, ¿quién le hablaría?

MUY graciosa es la doncella,
¡cómo es bella y hermosa!

Digas tú, el marinero
que en las naves vivías,
si la nave o la vela o la estrella
es tan bella.

Digas tú, el caballero
que las armas vestías,
si el caballo o las armas o la guerra
es tan bella.

Digas tú, el pastorcico
que el ganadico guardas,
si el ganado o las valles o la sierra
es tan bella.

IN the garden is born the rose. I want to go there to see the nightingale, how he sings.

On the banks of the river, the maiden gathers lemons. I want to go there, to see the nightingale, how he sings.

The maiden was gathering lemons to give to her love. I want to go there to see the nightingale, how he sings.

To give them to her love in a hat of silken stuff. I want to go there to see the nightingale, how he sings.

I HAVE come from the rose-bush, mother, from the rose-bush.

On the banks of that ford, I saw a red rose-bush, I have come from the rose-bush.

On the banks of that river I saw that flowering rose-bush. I have come from the rose-bush.

I saw that flowering rose-bush, and I gathered roses with a sigh. I have come from the rose-bush.

I have come from the rose-bush, mother, I have come from the rose-bush.

EN la huerta nasce la rosa:
quiérome ir allá
por mirar el ruiseñor
cómo cantabá.

Por las riberas del río
limones coge la virgo:
quiérome ir allá
por mirar el ruiseñor
cómo cantabá.

Limones cogía la virgo
para dar al su amigo:
quiérome ir allá
para ver el ruiseñor
cómo cantabá.

Para dar al su amigo
en un sombrero de sirgo:
quiérome ir allá
para ver el ruiseñor
cómo cantabá.

DEL rosal vengo, mi madre,
vengo del rosale.

A riberas de aquel vado
viera estar rosal granado:
vengo del rosale.

A riberas de aquel río
viera estar rosal florido:
vengo del rosale.

Viera estar rosal florido,
cogí rosas con sospiro:
vengo del rosale.

Del rosal vengo, mi madre,
vengo de rosale.

Carol

TO war, gallant knights! For the holy angels have come on earth to help us. To war!

In their shining armour, they come flying from the sky, crying on God and man to help our armies.

To war, noble knights! For the holy angels have come on earth to help us. To war!

Song

I WANT no mistress in England, for I have others better in my own land.

I neither want nor value their favour. I renounce love, for it is a waste of time to follow Cupid in England, since I have others better at home.

Vilancete

¡A LA guerra,
caballeros esforzados!
Pues los ángeles sagrados
a socorro son en tierra,
¡a la guerra!

Con las armas resplandecientes
vienen del cielo volando,
Dios y Hombre apellidando
en socorro de las gentes.

¡A la guerra,
caballeros esmerados!
Pues los ángeles sagrados
a socorro son en tierra,
¡a la guerra!

ANÓNIMO

Canción

QUE no quiero amores
en Ingalaterra,
pues otros mejores
tengo yo en mi tierra.

No quiero ni estimo
ser favorecido;
de amores me eximo,
qu'es tiempo perdido
seguir a Cupido
en Ingalaterra,
pues otros mejores
tengo yo en mi tierra.

What favours can fortune give me in however many revolutions of the sun and moon, and what can any woman give me in England, for I have others better at home?

For when I return, I faithfully trust I shall be well-rewarded for my courtship. But to take a mistress in England would be madness, since I have others better at home.

I MET three highland girls at the foot of a great mountain, who by their looks and manners could not be keepers of flocks.

They wore beautiful veils and ruffs of silk, ropes of fine pearls tied round their hair, which in all of them was fair. They wore satin slippers, scarlet petticoats, and brocade cloaks.

¿Qué favores puede
darme la fortuna,
por mucho que ruede
el sol ni la luna,
ni mujer alguna
en Ingalaterra,
pues otros mejores
tengo yo en mi tierra?

Que cuando allá vaya,
a fe yo lo fío,
buen galardón haya
del servicio mío;
que son desvarío
los de Ingalaterra,
pues otros mejores
tengo yo en mi tierra.

JUAN DE TIMONEDA

TRES serranas he encontrado
al pie de una gran montaña,
que, según su gesto y maña,
no deben guardar ganado.

De seda traían y bellos
los velos y gorguerinas,
cordones de perlas finas
apretando sus cabellos,
rubios eran todos ellos
y de seda las servillas,
de escarlata las basquillas,
los monjiles de brocado.

The three garlands they wore were all adorned with laurel, and they wore diamonds and emeralds in bracelets and ear-rings. Their leggings were silvered, their pouches crimson, and each one carried her studded ivory crook.

They carried golden distaffs in their girdles and (golden) brooches, the knobs (of their distaffs) were of pearl, the spindles of pure silver. They were gravely spinning silk and singing this song: 'Where is my heart?' as they went into a valley.

I AM a pretty girl and lead a sad life, since I am ill-married.

I am – I don't deny it – beautiful beyond words, beloved by one and desired by a hundred. I am unhappy and good for nothing, because I am ill-married.

With this hair that looks so fine I would drive men off their heads. The man who might have it thinks nothing of it, because I am ill-married.

De laurel muy adornadas
traían sus tres guirnaldas,
con diamantes y esmeraldas,
en ejorcas y arracadas;
antiparas plateadas,
de carmesín los zurrones,
de marfil con sus tachones
cada una su cayado.

Ruecas de oro en su cintura
traían y prendederos,
de aljófar los rocaderos,
los husos de plata pura,
seda hilando con mesura
y cantando esta canción:
«¿Dónde está mi corazón?»
por un valle se han entrado.

SOY garridica
y vivo penada
por ser mal casada.

Yo soy, no repuno,
hermosa sin cuento,
amada de uno,
querida de ciento.
No tengo contento,
ni valgo yo nada
por ser mal casada.

Con estos cabellos
de bel parecer
haría con ellos
los hombres perder.
Quien los puede haber
no los tiene en nada
por ser mal casada.

THE hill is high and rough to climb, the conduits run water and flow into the balm.

Mother, dear Mother, with such a pretty body, one morning my handsome friend was walking on that hill with its high ridge. I signed to him with my hood and with my five fingers. The conduits run water and flow into the balm.

BENEATH the rock is born the rose that does not burn the air.

Beneath a poor gateway is a divine rose-tree, and an angelic queen with a most charming grace.

That most lovely queen has grown a rose, redder and more lovely than anyone has ever seen.

A white and red rose, a blessed and holy rose, a rose for which our first father's sin is forgiven.

PEDRO DE PADILLA

LA sierra es alta
y áspera de sobir,
los caños corren agua
y dan en el toronjil.

Madre, la mi madre,
del cuerpo atán garrido,
por aquella sierra
de aquel lomo erguido
iba una mañana
el mi lindo amigo.
Llaméle con mi toca
y con mis dedos cinco,
los caños corren agua
y dan en el toronjil.

ESTEBAN DE ZAFRA

BAJO de la peña nace
la rosa que no quema el aire.

Bajo de un pobre portal
está una divina rosal
y una reina angelical
de muy gracioso donaire.

Esta reina tan hermosa
ha producido una rosa
tan colorada y hermosa
cual nunca la vido nadie.

Rosa blanca y colorada,
rosa bendita y sagrada,
rosa por cual es quitada
la culpa del primer padre.

The rose-tree of which I spoke is the virgin Saint Mary, the rose that she grew is her son, husband, and father.

It is the rose of salvation for our redemption, to cure the harm done by our first mother.

THE osier, friend, under the young osier.

And the two friends have gone, gone under the green pines, under the young osier, the osier, friend.

And the two lovers have gone, together through the green meadows, under the young osier.

Hill-song of La Zarzuela

I WAS going, Mother, to Villa Real: I lost my way in a difficult place. I went seven days without eating bread, without my mule getting fodder or my hawk getting meat. Between La Zarzuela and Darazután, I lifted my eyes towards the sunrise and saw a cabin from which the smoke rose. I spurred

Es el rosal que decía
la Virgen Santa María,
la rosa que producía
es su hijo, esposo y padre.

Es rosa de salvación
para nuestra redención,
para curar la lisión
de nuestra primera madre.

LOPE DE RUEDA

MIMBRERA, amigo,
so la mimbrereta.

Y los dos amigos
idos se son, idos
so los verdes pinos,
so la mimbrereta,
mimbrera, amigo.

Y los dos amados
idos se son, ambos
so los verdes prados,
so la mimbrereta.

ANÓNIMO

Serranilla de la Zarzuela

YO me iba, mi madre, · a Villa Reale:
errara yo el camino · en fuerte lugare.
Siete días anduve · que no comí pane,
cebada mi mula, · carne el gavilán.
Entre la Zarzuela · y Darazután,
alzaba los ojos · hacia do el sol sale;
viera una cabaña, · della el humo sale.

my mule and rode to it; the shepherd's dogs came out to bark at me, and I saw a highland girl with a pretty grace.

'Come in, knight, and do not be shy; my father and mother have gone to the town, my darling Minguillo has gone for bread, and will not be back tonight or tomorrow to eat; you shall drink milk while the cheese is being made. We will make up the bed beside the broom field, and we will get a son, whose name shall be Pascual. He will either be an archbishop, a pope, or a cardinal, or he will be the swine-drover of Villa Real. Well, by my life, you must find this a joke.'

THE leaves murmur in the wind, Mother, and to their sound I sleep in their shade.

A mild wind blows lightly and softly, which moves the ship of my thoughts. It makes me so happy that it seems to offer me heaven well before my time, and to their sound I sleep in their shade.

If I happen to wake I find myself among flowers, and scarcely remember my sorrows. I lose them from sight, overwhelmed by sleep, and the rustle of the leaves gives me back life, and to their sound I sleep in their shade.

Picara mi mula · fuíme para allá;
perros del ganado · sálenme a ladrar:
vide una serrana · del bello donaire.
«Llegáos, caballero, · vergüenza no hayades;
mi padre y mi madre · han ido al lugar,
mi carillo Minguillo · es ido por pan,
ni vendrá esta noche · ni mañana a yantar;
comeréis de la leche · mientras el queso se hace.
Haremos la cama · junto al retamal;
haremos un hijo · llamarse ha Pascual;
o será arzobispo, · papa o cardenal,
o será porquerizo · de Villa Real.»
«Bien, por vida mía, · debéis de burlar.»

CON el viento murmuran,
madre, las hojas;
y al sonido me duermo
bajo su sombra.

Sopla un manso viento
alegre y suave,
que mueve la nave
de mi pensamiento;
dame tal contento
que me parece
que el cielo me ofrece
bien a deshora;
y al sonido me duermo
bajo su sombra.

Si acaso recuerdo
me hallo entre las flores,
y de mis dolores
apenas me acuerdo;
de vista las pierdo
del sueño vencida,
y dame la vida
el son de las hojas;
y al sonido me duermo
bajo su sombra.

MY pains, Mother, are the pains of love.

Come out, my lady, from under the orange grove. For you are so lovely that the air will burn you with love – yes, with love.

AS a heron flew past, the falcon swooped from the sky and, in catching her on the wing, got caught in a bramble.

Over the highest mountains the falcon God came down, to enclose himself in the womb of the Blessed Mary. So shrill was the heron's cry that 'ecce ancilla' (Behold the maid!) reached the sky, and the falcon dropped to the lure, and caught himself in a bramble.

Long were the leashes by which the falcon was caught, and made of those same cloths that Adam and Eve wove. But so (low and) humble was the wild heron's flight that when God came down from the sky he was caught (and held) by a bramble.

IF the night is dark and the way is so short, why do you not come, friend?

LAS mis penas, madre,
de amores son.

Salid, mi señora,
de s'ol naranjale,
que sois tan fermosa,
quemarvos ha el aire
de amores, sí.

AL revuelo de una garza
se abatió el neblí del cielo,
y por cogella de vuelo
quedó preso en una zarza.

Por las más altas montañas
el neblí Dios descendía
a encerrarse en las entrañas
de la sagrada María.
Tan alto gritó la garza
que «ecce ancilla» llegó al cielo
y el neblí bajó al señuelo
y se prendió en una zarza.

Eran largas las pihuelas
por do el neblí se prendió,
sacadas de aquellas telas
que Adán y Eva tramó.
Mas la zahareña garza
tan humilde hizo el vuelo
que al descender Dios del cielo
quedó preso en una zarza.

SI la noche hace escura
y tan corto es el camino,
¿cómo no venís, amigo?

Midnight is past, and my torturer does not come. My ill-luck keeps him away. How unlucky I have been from birth! He makes me live in torture, and shows himself my enemy. Why do you not come, friend?

BEAUTIFUL and unhappily married, among the pretty girls I saw, remember, lady, how much you were loved by me.

Shining morning-star, darkness of my delights, crown of women, glory of the present age, supreme and paramount among all those girls that I saw, remember how much, lady, you were loved by me.

BENEATH the ilex, the ilex, beneath the ilex.

I was going, Mother, on pilgrimage, and to be more devout I travelled without company, beneath the ilex. (Actually the holm-oak.)

To be more devout, I travelled without company; I turned into another road, I left the one I was on, beneath the ilex.

La media noche es pasada
y el que me pena no viene:
mi desdicha lo detiene,
¡que nascí tan desdichada!
Háceme vivir penada
y muéstraseme enemigo:
¿cómo no venís, amigo?

LA bella malmaridada
de las lindas que yo vi,
acuérdate cuán amada,
señora, fuiste de mí.

Lucero resplandeciente,
tiniebla de mis placeres,
corona de las mujeres,
gloria del siglo presente;
estremada y ecelente
sobre todas cuantas vi,
acuérdate cuán amada,
señora, fuiste de mí.

SO ell encina, encina,
so ell encina.

Yo me iba, mi madre,
a la romería;
por ir más devota
fui sin compañía:
so ell encina.

Por ir más devota
fui sin compañía;
tomé otro camino,
dejé el que tenía:
so ell encina.

I found that I had lost my way on a mountain. I lay down to sleep at the foot of the ilex, beneath the ilex.

In the middle of the night, poor girl, I woke up, and found myself in the arms of him I loved most, beneath the ilex.

Wretched me, I was sorry when the dawn broke, because I was enjoying the man I loved best, beneath the ilex.

Most blessed be that pilgrimage beneath the ilex.

THAT gentleman, Mother, who fell in love with me, he is suffering and I am dying.

Mother, that gentleman, who has been wounded by love, I feel his pains also, for I am dying of them too: his love is so true that rightly I say: he is suffering and I am dying.

Halléme perdida
en una montiña,
echéme a dormir
al pie dell encina:
so ell encina.

A la media noche
recordé, mezquina;
halléme en los brazos
del que más quería:
so ell encina.

Pesóme, cuitada,
de que amanecía,
porque yo gozaba
del que más quería:
so ell encina.

Muy biendita sía
la tal romería
so ell encina.

AQUEL caballero, madre,
que de mí se enamoró,
pena él y muero yo.

Madre, aquel caballero
que va herido de amores,
también siento sus dolores
porque dellas mismas muero;
su amor tan verdadero
merece que diga yo:
pena él y muero yo.

I SAW the ships, Mother, I saw them, but they are no good to me.

Mother, there are three girls, not from this town, washing their smocks in the flowing water. I saw them, but they are no good to me.

I DON'T want to be a nun, no, because I'm a pretty girl in love.

Leave me with my pleasure, with my pleasure and my joy. Leave me to my headstrong ways, because I'm a pretty lovesick girl.

THREE Moorish girls have caught my fancy, in Jaén – Axa, Fátima, and Marién.

Three very handsome Moorish girls were going to pluck olives, and found themselves plucked, in Jaén – Axa, Fátima, and Marién.

And found themselves plucked, and returned dismayed, their cheeks all pale, in Jaén – Axa, Fátima, and Marién.

Three very sprightly Moorish girls, three very sprightly Moorish girls, were going to pick apples in Jaén – Axa, Fátima, and Marién.

Vi los barcos, madre,
vilos y no me valen.

Madre, tres mozuelas,
no de aquesta villa,
en agua corriente
lavan sus camisas:
sus camisas, madre,
vilas y no me valen.

No quiero ser monja, no,
que niña namoradica só.

Dejadme con mi placer,
con mi placer y alegría,
dejadme con mi porfía,
que niña malpenadica só.

Tres morillas me enamoran
en Jaén:
Axa y Fátima y Marién.

Tres morillas tan garridas
iban a coger olivas,
y hallábanse cogidas
en Jaén:
Axa y Fátima y Marién.

Y hallábanse cogidas
y tornaban desmaídas
y las colores perdidas
en Jaén:
Axa y Fátima y Marién.

Tres moricas tan lozanas,
tres moricas tan lozanas
iban a coger manzanas
a Jaén:
Axa y Fátima y Marién.

I SHALL go to the lovers' bathing place alone, and there I shall bathe, so that I may be healed of this ill, caused me by misfortune, which is so mortal a pain that it destroys my looks. To the bathing place of sorrow I will go alone, and there I will bathe.

Glosa of the Cows*

KEEP my cows for me, darling boy, and I will kiss you: or else, you may kiss me and I will keep the cows for you.

You will not be cheated, Gil, by this exchange that I am offering you. Do not be put out at being wooed by me. I do not know who will make you a more advantageous offer – or else, you may kiss me, and I'll keep the cows for you.

In return for a little trouble, you will receive from me what I would give to nobody except as a special gift. The flock is not worth as much as what I shall give you – or else you may give it to me, and I'll keep the cows for you.

* A *Glosa* is a poem that repeats the rhymes of its refrain.

A LOS baños del amor
sola me iré
y en ellos me bañaré.

Porque sane deste mal
que me causa desventura,
que es un dolor tan mortal
que destruye mi figura.
A los baños de tristura
sola me iré
y en ellos me bañaré.

CRISTÓBAL DE CASTILLEJO

Glosa de las vacas

GUÁRDAME las vacas,
carillejo, y besarte he;
si no, bésame tú a mí,
que yo te las guardaré.

En el troque que te pido,
Gil, no recibes engaño;
no te me muestres extraño
por ser de mí requerido.
Tan ventajoso partido
no sé yo quien te lo dé;
si no, bésame tú a mí
que yo te las guardaré.

Por un poco de cuidado
ganarás de parte mía
lo que a ninguno daría
si no por don señalado.
No vale tanto el ganado
como lo que te daré;
si no, dame lo tú a mí
que yo te las guardaré.

I have no need to grant you this favour, except that need which has made my free-will the prisoner of love. And honesty forbids me to deny you the truth – or else, you may love me, and I'll keep the cows for you.

Oh, how many men would beg of me what I am begging of you, and would count themselves lucky if they got it from me. Take what they would like to have, and do what I shall tell you – or else, you may command me and I'll keep the cows for you.

But if you happen to be so lazy, Gil, as to value your rest more highly than the enjoyment of that pleasure, to save you trouble I will do the work, and you shall kiss me, while I keep the cows for you.

I will not be cross, but will be more industrious than you, for when there is a reward, work is no trouble, and I'll see that my pains are paid for in the currency of your kissing me and my keeping the cows for you.

No tengo necesidad
de hacerte este favor,
sino sola la que en amor
ha puesto mi voluntad.
Y negarte la verdad
no lo consiente mi fe;
si no, quiéreme tú a mí,
que yo te las guardaré.

Oh cuántos me pedirían
lo que yo te pido a ti,
y en alcanzarlo de mí
por dichosos se tendrían.
Toma lo que ellos querrían,
haz lo que te mandaré;
si no, mándame tú a mí,
que yo te las guardaré.

Mas tú, Gil, si por ventura
quieres ser tan perezoso,
que precias más tu reposo
que gozar de esta dulzura,
yo por darte a ti holgura
el cuidado tomaré
que tú me besas a mí,
que yo te las guardaré.

Yo seré más diligente
que tú sin darme pasión,
porque con el galardón
el trabajo no se siente;
y haré que se contente
mi pena con el porqué,
que es que me beses tú a mí,
que yo te las guardaré.

To Love

GIVE me, Love, innumerable kisses, bound fast in my hair, and one thousand one hundred after that, and after that one thousand one hundred, and after many thousands three; and then, so as to annoy nobody, let us destroy the accounts and count backwards.

LIKE one who receives pleasure in dreams, his pleasure proceeding from delirium, so imagination with its figments vainly invents its pleasures in me.

No good thing is inscribed on my sad heart, except what I gain by my thoughts; of all the good things that have happened to me only the imaginary part is alive.

My heart fears to advance, seeing that its pain is lying in ambush, and so it retires in an instant

to contemplate its past happiness. Oh, what a fleeting shadow of help it is, that what is best in me is what is nothing!

I AM like a man who lives in the desert, forgotten by the world and its affairs, and you see by chance a great friend approaching him whom he had taken for dead.

Al Amor

DAME, Amor, besos sin cuento,
asido de mis cabellos,
y mil y ciento tras ellos,
y tras ellos mil y ciento,
y después
de muchos millares, tres;
y porque nadie los sienta,
desbaratemos la cuenta
y contemos al revés.

JUAN BOSCÁN

COMO aquél que en soñar gusto recibe,
su gusto procediendo de locura,
así el imaginar con su figura
vanamente su gozo en mí concibe.

Otro bien en mí triste no se escribe,
si no es aquél que mi pensar procura;
de cuanto a sido hecho en mi ventura
lo solo imaginado es lo que vive.

Teme mi corazón de ir adelante,
viendo estar su dolor puesto en celada,
y así revuelve atrás en un instante

a contemplar su gloria ya pasada.
¡Oh sombra de remedio inconstante,
ser en mí lo mejor lo que no es nada!

SOY como aquél que vive en el desierto,
del mundo y de sus cosas olvidado,
y a descuido veis donde le ha llegado
un gran amigo, al cual tuvo por muerto.

At first he fears this strange occurrence; but after he has made quite sure, he begins to rejoice as he thinks of the past, very much alive with new feelings.

But when this friend goes away soon, since his business requires him to depart, solitude begins to be a new thing to him.

He does not reconcile himself to the mountain grasses, he lacks all taste for the wasteland, and he trembles each time he goes into his cave.

The First Eclogue

THE sweet lamentation of two shepherds, Salicio and Nemoroso together, I shall recount and imitate their plaints; whose sheep were most heedful to their delightful song, and forgot to graze while they listened to their tales of love. You who have gained by your labours worldwide renown and a place second to none, listen to me now, Albano, you who are alone, devoting yourself to the illustrious government of the Realm; or, turning in another direction, may now be brilliantly armed, the earthly representative of Mars,

Teme luego de un caso tan incierto;
pero después que bien sa ha asegurado,
comienza a holgar pensando en lo pasado,
con nuevos sentimientos muy despierto.

Mas cuando ya este amigo se le parte,
al cual partirse presto le conviene,
la soledad empieza a selle nueva;

con las yerbas del monte no se aviene,
para el yermo le falta toda el arte,
y tiembla cada vez que entra en su cueva.

GARCILASO DE LA VEGA

Égloga primera

El dulce lamentar de dos pastores,
Salicio juntamente y Nemoroso,
he de contar, sus quejas imitando;
cuyas ovejas al cantar sabroso
estaban muy atentas, los amores,
de pacer olvidadas, escuchando.
Tú, que ganaste obrando
un nombre en todo el mundo,
y un grado sin segundo,
agora estés atento, solo y dado
al ínclito gobierno del Estado,
Albano; agora vuelto a la otra parte,
resplandeciente, armado,
representando en tierra al fiero Marte;

the cruel; or, free from tiresome worries and affairs, may now, perhaps, be tearing down the mountainside, an eager horseman galloping after the timorous deer, who struggle in vain to postpone their deaths; wait, for when the leisure I have lost is restored to me, you shall see my pen busy with the infinite and countless sum of your virtues and famous deeds, ere I pine away for lack of you, who are greater than all the world.

Until that time, which I foresee, comes one day to release me from the debt which I owe to your fame and your glory – and which is a general debt, and not mine alone, but owed by any rare talent who celebrates what should be remembered – may the tree of victory, which closely girds your glorious brow, give place to the ivy which is planted in your shadow, and which climbs little by little, clinging to your praises. Until these are sung, listen to the singing of my shepherds.

agora de cuidados enojosos
y de negocios libre, por ventura
andas a caza, el monte fatigando
en ardiente jinete, que apresura
el curso tras los ciervos temorosos,
que en vano su morir van dilatando.
Espera, que en tornando
a ser restituido
al ocio ya perdido,
luego verás ejercitar mi pluma
por la infinita, innumerable suma
de tus virtudes y famosas obras;
antes que me consuma,
faltando a ti, que a todo el mundo sobras.

En tanto que este tiempo que adivino
viene de sacarme de la deuda un día,
que se debe a tu fama y a tu gloria;
que es deuda general, no sólo mía,
mas de cualquier ingenio peregrino
que celebra lo dino de memoria;
el árbol de vitoria
que ciñe estrechamente
tu gloriosa frente
dé lugar a la hiedra que se planta
debajo de tu sombra, y se levanta
poco a poco, arrimada a tus loores;
y en cuanto esto se canta,
escucha tú el cantar de mis pastores.

Rising on fire from the waves, the sun was streaking the mountain-tops when, lying on the grass at the foot of a tall beech, where a clear and sounding stream crossed the fresh, green meadow, Salicio, with his voice tuned to the sound of the moving water, complained as sweetly and softly as if she who was to blame for his grief had not been absent: and so, arguing with her as if she were present, he said:

SALICIO

Oh, harder than marble to my plaints, and colder than snow to the flaming fire in which I burn, oh, Galatea! I am dying, and yet I fear to live; and rightly fear it, since you abandon me, and without you there is no reason why life should be. I am ashamed that anyone should see me in this plight, forsaken by you, and now I blush for myself. Do you despise yourself for being the mistress of a soul, in which you have always dwelt, unable to leave it for an hour? Fall, tears, abundantly and flow.

The sun darts the rays of his fire over mountains and valleys, rousing birds, beasts, and men: those go flying through the clear air, those through the green valley, or over the lofty heights, safely and freely pasturing, and men, now that the sun is here, go once more to their work and to the customary

Saliendo de las ondas encendido,
rayaba de los montes el altura
el sol, cuando Salicio, recostado
al pie de una alta haya, en la verdura,
por donde un agua clara con sonido
atravesaba el fresco y verde prado.
Él, con canto acordado
al rumor que sonaba,
del agua que pasaba,
se quejaba tan dulce y blandamente
como si no estuviera de allí ausente
la que de su dolor culpa tenía;
y así, como presente,
razonando con ella, le decía:

SALICIO

¡Oh más dura que mármol a mis quejas,
y al encendido fuego en que me quemo,
más helada que nieve, Galatea!
Estoy muriendo, y aún la vida temo;
témola con razón, pues tú me dejas;
que no hay, sin ti, el vivir para qué sea.
Vergüenza he que me vea
ninguno en tal estado,
de ti desamparado,
y de mí mismo yo me corro agora.
¿De un alma te desdeñas ser señora,
donde siempre moraste, no pudiendo
della salir un hora?
Salid sin duelo, lágrimas, corriendo.

El sol tiende los rayos de su lumbre
por montes y por valles, despertando
las aves y animales y la gente:
cuál por el aire claro va volando,
cuál por el verde valle o alta cumbre
paciendo va segura y libremente,
cuál con el sol presente
va de nuevo al oficio,

employment to which their nature or their need inclines them. But this miserable creature is in tears when shadows come to cover the world or when the light draws near. Fall, tears, abundantly and flow.

And you, who have now forgotten this life of mine, and show not the smallest regret that sad Salicio is dying for you, do you permit the wind to bear away, unknown, the love and faith that should be kept eternally for me alone? Oh God, will she not perhaps receive some punishment from heaven, since You can see from aloft how this false oath-breaker drives her close friend to his death? If in return for my love I am dying, what will the enemy do? Fall, tears, abundantly and flow.

On your account the silence of the shady forest, on your account the indifference and remoteness of the solitary mountain pleased me; for you I desired the green grass, the fresh wind, the white lily and red rose, and the sweet spring. Oh, how I was deceived! How different and how contrary was the feeling hidden in your false breast! The ill-omened crow told me this very clearly, recounting my misfortune with his cawing. Fall, tears, abundantly and flow.

How often, when sleeping beneath the trees, though I have thought it the wandering of my mind, I have seen my unhappy and evil fate in dream! I dreamed that I was driving my herd in the summer to drink of the Tagus and

y al usado ejercicio
do su natura o menester le inclina:
siempre está en llanto esta ánima mesquina,
cuando la sombra el mundo van cubriendo
o la luz se avecina.
Salid sin duelo, lágrimas, corriendo.

¿Y tú, desta mi vida ya olvidada,
sin mostrar un pequeño sentimiento
de que por ti Salicio triste muera,
dejas llevar, desconocida, al viento
el amor y la fe que ser guardada
eternamente sólo a mí debiera?
¡Oh Dios! ¿Por qué siquiera,
pues ves desde tu altura
esta falsa perjura
causar la muerte de un estrecho amigo,
no recibe del cielo algún castigo?
Si en pago del amor yo estoy muriendo,
¿qué hará el enemigo?
Salid sin duelo, lágrimas, corriendo.

Por ti el silencio de la selva umbrosa,
por ti la esquividad y apartamiento
del solitario monte me agradaba;
por ti la verde hierba, el fresco viento,
el blanco lirio y colorada rosa
y dulce primavera deseaba.
¡Ay, cuánto me engañaba!
¡Ay cuán diferente era
y cuán de otra manera
lo que en tu falso pecho se escondía!
Bien claro con su voz me lo decía
la siniestra corneja, repitiendo
la desventura mía.
Salid sin duelo, lágrimas, corriendo.

¡Cuántas veces, durmiendo en la floresta,
reputándolo yo por desvarío,
vi mi mal entre sueños, desdichado!
Soñaba que en el tiempo del estío

there to spend the noonday heat; and when I got there – I do not know how – the water was flowing in an unusual place and down a new channel; then, burning with the summer heat, I went on along the course of the evasive water, with distracted mind. Fall, tears, abundantly and flow.

In whose ear does your sweet speech sound? On whom have you turned your bright gaze? Whom have you so inconsiderately put in my place? Your broken word, to whom have you given it now? Whose is the neck that you have embraced with the chain of your lovely arms? No heart, not even a heart of stone, would be so strong as not to dissolve itself in tears till its life ebbed away, on seeing my beloved ivy wrenched from me and clinging to another wall, and my vine entangled with another elm. Fall, tears, abundantly and flow.

What can we not expect henceforth, what difficult and doubtful event may not come to pass? Or what discord will not be reconciled? And, at the same time, what can a lover now count as certain, or what will he not fear worse from today, since you have given cause for every doubt? When you withdrew from my protection, you gave notable cause and example to all who live beneath the heavens, why the most secure should fear and suspect the loss of what he once possessed. Fall abundantly, fall abundantly, tears, and flow.

llevaba, por pasar allí la siesta,
a beber en el Tajo mi ganado;
y después de llegado,
sin saber de cuál arte,
por desusada parte,
y por nuevo camino el agua se iba.
Ardiendo yo con la calor estiva,
el curso, enajenado, iba siguiendo
del agua fugitiva.
Salid sin duelo, lágrimas, corriendo.

Tu dulce habla ¿en cúya oreja suena?
Tus claros ojos ¿a quién los volviste?
¿Por quién tan sin respeto me trocaste?
Tu quebrantada fe ¿dó la pusiste?
¿Cuál es el cuello que, como en cadena,
de tus hermosos brazos anudaste?
No hay corazón que baste,
aunque fuese de piedra,
viendo mi amada hiedra,
de mí arrancada, en otro muro asida,
y mi parra en otro olmo entretejida,
que no se esté con llanto deshaciendo
hasta acabar la vida.
Salid sin duelo, lágrimas, corriendo.

¿Qué no se esperará de aquí adelante,
por difícil que sea y por incierto?
O ¿qué discordia no será juntada?
y juntamente ¿qué tendrá por cierto,
o qué de hoy más no temerá el amante,
siendo a todo materia por ti dada?
Cuando tú enajenada
de mi cuidado fuiste,
notable causa diste
y ejemplo a todos cuantos cubre el cielo,
que el más seguro tema con recelo
perder lo que estuviese poseyendo.
Salid fuera sin duelo,
salid sin duelo, lágrimas, corriendo.

You gave the world cause to hope that it might attain the impossible and unthought of, and that it might join contraries, since you gave your wicked heart to whom you did, taking it from me with such inconstancy as will always be a legend among men. Now, the patient ewe will join with the hungry wolf, and bold serpents will now noiselessly make their nests with the simple birds; for I perceive an even greater disparity between you and the man you have chosen. Fall, tears, abundantly and flow.

I have always plenty of fresh milk in summer and winter; the butter and cheese are rich in my sheepfold; I saw you once so delighted by my singing, indeed, that the Mantuan Shepherd (Virgil) could not have received greater praise from you. I am surely not, if you look well at me, so deformed or ugly; for even now I can see myself in this clear and running stream, and I certainly would not change features with the man who is now laughing at me. But I would change my luck with him! Fall, tears, abundantly and flow.

How did I come into such contempt with you? How was I so speedily loathed by you? How did you come to lack understanding of me? If you had not a fierce nature, you would always have valued me, and I should not have known this separation from you. Do you not know that my sheep are numberless that seek the cool of the Cuenca hills in summer, and the pasturage of the sheltered Estremo in winter? But what is the good of

Materia diste al mundo de esperanza
de alcanzar lo imposible y no pensado,
y de hacer juntar lo diferente,
dando a quien diste el corazón malvado,
quitándolo de mí con tal mudanza,
que siempre sonará de gente en gente.
La cordera paciente
con el lobo hambriento
hará su ayuntamiento,
y con las simples aves sin ruido
harán las bravas sierpes ya su nido;
que mayor diferencia comprehendo
de ti al que has escogido.
Salid sin duelo, lágrimas, corriendo.

Siempre de nueva leche en el verano
y en el invierno abundo; en mi majada
la manteca y el queso está sobrado;
de mi cantar, pues, yo te vi agradada,
tanto, que no pudiera el mantuano
Títiro ser de ti más alabado.
No soy, pues, bien mirado,
tan disforme ni feo;
que aun agora me veo
en esta agua que corre clara y pura,
y cierto no trocara mi figura
con ese que de mí se está riendo;
¡trocara mi ventura!
Salid sin duelo, lágrimas, corriendo.

¿Cómo te vine en tanto menosprecio?
¿Cómo te fui tan presto aborrecible?
¿Cómo te faltó en mí el conocimiento?
Si no tuvieras condición terrible,
siempre fuera tenido de ti en precio,
y no viera de ti este apartamiento.
¿No sabes que sin cuento
buscan en el estío
mis ovejas el frío
de la sierra de Cuenca y el gobierno
del abrigado Estremo en el invierno?

ownership if I am dissolving in eternal weeping? Fall, tears, abundantly and flow.

With my weeping the stones are moved from their natural hardness and break it. The trees seem to bend down, and the birds to listen to me as they sing. With change of song they mourn, and prophesy my death in their singing. The wild beasts that rest their tired bodies, wake from their peaceful sleep to listen to my plaints. You alone have hardened yourself against me and do not even turn your eyes upon me, to see what you have done. Fall, tears, abundantly and flow.

But since you do not come here to rescue me, do not forsake the place that you so loved, for you will surely be able to come without fear of me. I will forsake the place where you forsook me. Come if it is only that which keeps you away. Here you see a meadow full of grass, here you see a thicket, here you see a clear stream which was once dear to you, to which I complain of you with my tears. Perhaps, since I am going away, you will meet him here who may rob me of all my treasure; for since I leave him my treasure, it matters little if he has the place too.

Here Salicio concluded his singing and, sighing, with his last note broke a deep vein of tears. The mountain, wishing to show some favour to the solemn utterance of that grief, echoes and booms with his sad voice. The fair

Mas ¡qué vale el tener, si derritiendo
me estoy en llanto eterno!
Salid sin duelo, lágrimas, corriendo.

Con mi llorar las piedras enternecen
su natural dureza y la quebrantan;
los árboles parece que se inclinan;
las aves que me escuchan, cuando cantan,
con diferente voz se condolecen,
y mi morir cantando me adivinan.
Las fieras que reclinan
su cuerpo fatigado,
dejan el sosegado
sueño por escuchar mi llanto triste.
Tú sola contra mí te endureciste,
los ojos aun siquiera no volviendo
a lo que tú heciste.
Salid sin duelo, lágrimas, corriendo.

Mas ya que socorrer aquí no vienes,
ne dejes el lugar que tanto amaste,
que bien podrás venir de mí segura.
Yo dejaré el lugar do me dejaste;
ven, si por sólo esto te detienes.
Ves aquí un prado lleno de verdura,
ves aquí un espesura,
ves aquí un agua clara,
en otro tiempo cara,
a quien de ti con lágrimas me quejo.
Quizá aquí hallarás, pues yo me alejo,
al que todo mi bien quitarme puede;
que pues el bien le dejo,
no es mucho que el lugar también le quede.

Aquí dio fin a su cantar Salicio,
y sospirando en el postrero acento,
soltó de llanto una profunda vena.
Queriendo el monte al grave sentimiento
de aquel dolor en algo ser propicio,
con la pesada voz retumba y suena.
La blanca Filomena

Philomel, almost as if in grief and moved to pity, sweetly answers the sound of his tears. What Nemoroso sang after this, relate, Pierides; that I cannot and dare not do, for I feel my weak song fail.

NEMOROSO

Flowing, pure and crystalline waters, trees that gaze at yourselves in them, green meadow full of cool shadow, birds that here scatter your laments, ivy that climbs up the trees, twisting your way up their green bosoms, I saw myself so removed from the deep grief I feel that I was enjoying your solitude in utter content and where I rested in a sweet sleep or rambled in my thoughts, in which I found nothing but the most joyful memories.

And in this same valley where now I find sadness and weariness, I was then contented and happy in my repose. Oh, perishable, vain, and swift-footed prosperity! I remember how once when I slept here I found Elisa by my side when I woke. Oh, miserable fate! Oh, delicate web, consigned prematurely to the sharp shears of death! Such a fate would have been more fitting to the weary years of my own life. But my life must be harder than iron, seeing that your departure has not snapped it.

casi como dolida
y a compasión movida,
dulcemente responde al son lloroso.
Lo que cantó tras esto Nemoroso,
decidlo vos, Piérides; que tanto
no puedo yo ni oso,
que siento enflaquecer mi débil canto.

NEMOROSO

Corrientes aguas, puras, cristalinas;
árboles que os estáis mirando en ellas,
verde prado de fresca sombra lleno,
aves que aquí sembráis vuestras querellas,
hiedra que por los árboles caminas,
torciendo el paso por su verde seno;
yo me vi tan ajeno
del grave mal que siento,
que de puro contento
con vuestra soledad me recreaba,
donde con dulce sueño reposaba,
o con el pensamiento discurría
por donde no hallaba
sino memorias llenas de alegría.

Y en este mismo valle, donde agora
me entristesco y me canso, en el reposo
estuve ya contento y descansado.
¡Oh bien caduco, vano y presuroso!
Acuérdome durmiendo aquí algún hora,
que despertando, a Elisa vi a mi lado.
¡Oh miserable hado!
¡Oh tela delicada,
antes de tiempo dada
a los agudos filos de la muerte!
Más convenible fuera aquesta suerte
a los cansados años de mi vida,
que es más que el hierro fuerte,
pues no la ha quebrantado tu partida.

Where now are those bright eyes that drew my soul after them, as if it were their prisoner, wherever they turned? Where is that white and delicate hand, full of those conquests and spoils that my senses offered her as my gifts? That hair that looked so scornfully upon gold as a lesser treasure, where is it now? Where is that soft breast? Where is the column that supported that golden crest with such grace and pride? All these, alas for me, are now buried in the cold, barren, and hard earth.

Who could have told me, Elisa, my dear life, when we were walking in this valley in the cool breeze, gathering the delicate flowers, that it would see the sad and solitary day come, with its wide separation, to put a bitter end to my love? The heavens have dealt me griefs with so heavy a hand that they have condemned me to perpetual tears and sad solitude; and what pains me more is to find myself bound to a heavy and tiresome life, alone, forsaken, blind, and lightless in a dark cell.

Since you have left us, the sheep no longer crop their fill, nor does the field produce plentifully for the farmer. There is no good that does not change and turn to evil; the weeds choke the wheat, and in its place wild oats spring

¿Dó están agora aquellos claros ojos
que llevaban tras sí, como colgada,
mi alma doquier que ellos se volvían?
¿Dó está la blanca mano delicada,
llena de vencimientos y despojos
que de mí mis sentidos le ofrecían?
Los cabellos que vían
con gran desprecio el oro,
como a menor tesoro,
¿adónde están? ¿Adónde el blando pecho?
¿Dó la coluna que el dorado techo
con presunción graciosa sostenía?
Aquesto todo agora ya se encierra,
por desventura mía,
en la fría, desierta y dura tierra.

¿Quién me dijera, Elisa, vida mía,
cuando en aqueste valle al fresco viento
andábamos cogiendo tiernas flores,
que había de ver con largo apartamiento
venir el triste y solitario día
que diese amargo fin a mis amores?
El cielo en mis dolores
cargó la mano tanto,
que a sempiterno llanto
y a triste soledad me ha condenado;
y lo que siento más es verme atado
a la pesada vida y enojosa,
solo, desamparado,
ciego, sin lumbre en cárcel tenebrosa.

Después que nos dejaste, nunca pace
en hartura el ganado ya, ni acude
el campo al labrador con mano llena.
No hay bien que en mal no se convierta y mude:
la mala hierba al trigo ahoga, y nace
en lugar suyo la infelice avena;
la tierra, que de buena
gana nos producía
flores con que solía

up. The soil that gladly bore us flowers, the mere sight of which would dispel countless troubles, now bears these thistles instead, and is so encumbered with thorns as to be unworkable; with the water from my eyes I nourish this miserable crop.

As when the sun departs the shadows grow and, as its rays sink, the black darkness rises to cover the world, whence comes the fear that strikes us and the fearful shape assumed by what the night hides from us, until the sun reveals its pure and lovely light; even so is the dark night of your departure, in which I am left troubled by shadow and fear till death shall fix the time when I shall set out to see the welcome sun of your clear gaze.

As the nightingale, hidden among the leaves, is wont to complain with sad song of the harsh countryman who has cunningly despoiled her dear, sweet nest of its tender fledglings whilst she was away from her favourite branch; and as she, in so changed a plight, expresses the grief she feels with her sweet voice; and as the air resounds with her song, and the silent night does not hold back her doleful dirge and her complaints, but calls on the skies and the stars to witness her sorrow; even so do I give full rein to my grief, and thus lament in vain the sternness of proud death. She put her hand on my heart, and took away my sweet treasure, for my heart was its nest and its dwelling-

quitar en sólo vellas mil enojos,
produce agora en cambio estos abrojos,
ya de rigor de espinas intratable;
yo hago con mis ojos
crecer, lloviendo, el fruto miserable.

Como al partir del sol la sombra crece,
y en cayendo su rayo se levanta
la negra escuridad que el mundo cubre,
de do viene el temor que nos espanta,
ya la medrosa forma en que se ofrece
aquello que la noche nos encubre,
hasta que el sol descubre
su luz pura y hermosa,
tal es la tenebrosa
noche de tu partir, en que he quedado
de sombra y de temor atormentado,
hasta que muerte el tiempo determine
que a ver el deseado
sol de tu clara vista me encamine.

Cual suele el ruiseñor con triste canto
quejarse, entre las hojas escondido,
del duro labrador, que cautamente
le despojó su caro y dulce nido
de los tiernos hijuelos, entre tanto
que del amado ramo estaba ausente,
y aquel dolor que siente,
con diferencia tanta
por la dulce garganta
despide, y a su canto el aire suena,
y la callada noche no refrena
su lamentable oficio y sus querellas,
trayendo de su pena
al cielo por testigo y las estrellas;

desta manera, suelta ya la rienda
a mi dolor, y así me quejo en vano
de la dureza de la muerte airada.
Ella en mi corazón metió la mano,
y de allí me llevó mi dulce prenda,

place. Oh, harsh death, you are the cause of my complaining to the heavens and troubling the whole world with my importunate tears. Such extreme grief allows of no moderation. No one can rid me of my grievous feelings unless they relieve me first of all feelings.

Here I have a lock of your hair, Elisa, wrapped in a white cloth, and it is never away from my heart. I unfold it, and feel myself moved by so great a grief that my eyes can never weep their fill over it. Without taking it from there, I dry it of my tears with burning sighs that are hotter than the fire; and at the same time almost view and count the hairs over one by one. Then, putting them together, I tie them with a cord, and after this my wearisome grief gives me a little rest.

But immediately there comes to my mind that dark and gloomy night which so afflicts this wretched soul of mine with the memory of my misfortune. I seem to see you before me in that harsh ordeal of Lucina (Diana, the goddess who presides over childbirth), to hear that divine voice with whose sound and words you might have calmed the angry winds, and which is now mute. I seem to hear you calling on that cruel and inexorable goddess for her help in your predicament. And you, oh, rural goddess, where were you?

que aquél era su nido y su morada.
¡Ay muerte arrebatada!
Por ti me estoy quejando
al cielo y enojando
con importuno llanto al mundo todo.
El desigual dolor no sufre modo.
No me podrán quitar el dolorido
sentir, si ya del todo
primero no me quitan el sentido.

Tengo una parte aquí de tus cabellos,
Elisa, envueltos en un blanco paño,
que nunca de mi seno se me apartan.
Descójolos, y de un dolor tamaño
enternecerme siento, que sobre ellos
nunca mis ojos de llorar se hartan.
Sin que de allí se partan,
con suspiros calientes,
más que la llama ardientes,
los enjugo del llanto, y de consuno
casi los paso y cuento uno a uno;
juntándolos, con un cordón los ato.
Tras esto el importuno
dolor me deja descansar un rato.

Mas luego a la memoria se me ofrece
aquella noche tenebrosa, escura,
que tanto aflige esta ánima mesquina
con la memoria de mi desventura.
Verte presente agora me parece
en aquel duro trance de Lucina,
y aquella voz divina,
con cuyo son y acentos
a los airados vientos
pudieras amansar, que agora es muda,
me parece que oigo que a la cruda,
inexorable diosa demandabas
en aquel paso ayuda;
y tú, rústica diosa, ¿dónde estabas?

Were you so taken up with hunting the wild beasts? Were you so taken up with a shepherd (Ganymede)? Could anything be enough to make you so cruel that, when implored for compassion, you did not give ear to these vows and supplications, either lest you might see such beauty reduced to dust, or lest you might see the sad state in which your Nemoroso is left, whose pleasure it was to follow your ritual, pursuing the wild beasts in the mountains, and offering their remains at your sacred altars? And do you laugh, ungrateful one, and let my treasure die before my eyes?

Divine Elisa, since now you tread and measure the sky with immortal feet, and see its changes, being yourself unmoving, why do you forget me, and why do you not beg that the time may come soon when this veil of my body may be rent, and I may find myself free; and that we may in the third sphere, hand in hand, seek another plain, other mountains and other rivers, other flowered and shady valleys, where I may rest and always be able to see you before my eyes, without the fear and dread of losing you?

The shepherds would never have put an end to their sad weeping, nor would their songs, which only the mountain heard, have ended, if they had not seen red clouds edged with gold as the sun sank behind the mountains and realized that day was done. The shadows could be seen now hurrying apace down the thick slope of the highest mountain; and, both awaking as if

¿Íbate tanto en perseguir las fieras?
¿Íbate tanto en un pastor dormido?
¿Cosa pudo bastar a tal crueza,
que, conmovida a compasión, oído
a los votos y lágrimas no dieras
por no ver hecha tierra tal belleza,
o no ver la tristeza
en que tu Nemoroso
queda, que su reposo
era seguir tu oficio, persiguiendo
las fieras por los montes, y ofreciendo
a tus sagradas aras los despojos?
¿Y tú, ingrata, riendo,
dejas morir mi bien ante mis ojos?

Divina Elisa, pues agora el cielo
con inmortales pies pisas y mides,
y su mudanza ves, estando queda,
¿por qué de mí te olvidas, y no pides
que se apresure el tiempo en que este velo
rompa del cuerpo, y verme libre pueda,
y en la tercera rueda
contigo mano a mano
busquemos otro llano,
busquemos otros montes y otros ríos,
otros valles floridos y sombríos,
donde descanse y siempre pueda verte
ante los ojos míos,
sin miedo y sobresalto de perderte?

Nunca pusieran fin al triste lloro
los pastores, ni fueran acabadas
las canciones que sólo el monte oía
si, mirando las nubes coloradas,
al tramontar del sol bordadas de oro,
no vieran que era ya pasado el día.
La sombra se veía
venir corriendo apriesa
ya por la falda espesa
del altísimo monte, y recordando
ambos como de sueño, y acabando

from sleep when the fleeting sun went down, they drove their flocks off in the thin light and returned step by step homeward.

To 'The Flower of Gnido'
[Doña Violante Sanseverino]

IF the sound of my humble lyre could so prevail as in one moment to calm the anger of the mighty wind and the fury and tossing of the sea;

and on the harsh mountains could tame the wild beasts with its song, moving the trees and confusedly drawing them into its rhythms;

do not think, fair flower of Gnido, that I would sing of fierce and angry Mars, transformed in death and stained with dust, blood, and sweat;

or of those captains, raised on their triumphal chariots, who loaded the necks of fierce Germans with chains and tamed the French.

Nothing but the power of your beauty would be the subject of my song, and at times I would also reproach you for the fierceness with which you are armed;

and how for you alone, and on account of your great prowess and beauty, the miserable lover, turned to a viola,* weeps his misfortune in its symbol.

* A reference to the lady's name, and to the viola as a symbol of the lover's pallor.

el fugitivo sol, de luz escaso,
su ganado llevando,
se fueron recogiendo paso a paso.

A la Flor de Gnido

SI de mi baja lira
tanto pudiese el son, que en un momento
aplacase la ira
del animoso viento,
y la furia del mar y el movimiento;

y en ásperas montañas
con el süave canto enterneciese
las fieras alimañas,
los árboles moviese,
y al son confusamente los trajese;

no pienses que cantado
sería de mí, hermosa flor de Gnido,
el fiero Marte airado,
a muerte convertido,
de polvo y sangre y de sudor teñido;

ni aquellos capitanes
en las sublimes ruedas colocados,
por quien los alemanes
el fiero cuello atados,
y los franceses van domesticados.

Mas solamente aquella
fuerza de tu beldad sería cantada,
y alguna vez con ella
también sería notada
el aspereza de que estás armada;

y cómo por ti sola,
y por tu gran valor y hermosura,
convertido en viola,
llora su desventura
el miserable amante en su figura.

I speak of that prisoner, who should be shown more care since he is dying of love, condemned to the oar and tied to Venus' shell (a ship).

Because of you he does not break the furious plunging of wild horses as he used to, nor guide them with the bit, nor prick them with sharp spurs.

Because of you he does not wield the quick sword with his nimble hand, and on the doubtful field he flees the dusty lists like a poisonous serpent.

Because of you his gentle Muse resorts not to the resounding cither, but to sad complaints, which bathe the lover's face with plenteous tears.

Because of you his best friend is unwelcome, vexatious, and tiresome, as I can bear witness, since I was once his haven and resting-place after perilous shipwreck.

And now his grief so overwhelms his lost reason that no poisonous creature was ever so loathed and feared as I am by him.

You were not begotten or born from the hard soil: she should not be criticized, for one who banishes every other error is committing the error of ingratitude.

Hablo de aquel cativo,
de quien tener se debe más cuidado
que está muriendo vivo,
al remo condenado,
en la concha de Venus amarrado.

Por ti, como solía,
del áspero caballo no corrige
la furia y gallardía,
ni con freno le rige,
ni con vivas espuelas ya le aflige.

Por ti, con diestra mano
no revuelve la espada presurosa,
y en el dudoso llano
huye la polvorosa
palestra como sierpe ponzoñosa.

Por ti, su blanda musa,
en lugar de la cítara sonante,
tristes querellas usa,
que con llanto abundante
hacen bañar el rostro del amante.

Por ti, el mayor amigo
le es importuno, grave y enojoso;
yo puedo ser testigo,
que ya del peligroso
naufragio fui su puerto y su reposo.

Y agora en tal manera
vence el dolor a la razón perdida,
que ponzoñosa fiera
nunca fue aborrecida
tanto como yo dél, ni tan temida.

No fuiste tú engendrada
ni producida de la dura tierra;
no debe ser notada
que ingratamente yerra
quien todo el otro error de sí destierra.

Let the case of Anaxerete frighten you and make you a coward, for she regretted her scorn very late, and so her soul burns together with the marble (into which she was turned).

Her stony breast was rejoicing in another's ill when, looking down, she saw the dead body of her wretched lover lying there.

And tied round his neck, the noose with which he had freed his careworn heart from the chain, and with his brief pain bought another's eternal punishment.

Then she felt her harshness turn to loving pity. Oh, late repentance, and last-moment tenderness! How did a greater hardness come upon you?

Her eyes were fixed on the outstretched corpse that they saw there; her bones became harder and swelled until they had taken over all her flesh;

her frozen bowels turned gradually into hard stone; in her wretched veins her blood ceased to know its form and its nature;

until finally, turned and transformed into hard marble, she aroused not so much the people's astonishment as their sense of being avenged for her ingratitude.

Hágate temerosa
el caso de Anajárete, y cobarde,
que de ser desdeñosa
se arrepintió muy tarde;
y así, su alma con su mármol arde.

Estábase alegrando
del mal ajeno el pecho empedernido,
cuando abajo mirando
el cuerpo muerto vido
del miserable amante, allí tendido.

Y al cuello el lazo atado,
con que desenlazó de la cadena
el corazón cuitado,
que con su breve pena
compró la eterna punición ajena.

Sintió allí convertirse
en piedad amorosa el aspereza.
¡Oh tarde arrepentirse!
¡Oh última terneza!
¿Cómo te sucedió mayor dureza?

Los ojos se enclavaron
en el tendido cuerpo que allí vieron;
los huesos se tornaron
más duros y crecieron,
y en sí toda la carne convirtieron;

las entrañas heladas
tornaron poco a poco en piedra dura;
por las venas cuitadas
la sangre su figura
iba desconociendo y su natura;

hasta que finalmente
en duro mármol vuelta y transformada,
hizo de sí la gente
no tan maravillada
cuanto de aquella ingratitud vengada.

Do not choose now, lady, for God's sake, to try the arrows of angry Nemesis; let it suffice that to the poets your perfect deeds and beauty

give immortal subjects, without their having to celebrate also in plaintive verse the horror of some sad and miserable tragedy, of which you may be the cause.

BY rough roads I have come to a place from which I cannot move for fear; and if I try to stir or take a step, then I am dragged back by the hair.

But I am such that, with death at my side, I seek new counsel from my life; and I know the best yet approve the worst, either out of bad habits or by my destiny.

Moreover, the brief time that I have, and the mistaken course of my years in their first beginnings and in their middle time,

my inclinations, which I do not resist, and the certainty of death, the end of all these disasters, make me neglect my remedy.

WHILST the colours of the rose and the lily show themselves in your face, and whilst your burning, direct glance inflames and restrains the heart,

and whilst the wind stirs, scatters, and disarranges the hair, which was mined from a vein of gold, as it suddenly blows on your lovely white and straight neck;

No quieras tú, señora,
de Némesis airada las saetas
probar, por Dios, agora;
baste que tus perfetas
obras y hermosura a los poetas

den inmortal materia,
sin que también en verso lamentable
celebren la miseria
de algún caso notable
que por ti pase triste y miserable.

POR ásperos caminos he llegado
a parte que de miedo no me muevo;
y si a mudarme o dar un paso pruebo,
allí por los cabellos soy tornado.

Mas tal estoy que con el muerte al lado
busco de mi vivir consejo nuevo;
conozco lo mejor y lo peor apruebo,
o por costumbre mala, o por mi hado.

Por otra parte el breve tiempo mío,
y el errado proceso de mis años,
en su primer principio y en su medio,

mi inclinación, con quien yo no porfío,
la cierta muerte, fin de tantos daños,
me hacen descuidar de mi remedio.

EN tanto que de rosa y azucena
se muestra la color en vuestro gesto,
y que vuestro mirar ardiente, honesto,
enciende el corazón y lo refrena,

y en tanto el cabello, que en la vena
del oro se escogió, con vuelo presto,
por el hermoso cuello blanco, enhiesto,
el viento mueve, esparce y desordena;

gather the sweet fruit of your happy Spring, before angry Time covers your lovely head with snow.

The icy wind will wither the rose; light-foot age, to make no change in his own customs, will change everything.

Madrigal

CLEAR and serene eyes, if you are praised for a sweet glance, why, if you look at me, do you look angrily?

If when you are kinder, you seem more beautiful to the gazer, do not look at me angrily, for fear of appearing less beautiful. Oh, raging torments!

Clear and serene eyes, since you look at me like that, at least look at me.

[*Sonnet Addressed to King Charles V*]

SIR, now the glorious age is drawing near, or has already arrived, in which Heaven, by a good fortune reserved for your days, promises that there shall be one flock and one shepherd only on the earth.

Now this great beginning, with a campaign like this, gives you a sight of the end of your blessed ambition, and announces to the world, for its greater comfort, one Monarch, one Empire, and one Sword.

coged de vuestra alegre primavera
el dulce fruto, antes que el tiempo airado
cubra de nieve la hermosa cumbre.

Marchitará la rosa el viento helado,
todo lo mudará la edad ligera,
por no hacer mudanza en su costumbre.

GUTIERRE DE CETINA

Madrigal

Ojos claros, serenos,
si de un dulce mirar sois alabados,
¿por qué, si me miráis, miráis airados?
Si cuando más piadosos,
más bellos parecéis a aquel que os mira,
no me miréis con ira,
porque no parezcáis menos hermosos.
¡Ay tormentos rabiosos!
Ojos claros, serenos,
ya que así me miráis, miradme al menos.

HERNANDO DE ACUÑA

Ya se acerca, señor, o ya es llegada,
la edad gloriosa en que promete el cielo
una grey y un pastor solo en el suelo,
por suerte a vuestros tiempos reservada.

Ya tan alto principio en tal jornada,
os muestra el fin de vuestro santo celo,
y anuncia al mundo, para más consuelo,
un Monarca, un Imperio y una Espada.

Now the world's sphere partly feels itself to be, and wholly hopes to be, your kingdom, conquered by you in righteous war;

for to whom Christ has given His banner He will give that second and happier day on which, after conquering the sea, he conquers the land.

The Retired Life

WHAT a life of repose is his who flees the din of the world and follows the hidden path down which have passed the few sages that there have been in the world!

For his heart is not perturbed by the state of proud grandees, nor does he admire the gilded roof, built by the cunning Moor, and held up by jasper columns.

Nor does he care if fame sings his name with a voice of praise, nor does he care if flattering tongues exalt what honest truth condemns.

What pleasure can it bring me to be pointed at by vain fingers, or to run in pursuit of that wind (of fame) breathless with sharp longings and mortal cares?

Oh, mountain! oh, spring! oh, river! oh, safe and delightful hiding-place! With my ship almost wrecked, I flee from that stormy sea to your dear quietness.

Ya el orbe de la tierra siente en parte
y espera en todo, vuestra monarquía
conquistada por vos en justa guerra;

que a quien ha dado Cristo su estandarte,
dará el segundo más dichoso día
en que, vencido el mar, venza la tierra.

FRAY LUIS DE LEÓN

Vida retirada

¡QUÉ descansada vida
la del que huye el mundanal ruido,
y sigue la escondida
senda por donde han ido
los pocos sabios que en el mundo han sido!

Que no le enturbia el pecho
de los soberbios grandes el estado,
ni del dorado techo
se admira, fabricado
del sabio moro, en jaspes sustentado.

No cura si la fama
canta con voz su nombre pregonera,
ni cura si encarama
la lengua lisonjera
lo que condena la verdad sincera.

¿Qué presta a mi contento
si soy del vano dedo señalado?
¿si en busca de esta viento
ando desalentado
con ansias vivas, con mortal cuidado?

¡Oh monte! ¡oh fuente! ¡oh río!
¡oh secreto seguro deleitoso!
Roto casi el navío,
a vuestro almo reposo,
huyo de aqueste mar tempestuoso.

I want an unbroken sleep, a pure, happy, free day: I do not want to see the vain and angry frown of one whom blood or money exalt.

Let the birds wake me with their delicious and untaught song, not the heavy cares with which a man who is subject to another's will is always followed.

I want to live alone, I want to enjoy the wealth I owe to heaven, alone and without witnesses, free from love and enthusiasm, from hatred, hopes, and suspicions.

On the slope of the mountain I have a garden planted by my own hand. It was carpeted with lovely flowers in the Spring and now shows hopes of certain fruit.

And as if eager to see and increase its beauty, from the proud mountain top a pure spring hurries, running to reach it.

And there, in quiet, twisting its way among the trees, and clothing the ground it passes through with verdure, it goes scattering a variety of flowers.

The breeze fans the garden and offers a thousand odours to the senses. It sways the trees with a gentle sound, which puts gold and sceptres into oblivion.

Un no rompido sueño,
un día puro, alegre, libre quiero;
no quiero ver el ceño
vanamente severo
de a quien la sangre ensalza o el dinero.

Despiértenme las aves
con su cantar sabroso no aprendido,
no los cuidados graves
de que es siempre seguido
quien al ajeno arbitrio está atenido.

Vivir quiero conmigo,
gozar quiero del bien que debo al cielo,
a solas sin testigo,
libre de amor, de celo,
de odio, de esperanzas, de recelo.

Del monte en la ladera
por mi mano plantado tengo un huerto,
que con la primavera
de bella flor cubierto
ya muestra en esperanza el fruto cierto.

Y como codiciosa
de ver y acrecentar su hermosura,
desde la cumbre airosa
una fontana pura
hasta llegar corriendo se apresura.

Y luego sosegada
el paso entre los árboles torciendo,
el suelo de pasada
de verdura vistiendo,
y con diversas flores va esparciendo.

El aire el huerto orea,
y ofrece mil olores al sentido,
los árboles menea
con un manso ruido,
que del oro y del cetro pone olvido.

Let those who trust themselves to a weak ship have their treasure; it is not mine to see the tears of those who lose heart when the North wind and the South wind blow hard.

The mast creaks beneath the blast, and clear day turns to blind night; a confused clamour sounds up to the heavens, they rival one another in casting their riches into the sea.

Let a poor little table well stocked with lovely peace suffice for me. Let plate shaped from fine gold go to him who does not fear the sea when it is angry.

And whilst the rest are miserably burning with an insatiable thirst for impermanent authority, let me lie stretched in the shade, singing.

Stretched in the shade, and crowned with ivy and everlasting laurel, with my ear listening attentively to the measured sound of the cunningly plucked plectrum.

Ode to Francisco Salinas
Reader in Music at the University of Salamanca

THE air clears and puts on beauty and unaccustomed light, Salinas, when the consummate music sounds at the touch of your skilled hand.

Ténganse su tesoro
los que de un flaco leño se confían:
no es mío ver el lloro
de los que desconfían
cuando el cierzo y el ábrego porfían.

La combatida antena
cruje, y en ciega noche el claro día
se torna, al cielo suena
confusa vocería,
y la mar enriquecen a porfía.

A mí una pobrecilla
mesa de amable paz bien abastada
me baste, y la vajilla
de fino oro labrada
sea de quien la mar no teme airada.

Y mientras miserable-
mente se están los otros abrasando
con sed insaciable
del no durable mando,
tendido yo a la sombra esté cantando.

A la sombra tendido,
de hiedra y lauro eterno coronado,
puesto el atento oído
al son dulce acordado,
del plectro sabiamente meneado.

Oda a Francisco Salinas
Catedrático de música de la Universidad de Salamanca

EL aire se serena
y viste de hermosura y luz no usada,
Salinas, cuando suena
la música extremada
por vuestra sabia mano gobernada.

At this divine sound, my soul, which is sunk in apathy, once more recovers its sense and its lost memory of its first high origin.

And, as it remembers itself, its fate and thoughts improve: it forgets the perishable and deceptive beauty of gold which the blind crowd adores.

It soars through the whole air till it reaches the highest sphere, and there it hears another system of imperishable music, which is the first of all.

It sees how the great master, playing on that immense cither with skilled motions, produces the sacred sound by which this eternal temple is sustained.

And as it is composed of harmonious numbers, it sends out a reply in concord; and the two tunes mingle and compete in the sweetest harmony.

Here the soul sails through a sea of sweetness, and finally so drowns in it that it hears or is conscious of no strange or rare occurrence.

Oh, happy swoon! Oh, death that gives life! Oh, sweet oblivion! Might I but remain in your peace, and never be restored to this low and vile consciousness!

A cuyo son divino
mi alma que en olvido está sumida
torna a cobrar el tino
y memoria perdida
de su origen primera esclarecida.

Y como se conoce,
en suerte y pensamientos se mejora;
el oro desconoce
que el vulgo ciego adora,
la belleza caduca engañadora.

Traspasa el aire todo
hasta llegar a las más alta esfera,
y oye allí otro modo
de no perecedera
música, que es de todas la primera.

Ve cómo el gran maestro,
a aquesta inmensa cítara aplicado,
con movimiento diestro
produce el son sagrado,
con que este eterno templo es sustentado.

Y como está compuesta
de números concordes, luego envía
consonante respuesta,
y entrambas a porfía
mezclan una dulcísima armonía.

Aquí la alma navega
por un mar de dulzura, y finalmente
en él así se anega,
que ningún accidente
extraño o peregrino oye o siente.

¡Oh desmayo dichoso!
¡oh muerte que das vida! ¡oh dulce olvido!
¡durase en tu reposo
sin ser restituido
jamás a aqueste bajo y vil sentido!

To this good life I call you, glory of Apollo's sacred choir, friends whom I love above all treasure, since all things else are but tears.

Oh, go on for ever sounding your music in my ears, Salinas, music by which the feelings wake to the goodness of God, remaining still asleep to all other things.

Still Night: to Diego Olarte

WHEN I gaze on the sky spangled with innumerable lights, and look down on the earth with night all around it, buried in sleep and oblivion:

love and grief wake in my breast a burning desire: my eyes, which have become fountains, flow in a broad stream, the tongue says in doleful tones:

Abode of greatness, temple of radiance and beauty, what misfortune is it that holds my soul, which was born at your height, in this low, dark prison?

What deadly madness so alienates the senses from the truth that, forgetful and lost to your divine good, they follow this empty shadow, this feigned good?

A este bien os llamo,
gloria del apolíneo sacro coro,
amigos a quien amo
sobre todo tesoro,
que todo lo demás es triste lloro.

¡Oh! suene de continuo,
Salinas, vuestro son en mis oídos,
Por quien al bien divino
despiertan los sentidos,
quedando a lo demás amortecidos.

Noche serena: a Diego Olarte

CUANDO contemplo el cielo
de innumerables luces adornado,
y miro hacia el suelo
de noche rodeado,
en sueño y en olvido sepultado;

el amor y la pena
despiertan en mi pecho una ansia ardiente;
despiden larga vena
los ojos hechos fuente,
la lengua dice al fin con voz doliente:

Morada de grandeza,
templo de claridad y hermosura,
mi alma que a tu alteza
nació, ¿qué desventura
la tiene en esta cárcel baja, escura?

¿Qué mortal desatino
de la verdad aleja así el sentido,
que de tu bien divino
olvidado, perdido,
sigue la vana sombra, el bien fingido?

With no care for his destiny, man is consigned to sleep, and the heavens, as they slowly revolve, with quiet step, steal the hours of his life.

Oh, awake, mortals! Watch out carefully for your danger. Can immortal souls, made for so much good, live on shadows and deception?

Oh, raise your eyes to that celestial and eternal sphere, and you will laugh at the caprices of this flattering life with all its fears and all its hopes.

Is this low and heavy earth more than a tiny dot compared with that great copy of it where all that is, all that will be, and all that has passed, lives in a better state?

Whoever gazes on the great concert of those eternal luminaries, on their unchanging movements, and on their motions which are various, yet in their proportionate relationship concordant and equal;

on the moon, as she moves her silver circle, and on the light (Venus), as it follows in pursuit of her, that light in which wisdom rains down (Mercury), and on the gracious star of love which comes after her, resplendent and beautiful;

and (sees) how bloody and angry Mars follows another track, and kindly Jupiter, encircled with a thousand blessings, clears the sky with his beloved beams.

El hombre está entregado
al sueño, de su suerte no cuidando,
y con paso callado
el cielo vueltas dando
las horas del vivir le va hurtando.

¡Ay!, despertad, mortales;
mirad con atención en vuestro daño.
¿Las almas inmortales
hechas a bien tamaño,
podrán vivir de sombra, y de engaño?

¡Ay!, levantad los ojos
a aquesta celestial eterna esfera;
burlaréis los antojos
de aquesa lisonjera
vida, con cuanto teme y cuanto espera.

¿Es más que un breve punto
el bajo y torpe suelo, comparado
con ese gran trasunto
do vive mejorado
lo que es, lo que será, lo que ha pasado?

Quien mira el gran concierto
de aquestos resplandores eternales,
su movimiento cierto,
sus pasos desiguales
y en proporción concorde tan iguales;

la luna cómo mueve
la plateada rueda, y va en pos de ella
la luz do el saber llueve,
y la graciosa estrella
de amor le sigue reluciente y bella:

y cómo otro camino
prosigue el sanguinoso Marte airado,
y el Júpiter benino,
de bienes mil cercado,
serena el cielo con su rayo amado.

Saturn, father of the Golden Age, revolves at the zenith, and after him the multitude of the shining chorus come scattering their light and their treasure.

Who can look upon (all) this and prize the lowly earth, and not moan and sigh to break through what encloses his soul and cuts off from those blessings?

Here dwells happiness, here reigns peace; here, seated on a rich and high seat, is blessed love, surrounded by honour and delights.

Here mighty beauty shows herself in her fullness, and the most pure and radiant light shines out so that it is never dark; here blossoms eternal Spring.

Oh, fields of truth! Oh, truly green and delightful meadows! Oh, richest mines? Oh, pleasing retreat! Valleys stocked full of a thousand blessings!

On the Ascension

AND do you, blessed Shepherd, leave your flock in this deep, dark valley, in solitude and tears, while you yourself, cleaving the pure air, depart safely for immortality?

Rodéase en la cumbre
Saturno, padre de los siglos de oro;
tras él la muchedumbre
del reluciente coro
su luz va repartiendo y su tesoro.

¿Quién es el que esto mira
y precia la bajeza de la tierra,
y no gime y suspira
por romper lo que encierra
el alma, y de estos bienes la destierra?

Aquí vive el contento,
aquí reina la paz; aquí, asentado
en rico y alto asiento
está el amor sagrado,
de honra y de deleites rodeado.

Inmensa hermosura
aquí se muestra toda; y resplandece
clarísima luz pura,
que jamás anochece;
eterna primavera aquí florece.

¡Oh campos verdaderos!
¡oh prados con verdad frescos y amenos!
¡riquísimos mineros!
¡oh deleitosos senos,
repuestos valles de mil bienes llenos!

En la Ascensión

¿Y DEJAS, Pastor santo,
tu grey en este valle hondo, escuro,
con soledad y llanto,
y tú rompiendo el puro
aire, te vas al inmortal seguro?

To whom will they now turn, those who were once fortunate and those who are now sad and afflicted, nurtured at Your breasts and now without You?

What can eyes which once looked upon the beauty of Your face gaze at that will not fret them? Is there anything that one who has heard Your sweet tones will not find dull and calamitous?

Who will now calm that stormy sea? Who will give peace to the wild and stormy winds? Now that You are hidden away, what Northern point will guide the ship to port?

Oh, what grieves you, cloud, envious even of this brief joy? Where are you flying so hurriedly? How rich you are as you depart! How poor and how blind, alas, you leave us!

To Christ Crucified

IT is not the heaven that You have promised me, my God, that moves me to love You, nor is it the hell I so fear that moves me to cease sinning against You.

You move me, Lord; it moves me to see You nailed to that cross and despised; it moves me to see Your body so wounded; the insults You suffered and Your death move me.

Los antes bien hadados
y los agora tristes y afligidos
a tus pechos criados,
de ti desposeídos,
¿a dó convertirán ya sus sentidos?

¿Qué mirarán los ojos
que vieron de tu rostro la hermosura,
que no les sea enojos?
¿Quién oyó tu dulzura,
¿qué no tendrá por sordo y desventura?

Aqueste mar turbado
¿quién le pondrá ya freno? ¿quién concierto
al viento fiero airado?
Estando tú encubierto,
¿qué norte guiará la nave al puerto?

¡Ay!, nube envidïosa
aun de este breve gozo, ¿qué te aquejas?
¿dó vuelas presurosa?
¡cuán rica tú te alejas!
¡cuán pobres y cuán ciegos, ay, nos dejas!

MIGUEL DE GUEVARA

A Cristo crucificado

No me mueve, mi Dios, para quererte,
el cielo que me tienes prometido,
ni me mueve el infierno tan temido
para dejar por eso de ofenderte.

Tú me mueves, Señor; muéveme el verte
clavado en esa cruz, y escarnecido;
muéveme el ver tu cuerpo tan herido,
muévenme tus afrentas, y tu muerte.

Finally, Your love moves me, and so much that even if there were no heaven, I should love You; and even if there were no hell, I should fear You.

You have not to give me anything to make me love You; for even if I did not hope for what I do hope for, I should love You just as I do.

THREE things keep my heart the prisoner of love, the fair Inés, smoked ham and aubergines in (melted) cheese.

It is this Inés, lovers, who had such power over me as to make me hate all that was not Inés.

She kept me out of my senses for a year, until on one occasion she gave me for lunch smoked ham and aubergines in cheese.

Inés had the first triumph, but now it is difficult to judge which of all the three has the greatest share in my soul.

In taste, measure, and weight, I can see no distinction between them: now I love Inés, now smoked ham, and now aubergines in cheese.

Inés boasts her beauty, the ham that it is from Aracena, and the cheese and the aubergine their ancient Spanish extraction.

Muéveme, al fin, tu amor, y en tal manera,
que aunque no hubiera cielo, yo te amara,
y aunque no hubiera infierno te temiera.

No me tienes que dar porque te quiera;
pues aunque lo que espero no esperara,
lo mismo que te quiero te quisiera.

BALTASAR DEL ALCÁZAR

TRES cosas me tienen preso
de amores el corazón:
la bella Inés, el jamón
y berengenas con queso.

Esta Inés, amantes, es
quien tuvo en mí tal poder,
que me hizo aborrecer
todo lo que no era Inés.

Trájome un año sin seso,
hasta que en una ocasión
me dio a merendar jamón
y berengenas con queso.

Fue de Inés la primer palma,
pero ya júzgase mal
entre todos ellos cuál
tiene más parte en mi alma.

En gusto, medida y peso
no le hallo distinción;
ya quiero Inés, ya jamón,
ya berengenas con queso.

Alega Inés su beldad,
el jamón que es de Aracena,
el queso y la berengena
la española antigüedad.

And the weight is so equally balanced that, judged dispassionately, all are alike: Inés, smoked ham, and aubergines in cheese.

At least this matter of these new loves of mine will make Inés sell me her favours more cheaply,

for, if reason does not move her, she will have as counterweight, a slice of ham and aubergines in cheese.

For the Loss of the King Don Sebastian

LET a voice of grief and a song of lamentation and a spirit of fear blended with anger, make a bitter beginning to the memory of that fatal and abhorrent day for which wretched Portugal groans, naked of valour, stripped of glory; and let the mournful story strike with doleful and sad horror from the gulf of Lybia (the African Atlantic) and the burning gulf to where the sea wears another colour, and where the red boundary of the Orient and all its fierce and conquered peoples see the banners of Christ waving.

Alas for those who crossed, trusting in their horses and in the multitude of their chariots, into your desert, Lybia; and, miscalculating their vigour and strength, did not offer up their hopes to that summit of eternal light (God), but, with the pride of certainty, promised themselves the uncertain victory,

Y está tan en fiel el peso,
que, juzgado sin pasión,
todo es uno: Inés, jamón
y berengenas con queso.

A lo menos este trato
destos mis nuevos amores
hará que Inés sus favores
me los venda más barato,

pues tendrá por contrapeso,
si no hiciere la razón,
una lonja de jamón
y berengenas con queso.

FERNANDO DE HERRERA

Por la pérdida del Rey don Sebastián

VOZ de dolor, y canto de gemido,
y espíritu de miedo, envuelto en ira,
hagan principio acerbo a la memoria
d' aquel día fatal, aborrecido,
que Lusitania mísera suspira,
desnuda de valor, falta de gloria;
y la llorosa historia
asombre con horror funesto y triste
dend' el áfrico Atlante y seno ardiente
hasta do el mar de otro color se viste,
y do el límite rojo d' Oriente
y todas sus vencidas gentes fieras
ven tremolar de Cristo las banderas.

¡Ay de los que pasaron, confiados
en sus caballos y en la muchedumbre
de sus carros, en ti, Libia desierta,
y en su vigor y fuerzas engañados,
no alzaron su esperanza a aquella cumbre
d' eterna luz, mas con soberbia cierta

and without turning their gaze to God, with stiff neck and proud heart, merely waited always for the spoils! And the Holy One of Israel opened His hand and let them fall, and chariot, horse, and rider fell into the abyss.

There came the cruel day, the day full of wrath and anger and fury, that plunged the kingdom, empty of people and pleasure, into desolation and profound weeping. The sky did not grow bright, the new sun remained perplexed, in prophecy of all this evil, and with unexpected terror the Lord visited their ills upon them, to humble the strong and proud, and raised up the weaker barbarians, who with bold and constant hearts seek no gold, but with angry iron avenge the offence and guilty error (of the Portuguese).

These heathen and stout men, in their fury, unsheathed their burning swords against the clarity and beauty of your glory and valour and, not satisfied by your death, tarnished your whole honour, wretched and luckless Portugal; and with steadfast brows fearlessly brought your armoured squadrons and your bravery down in wild ruin. The sand became a lake of blood, the plain was piled with dead; some fought with their vigour, others with courage, but in others was dismay and heavy fear.

Can these be the famous, the strong, the warlike men who made the earth tremble with their fury, who shook mighty kingdoms, who tamed the

se ofrecieron la incierta
vitoria, y sin volver a Dios sus ojos,
con yerto cuello y corazón ufano
sólo atendieron siempre a los despojos!
Y el Santo d' Israel abrió su mano,
y los dejó, y cayó en despeñadero
el carro, y el caballo y caballero.

Vino el día crüel, el día lleno
d' indinación, de ira y furor, que puso
en soledad y en un profundo llanto,
de gente y de placer el reino ajeno.
El cielo no alumbró, quedó confuso
el nuevo sol, presagio de mal tanto,
y con terrible espanto
el Señor visitó sobre sus males,
para humillar los fuertes arrogantes,
y levantó los bárbaros no iguales,
que con osados pechos y constantes
no busquen oro, mas con hierro airado
venguen la ofensa y el error culpado.

Los impios y robustos, indinados,
las ardientes espadas desnudaron
sobre la claridad y hermosura
de tu gloria y valor, y no cansados
en tu muerte tu honor todo afearon,
mezquina Lusitania sin ventura;
y con frente segura
rompieron sin temor con fiero estrago
tus armadas escuadras y braveza.
L' arena se tornó sangriento lago,
la llanura con muertos aspereza;
cayó en unos vigor, cayó denuedo;
mas en otros desmayo y torpe miedo.

¿Son éstos, por ventura, los famosos,
los fuertes, los belígeros varones
que conturbaron con furor la tierra,
que sacudieron reinos poderosos,
que domaron las hórridas naciones,

savage nations, who laid waste in cruel war all that lies within the Indian Ocean, and destroyed proud cities? Where now is the steadfast heart and the daring? How could so much heroic valour end and perish in a single day, and they, overthrown far from their native land, not even be properly buried?

They were like a lovely cedar of high Lebanon, clothed in branches and leaves and exceedingly tall; the waters made it mighty and higher than the tall trees: and its branches increased in size and in beauty; and as its shade spread wider, the birds whom the great sky houses nested there, and the beasts had their young beneath its leaves, and it made a shady screen for many people: never did any tree equal its shape in loftiness and beauty.

But it stretched up its tall head and, utterly vain and confident, soared into presumption, valuing its height alone. For this God threw it down in destruction, and consigned it to the heathen and the stranger, cut down by the root; for overwhelmed by the angry mountains, branchless, leafless, and naked, men who had made a protection of its shade fled from it in alarm, and all the birds and the beasts that there were settled on its wreck and its branches.

Accursed Lybia, you on whose dry sand the conquered kingdom of Portugal died, and where his noble glory ended, do not be glad or full of pride, for it was by chance that your timorous and weak hand obtained so

que pusieron desierto en cruda guerra,
cuanto el mar Indo encierra,
y soberbias ciudades destruyeron?
¿Dó el corazón seguro y la osadía?
¿Cómo así se acabaron, y perdieron
tanto heroico valor en sólo un día;
y lejos de su patria derribados,
no fueron justamente sepultados?

Tales ya fueron éstos, cual hermoso
cedro del alto Líbano, vestido
de ramos, hojas, con excelsa alteza;
las aguas lo criaron poderoso
sobre empinados árboles crecido,
y se multiplicaron en grandeza
sus ramos con belleza;
y extendiendo su sombra, s' anidaron
las aves que sustenta el grande cielo,
y en sus hojas las fieras engendraron
y hizo a mucha gente umbroso velo;
no igualó en celsitud y en hermosura
jamás árbol alguno a su figura.

Pero elevóse con su verde cima,
y sublimó la presunción su pecho
desvanecido todo y confiado,
haciendo de su alteza sólo estima.
Por eso Dios lo derribó deshecho,
a los impíos y ajenos entregado,
por la raíz cortado;
qu' opreso de los montes arrojados,
sin ramos y sin hojas y desnudo,
huyeron dél los hombres, espantados,
que su sombra tuvieron por escudo;
en su ruina y ramos, cuantas fueron,
las aves y las fieras se pusieron.

Tú, infanda Libia, en cuya seca arena
murió el vencido reino lusitano,
y s' acabó su generosa gloria,
no estés alegre y d' ufanía llena;

great a victory, and that victory is unworthy of memory; for if ever righteous grief moves the brave heart of Spain to vengeance, shattered with the sharp lance, you will pay with your death for this outrage you have done, and the river Luco in fear will yield its tribute of African blood to the huge sea.

For the Victory of Lepanto

DEEP Pontus,* who roar thunder-struck with confusion and terror, lift your face from your troubled breast, full of dull fear, and see your bloodstained fields burning;

and (see), meeting together in this circle all the might of the Christians and the Saracens, and the heathen flying, trembling and broken, covered with smoke and fire and thunder.

Celebrate with a deep voice the greatest victory that ever the heavens saw, and the most hard-contested and unique achievement; and proclaim that the young Austrian† and the valour of Spain alone had deserved the glory that lends such renown to your sacred soil.

To Seville

FORTUNATE queen of the great Ocean, without whom Spain would lack greatness, and whose value and vigour are increased by valour, skill, and nobility

what shall I say that you are, lovely light of Europe? Not earth, for your riches and glory are not confined to earth's narrow bounds, but a heaven of marvellous virtue.

* The Black Sea.
† Don John of Austria.

porque tu temerosa y flaca mano
hubo sin esperanza tal vitoria,
indina de memoria;
que si el justo dolor mueve a venganza
alguna vez el español coraje,
despedazada con aguda lanza,
compensarás muriendo el hecho ultraje;
y Luco amedrentado, al mar inmenso
pagará d' africana sangre el censo.

Por la vitoria de Lepanto

HONDO Ponto, que bramas atronado
con tumulto y terror, del turbio seno
saca el rostro, de torpe miedo lleno;
mira tu campo arder ensangrentado;

y junto en este cerco y encontrado
todo el cristiano esfuerzo y sarraceno,
y cubierto de humo y fuego y trueno,
huir temblando el impio quebrantado.

Con profundo murmurio la vitoria
mayor celebra que jamás vio el cielo,
y más dudosa y singular hazaña;

y di que sólo mereció la gloria
que tanto nombre da a tu sacro suelo
el joven de Austria y el valor de España.

A Sevilla

REINA del grand' Océano dichosa,
sin quien a España falta la grandeza,
a quien valor, ingenio y la nobleza
hacen más estimada y generosa,

¿Cuál diré que tú seas, luz hermosa
de Europa? Tierra no, que tu riqueza
y gloria no se cierra en su estrecheza;
cielo sí, de virtud maravillosa.

He who gazes on your power and abundance listens and is amazed and does not believe in you, so fame is dwarfed in the presence of reality.

You are not a city, but a world; in you everything that is scattered among other cities can be admired together, oh part of Spain that is much greater than the whole.

ALONE, along a road exposed to the sun, and foully sown with thorns and thistles, I make my slow way and wearily go where the unstable sea will cut off my return.

Sad silence inhabits this desert, and the pain that here one must be silent; when I think as I ride, I see the way increase and my labours certain.

On one side the assembled peaks rise, soaring to the sky; on the other yawns a great precipice.

I do not know to whom to turn in my plight for liberation from Love and these evils, for I expect no remedy, oh my light, except from you.

NIGHT, you that, in your loving and sweet oblivion, hide and harbour the cares of hostile day, and compensate the senses for their past labours,

You that have led me from my grief to contemplate you and contemplate my hostile fates, now banded together against a man persecuted by the heavens,

Oye y se espanta y no te cree el que mira
tu poder y abundancia; de tal modo
con la presencia ve menor la fama.

No ciudad, eres orbe; en ti se admira
junto cuanto en las otras se derrama,
parte de España más mejor que el todo.

POR un camino, solo, al sol abierto,
de espinas y de abrojos mal sembrado,
el tardo paso muevo, y voy cansado
a do cierra la vuelta el mar incierto.

Silencio triste habita este desierto:
y el mal que ahí conviene ser callado;
cuando pienso a caballo, acrecentado
veo el camino, y mi trabajo cierto.

A un lado levantan su grandeza
los riscos juntos, con el cielo iguales,
al otro cae un gran despeñadero.

No sé de quién me valga en mi estrecheza,
que me libre de Amor y destos males,
pues remedio sin vos, mi Luz, no espero.

FRANCISCO DE LA TORRE

NOCHE que en tu amoroso y dulce olvido
escondes y entretienes los cuidados
del enemigo día y los pasados
trabajos recompensas al sentido.

Tú que de mi dolor me has conducido
a contemplarte y contemplar mis hados
enemigos agora conjurados
contra un hombre del cielo perseguido,

May the bright lamps of heaven always light you, and may your friendly brow always be bound with night-shade and cypress.

May the bright sun never shed his light on this spot whilst I deplore my absence from my love. For well you know my life!

Ode

BRIGHT lights of the heavens and bright eyes in the dread face of night, bright crown, and bright Cassiopea, Andromeda, and Perseus,

You with whom the divine virgin, daughter of the ruler of mighty Olympus, passes the long periods of the watch that falls to her lot,

listen to my plaint, for my tears are the sign of no mild grief; let them not be lost as such tears once shed are always lost.

How many times have you seen me, and has Cynthia seen me, weeping in my distress for that lukewarm passion with which that sleeping shepherd of hers adored her beauty!

How many times did the bright dawn find me, a woeful spirit wandering through solitary and deserted valleys, lamenting my lot!

How many times, when she saw me so sad, did her pity for my grief make her shed bitter and piteous tears, with which she beautified the flowers!

así las claras lámparas del cielo
siempre te alumbren, y tu amiga frente
de beleño y ciprés tengas ceñida.

Que no vierta su luz en ese suelo
el claro sol, mientras me quejo ausente
de mi pasión. Bien sabes tú mi vida.

Oda

CLARAS lumbres del cielo y ojos claros
del espantoso rostro de la noche,
corona clara y clara Casiopea,
    Andrómeda y Perseo,

vos, con quien la divina Virgen, hija
del Rector del Olimpo inmenso, pasa
los espaciosos ratos de la vela
    nocturna que le cabe,

escuchad vos mis quejas, que mi llanto
no es indicio de no rabiosa pena;
no vayan tan perdidas como siempre
    tan bien perdidas lágrimas.

¡Cuántes veces me vistes y me vido
llorando Cintia, en mi cuidado el tibio
celo con que adoraba su belleza
    un su pastor dormido!

¡Cuántas veces me halló la clara Aurora
espíritu doliente, que anda errando
por solitarios y desiertos valles,
    llorando mi ventura!

¡Cuántas veces mirándome tan triste
la piedad de mi dolor la hizo
verter amargas y piadosas lágrimas
    con que adornó las flores!

You saw me alone, too, oh stars, a faithful companion of your silence, walking through the quiet night, full of evil suspicions.

I saw the cruel Circe, who tortures me, making fierce spells from the leaves and flower of my hope, prematurely and wrongfully cut down.

A cruel vision, in which the glory, whose firmness I once worshipped, fell away, and the hopes of a life envied by fortune itself were imperilled.

Oh leave me alone, you visions of heaven, for the glory that can only come by good fortune and by her hand will not for ever be desired by my afflicted spirit.

WHITE ivory inlaid in ebony, soft voice heard by one unworthy, sweet glance – on whose account I carry a great wound in my heart – ill-tenanted;

white foot, guided by another foot, ear deaf to the remedying of my life, but attentive to the voice of unreason, by the side of another I know not why,

rare and high good fortune, will not courteous Fate allow me to enjoy one hour of the noble benefits that flow from you?

Oh, the sun, which beautifies and colours all that it looks on – will it not keep away from me here so that it may not see a brighter sun in so dark a place?

Vos, estrellas, también me vistes solo,
fiel compañero del silencio vuestro,
andar por la callada noche, lleno
de sospechosos males.

Vi la Circe cruel que me persigue,
de las hojas y flor de mi esperanza,
antes de tiempo y sin razón cortadas,
hacer encantos duros.

Cruda visión, donde la gloria, un tiempo
adorada por firme, cayó, y donde
peligró la esperanza de una vida
de fortuna invidiada.

¡Ay, déjenme los cielos, que la gloria,
que por fortuna y por su mano viene,
no será deseada eternamente
de mi afligido espíritu!

FRANCISCO DE FIGUEROA

BLANCO marfil en ébano entallado,
suave voz indignamente oída,
dulce mirar – por quien larga herida
traigo en el corazón – mal ocupado;

blanco pie por ajeno pie guiado,
oreja sorda a remediar mi vida
y atenta al son de la razón perdida,
lado, no sé por qué, junto a tal lado;

raras, altas venturas, ¿no me diera
la Fortuna cortés gozar una hora
del alto bien que desde vos reparte?

¿Oh el Sol, que cuanto mira orna y colora,
no me faltara aquí, porque no viera
un sol más claro en tan oscura parte?

Description of a Sentinel in a Camp

HAVE you ever seen the fierce and active Spanish army in the field when black-winged night is scattering silence, sleep, fear, and alarm on the dark air?

Have you ever seen it sleeping and taking its rest under the waking vigilance of the royal sentry of the night, who is looking around him cautiously and restlessly on his own behalf, and for the others?

Casting his watchful and steadfast eye, and verifying (his observations) with vigilant ear, he descries, or thinks he can dimly make out in the distance, indistinct in the shadows, the squat figure of some stealthy enemy on the watch.

He looks and looks again, crouches and straightens up, advances a pace and returns to his post, takes notice, takes warning, prepares his arms, stands on tiptoe, stops, moves off, feels the ground, and moves step by step from one spot to another, and so makes his examination with speed.

He continually keeps his eyes on this shape, and is uncertain, and cannot make up his mind; he would like to shout: 'To arms, to arms!' but holds back for fear of causing a general alarm; for if the shape were not a reality he would detract from the reputation and esteem which any good soldier should enjoy.

But lo, suddenly the enemy discharges his fury against his breast. 'To arms, to arms! Saint James! To arms, to arms!' he cries. Then you will hear his cry multiplied, spread, and repeated in every mouth.

FRANCISCO DE ALDANA

Descripción de un centinela en un campamento

¿VISTES alguna vez en la campaña
ejército español, fiero y lozano,
cuando la noche con sus alas negras
esparce por el aire tenebroso
silencio, sueño, miedo y sobresalto?
¿Vistesle estar durmiendo y reposando
debajo la despierta vigilancia
de la real nocturna centinela,
que está con recatado azoramiento
mirando alrededor por sí y por otros?
La cual echando el ojo atento y firme,
retificando con la oreja atenta,
descubre, o le parece que columbra
confusamente umbroso y bajo bulto
de algún acechador cauto enemigo.
Mira y torna a mirar, se abaja y alza,
echa adelante un paso y vuelve al puesto,
se impone, se apercibe, se apareja,
se empina, pára, parte, prueba y pasa
su paso a paso de una en otra parte,
y requiere asimismo no despacio.
Tiene continuado el rostro siempre
al bulto, y duda y no se determina;
quiere gritar: «¡Arma, arma!» y se detiene
por no causar común desasosiego;
que si no fuese el bulto cierta cosa,
viene a disminuir de aquel concepto
y estimación debida a buen soldado.
Mas héte de improviso que descarga
el contrario furor sobre su pecho.
«¡Arma, arma; Santiago; arma, arma!» grita.
Luego veréis la voz multiplicada,
difusa y repetida en toda boca.

To the Heavens

CLEAR fountain of light, oh, new and lovely fatherland of heaven, rich with shiners, home of the truth, without shadow or veil, cheerful and kindly dwelling of intelligent spirits!

Oh, how far distant you are there, body of glory, from mortal and perishable desires, like a divine Argus, risen upon wings, free from our human error and merciful.

Oh, beloved fatherland, this migrant soul sighs and weeps for you in its cell, and is borne off on its wanderings between one minute and another.

May this true beauty, which has my love, grant me so kind a fate and chance that the lover may reach the heights to which love rises.

Song of the Ascent of Mount Carmel

IN a dark night, inflamed by love's desires – oh, lucky chance! – I went out unnoticed, all being then quiet in my house.

In darkness and safe, by the secret staircase, and disguised – oh, lucky chance! – in darkness and by stealth, all being then quiet in my house.

On that lucky night, in secret, since no one saw me nor did I see anything, with no other light or guide except the light that was burning in my heart.

Al cielo

¡CLARA fuente de luz nuevo y hermoso,
rico de luminarias patrio cielo!
¡Casa de la verdad, sin sombra o velo,
de inteligencias ledo almo reposo!

¡Oh, cómo allá te estás, cuerpo glorioso,
tan lejos del mortal caduco anhelo,
casi un Argos divino alzado a vuelo,
de nuestro humano error libre y piadoso!

¡Oh patria amada! a ti suspira y llora
ésta, en su cárcel, Alma peregrina,
llevada errando de uno en otro instante.

Esa cierta beldad que me enamora,
suerte y sazón me otorgue tan benina,
que do sube el amor llegue el amante.

SAN JUAN DE LA CRUZ

Canción de la subida del Monte Carmelo

EN una noche oscura,
con ansias en amores inflamada,
¡oh dichosa ventura!,
salí sin ser notada,
estando ya mi casa sosegada.

A oscuras y segura
por la secreta escala, disfrazada,
¡oh dichosa ventura!,
a oscuras y en celada,
estando ya mi casa sosegada.

En la noche dichosa,
en secreto, que nadie me veía,
ni yo miraba cosa,
sin otra luz y guía
sino la que en el corazón ardía.

This guided me more certainly than the light of midday, to where one awaited me whom I knew well, in a place where no one was to be seen.

Oh, night that was the guide; oh, night more delightful than the dawn; oh, night that joined Lover with Mistress, the Mistress transformed into the Lover!

In my burgeoning heart, which kept itself wholly for Him alone, there He stayed asleep, and I entertained Him, and the cedars were the fan that made the breeze.

The wind from the battlements, as it scattered His hair, wounded me on the neck with its smooth hand, and suspended all my senses.

I remained and forgot myself, I laid my face against the Lover, everything stopped and left me, leaving my cares forgotten among the lilies.

Song of the Living Flame of Love

OH, flame of living love that deals a tender wound right in the deepest centre of my soul, since now you are not elusive, be pleased to finish now, and break the web of this sweet meeting!

Aquesta me guiaba
  más cierto que la luz de mediodía,
  adonde me esperaba
  quien yo bien me sabía,
  en parte donde nadie parecía.

¡Oh noche que guiaste,
  oh, noche amable más que la alborada,
  oh, noche que juntaste
  Amado con Amada,
  Amada en el Amado transformada!

En mi pecho florido,
  que entero para él sólo se guardaba,
  allí quedó dormido,
  y yo le regalaba
  y el ventalle de cedros aire daba.

El aire del almena,
  cuando ya sus cabellos esparcía,
  con su mano serena
  en mi cuello hería
  y todos mis sentidos suspendía.

Quedéme y olvidéme,
  el rostro recliné sobre el Amado,
  cesó todo, y dejéme,
  dejando mi cuidado
  entre las azucenas olvidado.

Canción de la llama de amor viva

¡OH llama de amor viva
  que tiernamente hieres
de mi alma en el más profundo centro,
  pues ya no eres esquiva,
  acaba ya, si quieres;
rompe la tela de este dulce encuentro!

Oh, gentle cautery! oh, delicate wound! oh, soft hand! oh, gentle touch that tastes of eternal life and pays all debts, by killing you have transformed death into life!

Oh, lamps of fire in whose brightness the deep caverns of the senses, which were dark and blind, give warmth and light to the lover, together with strange perfections!

How mildly and lovingly you rouse memory in my breast, where you dwell alone; and sweet in your breathing, full of goodness and glory, how delicately you capture my love!

Verses of the Soul that Pines to See God

I LIVE and do not live in myself, and so strong are my hopes that I am dying of not dying.

I do not live in myself now, and without God I cannot live; since I am left without Him and without myself, what will this living be? It will deal me a thousand deaths, since I am hoping for my own life, dying because I am not dying.

¡Oh cauterio suave!
¡oh regalada llaga!
¡oh mano blanda! ¡oh toque delicado
que a la vida eterna sabe
y toda deuda paga!
¡matando, muerte en vida la has trocado!

¡Oh lámparas de fuego
en cuyos resplandores
las profundas cavernas del sentido
que estaba oscuro y ciego,
con extraños primores,
calor y luz dan junto a su querido!

¡Cuán manso y amoroso
recuerdas en mi seno,
donde secretamente solo moras;
y en tu aspirar sabroso
de bien y gloria lleno,
cuán delicadamente me enamoras!

Coplas del alma que pena por ver a Dios

VIVO sin vivir en mí,
y de tal manera espero
que muero porque no muero.

En mí yo no vivo ya,
y sin Dios vivir no puedo,
pues sin Él y sin mí quedo,
este vivir, ¿qué será?
pues mi misma vida espero.
Mil muertes se me hará,
pues mi misma vida espero,
muriendo porque no muero.

This life that I live is a privation of living, and so it is a continual death until I live with You. Listen, my God, to what I say, for I do not want this life, since I am dying of not dying.

Being absent from You, what life can I lead without suffering the greatest death I ever saw? I pity myself because I persevere in such fashion that I am dying of not dying.

The fish that leaves the water still does not lack alleviation, for the death he suffers finally serves him as death. What death could there be equal to my pitiful life, since the more I live the more I die?

When I begin to draw alleviation from seeing You in the Sacrament, it increases my grief, not to be able to enjoy You. All makes for my greater grief, since I do not see You as I wish, for I am dying of not dying.

And if I gladden myself, Lord, with the hope of seeing You, in seeing that I may lose You my grief is redoubled. Living in such fear and hoping as I hope, I die of not dying.

Esta vida que yo vivo,
es privación de vivir;
y así, es continuo morir
hasta que vivo contigo.
Oye, mi Dios, lo que digo,
que esta vida no la quiero,
que muero porque no muero.

Estando ausente de Ti,
¿Qué vida puedo tener
sino muerte padecer
la mayor que nunca ví?
Lástima tengo de mí,
pues de suerte persevero,
que muero porque no muero.

El pez que del agua sale
aun de alivio no carece,
que la muerte que padece
al fin de muerte le vale.
¿Qué muerte habrá que se iguale
a mi vivir lastimero,
pues si más vivo más muero?

Cuando me empiezo a aliviar
de verte en el Sacramento,
háceme más sentimiento
el no te poder gozar.
Todo es para más penar
por no verte como quiero
que muero porque no muero.

Y, si me gozo, Señor,
con esperanza de verte,
en ver que puedo perderte
se me dobla mi dolor,
viviendo en tanto pavor
y esperando como espero,
que muero porque no muero.

Rescue me from this death, my God, and give me life; do not keep me in such strong bonds as these. See that I am dying for the sight of You, and that my pain is so complete that I am dying of not dying.

I will mourn my death now, and lament my life, since it is prolonged for my sins. Oh, my God, when will it be that I shall truly say: I live because I am not dying?

Seguidilla

I WILL tread the small dust* so very fine:† I will tread the dust so fine.

I will tread the soil, however hard it is, so that love may open me a tomb in it, for love trod my good fortune so small.

I shall tread gaily on the hardest soil if by chance you tread there on the evil that I fear; my happiness has flown away and left the dust so small.

* *El polvico* is also the name of a dance.

† Or 'so often'.

Sácame de aquesta muerte,
mi Dios, y dame la vida;
no me tengas impedida
en este lazo tan fuerte.
Mira que muero por verte,
y mi mal es tan entero
que muero porque no muero.

Lloraré mi muerte ya,
y lamentaré mi vida
en tanto que detenida
por mis pecados está.
¡Oh mi Dios! ¿Cuándo será?
cuando yo diga de vero:
vivo ya porque no muero.

MIGUEL DE CERVANTES SAAVEDRA

Seguidilla

PISARÉ yo el polvico
atán menudico;
pisaré yo el polvó
atán menudó.

Pisaré yo la tierra
Por más que esté dura,
puesto que me abre en ella
amor sepultura,
pues ya mi buena ventura
amor la pisó
atán menudó.

Pisaré yo lozana
el más duro suelo,
si en él acaso pisas
el mal que recelo;
mi bien se ha pasado en vuelo
y el polvo dejó
atán menudó.

The Gipsy Girl

WHEN Preciosa beats her tambourine and the sweet music wounds the empty air, it is pearls that drop from her hands, flowers that she sends from her mouth.

The soul is wonderstruck and the judgement amazed by her sweet and superhuman movements; for their purity, their frankness and their modesty her fame soars up till it touches the sky.

She carries a thousand souls hanging on her lightest hair, and at her feet Love has surrendered both his arrows.

She blinds and sheds light with her two suns; by them Love maintains his empire, and thinks himself capable of performing even greater prodigies.

Elegy

IF one could be the sky, oh nymph brighter than the sky, to enjoy the infinity of your face with a thousand lights, when you look at its stars,

or because you are glad of them sometimes, or to enjoy such richness for ever, since certainly you will see yourself accounted one of them (the stars),

or, naked of the mortal sheath, to preserve your beauty for a thousand centuries, eternalized with that other incorruptible beauty!

One would make the air in your region mild, and give a good sign and a good planet to the rich soil trodden by your feet.

La gitanilla

CUANDO Preciosa el panderete toca
y hiere el dulce son los aires vanos,
perlas son que derrama con las manos,
flores son que despide con la boca.

Suspensa el alma y la cordura loca
queda a los dulces actos sobrehumanos,
que de limpios, de honestos y de sanos
su fama al cielo levantado toca.

Colgada del menor de sus cabellos
mil almas lleva y a sus plantas tiene
amor rendidas una y otra flecha.

Ciega y alumbra con sus soles bellos,
su imperio Amor por ellos le mantiene,
y aun más grandezas en su ser sospecha.

LUIS BARAHONA DE SOTO

Elegía

¡QUIÉN fuera cielo, ninfa más que él clara,
por gozar, cuando miras sus estrellas
con luces mil, la inmensa de tu cara,

o porque alguna vez te agradas dellas,
o por gozar por siempre tal riqueza,
pues cierto te has de ver contada entre ellas,

o por, desnudo de mortal corteza,
con otra incorruptible eternizado,
conservar por mil siglos tu belleza!

Hiciera el aire en tu región templado,
y diérale buen signo y buen planeta
al rico suelo de tus pies pisado.

Never would a tragic freak of nature or a comet, lightning, or thunder, snow or hail, disturb the region tranquil for your sake,

and there, like rain, into your white hands, a whirlwind of gold and emeralds – and even the sky that made them – would fall.

One would cover your shoulders with stars, and put the moon on your breast and a thousand lights together on your skirts.

There fame, not gain, would grow, so that to give all this great beauty to your loveliness would be no more than to declare what was already done.

I would display my desire and the sagacity born of my love, since I could display no more greatness (than yours) even if I would.

One could add no more (greatness) than is yours, nor could any be obtained, for if the earth could hold more it would give you more.

This I would do for my consolation, and so that you should owe to my hand what you owe to what are now the heavens.

Finally, I would give you, since everything else is vain, that food which confers countless years, and remove your life from the human course and, what is more, I should keep you happy.

Moral Epistle to Fabio

FABIO, the hopes of Court are fetters in which the ambitious man dies, and where the most astute get grey hairs.

Jamás prodigo triste ni cometa,
rayo ni trueno, nieve ni granizo,
turbara la región por ti quïeta,

y allí en tus blancas manos, llovedizo,
un torbellino de oro y esmeraldas
cayera, y aun el cielo que lo hizo.

De estrellas te cubriera las espaldas,
la luna te pusiera sobre el pecho,
y mil luceros juntos en tus faldas.

Creciera allí la fama, no el provecho,
que dalle a tu beldad tan gran belleza
no fuera más que declarar lo hecho.

Mostrar mi deseo y sutileza
nacida del amor, pues no pudiera
mostrar aunque quisiera más grandeza.

Ninguna más que tienes le añadiera,
ni puede procurarse, pues si el suelo
pudiera caber más, más se te diera.

Esto hiciera yo por mi consuelo
y porque le debieras a mi mano
lo que le debes al que agora es cielo.

Al fin te diera, pues esotro es vano,
el manjar que los años da sin cuenta,
sacando tu vivir del curso humano,
y lo que es más, tuviérate contenta.

ANDRÉS FERNÁNDEZ DE ANDRADA

Epístola moral a Fabio

FABIO, las esperanzas cortesanas
prisiones son do el ambicioso muere
y donde al más astuto nacen canas.

Anyone who has not filed them through or broken them has not deserved the name of a man, nor to attain the honours at which he aimed.

Let the mean and common spirit, timorous in his endeavours, choose rather to hang in suspense than to fall:

but the sound and noble heart would rather bend his forehead to adversity than his knee to the mighty.

Fortune has given more triumphs and crowns to the prudent man who has known how to retire, than to one who has obstinately and crazily gone on hoping.

This awful and tedious onslaught of adversities awaits us from our first sob in the cradle.

Let us let it pass like the wild spate of the Guadalquivir, when it angrily broadens its banks to the mountains.

The man who has deserved the prize is counted among the heroes, not he who attains it for empty considerations of state.

Everything that was Astraea's,* everything that she ruled with her dread sword and her scales, is now the private property of favour.

Gold, evil, and tyranny proceed from the wicked and pass to the good. What does virtue expect, or what does it trust in?

Come and rest in the maternal bosom of ancient Romúlea, whose climate will be kinder to you and calmer:

where at least, when the earth lies on our body, someone will say: 'May it be soft', as he scatters it over us;

* Goddess of Justice.

El que no las limare o las rompiere,
ni el nombre de varón ha merecido,
ni subir al honor que pretendiere.

El ánimo plebeyo y abatido
elija, en sus intentos temeroso,
primero estar suspenso que caido;

que el corazón entero y generoso
al caso adverso inclinará su frente,
antes que la rodilla al poderoso.

Más triunfos, más coronas dio al prudente
que supo retirarse, la fortuna,
que al que esperó obstinada y locamente.

Esta invasión terrible e importuna
de contrarios sucesos nos espera
desde el primer sollozo de la cuna.

Dejémosla pasar como a la fiera
corriente del gran Betis, cuando airado
dilata hasta los montes la ribera.

Aquel entre los héroes es contado
que el premio mereció, no quien le alcanza
por vanas consecuencias del estado.

Peculio propio es ya de la privanza
cuando de Astrea fue, cuando regía
con su temida espada y su balanza.

El oro, la maldad, la tiranía
del inicuo procede y pasa al bueno.
¿Qué espera la virtud o qué confía?

Ven y reposa en el materno seno
de la antigua Romúlea, cuyo clima
te será más humano y más sereno;

adonde, por lo menos, cuando oprima
nuestro cuerpo la tierra, dirá alguno:
«Blanda le sea», al derramarla encima;

where you will not leave the table fasting, even when it lacks the rare fish or when Juno denies us her peacock.

Seek sweet and dear tranquillity then, as the pilot seeks the upstanding lighthouse in the dark night on the Aegean;

for if you reduce and confine your desires you will say: 'What I despise has come to me: for public opinion is madness.'

The nightingale prefers its poor nest of feathers and light straw, prefers its plaints in the well-stocked and secret wood,

to pleasing the ears of some famous prince with flattery, imprisoned in the metal of its gilt cage.

How miserable is the man who is destined for that old settlement of the vices, to read the auguries in the faces of the great.

Give up desire and thirst for position; for the idol to whom you now sacrifice accepts the gift and laughs at its intention.

Bring your thoughts into conformity with life, and you will not soar above it between today and tomorrow, nor even between one moment and another.

You have hardly an empty shadow of our ancient Itálica* – and yet do you hope? Such is the perpetual error of humankind!

The Grecian standards, the banners of the Roman senate and monarchy, have perished, and their course is spent.

What is our life more than a brief day, in which the sun no sooner rises than it loses itself in the darkness of the cold night?

* A ruined Roman city near Seville.

donde no dejarás la mesa ayuno
cuando te falte en ella el pece raro
o cuando su pavón nos niegue Juno.

Busca, pues, el sosiego dulce y caro,
como en la oscura noche del Egeo
busca el piloto el eminente faro;

que si acortas y ciñes tu deseo,
dirás: «Lo que desprecio he conseguido;
que la opinión vulgar es devaneo.»

Más precia el ruiseñor su pobre nido
de pluma y leves pajas, más sus quejas
en el bosque repuesto y escondido,

que agradar lisonjero las orejas
de algún principe insigne, aprisionado
en el metal de las doradas rejas.

Triste de aquel que vive destinado
a esa antigua colonia de los vicios,
augur de los semblantes del privado.

Cese el ansia y la sed de los oficios;
que acepta el don y burla del intento
el ídolo a quien haces sacrificios.

Iguala con la vida el pensamiento,
y no le pasarás de hoy a mañana,
ni quizá de un momento a otro momento.

Casi no tienes ni una sombra vana
de nuestra antigua Itálica, y ¿esperas?
¡Oh error perpetuo de la suerte humana!

Las enseñas grecianas, las banderas
del senado y romana monarquía
murieron, y pasaron sus carreras.

¿Qué es nuestra vida más qu un breve día
do apenas sale el sol cuando se pierde
en las tinieblas de la noche fría?

What more is it than the grass, green in the morning and dry by evening? Oh, blind confusion! Shall I ever wake up from this dream?

Shall I ever be able to see that as I live I depart from life, and that wary death and my simple living are one?

Like the rivers that flow in a rapid stream to the sea, so am I carried to the last breath of my life.

What has remained to me of my past years? What happiness can I hope for in a future life, with no knowledge of my destiny?

Oh if, as I see myself dying, I could finally learn to die before I reach that necessary last end;

before the harsh hand of cruel death reaps this useless grain, and consigns it to the common store!

The flowers of summer have passed, autumn has passed with its grapes, and winter has passed whiteheaded with snow;

the leaves which we saw in the tall woods have fallen – and we persist in living, constant in our illusion!

Let us fear the Lord, who sends us the year's wheat and plenty, and the early rains and the late.

Do not let us imitate the soil, which always resists the waters of the heavens and the plough, nor the vine whose fruit never ripens.

Surely you do not think that man was created to be a thunderbolt of war, to plough the salt sea,

¿Qué más que el heno, a la mañana verde,
seco a la tarde? ¡Oh ciego desvarío!
¿Será que de este sueño me recuerde?

¿Será que pueda ver que me desvío
de la vida viviendo, y que está unida
la cauta muerte al simple vivir mío?

Como los ríos, que en veloz corrida
se llevan a la mar, tal soy llevado
al último suspiro de mi vida.

De la pasada edad ¿qué me ha quedado?
Oh ¿qué tengo yo, a dicha, en la que espero,
sin ninguna noticia de mi hado?

¡Oh, si acabase, viendo cómo muero,
de aprender a morir antes que llegue
aquel forzoso término postrero;

antes que aquesta mies inútil siegue
de la severa muerte dura mano,
y a la común materia se la entregue!

Pasáronse las flores del verano,
el otoño pasó con sus racimos,
pasó el invierno con sus nieves cano;

las hojas que en las altas selvas vimos
cayeron ¡y nosotros a porfía
en nuestro engaño inmóviles vivimos!

Temamos al Señor que nos envía
las espigas del año y la hartura,
y la temprana lluvia y la tardía.

No imitemos la tierra siempre dura
a las aguas del cielo y el arado,
ni la vid cuyo fruto no madura.

¿Piensas acaso tú que fue criado
el varón para rayo de la guerra,
para surcar el piélago salado,

to measure the earth's sphere and the circle in which the sun moves for ever? If anyone believes that, oh, how wrong he is!

This exalted and divine portion of us is called to greater deeds and aims at nobler objects.

So it is that pure and holy reason, which is given to man alone, wakes me with its crown of splendour and light,

and kindles a fresh flame in the cold, hard, and empty region of this breast, and the light which was dead burns again.

I wish, Fabio, to follow Him who calls me, and to move quietly among people, for I desire neither titles nor fame.

The proud tyrant of the Orient who packs his towers with a hundred cubits of the pure and shining white metal,

can hardly afford the means to sin; virtue is cheaper and woos everyone by her very presence.

Poor is he who runs in pursuit of gold and silver, extending his travels to every climate and every sea!

Enough for me is a corner among my household gods, a book and a friend and a brief sleep, untroubled by debts or cares.

This is all that Nature owes to the simple and prudent man, and with it a little ordinary, honest, and light food.

Do not imagine because I write to you like this that I practise virtue; for this was difficult even for Epictetus.

para medir el orbe de la tierra
y el cerco donde el sol siempre camina?
¡Oh, quien así lo entiende, cuánto yerra!

Esta nuestra porción, alta y divina,
a mayores acciones es llamada
y en más nobles objetos se termina.

Así aquella, que al hombre sólo es dada,
sacra razón y pura, me despierta,
de esplendor y de rayos coronada;

y en la fría región dura y desierta
de aqueste pecho, enciende nueva llama,
y la luz vuelve a arder que estaba muerta.

Quiero, Fabio, seguir a quien me llama,
y callado pasar entre la gente,
que no afecto los nombres ni la fama.

El soberbio tirano del Oriente
que maciza las torres de cien codos
del cándido metal puro y luciente,

apenas puede ya comprar los modos
del pecar; la virtud es más barata,
ella consigo misma ruega a todos.

¡Pobre de aquél que corre y se dilata
por cuantos son los climas y los mares,
perseguidor del oro y de la plata!

Un ángulo me basta entre mis lares,
un libro y un amigo, un sueño breve,
que no perturben deudas ni pesares.

Esto tan solamente es cuanto debe
Naturaleza al simple y al discreto,
y algún manjar común, honesto y leve.

No, porque así te escribo, hagas conceto
que pongo la virtud en ejercicio;
que aun esto fue difícil a Epiteto.

Let it suffice for the beginner to loathe vice, and to teach his soul modesty; the heavens will be kinder to him afterwards.

To despise pleasures is not a sign of solid virtue; for even the wicked man finds them tiresome in his heart.

But you will not be able to deny me how necessary this road is that leads to the high seat, the abode of peace and repose.

It takes more than a single moment for that intelligence which measures the duration of all things by their qualities to ripen a fruit;

we see it first as a beautiful and pure flower, then as a bitter and unpalatable substance, and later, when it is perfect, as sweet and ripe.

Even so human moderation should measure and apportion and divide the actions which are the necessary accompaniments of life.

God forbid that you should imitate those men who haunt our public squares, lean men and wicked pretenders to virtue:

these filthy tragic actors, who court the common applause, and whose hearts are accursed and dark tombs.

How quietly the breeze passes over the mountains, gently breathing! How talkative and noisy it is in the reeds!

How dumb is virtue in the man of moderation! How repetitive and noisy in the vain, ambitious and showy!

I should like to copy the common people in their clothes, and in my habits only the best, and never to boast of being ragged or ill dressed.

Basta, al que empieza, aborrecer al vicio,
y el ánimo enseñar a ser modesto;
después le será el cielo más propicio.

Despreciar el deleite no es supuesto
de sólida virtud; que aun el vicioso
en sí propio le nota de molesto.

Mas no podrás negarme cuán forzoso
este camino sea al alto asiento,
morada de la paz y del reposo.

No sazona la fruta en un momento
aquella inteligencia que mensura
la duración de todo a su talento;

flor la vimos primero hermosa y pura,
luego materia acerba y desabrida,
y perfecta después, dulce y madura.

Tal la humana prudencia es bien que mida
y dispense y comparta las acciones
que han de ser compañeras de la vida.

No quiera Dios que imite estos varones
que moran nuestras plazas, macilentos,
de la virtud infames histrïones;

esos inmundos trágicos, atentos
al aplauso común, cuyas entrañas
son infaustos y oscuros monumentos.

¡Cuán callada que pasa las montañas
el aura, respirando mansamente!
¡Qué gárrula y sonante por las cañas!

¡Qué muda la virtud por el prudente!
¡Qué redundante y lleno de ruido
por el vano, ambicioso y aparente!

Quiero imitar al pueblo en el vestido,
en las costumbres sólo a los mejores,
sin presumir de roto y mal ceñido.

Do not let our clothes be resplendent with gold and colour, nor yet let them be like those of the Doric singers.

Let me possess a moderate livelihood and follow an ordinary and middling style of living, that is not criticized by any who see it.

There have been people who have drunk as ambitiously from ill-baked common clay as from a prized *Murrhine* beaker,

and there have been some so noble and generous that they used transparent and shining glass as if it were vile clay.

Where temperance is lacking, have you ever seen anything perfect? Oh, death, come silently as is your custom when you come on an arrow,

not on a thundering engine, loaded with fire and noise: for my door is not made of reinforced metal.

So, Fabio, truth shows me her essence revealed, and my will is reconciled and agreeable to it.

Do not mock when you see how great is my trust, nor attribute the ardour of this courage to vain and pompous rhetoric.

Is virtue by chance less powerful than vice? Is virtue less strong? Do not argue that it is weak and timorous.

Greed in the hands of fate casts itself into the sea, anger throws itself against swords, and ambition laughs at death.

And will not the contrary qualities be at least as bold as when I see them aided by the most illustrious spirits?

No resplandezca el oro y los colores
en nuestro traje, ni tampoco sea
igual al de los dóricos cantores.

Una mediana vida yo posea,
un estilo común y moderado,
que no lo note nadie que lo vea.

En el plebeyo barro mal tostado
hubo ya quien bebió tan ambicioso
como en el vaso múrrino preciado;

y alguno tan ilustre y generoso
que usó, como si fuera vil gabeta,
del cristal transparente y luminoso.

Sin la templanza ¿viste tú perfeta
alguna cosa? ¡Oh muerte!, ven callada,
como sueles venir en la saeta,

no en la tonante máquina preñada
de fuego y de rumor; que no es mi puerta
de doblados metales fabricada.

Así, Fabio, me muestra descubierta
su esencia la verdad, y mi albedrío
con ella se compone y se concierta.

No te burles de ver cuánto confío,
ni al arte de decir, vana y pomposa,
el ardor atribuyas de este brío.

¿Es por ventura menos poderosa
que el vicio la virtud? ¿Es menos fuerte?
No la arguyas de flaca y temerosa.

La codicia en las manos de la suerte
se arroja al mar, la ira a las espadas,
y la ambición se ríe de la muerte,

Y ¿no serán siquiera tan osadas
las opuestas acciones, si las miro
de más ilustres genios ayudadas?

Now, sweet friend, I flee and retire from what I loved in my simplicity; I have broken the bonds. Come and you will see the high end to which I aspire, before time dies in our arms.

ALARMING image of death, cruel dream, no longer disturb my breast, by showing me the cutting of that tight knot that is the sole consolation of my unhappy fate!

Seek the strong outer wall, the jasper partitions, the golden roof of some tyrant, or make the rich miser wake in his narrow bed, trembling and sweating.

Let the former see the mob furiously break down his bolted doors, or the hidden sword of his bribed slave.

Let the latter see his riches laid bare with a false key or by a violent attack, and leave love assured in his triumphs.

OCTOBER has taken the vine-leaves with it, and swollen with the great rains, Ebro will suffer neither banks nor bridges, but rather covers the neighbouring fields.

Moncayo, as usual, now reveals her tall brow crowned with snow, and no sooner do we see the sun in the East than the opaque earth conceals it from us.

Ya, dulce amigo, huyo y me retiro
de cuanto simple amé; rompí los lazos;
vea y verás al alto fin que aspiro,
antes que el tiempo muera en nuestros brazos.

LUPERCIO LEONARDO DE ARGENSOLA

¡IMAGEN espantosa de la muerte,
sueño crüel, no turbes más mi pecho,
mostrándome cortado el nudo estrecho,
consuelo solo de mi adversa suerte!

Busca de algún tirano el muro fuerte,
de jaspe las paredes, de oro el techo;
o el rico avaro en el angosto lecho
haz que temblando con sudor despierte.

El uno vea el popular tumulto
romper con furia las herradas puertas,
o al sobornado siervo el hierro oculto.

El otro sus riquezas, descubiertas
con llave falsa o con violento insulto
y déjale al amor sus glorias ciertas.

LLEVÓ tras sí los pámpanos otubre,
y con las grandes lluvias insolente,
no sufre Ibero márgenes ni puente,
mas antes los vecinos campos cubre.

Moncayo, como suele, ya descubre
coronada de nieve la alta frente,
y el sol apenas vemos en Oriente
cuando la opaca tierra nos lo encubre.

Now the sea and the woods feel the north-wind's anger, and its roaring shuts people up in port and people in their cottages.

And Fabio, lying on Thais' threshold, wets it with shameful tears, his debt to the time that he has wasted.

ALTHOUGH you may be the descendant of illustrious Goths, and hang your coats-of-arms with their Roman eagles and the spoils of barbarian wars on the Egyptian pyramids;

although you may give Jove rich offerings, Asian incense and Mexican plumes, and pull down the banners of Africa and spread your name from Pole to Pole;

although laurel and gold may swathe your brows, and you may control Fortune's wheel, and impose laws on the world at your whim;

although you tread the forehead of the moon, and trample upon kings' crowns, if virtue is lacking in you, you have nothing.

Ballad of the Epiphany
On the Exposure of the Holy Sacrament

THEY are beating the drums in Bethlehem, shepherd: they are sounding the little trumpets, and the sound rejoices me.

Sienten el mar y selvas ya la saña
del aquilón, y encierra su bramido
gente en el puerto y gente en la cabaña.

Y Fabio, en el umbral de Tais tendido,
con vergonzosos lágrimas lo baña,
debiéndolas al tiempo que ha perdido.

LUPERCIO or BARTOLOMÉ LEONARDO DE ARGENSOLA

AUNQUE de godos ínclitos desciendas
y cuelgues de pirámides gitanas
tus armas con las águilas romanas
y despojos de bárbaras contiendas;

aunque a Jove le des ricas ofrendas,
olores de Asia, plumas mexicanas,
y arrastres las banderas africanas,
y tu nombre de polo a polo estiendas;

aunque ciñan laurel y oro tus sienes,
y gobiernes la rueda de Fortuna,
y pongas a tu gusto al mundo leyes;

aunque pises la frente de la Luna,
y huelles las coronas de los reyes,
si la virtud te falta, nada tienes.

JOSÉ DE VALDIVIELSO

Romance
Día de la Epifanía, descubierto el Santísimo Sacramento

ATABALES tocan
en Belén, pastor;
trompeticas suenan;
alégrame el son.

From where the dawn opens her balcony and, smiling, brings out the sun in her arms, come Balthasar, Gaspar, and Melchior, joyfully asking for the God of love. They all bring presents of great value, gold, incense, and myrrh, to the King, Man, and God. They are beating the drums, etc.

The virginal Mother King Solomon spoke of came out dressed in her best for the visit. She put on a bodice of stars and a lustrous mantle, scalloped with the sun. For her slippers, which were embroidered, the moon gave her silver spangles. They are beating the drums, etc.

She brought out the best of the earth and the sky in the *Lamb of God*, that hung at her neck. The pretty child cried at the harshness of the frost, but

De donde la aurora
abre su balcón
y saca risueña
en brazos el sol,
vienen Baltasar,
Gaspar y Melchor,
preguntando alegres
por el Dios de amor.
Todos traen presentes
de rico valor,
oro, incienso y mirra
al Rey, Hombre y Dios.
　　Atabales tocan
　　en Belén, pastor;
　　trompeticas suenan;
　　alégrame el son.

La virginal Madre
del rey Salomón
para la visita
de fiesta salió.
De estrellas se puso
un apretador,
y un manto de lustro
con puntas de sol.
Para los chapines,
que bordados son,
virillas de plata
la luna le dió.
　　Atabales tocan
　　en Belén, pastor;
　　trompeticas suenan;
　　alégrame el son.

De la tierra y cielo
sacó lo mejor,
en el *Agnus Dei*
que al cuello colgó.
Lloró el niño hermoso
del hielo al rigor,

when she gave him his three pennies (a reference to the Three Kings) she straightway made him quiet. Although they see him poor and give him presents, they know that he will turn into a better Judge (that is, one who will not take bribes). They are beating the drums, etc.

Christmas Carol
On the Exposure of the Holy Sacrament

IN the holy Church they are ringing for Matins, and the heavenly choirboys are singing the Lauds.

In the church where the Virgin came down between white swans to turn it into heaven; where the bread of life, on which Heaven lives, lies among the straw, which is his monstrance.

At midnight they ring for Matins, and the heavenly choirboys sing the Lauds.

They wear cassocks of flesh-coloured roses, with surplices of lilies. They find in the choir that the God they fear is a child, and see that he is laughing joyfully at his mother.

mas dándole el tres
luego le acalló.
Aunque le ven pobre
y le dan por Dios,
saben que Jüez
volverá mejor.
    Atabales tocan
    en Belén, pastor;
    trompeticas suenan;
    alégrame el son.

Letra de Navidad, descubierto el Santísimo Sacramento

    EN la santa Iglesia
    tocan a maitines,
    y los seises del cielo
    los laudes dicen.

En la Iglesia adonde
entre blancos cisnes
a volverla cielo
descendió la Virgen;
donde pan de vida
con que el cielo vive
está entre las pajas,
que son sus viriles.
    A la media noche
    tocan a maitines,
    y los seises del cielo
    los laudes dicen.

De encarnadas rosas
sotanas se visten,
siendo de azucenas
las sobrepellices.
Hallan en el coro
niño el Dios terrible;
ven que con su Madre
gozoso se ríe.

Meanwhile they are ringing for Matins in the tower, and the heavenly choirboys are singing the Lauds.

In their beauty they are seraphim reciting the *Ave Regina* to their Queen. The divine trebles are singing carols and the *Te Deum laudamus* with the flute-players.

And with the ringing of the bells they sound for Matins, and the heavenly choirboys sing the Lauds.

The midnight Mass is solemnly read, and with the shepherds they go on in the *Gloria*. The choir repeats *Homo factus est*, and they all kneel down in joy and humility.

And in the holy Church they ring for Matins, and the heavenly choirboys sing the Lauds.

En tanto en la torre
tocan a maitines,
y los seises del cielo
los laudes dicen.

Son en hermosura
unos serafines,
que el *Ave Regina*
a su Reina dicen.
Villancicos cantan
los divinos tiples,
y *Te Deum laudamus*
con los ministriles.
Y al son de las campanas
tocan a maitines,
y los seises del cielo
los laudes dicen.

La misa del gallo
solemne se dice,
y con los pastores
la *Gloria* prosiguen.
Homo factus est,
el coro repite,
y postránse todos
alegres y humildes.
Y en la santa Iglesia
tocan a maitines,
y los seises del cielo
los laudes dicen.

To Christ our Lord, Praying in the Garden

WHAT stratagem are you laying, oh my warrior? Or rather what ineffable sacrament? That the mere thought that the time for the struggle is drawing near should bathe you in blood!

Spill from your soul a different dew that shall soothe or fortify your weak (human) feelings. But you do not wish your sufferings to give you (supernatural) strength, which will increase your (human) courage.

For it is not fear that has opened your veins, and made them ooze through your red pores, for fear rather banishes the spirits.

It is that as my guilt comes before your eyes you burn with noble anger, and in this struggle I increase your pains.

After Suffering a Great Misfortune

IF I may offer You, Lord, an affection intent on the worship of its own idols, I present it to You with tears of love; and may You turn it into a perfect sacrifice.

For in this very deep and strong sleep, which is the working of Your mercy, what I perceive is no feigned image but a brief and mysterious presentation of death,

on which I look with a higher gaze, my inner workings being plunged in darkness. Let that light bathe it, Lord, that light

which breathes perfections into life, since You permit me without losing life to enjoy the experiences of the last breath.

BARTOLOMÉ LEONARDO DE ARGENSOLA

A Cristo nuestro señor, orando en el huerto

¿QUÉ estratagema hacéis, guerrero mío?
Mas antes ¿qué inefable sacramento?
¡Que os bañe en sangre sólo el pensamiento
de que se llega el plazo al desafío!

Derramad de vuestra alma otro rocío
que aduerma o arme el flaco sentimiento;
mas vos queréis que vuestro sufrimiento
no cobre esfuerzo por cobrar más brío.

Que no es temor el que os abrió las venas
y las distila por los poros rojos,
que antes él los espíritus retira,

sino como se os viene ante los ojos
mi culpa, ardéis de generosa ira,
y en esta lucha aumento vuestras penas.

Habiendo padecido un gran desmayo

SI un afecto, Señor, puedo ofrecerte
al culto de sus ídolos atento,
con lágrimas de amor te lo presento;
tú en víctima perfecta lo convierte.

Que en este sueño tan intenso y fuerte,
de tus misericordias instrumento,
no imagen imitada es lo que siento,
sino un breve misterio de la muerte,

en quien con ojos superiores miro
mi fábrica interior oscurecida.
Bañela aquella luz, Señor, aquella

que inspira perfecciones a la vida;
pues permites que goce, sin perdella,
experiencias del último suspiro.

FORTUNE presents gifts, not according to the book. When (you expect) whistles, it's flutes; when (you expect) flutes, it's whistles.

What various paths are followed in distributing honours and possessions. She gives awards to some, and penitents' cloaks to others. When (you expect) whistles, it's flutes; when (you expect) flutes, it's whistles.

Sometimes she robs the chief goatherd of his cottage and goat-pen; and to whomever she fancies the lamest goat has borne two kids. When (you expect) whistles, it's flutes; when (you expect) flutes, it's whistles.

Because in a village a poor lad has stolen one egg, he swings in the sun; and another gets away with a hundred thousand crimes. When (you expect) whistles, it's flutes; when (you expect) flutes, it's whistles.

OH lucent honour of the liquid element, sweet brook of running silver, whose water stretches through the grass with an exquisite sound, at a slow pace!

LUIS DE GÓNGORA

DA bienes Fortuna
que no están escritos:
cuando pitos, flautas,
cuando flautas, pitos.

¡Cuán diversas sendas
se suelen seguir
en el repartir
honras y haciendas!
A unas da encomiendas
a otros sambenitos.
Cuando pitos, flautas,
cuando flautas, pitos.

A veces despoja
de choza y apero
al mayor cabrero;
y a quien se le antoja
la cabra más coja
parió dos cabritos.
Cuando pitos, flautas,
cuando flautas, pitos.

Porque en una aldea
un pobre mancebo
hurtó solo un huevo,
al sol bambolea,
y otro se pasea
con cien mil delitos.
Cuando pitos, flautas,
cuando flautas, pitos.

¡OH claro honor del líquido elemento,
dulce arroyuelo de corriente plata
cuya agua entre la hierba se dilata
con regalado son, con paso lento!

Since Love portrays in your quiet and smooth stream the snow and scarlet of her face, for whom I feel myself freeze and burn whilst she gazes at herself in you,

go as you do; do not slacken the wavy rein on the crystal bit with which you guide your swift current;

for it is not right for the great lord of the watery trident to catch so much beauty in confusion in his deep breast.

To Córdoba

OH lofty wall, oh towers crowned with honour, majesty, and gallantry! Oh great river, great king of Andalusia, with your noble, if not golden sands!

Oh fertile plain, oh soaring hills, favoured by the sky and gilded by the day! Oh my fatherland for ever glorious, both for the pen and the sword!

If among those ruins and relics which Genil enriches and Dauro waters your memory were not a nourishment to me, never let my absent eyes deserve to see your wall, your towers and your river, your plain and hills, oh fatherland, oh flower of Spain!

WHILST, in competition with your hair, the sun, like burnished gold, gleams in vain, whilst your white forehead despises the lovely lily in the midst of the plain,

whilst more eyes follow each lip, to catch it, than follow the early pink, and whilst your delicate neck triumphs with gentle disdain over the lucent crystal,

Pues la por quien helar y arder me siento,
mientras en ti se mira, Amor retrata
de su rostro la nieve y la escarlata
en tu tranquilo y blando movimiento,

véte como te vas; no dejes floja
la undosa rienda al cristalino freno
con que gobiernas tu veloz corriente;

que no es bien que confusamente acoja
tanta belleza en su profondo seno
el gran señor del húmido tridente.

A Córdoba

¡Oh excelso muro, oh torres coronadas
de honor, de majestad, de gallardía!
¡Oh gran río, gran rey de Andalucía,
de arenas nobles, ya que no doradas!

¡Oh fértil llano, oh sierras levantadas,
que privilegia el cielo y dora el día!
¡Oh siempre gloriosa patria mía,
tanto por plumas cuanto por espadas!

¡Si entre aquellas ruinas y despojos
que enriquece Genil y Dauro baña
tu memoria no fue alimento mío,

nunca merezcan mis ausentes ojos
ver tu muro, tus torres y tu río,
tu llano y sierra, oh patria, oh flor de España!

Mientras por competir con tu cabello,
oro bruñido, el Sol relumbra en vano,
mientras con menosprecio en medio el llano
mira tu blanca frente el lilio bello;

mientras a cada labio, por cogello,
siguen más ojos que al clavel temprano,
y mientras triunfa con desdén lozano
del luciente cristal tu gentil cuello;

enjoy neck, hair, lip, and forehead, before what was in your golden age gold, lily, pink, and lucent crystal not only turns to silver or plucked violet, but you and it together become earth, smoke, dust, shadow, nothing.

AS the sun comes up over the mountains, my nymph, despoiling the green plain of flowers, made as many grow with her white foot as she plucked with her lovely hand.

The wind, as it ran in sprightly error through the fine gold (of her hair), rippled it as the green leaves of the luxuriant poplar stir in the red dawn of day.

But when she bound her fair brows with the various spoils in her skirt, and laid a boundary between the gold and the snow

I would swear that her garland shone more brightly, though it was of flowers, than the one* which decorates the heavens with its nine lights.

Angelica and Medoro

IN a pastoral shelter among oaks, which the war had passed by as hidden or spared as poor,

where peace wears sheepskin and, among the shepherds, leads sheep from the hill to the plain, goats from the plain to the hill,

ill-wounded and well-cured, a happy youth takes shelter, one whom Love has crowned with favours without piercing him with his arrow.

* The constellation known as Ariadne's Crown.

goza cuello, cabello, labio y frente,
antes que lo que fue en tu edad dorada
oro, lilio, clavel, cristal luciente,

no sólo en plata o vïola troncada
se vuelva, mas tú y ello juntamente
en tierra, en humo, en polvo, en sombra, en nada.

AL tramontar del sol, la ninfa mía
de flores despojando el verde llano,
cuantas troncaba la hermosa mano
tantas el blanco pie crecer hacía.

Ondeábale el viento que corría
el oro fino con error galano,
cual verde hoja de álamo lozano
se mueve al rojo despuntar de día.

Mas luego que ciñó sus sienes bellas
de los varios despojos de su falda,
término puesto al oro y la nieve,

juraré que lució más su guirnalda
con ser de flores, la otra ser de estrellas
que la que ilustra el cielo en luces nueve.

Angélica y Medoro

EN un pastoral albergue,
que la guerra entre unos robles
lo dejó por escondido
o le perdonó por pobre,

do la paz viste pellico
y conduce entre pastores
ovejas del monte al llano
y cabras del llano al monte,

mal herido y bien curado,
se alberga un dichoso joven,
que sin clavarle Amor flecha
le coronó de favores.

With little blood in his veins, and deep night in his eyes, that life and death of men found him in the field.

She gets down from her palfrey, not because she knows the Moor, but because she saw the grass repaying so much blood with flowers.

She wipes his face, and her hand feels Love, who is hidden behind the roses, whose colours death is already stealing.

He hid behind the roses so that his shafts might work the diamond of Cathay (Angelica) with that noble blood.

And now he charms her eyes and now there enters in, without seeing where, pity, ill-born between sweet scorpion-stings.

Now the flint is wounded, now the first blow strikes sparks of water. Oh pity, daughter of treacherous parents!

She applies herbs to his wounds, and if they do not heal them immediately, at least, in virtue of those hands, they make up to the pain.

Love offers her his bandage, but she tears her veils to bind his wounds: may the sun's rays spare her.

She was tying the last knots, when the heavens sent to her aid a peasant on a mare, who was riding through the wood.

Las venas con poca sangre,
los ojos con mucha noche
le halló en el campo aquella
vida y muerte de los hombres.

Del palafrén se derriba,
no porque al moro conoce,
sino por ver que la hierba
tanta sangre paga en flores.

Límpiale el rostro, y la mano
siente al Amor que se esconde
tras las rosas, que la muerte
va violando sus colores.

Escondióse tras las rosas
porque labren sus arpones
el diamente de Catay
con aquella sangre noble.

Ya le regala los ojos,
ya le entra, sin ver por dónde,
una piedad mal nacida
entre dulces escorpiones.

Ya es herido el pedernal,
ya despide el primer golpe
centellas de agua. ¡Oh, piedad,
hija de padres traidores!

Hierbas aplica a sus llagas,
que si no sanan entonces,
en virtud de tales manos
lisonjean los dolores.

Amor le ofrece su venda,
mas ella sus velos rompe
para ligar sus heridas:
los rayos del Sol perdonen.

Los últimos nudos daba
cuando el cielo la socorre
de un villano en una yegua
que iba penetrando el bosque.

The fair maid's sad and piteous cries, which move the stout trees and which the deaf stones hear, bring him to a stop,

and simple kindness, which is more at home in the woodlands than at court, politely accedes to her request for help.

Humbly the peasant gets down, and lays across his mare a body with little blood, but with two hearts.

He guides them to his hut as the sun dips beneath the horizon, and the smoke of his hut serves them for direction.

They come to it soon, and there a farmer's wife receives a living sickness with two souls and a blinded woman with two bright eyes.

Soft straw for feathers makes them their bed, which will speedily be the bridal bed where the young man receives his happiness.

Then those hands, whose fingers were the gods of this life, restore to Medoro new health and redoubled strength,

and give him, when least he expects it, her beauty and a kingdom for dowry, the second desire of Mars, the first blessing of Adonis.*

A wanton swarm of little Cupids forms a crown around the hut, as bees do around the hollow trunk of a cork-tree.

* That is the goddess Venus.

Enfrénanle de la bella
las tristes piadosas voces,
que los firmes troncos mueven
y las sordas piedras oyen;

y la que mejor se halla
en las selvas que en la corte
simple bondad al pío ruego
cortesmente corresponde.

Humilde se apea el villano
y sobre la yegua pone
un cuerpo con poco sangre,
pero con dos corazones;

a su cabaña los guía,
que el Sol deja su horizonte
y el humo de su cabaña
les va sirviendo de norte.

Llegaron temprano a ella,
do una labradora acoge
un mal vivo con dos almas
y una ciega con dos soles.

Blando heno en vez de pluma
para lecho les compone,
que será tálamo luego
do el garzón sus dichas logre.

Las manos, pues, cuyos dedos
desta vida fueron dioses,
restituyen a Medoro
salud nueva, fuerzas dobles,

y le entregan, cuando menos,
su beldad y un reino en dote,
segunda invidia de Marte,
primera dicha de Adonis.

Corona un lascivo enjambre
de Cupidillos menores
la choza, bien como abejas
hueco tronco de alcornoque.

How many knots does vile envy tie in her asp, as she counts the plaintive cooing of the doves!

How soundly Love drives her away, making a whip of his bow, so that this event shall not be dishonoured or the place be contaminated!

The African is all gallantry, his clothes give out sweet odours, he hangs up his crescent bow and takes off his curved scimitar.

Enamoured turtle-doves are his hoarse drums, and the birds of Venus his well-followed banners.

She goes with naked breast, her hair flying in disorder; if she pins it up it is with pinks, if she ties it, it is with jasmine.

Her feet are shod in golden thongs for their snow to be enjoyed, and so that beauty shall not escape from the world.

Everything serves the lovers: swift feathers fan them, little airs flatter but do not gossip.

The fields give them carpets, the trees pavilions, the peaceful fountain gives them sleep, and the nightingales music.

The tree-trunks give them bark in which their names will remain better than on marble slabs or on sheets of bronze.

¡Qué de nudos le está dando
a un áspid la invidia torpe,
contando de las palomas
los arrullos gemidores!

¡Qué bien la destierra Amor,
haciendo la cuerda azote,
por que el caso no se infame
y el lugar no se inficione!

Todo es gala el Africano,
su vestido espira olores,
el lunado arco suspende,
y el corvo alfanje depone.

Tórtolas enamoradas
son sus roncos atambores,
y los volantes de Venus
sus bien seguidos pendones.

Desnuda el pecho anda ella,
vuela el cabello sin orden;
si le abrocha, es con claveles,
con jazmines si le coge.

El pie calza en lazos de oro,
porque la nieve se goce,
y no se vaya por pies
la hermosura del orbe.

Todo sirve a los amantes:
plumas les baten, veloces,
airecillos lisonjeros,
si no son murmuradores.

Los campos les dan alfombras,
los árboles pabellones,
la apacible fuente sueño,
música los ruiseñores.

Los troncos les dan cortezas
en que se guarden sus nombres,
mejor que en tablas de mármol
o que en láminas de bronce.

There is no green ash without its sentence, no white poplar without its inscription; if one valley resounds with 'Angelica', the other replies 'Angelica'.

Caves where silence hardly permits shadows to dwell, they profane with their embraces, in spite of their horrors.

So, cottage and bed, courteous peasants, breezes, fields, fountains, plains, caves, tree-trunks, birds, flowers, ashes, poplars, hills, and valleys, all witnesses of this love, may heaven save you if it can from the Count's* madness.

IN the pinewoods of Júcar I saw some highland girls dancing, to the sound of the water on the stones and the sound of the wind in the branches. This is no white band of nymphs such as lodge in the water, or such as the woods worship, followers of Diana: they were country girls from Cuenca, an honour to that hill, whose foot two rivers kiss in order to kiss the soles of their feet. They were weaving happy dances, giving one another their white hands in friendship, perhaps in fear that the changes in the dance might alter it (their friendship). How well the highland-girls dance! How well they dance!

* The Count is the Orlando Furioso of Ariosto's poem, and this *romance* is a treatment of an incident from Canto XIX, in which the love of Angelica for the Saracen Medoro provokes the madness for which the poem's hero is famous.

No hay verde fresno sin letra,
ni blanco chopo sin mote;
si un valle «Angélica» suena
otro «Angélica» responde.

Cuevas do el silencio apenas
deja que sombras las moren
profanan con sus abrazos
a pesar de sus horrores.

Choza, pues, tálamo y lecho,
cortesanos labradores,
aires, campos, fuentes, vegas,
cuevas, troncos, aves, flores,

fresnos, chopos, montes, valles,
contestes de estos amores,
el cielo os guarde, si puede,
de las locuras del Conde.

EN los pinares de Júcar
vi bailar unas serranas,
al son del agua en las piedras
y al son del viento en las ramas.
No es blanco coro de ninfas
de las que aposenta el agua
o las que venera el bosque,
seguidoras de Diana:
serranas eran de Cuenca,
honor de aquella montaña,
cuyo pie besan dos ríos
por besar de ellas las plantas.
Alegres corros tejían,
dándose las manos blancas
de amistad, quizá temiendo
no la truequen las mudanzas.
¡Qué bien bailan las serranas!
¡Qué bien bailan!

Their hair in crisp curls gives light to the sun, and gold to Arabia, some have it bound with flowers, others in silver cords. They wear country cloth, of the colour of the sky if not of hope, (cloth) that eclipses the sapphire and the emerald. Their feet, when the spy-hole of their skirt allows, wear thongs and reveal pieces of snow and mother-of-pearl. Those girls who in their movements so modestly lift the crystal of the column on its small base – How well they dance, the highland-girls! How well they dance!

One, bruising black stones (castanets) between her white fingers, an ivory instrument that the Muses would envy, silenced the birds and checked the flow of the water; the leaves did not stir, so as not to interrupt what she sings:

'The highland girls of Cuenca went to the pinewood, some for pine-nuts, others to dance.

'The pretty highland-girls, dancing and dividing one pine-nut with another pine-nut, if not with pearls (their teeth), rejoice in exchanging the arrows of Cupid, some for pine-nuts, others to dance.

El cabello en crespos nudos
luz da al Sol, oro a la Arabia,
cuál de flores impedido,
cuál de cordones de plata.
Del color visten del cielo,
si no son de la esperanza,
palmillas que menosprecian
al zafiro y la esmeralda.
El pie (cuando lo permite
la brújula de la falda)
lazos calza, y mirar deja
pedazos de nieve y nácar.
Ellas, cuyo movimiento
honestamente levanta
el cristal de la columna
sobre la pequeña base,
¡*Qué bien bailan las serranas*!
¡*Qué bien bailan*!

Una entre los blancos dedos
hiriendo negras pizarras,
instrumento de marfil
que las musas invidiaran,
las aves enmudeció,
y enfrenó el curso del agua;
no se movieron las hojas,
por no impedir lo que canta:

«Serranas de Cuenca
iban al pinar,
unas por piñones,
otras por bailar.

Bailando y partiendo
las serranas bellas,
un piñon con otro,
si ya no es con perlas,
de Amor las saetas
huelgan de trocar,
unas por piñones,
otras por bailar.

'Between branch and branch, when the blind god begs the sun for eyes to see them better, you will see them treading on the eyes of the sun,* some for pine-nuts, others to dance.'

THE flowers of the rosemary, Mistress Isabel, are blue flowers today, and tomorrow will be honey.

You are jealous, Mistress, jealous of that happy man, for you seek him, blind because he does not see you, ungrateful because he angers you, and presumptuous because he does not excuse himself today for what he did yesterday. Let hopes wipe away the tears you weep for him; for jealousies between those who have loved one another dearly are blue flowers today, and tomorrow will be honey.

You that are your own sunrise whom, when you begin to dawn at your pleasure, your pleasure eclipses, let your eyes clear and drop no more pearls, for what becomes the dawn ill becomes the sun. Disperse like mists all that

* The patches of sunlight beneath the trees.

Entre rama y rama
cuando el ciego dios
pide al Sol los ojos
por verlas mejor,
los ojos del Sol
las veréis pisar,
unas por piñones,
otras por bailar.»

LAS flores del romero,
niña Isabel,
hoy son flores azules,
mañana serán miel.

Celosa estás, la niña,
celosa estás de aquel
dichoso, pues le buscas,
ciego, pues no te ve,
ingrato, pues te enoja
y confiado, pues
no se disculpa hoy
de lo que hizo ayer.
Enjuguen esperanzas
lo que lloras por él;
que celos entre aquellos
que se han querido bien
hoy son flores azules,
mañana serán miel.

Aurora de ti misma,
que cuando a amanecer
a tu placer empiezas,
te eclipsa tu placer,
serénense tus ojos,
y más perlas no des,
porque al Sol le está mal
lo que a la aurora bien.
Desata como nieblas
todo lo que no ves;

you cannot see; for lovers' suspicions with quarrels to follow are blue flowers today, and tomorrow will be honey.

Of the Chapel of Our Lady of the Sacristy, in the holy Church of Toledo, the Burial-place of Cardinal Sandoval

THIS fabric which you gaze on, this prime glory of sculpture, oh traveller, of porphyry too hard for the diamond and metals cut smooth with the file, seals up earth (the corpse) which let the earth never oppress; if you do not know whose (earth or bones), stay your ignorant foot and study this inscription, which delicately makes bronze speak and calls marble to life.

Liberal piety links urns, today beautiful, with majesty, with propriety, to the heroic and now sacred ashes of those who, leaving five blue stars on a field of gold,* with better feet tread golden stars on a blue field.

KEEP your flocks, shepherd girl. Shepherd girl, don't keep faith. For the man who made you a shepherd did not exempt you from being a woman.

The purity of the ermine that is so celebrated, put it on with your sheepskin and take it off with it too.

Leave firmness to stones, taking note that sometimes, despite their hardness, they obey the chisel.

* The coat of arms of the Sandoval family.

que sospechas de amantes
y querellas después
hoy son flores azules,
mañana serán miel.

De la capilla de Nuestra Señora del Sagrario, de la santa Iglesia de Toledo, entierro del Cardenal Sandoval

ESTA que admiras fábrica, esta prima
pompa de la escultura, oh caminante,
en pórfidos rebeldes al diamante,
en metales mordidos de la lima,

tierra sella que tierra nunca oprima;
si ignoras cúya, el pie enfrena ignorante,
y esta inscripción consulta, que elegante
informa bronces, mármoles anima.

Generosa piedad urnas hoy bellas
con majestad vincula, con decoro,
a las heróicas ya cenizas santas

de los que, a un campo de oro cinco estrellas
dejando azules, con mejores plantas
en campo azul estrellas pisan de oro.

GUARDA corderos, zagala,
zagala, no guardes fe;
que quien te hizo pastora
no te excusó de mujer.

La pureza del armiño,
que tan celebrada es,
vístela con el pellico
y desnúdala con él.

Deja a las piedras lo firme,
advirtiendo que tal vez,
a pesar de su dureza,
obedecen al cincel.

Let the ilex resist the wind rather with its peasant foot: for with its courtier-like leaves it believes in every breeze.

That lovely vine that you see clinging to the elm discreetly divides its leaves with the neighbouring laurel.

The moaning turtle-dove, laying its chaste scorn aside, made the boughs of that cypress a second marriage-bed.

The pink does not keep its leaves for one bee alone; others drink the pearly dew that edges its rosiness.

The crystal of that stream, faithful as the wave, refuses the absent one his image until it sees him again.

Inconstancy, in the end, gives feathers to Venus's son, with which he covers his wings and flights his arrows as well.

So do not let interest triumph over your free will, nor love either, of a kind more single-minded than fickle.

Shake off the yoke of riches; let woollen fillets, not gold chains tie back your loose hair.

Bad luck to you if you look constantly at the sun, and may anyone so like an eagle in this be twice and three times unlucky.

Resiste al viento la encina,
más con el villano pie;
que con las hojas corteses
a cualquier céfiro cree.

Aquella hermosa vid
que abrazada al olmo ves
parte pámpanos, discreta,
con el vecino laurel.

Tortolilla gemidora,
depuesto el casto desdén,
tálamo hizo segundo
los ramos de aquel ciprés.

No para una abeja sola
sus hojas guarda el clavel,
beben otras el aljófar
que borda su rosicler.

El cristal de aquel arroyo,
undosamente fïel,
niega al ausente su imagen
hasta que le vuelve a ver.

la inconstancia al fin da plumas
al hijo de Venus, que
poblando dellas sus alas,
viste sus flechas también.

No, pues, tu libre albedrío
lo tiranice interés,
ni amor que de singular
tenga más que de infïel.

Sacude preciosos yugos,
coyundas de oro no den,
sino cordones de lana,
al suelto cabello ley.

Mal hayas tú si constante
mirares al sol, y quien
tan águila fuere en esto,
dos veces mal haya y tres.

Bad luck to you if you imitate in their wanton simplicity the birds of that goddess who was once foam.

Once after lengthily wooing an ungrateful young man, a nymph of these woods turned into a speaking shadow (the nymph Echo).

So if you intend, shepherd girl, the whole valley to know of your cruel beauty, then refuse my suit.

Of the Deceptive Brevity of Life

THE swift arrow sought less eagerly its assigned target, into which it sharply bit, the festal Roman chariot over the dumb sand did not crown the winning-post more silently than precipitately, silently, our age runs to its end. Even for one who doubts it, beast that he is and naked of reason, each sun as it is repeated is (as fatal as) a comet.

Does Carthage confess it and you not know it? You are running into danger, Licio, if you persist in following shadows and embracing deceptions.

The hours will hardly forgive you, those hours that are wearing away the days, those days that are gnawing away the years.

Mal hayas tú si imitares,
en lasciva candidez,
las aves de la deidad
que primero espuma fue.

Solicitando prolija
la ingratitud de un doncel,
ninfa de las selvas ya
vocal sombra vino a ser.

Si quieres, pues, zagaleja,
de tu hermosura cruel
dar entera voz al valle,
desprecia mi parecer.

De la brevedad engañosa de la vida

MENOS solicitó veloz saeta
destinada señal, que mordió aguda;
agonal carro por la arena muda
no coronó con más silencio meta,

que presurosa corre, que secreta
a su fin nuestra edad. A quien lo duda,
fiera que sea de razón desnuda,
cada sol repetido es un cometa.

¿Confiésalo Cartago, y tú lo ignoras?
Peligro corres, Licio, si porfías
en seguir sombras y abrazar engaños.

Mal te perdonarán a ti las horas;
las horas que limando están los días,
los días que royendo están los años.

BELARDO was gardener of the gardens in Valencia, for hardships oblige a man to do what he would not think possible. When wild February is over he sows flowers for May, for he wants his hopes to bear fruit in the Spring. Clover for the girls he puts on one side of the garden, so that the fruit of love may learn from its three leaves. Yellow sweet-basil, some green and some dry, he transplants for the married ladies who are now passing thirty, and for the widows heplants lilies and verbena in plenty, because their black skirts conceal green souls. Balm-gentle for young girls of the kind who are beginning to spell out lies, for there is not much truth in them. Celery for the anaemic and almonds for the pregnant, thistles for the prudish, and nettles for old women. Lettuces for the mettlesome who burn when it rains, common cress for the cold, and wormwood for the ugly. Out of the silken clothes that once he wore at court he made, for the birds, a fig-

LOPE DE VEGA CARPIO

HORTELANO era Belardo
de las huertas en Valencia,
que los trabajos obligan
a lo que el hombre no piensa.
Pasado el febrero loco,
flores para mayo siembra,
que quiere que su esperanza
dé fruto a la primavera.
El trébol para las niñas
pone al lado de la huerta,
por que la fruta de amor
de las tres hojas aprenda.
Albahacas amarillas,
a partes verdes y secas,
trasplanta para casadas
que pasan ya de los treinta
y para las viudas pone
muchos lirios y verbena,
porque lo verde del alma
encubre la saya negra.
Toronjil para muchachas
de aquellas que ya comienzan
a deletrear mentiras,
que hay poca verdad en ellas.
El apio a las opiladas
y a las preñadas almendras,
para melindrosas cardos
y ortigas para las viejas.
Lechugas para briosas
que cuando llueve queman,
mastuerzo para las frías
y ajenjos para las feas.
De los vestidos que un tiempo
trujo en la Corte, de seda,
ha hecho para las aves
un espantajo de higuera.
Las lechuguillazas grandes,
almidonadas y tiesas

tree scarecrow. Great wide ruffs, starched and stiff, and the hat pulled down, that adorns neck and head, and over a silk doublet the best garnished leather, not to forget the breeches, both Spanish style and German. As he was out watering one day, he saw it in the middle of the fig-tree and, laughing at the sight of it, addressed it thus: 'Oh rich spoils of my early years and living trophies of our hopes! How fine you look, inside and out, in addition to having put an end to my tragedy! Finery and plumes of my soldiering days, once a grand show and now just sad. One Easter day I wore you in my village, as costly finery and the last thing in fashion. From her balcony a young lady saw me, with a white breast and black brows. She let herself be taken in, and I married her, for it is right to pay one's honest debts. She knew of my crime, that dark-skinned girl who reigned in Troy when she was my

y el sombrero boleado
que adorna cuello y cabeza,
y sobre un jubón de raso
la más guarnecida cuera,
sin olvidarse las calzas
españolas y tudescas.
Andando regando un día,
vióle en medio de la higuera
y riéndose de velle,
le dice desta manera:
«¡Oh ricos despojos
de mi edad primera
trofeos vivos
de esperanzas nuestras!
¡Qué bien parecéis
de dentro y de fuera,
sobre que habéis dado
fin a mi tragedia!
¡Galas y penachos
de mi soldadesca,
un tiempo colores
y agora tristeza!
Un día de Pascua
os llevé a mi aldea
por galas costosas,
invenciones nuevas.
Desde su balcón
me vio una doncella
con el pecho blanco
y la ceja negra.
Dejóse burlar,
caséme con ella,
que es bien que se paguen
tan honrosas deudas.
Supo mi delito
aquella morena
que reinaba en Troya
cuando fue mi reina.
Hizo de mis cosas

queen. She made a great bonfire of my possessions, and took her vengeance on pen and paper.'

May-song

In the early mornings of the month of May the nightingales sing, and the field re-echoes.

In the early mornings, when they are fresh, the nightingales cover the poplar trees.

The fountains laugh as they toss pearls at the little flowers that are closest to them.

The plants put on various silks, for to come out in colours costs them little.

Different-coloured carpets rejoice the fields, the nightingales sing and the field re-echoes.

una grande hoguera,
tomando venganzas
en plumas y letras.»

Maya

EN las mañanicas
del mes de mayo
cantan los ruiseñores,
retumba el campo.

En las mañanicas,
como son frescas,
cubren ruiseñores
las alamedas.

Ríense las fuentes
tirando perlas
a las florecillas
que están más cerca.

Vístense las plantas
de varias sedas,
que sacar colores
poco les cuesta.

Los campos alegran
tapetes varios,
cantan los ruiseñores,
retumba el campo.

Clover

CLOVER – Jesus, how good it smells! Clover – oh Jesus, what a scent! The married woman's clover when she loves her husband; and the young lady's who is kept indoors and easily deceived, follows her first love. Clover – Jesus, how good it smells! Clover – oh Jesus, what a scent!

OH Fortune, pick me that olive.

Flattering olive, green and tender outside, but wooden within: hard and importunate fruit.

Oh Fortune, pick me that olive.

Fruit so slow in ripening that it is bitter without condiments, and even if you pick a load you must only eat one. Oh Fortune, pick me that olive.

'WATCHMAN who watches on the castle, watch it well and look out for yourself, for when I was watching there I came to grief.'

'Look at the country full of so many armed foes.'

Trébole

TRÉBOLE, ¡ay Jesús, cómo huele!
Trébole, ¡ay Jesús, qué olor!
Trébole de la casada
que a su esposo quiere bien;
de la doncella también
entre paredes guardada,
que fácilmente engañada
sigue su primer amor.
Trébole, ¡ay Jesús, cómo huele!
Trébole, ¡ay Jesús, qué olor!

¡AY fortuna:
cógeme esta eceituna!

Aceituna lisonjera,
verde y tierna por defuera
y por de dentro madera:
fruta dura y importuna.
¡Ay fortuna:
cógeme esta aceituna!

Fruta en madurar tan larga
que sin aderezo amarga
y aunque se coja una carga
se ha de comer sólo una.
¡Ay fortuna:
cógeme esta aceituna!

«VELADOR que el castillo velas,
vélale bien y mira por ti,
que velando en él me perdí.»

«Mira las campañas llenas
de tanto enemigo armado.»

'I am wakeful now, love, from watching on the battlements. Now that you are sounding the bells take a warning and look at me, who when watching there came to grief.'

IT was by night they killed the knight, the pride of Medina, the flower of Olmedo.

Shadows warned the knight not to go out, and advised him not to depart, the pride of Medina, the flower of Olmedo.

I WAS fair of skin when I went to the reaping; the sun caught me and now I am dark.

I used to be fair, before I came out to reap. But the sun would not let the fire I wielded stay fair. At dawn my youth was a bright lily; the sun caught me and now I am dark.

«Ya estoy, amor, desvelado
de velar en las almenas.
Ya que las campanas suenas
toma ejemplo y mira en mí
que velando en él me pedí.»

QUE de noche le mataron
al caballero,
la gala de Medina,
la flor de Olmedo.

Sombras le avisaron
que no saliese
y le aconsejaron
que no se fuese
el caballero,
la gala de Medina,
la flor de Olmedo.

BLANCA me era yo
cuando entré en la siega;
dióme el sol y ya soy morena.

Blanca solía yo ser
antes que a segar viniese,
mas no quiso el sol que fuese
blanco el fuego en mi poder.
Mi edad al amanecer
era lustrosa azucena;
dióme el sol y ya soy morena.

THE bull caught me at your door, fair young bride. You did not say: 'God preserve you!'

The young bull you wedded caught me at your door; the whole village laughed at the fall he gave me, and you, grave and mocking, fair young bride, did not say: 'God preserve you!'

THE girl throws me little oranges in Valencia at Christmas, but I swear that if I throw them at her they will be sure to turn back into blossom.

I went out to a masquerade and stopped at her window; her morning dawned and I saw the sun in her eyes. She frantically flung little oranges from there; as she knows nothing of love she thinks that everything is a joke. But I swear that if I throw them at her they will be sure to turn back into blossom.

The girl throws me little oranges in Valencia at Christmas, but I swear that if I throw them at her they will be sure to turn back into blossom.

BLOSSOMING early mornings of cold winter, remember my child who is sleeping in the frost.

Fortunate mornings of cold December, although the sky scatters flowers

COGIÓME a tu puerta el toro,
linda casada:
no dijiste: «Dios te valga.»

El novillo de tu boda
a tu puerta me cogió;
de la vuelta que me dio
se rio la aldea toda,
y tú, grave y burladora,
linda casada,
no dijiste: «Dios te valga.»

NARANJITAS me tira la niña
en Valencia por Navidad,
pues a fe que si se las tiro
que se le han de volver azahar.

A una máscara salí
y paréme a su ventana;
amaneció su mañana
y el sol en sus ojos vi.
Naranjitas desde allí
me tiró para furor;
como no sabe de amor
piensa que todo es burlar,
pues a fe que si se las tiro
que se le han de volver azahar.

Naranjitas me tira la niña
en Valencia por Navidad,
Pues a fe que si se las tiro
que se le han de volver azahar.

MAÑANICAS floridas
del frío invierno,
recordad a mi niño
que duerme al hielo.
Mañanas dichosas
del frío diciembre,

and roses on you, you being strict and God being tender, remember my child, who is sleeping in the frost.

THE carters call me sweet young Mary; sweet young Mary they call me . . . and I go off with them.

To the Virgin

WHERE are you going, shepherd-girl, alone in the forest? But who carries the sun has no fear of night. Where are you going, Mary, bride of God, glorious mother of your own Creator? What will you do if day goes down in the west, and perhaps on the mountain night catches you? But who carries the sun has no fear of night. The sight of the stars is tiresome to me, but your eyes shine more than they. Now the dark night appears with them; the light hides away your beauty; but who carries the sun has no fear of night.

aunque el cielo os siembre
de flores y rosas,
pues sois rigurosas
y Dios es tierno,
recordad a mi niño
que duerme al hielo.

MARIQUITA me llaman
los carreteros;
Mariquita me llaman . . .
voyme con ellos.

A la Virgen

¿DÓNDE vais, zagala,
sola en el monte?
Mas quien lleva el sol
no teme la noche.
¿Dónde vais, María,
divina esposa,
madre gloriosa
de quien os cría?
¿Qué haréis si el día
se va al Ocaso
y en el monte acaso
la noche os coge?
Mas quien lleva el sol
no teme la noche.
El ver las estrellas
me causa enojos,
pero vuestros ojos
más lucen que ellas.
Ya sale con ellas
la noche oscura;
a vuestra hermosura
la luz se esconde;
mas quien lleva el sol
no teme la noche.

The Virgin's Carol

SINCE you are walking under the palms, holy angels, hold back your branches, for my child is asleep.

Oh palms of Bethlehem, which the furious winds toss violently, and which make so much noise, make no noise for him, and sway more gently, hold back your branches, for my child is asleep.

The divine child, who is tired from weeping for his repose on earth, wants to rest a little from his tender tears. Hold back your branches for my child is asleep.

Harsh frosts are all around him, you can see that I have nothing with which to protect him. Divine angels who are flying past, hold back your branches for my child is asleep.

TO the sound of the brooks, the birds sing from flower to flower, for there is no greater glory than love, no greater pain than jealousy.

Cantorcillo de la Virgen

PUES andáis en las palmas,
ángeles santos,
que se duerme mi niño,
tened los ramos.

Palmas de Belén
que mueven airados
los furiosos vientos
que suenan tanto,
no le hagáis ruido,
corred más paso,
que se duerme mi niño,
tened los ramos.

El niño divino,
que está cansado
de llorar en la tierra
por su descanso,
sosegar quiere un poco
del tierno llanto.
Que se duerme mi niño,
tened los ramos.

Rigurosos hielos
le están cercando;
ya veis que no tengo
con que guardarlo.
Ángeles divinos
que vais volando,
que se duerme mi niño,
tened los ramos.

AL son de los arroyuelos
cantan las aves de flor en flor
que no hay más gloria que amor
ni mayor pena que celos.

All through these pleasant woods, to the sound of the noisy streams, the birds sing in choirs of the pains of jealousy and love. The streams of water play Nature's own instrument, and as its crystal sweetness loosens the bonds of frost, to the sound of the brooks, the birds sing from flower to flower, for there is no greater glory than love, no greater pain than jealousy.

The daffodils and pinks celebrate love's glories, the violets and pansies do not woo one another for jealousy. One after another, the waves break on the banks, and as they see the small sand through crystalline veils, to the sound of the brooks, the birds sing from flower to flower, for there is no greater glory than love, no greater pain than jealousy.

Streams that murmur of love's faith forsworn string pearls on flowers with threads of pure silver. All is jealousy, all is love, and whilst I weep the pains that love has dealt me with its jealous anxieties, to the sound of the brooks, the birds sing from flower to flower, for there is no greater glory than love, no greater pain than jealousy.

Por estas selvas amenas,
al son de arroyos sonoros,
cantan las aves a coros
de celos y amor las penas.
Suenan del agua las venas,
instrumento natural,
y como el dulce cristal
va desatando los hielos,
al son de los arroyuelos
cantan las aves de flor en flor
que no hay más gloria que amor
ni mayor pena que celos.

De amor las glorias celebran
los narcisos y claveles,
las violetas y penseles
de celos no se requiebran.
Unas y otras se quiebran
las ondas por las orillas
y como las arenillas
ven por cristalinos velos,
al son de los arroyuelos
cantan las aves de flor en flor
que no hay más gloria que amor
ni mayor pena que celos.

Arroyos murmuradores
de la fe de amor perjura,
por hilos de plata pura
ensartan perlas en flores.
Todo es celos, todo amores,
y mientras que lloro yo
las penas que amor me dio
con sus celosos desvelos,
al son de los arroyuelos
cantan las aves de flor en flor
que no hay más gloria que amor
ni mayor pena que celos.

Interest's Chorus

LOVE, your harsh powers are cowardly and weak against famous persons difficult to conquer. Exploits are easy for Interest, the resplendent, with his Dalmatian gold and his Scythian diamonds. That liberal contriver Munificence has made chaste women adultresses; for not all women are Euridices, Evadnes, and Penelopes. Nowadays Pyramus does not kill himself, nor are the Daphnes trees to the sacred purple of the golden eagles. What Caucasus or Rhodope, what Ligurian marbles does this sweet-sounding metal not turn to liquid wax? Love wept tears of tenderness for fair Venus when he saw her in the beastly arms of an ugly satyr. The shameless goddess exchanged cruel and dauntless Mars and bright Apollo of Delphi for a ridiculous faun. Let love not imagine in his anxiety for Hercules' victories that he is going to record his tragic stories in porphyry; for my Hesperian apples will conquer his artifices and the greatest triumphs of the Roman Caesars.

Coro de interés

AMOR, tus fuerzas rígidas
cobardes son y débiles
para sujetos ínclitos
de conquistar difíciles.
Al interés espléndido
son las empresas fáciles,
con el oro dalmático
y los diamantes scíticos.
El dar, pródigo artífice,
constantes hizo adúlteras;
no todas son Eurídices,
Evadnes y Penélopes.
Ya no se mata Píramo,
ni son las Dafnes árboles
para la sacra púrpura
de las doradas águilas.
¿Qué Cáucaso, qué Ródope,
qué mármoles ligústicos,
no vuelve en cera líquida
este metal dulcísono?
Amor a Venus cándida,
porque en los brazos hórridos
la vio de un feo sátiro,
lloró con tiernas lágrimas.
Al fiero Marte indómito
y al claro Apolo Délfico,
por un Fauno ridículo
trocó la diosa impúdica.
No piense amor solícito
por las victorias de Hércules,
que sus historias trágicas
ha de escribir en pórfidos;
que mis pomas hespérides
han de vencer sus máquinas
y los mayores triunfos
de los romanos Césares.

SHEPHERD, who with your lover's whistling woke me out of my deep sleep, you who made this trunk into a crook on which you stretch your mighty arms,

turn your kindly eyes upon my faith, for I confess you to be my love and master, and pledge my word to follow your lover's whistling and your lovely feet.

Listen, shepherd, since you are dying of love, do not let the harshness of my sins frighten you, for you are so much a friend to the weary.

Wait then and listen to my cares . . . But why do I ask you to wait for me, if your feet are nailed to make you wait?

BELOVED, favourite sheep, you who have come countless times, beside this rock, for salt and put your mouth and the pink of your tongue to my coarse hand,

Why did you climb harsh mountains, for savagery like them touches your soul? What rage drove you to such madness that you lost memory and reason?

Graze upon cashew-nuts that you may be restored from that cruel and mercenary dream, and do not drink the waters of oblivion.

Here is your plain, your mountain, and your wood, I am your shepherd and you are my lord, you are my flock and I am your lover.

WHAT have I that you sue for my friendship? What interest brings you, dear Jesus, to spend the dark winter nights at my door, covered in dew?

PASTOR que con tus silbos amorosos
me despertaste del profundo sueño;
tú, que hiciste cayado de ese leño
en que tiendes los brazos poderosos,

vuelve los ojos a mi fe piadosos
pues te confieso por mi amor y dueño
y la palabra de seguirte empeño
tus dulces silbos y tus pies hermosos.

Oye, pastor, pues por amores mueres,
no te espante el rigor de mis pecados
pues tan amigo de rendidos eres.

Espera, pues, y escucha mis cuidados . . .
Pero ¿cómo te digo que me esperes
si estás para esperar los pies clavados?

QUERIDO manso mío que venistes
por sal mil veces junto aquella roca
y en mi grosera mano vuestra boca
y vuestra lengua de clavel pusistes,

¿por qué montañas ásperas subistes
que tal selvatiquez el alma os toca?
¿qué furia os hizo condición tan loca
que la memoria y la razón perdistes?

Paced la anacardina por que os vuelva
de ese cruel y interesable sueño
y no bebáis del agua del olvido.

Aquí está vuestra vega, monte y selva,
yo soy vuestro pastor y vos mi dueño,
vos mi ganado y yo vuestro perdido.

¿QUÉ tengo yo que mi amistad procuras?
¿Qué interés se te sigue, Jesús mío,
que a mi puerta, cubierto de rocío,
pasas las noches del invierno escuras?

Oh how hard was my heart that I did not open to you! What strange madness was it if the cold frost of my ingratitude chapped the wounds on your pure feet?

How many times did the angel say to me: 'Now, soul, look out of your window, and you will see how lovingly he persists in knocking!'

And how many times, oh supreme beauty, did I reply: 'I will open tomorrow', only to make the same reply upon the morrow!

Narcissus

THE insane love increases, the illusion increases in him who saw his fair image in the waters; and he, sole cause of his own mortal plaint, seeks the remedy and makes his plight worse.

He looks into the pool once more, and sees – rare prodigy! – that it spouts fire; he imagines that he can quench it in the water, and his unhappy star closes his eyes to his easy deception.

His powers departed from this blind beloved lover, and his senses left him, for fatal beauty fell a victim to his fate; and now that he is transformed into a purple flower, the water that was the cause of his death makes him grow, and tries to give him life.

¡Oh, cuánto fueron mis entrañas duras
pues no te abrí! ¡Qué extraño desvarío
si de mi ingratitud el hielo frío
secó las llagas de tus plantas puras!

¡Cuántas veces el ángel me decía:
«¡Alma, asómate agora a la ventana,
verás con cuanto amor llamar porfía!»

Y cuántas, hermosura soberana:
«Mañana te abriremos» – repondía,
para lo mismo responder mañana!

JUAN DE ARGUIJO

Narciso

CRECE el insano amor, crece el engaño
del que en las aguas vio su imagen bella;
y él, sola causa en su mortal querella,
busca el remedio y acrecienta el daño.

Vuelve a ver en la fuente ¡caso extraño!
que della sale el fuego; mas en ella
templarlo piensa, y la enemiga estrella
sus ojos cierra al fácil desengaño.

Fallecieron las fuerzas y el sentido
al ciego amante amado; que a su suerte
la belleza fatal cayó rendida;

y ahora, en flor purpúrea convertido
la agua, que fue principio de su muerte,
hace que crezca, y prueba a darle vida.

Storm and Calm

I SAW the calm light of the red sun clouded, and its pleasant face disappear in a moment, and the sky all around obscured by a most horrible darkness.

The stormy South wind roars angrily, its fury rises, the storm increases, and tall Olympus shakes on Atlas's shoulders, thundering in alarm;

but later I saw the black veil break, dissolving into water, and the clear day happily restored to its original brightness,

and gazing on the sky lovely with a new splendour, I said: 'Who knows if a similar change is not in store for my fortunes?'

Ode

NOW insistent suitors knock less often at your closed windows and do not break your sleep, and wakeful lads do not disturb your neighbours as they did; and you who used to wear out the threshold and the door-hinges with your activities, now hear the knocker less often, and sleep, Licisca, right through the nights, or weep in envy as you turn your memory to the long wrangles of the rivals whom you dragged into dangerous feuds. And now,

La tempestad y la calma

Yo vi del rojo sol la luz serena
turbarse, y que en un punto desparece
su alegre faz, y en torno se oscurece
el cielo con tiniebla de horror llena.

El austro proceloso airado suena,
crece su furia, y la tormenta crece,
y en los hombros de Atlante se estremece
el alto Olimpo y con espanto truena;

mas luego vi romperse el negro velo
deshecho en agua, y a su luz primera
restituirse alegre el claro día,

y de nuevo esplandor ornado el cielo.
Miré, y dije: ¿Quién sabe si le espera
igual mudanza a la fortuna mía?

FRANCISCO DE MEDRANO

Oda

Menos veces te baten las cerradas
ventanas ya mancebos porfiados,
ni te rompen el sueño, y desvelados
no traen así alteradas

tus vecinas; y tú, que los umbrales
solícita y los quicios fatigabas,
menos ya, menos oyes las aldabas,
y las noches cabales,

duermes, Licisca, o lloras envidiosa,
la memoria ocupando en las porfías
luengas de los rivales que traías
en guerra peligrosa.

old and lonely, when the moon wanes or the Spring winds blow, when Venus rouses you and drives you to fury, you vexatiously attack the lads who peevishly scorn roses that a cold evening has wilted, and delight to crown themselves with those that today's morning has hardly opened.

To Don Juan de Arguijo, against Artifice

THE greater is human artifice the sooner it tires the gaze; the clearest spring and garden arranged by man tell us reproachfully that our skill and our hands are short-lived.

That supreme carelessness of Nature, who is never miserly, stops and holds anyone who gazes on it with sound senses, in long admiration.

To see how a river runs for ever, how the field stretches out into the plains, and in the mountains twists and grows small, is an ever new and welcome glory, Argío, but the author who created them – Infinite God! – is like this in all his creatures.

To St Peter, in a Storm on the Way Back from Rome

SOVEREIGN fisherman in whose nets the greatest monarchs have been fortunate enough to be caught and have exchanged their prisons for glory and favours,

you who are able to open and close the gates of Heaven for your flock with a great key, and have won a palace on earth with porphyry columns and walls,

Y vieja, y sola ya, cuando la luna
descrece más o el cefiro más crece,
cuando te enciende Venus y enfurece,
acusas importuna

los mozos, que desprecian con enfado
rosas que desmayó una tarde fría,
y de las que hoy apenas abrió el día
se coronan de grado.

A don Juan de Arguijo, contra el artificio

CANSA la vista el artificio humano
cuanto mayor más presto; la más clara
fuente y jardín compuestos dan en cara
que nuestro ingenio es breve y nuestra mano.

Aquel, aquel descuido soberano
de la naturaleza, en nada avara,
con luenga admiración suspende y para
a quien lo advierte con sentido sano.

Ver cómo corre eternamente un río,
cómo el campo se tiende en las llanuras,
y en los montes se anuda y se reduce,

grandeza es siempre nueva y grata, Argío,
tal, pero es el autor que las produce
¡Oh Dios inmenso! en todas sus criaturas.

A San Pedro, en una borrasca, viniendo de Roma

PESCADOR soberano, en cuyas redes
los monarcas mayores han estado
dichosamente presos, y cambiado
en gloria sus prisiones, y en mercedes;

tú que abrir y cerrar el cielo puedes
con poderosa llave a tu ganado,
y alcázar en la tierra has alcanzado
con colunas de pórfido y paredes,

turn your gaze on the enraged sea, and since it once dared to wet your foot, although trodden by your courageous faith,

break its swell, calm its roaring, and, as a skilled disciple, raise my faith and my feet with your mighty hand.

I DO not know how or when or what I felt that filled me with sweetness; I know that beauty came to my arms eager to take pleasure in me;

I know that she came, although with frightened glance I could hardly endure her face; then I was struck still, like one who in a dark night has lost his sense of direction and dare not stir a step.

A great joy followed this seizure or sleep; I do not know when or how or what it was that put all that is known to the senses into a state of calm.

Not to know it is to know; for what the senses alone can embrace is very small, and this could be contained only in the soul.

MAKE way, reapers, make way, and let the little gleaning girl come.

If I were a grain of wheat in the hands that I bless, I say she could make me into flour and then into cake or biscuit, so that she could eat me then.

Make way, reapers, make way, and let the little gleaning girl come.

los ojos vuelve al mar enfurecido;
y pues tal vez osó mojar tu planta
aun siendo hollado de tu fe animosa,

su hinchazón rompe, acalla su ruido,
y, enseñado discípulo, levanta
mi fe y mis pies con mano poderosa.

NO sé cómo ni cuándo ni qué cosa
sentí que me llenaba de dulzura;
sé que llegó a mis brazos la hermosura,
de gozarse conmigo codiciosa;

sé que llegó, si bien con temerosa
vista resistí apenas su figura;
luego pasmé como el que en noche oscura,
perdido el tino, el pie mover no osa.

Siguió un gran gozo a aqueste pasmo o sueño;
no sé cuándo ni cómo ni qué ha sido,
que lo sensible todo puso en calma.

Ignorarlo es saber; que es bien pequeño
el que puede abarcar solo el sentido,
y éste pudo caber en sola la alma.

TIRSO DE MOLINA

SEGADORES, ¡afuera, afuera!:
dejen llegar a la espigaderuela.

Si en las manos que bendigo
fuera yo espiga de trigo,
que me hiciera harina digo
y luego torta o bondigo,
porque luego me comiera.

Segadores, ¡afuera, afuera!:
dejen llegar a la espigaderuela.

At the Ruins of Itálica

ALAS, these solitary fields, this parched mound, that you see here, Fabio, were once Itálica the famous; here was the victorious colony of Scipio; thrown to the ground lies the dread honour of that terrifying wall, and it is no more than a pitiful relic of its invincible people. Only deathly memories remain where once wandered shades that were an exalted pattern (to men); this level place was a forum, here was a temple; of all this scarcely the signs remain: the unhappy ashes of the gymnasium and the refreshing baths float lightly on the breeze; the towers which scorned the air have collapsed beneath their mighty weight.

This ruined amphitheatre, a pagan monument to the gods, whose disgrace is proclaimed by the yellow mustard, now reduced to a tragic stage – Oh laughing-stock of Time! – proclaims the magnitude of its former greatness, the extent of its present devastation. How is it that, in the ill-defined circle of its deserted arena, that great people does not shout? Since there are wild beasts here where is the naked swordsman? Where is the mighty athlete? All has disappeared; fate has reduced its happy voices to mute silence. Yet in these ruins Time still presents cruel spectacles to the eye; they stare in such disorder on the present that the soul hears their cries of grief.

RODRIGO CARO

A las ruinas de Itálica

ESTOS, Fabio, ¡ay dolor! que ves ahora
campos de soledad, mustio collado,
fueron un tiempo Itálica famosa;
aquí de Cipión la vencedora
colonia fue; por tierra derribado
yace el temido honor de la espantosa
muralla, y lastimosa
reliquia es solamente
de su invencible gente.
Sólo quedan memorias funerales
donde erraron ya sombras de alto ejemplo;
este allano fue plaza, allí fue templo;
de todo apenas quedan las señales;
del gimnasio y las termas regaladas
leves vuelan cenizas desdichadas:
las torres que desprecio al aire fueron
a su gran pesadumbre se rindieron.

Este despedazado anfiteatro,
impío honor de los dioses, cuya afrenta
publica el amarillo jaramago,
ya reducido a trágico teatro,
¡oh fábula del tiempo! representa
cuánta fue su grandeza, y es su estrago.
¿Cómo en el cerco vago
de su desierta arena
el gran pueblo no suena?
¿Dónde, pues fieras hay, está el desnudo
luchador? ¿Dónde está el atleta fuerte?
Todo despareció, cambió la suerte
voces alegres en silencio mudo;
mas aun el tiempo da en estos despojos
espectáculos fieros a los ojos,
y miran tan confuso lo presente
que voces de dolor el alma siente.

Here was born that thunderbolt of war, great father of his country and honour to Spain, the pious, happy, and triumphant Trajan, before whom there fell down in silence that land which looks on the cradle of the sun and that which is washed by the sea of Cadiz, which he also conquered. Here rocked the ivory and golden cradles of Elius Adrianus, of the divine Theodosius, and of Silius the strange. Here the gardens saw them crowned with laurel or with jasmine, gardens that are now all brambles and swamps. The house that was built for Caesar is now, alas, the wretched haunt of lizards; houses, gardens, Caesars have perished, and even the stones on which their deeds were recorded.

If you are not weeping, Fabio, turn an attentive eye on the long ruined streets, gaze on the marble and the shattered arches, gaze on the proud statues which violent Nemesis has overthrown, see now their famous originals buried in huge silence. So I imagine Troy, like this its ancient wall, and you, Rome, whose name scarcely survives, fatherland of the gods and kings, and you to whom just laws were of no avail, the creation of Minerva, wise Athens, once the envy of the ages, today ashes and vast solitudes; for fate did not respect your wisdom, nor did death, alas, spare your strength.

Aquí nació aquel rayo de la guerra,
gran padre de la patria, honor de España,
pío, felice, triunfador Trajano,
ante quien muda se postró la tierra
que ve del sol la cuna, y la que baña
el mar, también vencido, gaditano.
Aquí de Elio Adriano,
de Teodosio divino,
de Silio peregrino
rodaron de marfil y oro las cunas.
Aquí ya de laurel, ya de jazmines
coronados los vieron los jardines,
que ahora son zarzales y lagunas.
La casa para el César fabricada,
¡ay! yace de lagartos vil morada;
casas, jardines, Césares murieron,
y aun las piedras que de ellos se escribieron.

Fabio, si tú no lloras, pon atenta
la vista en luengas calles destruidas,
mira mármoles y arcos destrozados,
mira estatuas soberbias que violenta
Némesis derribó, yacer tendidas,
y ya en alto silencio sepultados
sus dueños celebrados.
Así a Troya figuro,
así a su antiguo muro,
y a ti, Roma, a quien queda el nombre apenas,
¡oh patria de los dioses y los reyes!
y a ti, a quien no valieron justas leyes,
fábrica de Minerva, sabia Atenas,
emulación ayer de las edades,
hoy cenizas, hoy vastas soledades;
que no os respetó el hado, no la muerte,
¡ay! ni por sabia a ti, ni a ti por fuerte.

But why does the mind devote itself to seeking arguments for fresh griefs? A better example is enough, the present is enough; for still the smoke can be seen here, still the flame can be seen; still today tears can be heard, today hoarse cries; some spirit or cult controls the minds of the people hereabouts, who relate in wonder how in the silent night a sad voice is heard, crying in tears: 'Itálica has fallen!' and mournful Echo calls 'Itálica!' in the leafy wood, which confronts it with 'Itálica!' resounding, and countless noble ghosts from its great ruin, when they hear that famous name of 'Itálica!', sigh yet again. So much are even the common people moved to grief!

This short tribute that, as a grateful guest, I owe your holy shades I give and consecrate to them, famous Itálica. For yourself (if those ungrateful ashes of which I bring some sweet news, though sad, have accepted a gift so tearful) permit me, as pious payment for my fond tears, to see the blessed body of Geroncio, your martyr and priest; show me some traces of his tomb, and with my tears I will dig the rocks that hide his holy coffin: but I have no right to ask for the one consolation for all that good which heaven in her anger has taken away. Enjoy his fair remains with your own and be the envy of the world and the stars!

Mas ¿para qué la mente se derrama
en buscar al dolor nuevo argumento?
Basta ejemplo mejor, basta el presente;
que aun se ve el humo aquí, se ve la llama,
aun se oyen llantos hoy, hoy ronco acento;
tal genio o religión fuerza la mente
de la vecina gente,
que refiere admirada
que en la noche callada
una voz triste se oye, que llorando
«¡cayó Itálica!»: y lastimosa
Eco reclama «¡Itálica!» en la hojosa
selva, que se le opone resonando
«¡Itálica!» y el claro nombre oído
de «¡Itálica!» renuevan el gemido
mil sombras nobles de su gran ruina:
¡tanto aun la plebe a sentimiento inclina!

Esta corta piedad que agradecido
huésped a tus sagrados Manes debo,
les dó y consagro, Itálica famosa.
Tú (si lloroso don han admitido
las ingratas cenizas de que llevo
dulce noticia asaz, si lastimosa),
permíteme, piadosa
usura a tierno llanto,
que vea el cuerpo santo
de Geroncio, tu mártir y prelado;
muestra de su sepulcro algunas señas,
y cavaré con lágrimas las peñas
que ocultan su sarcófago sagrado:
pero mal pido el único consuelo
de todo el bien que airado quitó el cielo.
¡Goza en las tuyas sus reliquias bellas
para envidia del mundo y las estrellas!

In a shattered ship, without helm or mast, I sail the broad gulf of love, in whose sea the waves are fire, and break on hearts, not sand.

Here I weep, so blind to my own good, moored to the chain of a thought, which hopes to find some relief: where they cry fire, fire roars.

Confused in this sea of my defeat, I strain my eyes, which are tired with weeping, and very far away the port appears before me.

And no sooner do I joyfully greet the port than a great storm of troubles drives me back, and it disappears from view.

On the green amaranth and reeds that Guadalhorce washes, sleep with his golden key held closed both eyes, bright suns, of my fair mistress, and the red skies of her face bathed in a sweet-scented sweat. The crystalline river-god saw her, and leaves his rippling lodging for the land, his body clad in spawn and dew, and with his frozen lips he drinks and touches the delicate breath of her mouth. Sleep felt this cold and opened the twin suns of the clear sky, which so offend the god who is made of frost that now his breast pounds like a forge, and he fears that the rays, which set him on fire, may turn him to water; and so, confused and blind, he jumped into the water and escaped the fire.

LUIS MARTÍN DE LA PLAZA

EN rota nave, sin timón ni antena,
el ancho golfo del amor navego,
en cuya mar las olas son de fuego,
y en pechos se quebrantan, no en arena.

Aquí lloro, amarrado en la cadena
de un pensamiento, para el bien tan ciego,
que pretende hallar algún sosiego:
donde fuego dan voces, fuego suena.

En este mar de mi derrota incierto,
tiendo los ojos, de llorar cansados,
y muy lejos el puerto se me ofrece.

Y apenas con placer saludo el puerto,
cuando grande tormenta de cuidados
atrás me vuelve a y él se desparece.

SOBRE el verde amaranto y espadaña
que Guadalhorce baña
tenía con dorada llave el sueño
cerrados los dos ojos, claros soles,
de mi hermoso dueño,
y del rostro los rojos arreboles
con un sudor cubiertos oloroso.
Vídola el cristalino dios del río,
y a tierra sale de su albergue undoso,
vestido el cuerpo de ovas y rocío,
y con helados labios bebe y toca
el delicado aliento de su boca.
El sueño sintió el hielo,
y abrió los soles del sereno cielo,
y al dios hecho de escarcha así le ofenden,
que suena ya su pecho como fragua,
y teme que los rayos que los encienden
lo conviertan en agua,
y así turbado y ciego
saltó en el agua y escapó del fuego.

THESE purple roses that today fell from Dawn's white breast, and a vase full of brightly coloured flowers, I offer you now, oh sweet breezes,

if with your wings you will protect my divine Flora from being tanned by the sun which, burning and a stranger to pity, offends her face, because it is gilding the fields.

Oh roaming daughters of the earth, see if May has fresher roses in her garlands (or) lovelier flowers.

The dawn, as it wept, gave them fine pearls, the sun (gave them) colours, my affection (gave them) my beautiful Flora's skirt, and she (gave them) perfume.

On the Assumption of the Virgin Mary

IN turquoise clouds and wisps (of cloud), with white torches and white candles, the sovereign pages of (our) holy God, stand in the imperial castle.

Between amaranth and silver lilies, on carpets of knots and foliage, they burn Indian incense and Syrian gums of a thousand sorts and species.

With the sun for cloak and the moon for slippers, the Virgin arrived in the imperial hall (a visit that the heavens longed for).

The seraphim threw themselves at her feet, the angels sang her welcome, and the holy Word seated her at His side.

PEDRO ESPINOSA

ESTAS purpúreas rosas, que a la aurora
se le cayeron hoy del blanco seno,
y un vaso de pintadas flores lleno,
¡oh dulces auras!, os ofrezco agora,

si defendéis de mi divina Flora
con vuestras alas el color moreno,
del sol, que ardiente y de piedad ajeno,
su rostro ofende porque el campo dora.

¡Oh hijas de la tierra peregrinas!
mirad si tiene mayo en sus guirnaldas
más frescas rosas, más bizarras flores.

Llorando les dio el alba perlas finas;
el sol colores, mi afición, la falda
de mi hermosa Flora, y ella, olores.

A la Asunción de la Virgen María

EN turquesadas nubes y celajes
estàn en los alcázares impirios,
con blancas hachas y con blancos cirios,
del sacro Dios los soberanos pajes;

humean de mil suertes y linajes,
entre amaranto y plateados lirios,
inciensos indios y pebetes sirios,
sobre alfombras de lazos y follajes.

Por manto el sol, la luna por chapines,
llegó la Virgen a la impírea sala,
(visita que esperaba el cielo tanto);

echáronse a sus pies los serafines,
cantáronle los ángeles la gala,
y sentóla a su lado el Verbo santo.

To the Most Blessed Virgin Mary

LIKE the unhappy pilot who, on the inconstant sea, sees himself with troubled eyes, subjected to torture on the tossing waves which throw up sand, and spatter and cover him with foam,

when, quite hopeless and half dead with fear, he sees St Elmo's fire burning on the mast and, bowing to its light, his soul quite full of joy, finds his shattered ship anchored in the welcome port,

so I was ploughing the sea of annoyance and anxieties and, in a fierce storm, was already half covered by the deep waters, my strength and light lost,

when I looked on the brightness of your eyes, oh Virgin, by whose glow, the waves growing quiet, I reached the happy port where I saved my life.

On Self-knowledge

THIS river has forgotten his humble beginnings, and by the wide fords frightens with his foam the valiant hill that stands up, armed with oaks, to challenge his strength.

With fickle majesty, proud of his waves, he passes and advances his irrevocable steps to the wide sea, in which he drowns his name and loses his strength.

How three and four times wretched are you, human misery, that can proudly disguise yourself in a flattering shadow!

Man, child of the earth and of nothingness, how on your way to death can you allow yourself basely to forget the country of your beginnings?

A la Santísima Virgen María

COMO el triste piloto que por el mar incierto
se ve, con turbios ojos, sujeto de la pena
sobre las corvas olas, que vomitando arena
lo tienen de la espuma salpicado y cubierto,

cuando, sin esperanza, de espanto medio muerto,
ve el fuego de Santelmo lucir sobre el antena,
y, adorando su lumbre, de gozo el alma llena,
halla su nave cascada surgida en dulce puerto,

así yo el mar surcaba de penas y de enojos,
y, con tormenta fiera, ya de las aguas hondas
medio cubierto estaba, la fuerza y luz perdida,

cuando miré la lumbre ¡oh Virgen! de tus ojos,
con cuyos resplandores, quietándose las ondas,
llegué al dichoso puerto donde escapé la vida.

Al conocimiento de sí propio

SU pobre origen olvidó este río,
y en anchos vados espumoso espanta
al que armado de robles se levanta
valiente monte a contrastar su brío.

Pasa con inconstante señorío,
de sus ondas ufano, y adelanta
al ancho mar la irrevocable planta,
en donde ahoga el nombre y pierde el brío.

¡Oh tres y cuatro veces desdichada
miseria humana, que soberbia puedes
disimularte en sombra lisonjera!

Hombre, hijo de la tierra y de la nada,
¿cómo, yendo a la muerte, te concedes
olvido vil de tu nación primera?

The Various Motions of his Heart, Floating on the Waves of Lisi's Hair

IN the curled tempest of wavy gold my heart, thirsty for beauty, swims gulfs of pure and burning light, if you let down your beautiful hair.

Leander on a sea of stormy fire displays his love and consumes his life; Icarus on an unsafe path of gold burns his wings to die gloriously.

With the ambition of a Phoenix, fired with hopes for whose extinction I weep, it attempts to breed lives by its death.

Greedy and rich, and poor in treasure, it copies Midas in its punishment and its hunger, Tantalus in its fleeting fountain of gold.

To a Nose

THERE was once a man stuck on to a nose. It was a superlative nose, it was a constable and scribe of a nose, it was a most hairy swordfish.

It was an ill-adjusted sundial, it was an alembic deep in thought, it was an elephant upside down, it was a nosier Ovidius Naso.

It was the prow of a galley, it was a pyramid of Egypt, it was the twelve tribes of noses.

It was an infinity of nosishness, very much of a nose, and such a fierce nose that it would have been a crime in the face of Annas.*

* A-nas, by an etymological pun, suggests noselessness or a-nasality.

FRANCISCO DE QUEVEDO Y VILLEGAS

Afectos varios de su corazón, fluctuando en las ondas de los cabellos de Lisi

EN crespa tempestad del oro undoso
nada golfos de luz ardiente y pura
mi corazón, sediento de hermosura,
si el cabello deslazas generoso.

Leandro en mar de fuego proceloso
su amor ostenta, su vivir apura;
Ícaro en senda de oro mal segura
arde sus alas por morir glorioso.

Con pretensión de fénix, encendidas
sus esperanzas, que difuntas lloro,
intenta que su muerte engendre vidas.

Avaro y rico, y pobre en el tesoro,
el castigo y la hambre imita a Midas,
Tántalo en fugitiva fuente de oro.

A una nariz

ÉRASE un hombre a una nariz pegado,
érase una nariz superlativa,
érase una nariz sayón y escriba
érase un peje espada muy barbado,

Era un reloj de sol mal encarado,
érase una alquitara pensativa,
érase un elefante boca arriba,
era Ovidio Nasón más narizado,

Érase un espolón de una galera,
érase una pirámide de Egito:
las doce tribus de narices era,

Érase un naricísimo infinito,
muchísima nariz, nariz tan fiera,
que en la cara de Anás fuera delito.

Lyrical Song

ROSE-BUSH, less presumption where the little pinks are, for what are roses today tomorrow will be thorns.

What good does it do you, rose-bush, to presume on your fine looks, when no sooner are you born than you begin to die? Your red in its life and death brings tears and laughter, in a single day or in a single sun. From its rise to its setting your beauty passes in a single step, and your perfection in less.

Rose-bush, less presumption, etc.

The advantage that your quality procures is not very great: if the dawn is your fine shawl, the night is your winding-sheet. There is no little flower so modest that it does not equal you in days, and as for your nobility* as a descendant of the dawn, the mallow laughs at it, riding* on its hummuck.

Rose-bush, less presumption, etc.

* The pun is obvious in Spanish, but cannot be translated, *caballero* being both a horseman and a gentleman.

Letrilla lírica

ROSAL, menos presunción
donde están las clavellinas,
pues serán mañana espinas
las que agora rosas son.

¿De qué sirve presumir,
rosal, de buen parecer,
si aun no acabas de nacer
cuando empiezas a morir?
Hace llorar y reír
vivo y muerto tu arrebol,
en un día o en un sol;
desde el oriente al ocaso
va tu hermosura en un paso,
y en menos tu perfección.

Rosal, menos presunción
donde están las clavellinas,
pues serán mañana espinas
las que agora rosas son.

No es muy grande la ventaja
que tu calidad mejora:
si es tu mantilla la aurora,
es la noche tu mortaja:
no hay florecilla tan baja
que no te alcance de días,
y de tus caballerías
por descendiente del alba,
se está riyendo la malva,
caballera de un terrón.

Rosal, menos presunción
donde están las clavellinas,
pues serán mañana espinas
las que agora rosas son.

HOW you slip from between my hands! Oh how you slide away, years of my life! What silent steps you take, cold death, when you bring all things to equality with your quiet tread!

Fiercely you climb the weak earthen wall on which vigorous youth relies; already my heart is waiting for the invisible flight of your wings on the last day.

Oh condition of humanity! Oh hard fate, that I cannot hope to live tomorrow without paying towards the purchase of my death!

Every moment of human life is a new summons warning me how fragile, how miserable, and how vain it is.

THE brief year of mortal life takes everything with it, mocking the dash, the brave steel, and the cold marble which pits its hardness against time.

Before the foot learns how to walk it travels the road of death, along which I am sending my obscure life: a poor and muddy river that the black sea swallows with its high waves.

Every short moment is a long step which I take, to my regret, on this journey, since standing or sleeping I always spur on.

Death, which is our unavoidable heritage, is a brief, final, and bitter breath: but if it is the law and not a punishment, why do I complain?

I LOOKED on the walls of my fatherland, so strong once, but now mouldered away, weary with the passage of time, by which their valour is already decaying.

¡Cómo de entre mis manos te resbalas!
¡Oh cómo te deslizas, edad mía!
¡Qué mudos pasos traes, oh muerte fría,
pues con callado pie todo lo igualas!

Feroz, de tierra del débil muro escalas,
en quien lozana juventud se fía;
mas ya mi corazón del postrer día,
atiende al vuelo sin mirar las alas.

¡Oh condición mortal! ¡Oh dura suerte!
¡Que no puedo querer vivir mañana
sin la pensión de procurar mi muerte!

Cualquier instante de la vida humana
es nueva ejecución con que me advierte
cuán frágil es, cuán mísera, cuán vana.

Todo tras sí lo lleva el año breve
de la vida mortal, burlando el brío,
al acero valiente, al mármol frío
que contra el tiempo su dureza atreve.

Antes que sepa andar el pie, se mueve
camino de la muerte, donde envío
mi vida oscura: pobre y turbio río,
que negro mar con altas ondas bebe.

Todo corto momento es paso largo
que doy, a mi pesar, en tal jornada,
pues, parado y durmiendo siempre aguijo.

Breve suspiro, y último, y amargo,
es la muerte, forzosa y heredada;
mas si es ley y no pena, ¿qué me aflijo?

Miré los muros de la patria mía,
si un tiempo fuertes, ya desmoronados,
de la carrera de la edad cansados
por quien caduca ya su valentía.

I went out to the fields, and saw the sun drinking up the streams, which were released from the frost, and the cattle complaining to the woods that they stole the daylight with their shadows.

I went into my house, and saw that it was the discoloured ruin of an ancient habitation; that my shepherd's crook was more bent and less strong.

I felt my sword conquered by the years, and found nothing to look upon that was not a memory of death.

THE last shadow that takes white day from me may close my eyes, and now, flattering its eager anxiety, may release this soul of mine;

but it will not leave the memory of where it burned on the further shore; my passion is capable of swimming the cold water, and losing its respect for strict law.

A soul which has imprisoned a whole god, veins that have given liquid (fuel) to so much fire, marrow that has burned in glory,

will forsake their body but not their passion; will be ashes but will retain their feeling, will be dust but dust in love.

Satirical Letter of Censure

against the present habits of the Spaniards, addressed to Don Gaspar de Guzmán, Count of Olivares, when he was royal favourite

I MUST not be silent even though you put your finger first on your lips and then on your forehead to advise silence and counsel fear.

Should there not be a brave spirit? Must one always regret what one says? Must one never say what one feels?

Salíme al campo, vi que el sol bebía
los arroyos del hielo desatados;
y del monte quejosos los ganados
que con sombras hurtó su luz al día.

Entré en mi casa; vi que, amancillada,
de anciana habitación era despojos;
mi báculo, más corvo y menos fuerte.

Vencida de la edad sentí mi espada,
y no hallé cosa en que poner los ojos
que no fuese recuerdo de la muerte.

CERRAR podrá mis ojos la postrera
sombra, que me llevare el blanco día:
y podrá desatar esta alma mía
hora, a su afán ansioso lisonjera;

mas no de esotra parte en la ribera
dejará la memoria en donde ardía;
nadar sabe mi llama la agua fría
y perder el respeto a ley severa.

Alma a quien todo un dios prisión ha sido,
venas que humor a tanto fuego han dado,
medulas que han gloriosamente ardido,

su cuerpo dejarán, no su cuidado:
serán ceniza, mas tendrá sentido,
polvo serán, mas polvo enamorado.

Epístola satírica y censoria

contra las costumbres presentes de los castellanos, escrita a Don Gaspar de Guzmán, Conde de Olivares, en su valimiento

NO he de callar, por más que con el dedo,
ya tocando la boca y ya la frente,
silencio avises o amenaces miedo.

¿No ha de haber un espíritu valiente?
¿Siempre se ha de sentir lo que se dice?
¿Nunca se ha de decir lo que se siente?

Today, without fear of offending by his freedom, a man of intelligence may speak, safe from intimidation by stronger men.

In other centuries strict criticism, the naked truth and the eloquent man's breaking of his silence, might be accounted crimes.

Now, let anyone who denies or doubts it know that Truth is the tongue of a harsh God, and that God's tongue was never mute.

Truth and God together are the true God: divine eternity does not sunder them, nor was either of the two first in time.

If God had come in advance of Truth, being the Truth, there would have been a contradiction in His existing and Truth's not doing so.

God's justice is true, and mercy and all things divine, all must be Truth entire.

Most excellent sir, my tears will not now brook limits or banks; my song will break like a flood.

Now I see my cheeks submerged, my eyes spilling like twin urns over the altars of the two Castiles.

That virtue lies disordered that was once, though not rich, yet still feared; and is buried in vanity and sleep.

So does that noble liberty which never chose to seek a longer life when it knew where to find an honourable death.

Once the strong nation, lavish with its spirit, counted growing old in the arms of its destiny an insult offered by the years.

Hoy, sin miedo que libre escandalice,
puede hablar el ingenio, asegurado
de que mayor poder le atemorice.

En otros siglos pudo ser pecado
severo estudio, y la verdad desnuda,
y romper el silencio el bien hablado.

Pues sepa, quien lo niega y quien lo duda,
que es lengua la verdad de Dios severo,
y la lengua de Dios nunca fue muda.

Son, la verdad y Dios, Dios verdadero:
ni eternidad divina los separa,
ni de los dos alguna fué primero.

Si Dios a la verdad se adelantara,
siendo verdad, implicación hubiera
en ser, y en que verdad de ser dejara.

La justicia de Dios es verdadera,
ya la misericordia y todo cuanto
es Dios, todo ha de ser verdad entera.

Señor excelentísimo, mi llanto
ya no consiente márgenes ni orillas:
inundación será la de mi canto.

Ya sumergirse miro mis mejillas,
la vista por dos urnas derramada
sobre las aras de las dos Castillas.

Yace aquella virtud desaliñada
que fue, si rica menos, más temida,
en vanidad y en sueño sepultada.

Y aquella libertad esclarecida
que, en donde supo hallar honrada muerte,
nunca quiso tener más larga vida.

Y, pródiga del alma, nación fuerte,
contaba por afrenta de los años
envejecer en brazos de la suerte.

Our people were strangers to the idle torpor of time, the deceptive passage of the hours and the days.

Nobody reckoned the number of his years, but the manner of his living; a brave heart did not pass a single hour without noble aspirations.

Stout virtue was mistress, and she alone ruled the rough people; though an ineloquent age it was a conquering one.

Fear of the hand was a shield to the heart which, trusting in it, nakedly defied all arms.

A single soldier, armed with no more than his honest duty, multiplied his precious honour and his valiant spirit to the power of squadrons.

And in the open field this people directed their eyes, though not their thoughts, to a dream, not of greater leisure but of greater honour.

The wife spun her husband's winding sheet before his suit; she saw him less often in his finery than in danger.

She was more often at her husband's side in the army than in bed. She risked losing him when he was sound, and avenged him when he was wounded.

All were matrons, and there were no fine ladies, for reputation was too strict to admit of courtly flattery.

The wide and noisy Ocean cut them off from the golden mines, which have driven peace from the human heart.

Nor did harsh money bring them foreign customs, nor the East corrupt their honour with precious stones.

Del tiempo el ocio torpe, y los engaños
del paso de las horas y del día,
reputaban los nuestros por extraños.

Nadie contaba cuánta edad vivía,
sino de qué manera; ni aun un hora
lograba sin afán su valentía.

La robusta virtud era señora,
y sola dominaba al pueblo rudo:
edad, si mal hablada, vencedora.

El temor de la mano daba escudo
al corazón que, en ella confiado,
todas las armas despreció desnudo.

Multiplicó en escuadras un soldado
su honor precioso, su ánimo valiente,
de sola honesta obligación armado.

Y, debajo del cielo, aquella gente,
si no a más descansado, a más honrado
sueño entregó los ojos, no la mente.

Hilaba la mujer para su esposo
la mortaja primero que el vestido;
menos le vió galán que peligroso.

Acompañaba el lado del marido
más veces en la hueste que en la cama.
Sano le aventuró, vengóle herido.

Todas matronas, y ninguna dama;
que nombres de halago cortesano
no admitió lo severo de su fama.

Derramado y sonoro el Oceano,
era divorcio de las rubias minas
que usurparon la paz del pecho humano.

Ni los trujo costumbres peregrinas
el áspero dinero, ni el Oriente
compró la honestidad con piedras finas.

Pure and burning virtue was their jewel; merit and praise their decoration, and only what was honest was desired.

The lance did not depend upon the pen, nor had the Cantabrian with his chests and ink-wells made the fields hereditary: they were fields of slaughter.

And Spain with her legitimate currency, begging no credit from Liguria (the bankers of Genoa) was more concerned with turbans than with figures.

It would mean less loss and injury if loans were to turn to Moorish captains, for their usury is worse than the Moorish fury.

Birds grew old in the air, and game died of old age, decrepitude living to a great age beneath the elements.

For the stomach, well disciplined in those days, sought repletion rather than surfeit, and the gullet knew no sin.

One cow gave food and leather enough for the greatest nobleman in that pure nation of great men.

The wrinkled pepper, and the foreign and fragrant flattery of the clove, had not yet come to tickle the palate.

Mutton and beef were the first course and the last, cooked with red peppers and tough garlic, and the servant ate as richly as his master.

Thirst drank from pure streams; afterwards unsteady toasts pointed the way to the winecup.

A thin face and a lean body were the signs of honest labour, and honour and profit lay in the same sack.

Joya fue la virtud pura y ardiente;
gala el merecimiento y alabanza;
sólo se codiciaba lo decente.

No de la pluma dependió la lanza,
ni el cántabro con cajas y tinteros
hizo el campo heredad, sino matanza.

Y España, con legítimos dineros,
no mendigando el crédito a Liguria,
más quiso los turbantes que los ceros.

Menos fuera la pérdida y la injuria
si se volvieran Muzas los asientos;
que esta usura es peor que aquella furia.

Caducaban las aves en los vientos
y expiraba decrépito el venado:
grande vejez duró en los elementos.

Que el vientre, entonces bien disciplinado,
buscó satisfacción y no hartura,
y estaba la garganta sin pecado.

Del mayor infanzón de aquella pura
república de grandes hombres era
una vaca sustento y armadura.

No había venido, al gusto lisonjera,
la pimienta arrugada, ni del clavo
la adulación fragante forastera.

Carnero y vaca fue principio y cabo,
y con rojos pimientos y ajos duros,
también como el señor comió el esclavo.

Bebió la sed los arroyuelos puros;
después mostraron del carquesio a Baco
el camino los brindis mal seguros.

El rostro macilento, el cuerpo flaco,
eran recuerdo del trabajo honroso,
y honra y provecho andaban en un saco.

An unbarbered Spaniard could safely call the Germans drunkards and the Dutch heretical traitors.

He could accuse Italy of disordinate jealousy: but today we copy them in many fashions and they are the originators.

Many of Gothic blood waste their inheritances: all wear their arms, but few imitate the Goths; they are not their successors, but merely sport the name.

There came that precious oil which is either thrown up by the whale or by the foam of the waves, and which gives us rather a reputation for luxury than a sweet odour.

And the hosts of Spain became sweetly perfumed but ill-led, and where once had been simple skins were now jewels.

Great deeds were ill-clad, and even the vanity of presumptuous women was not sated with coarse cloth and wool.

The Roman and his gold turned showy Sicilian silk, dyed with bright murex, into a harsh tyrant.

The silkworm could never persuade the tough Spaniard to wear its winding-sheet in summer, at the instance of the dog-star.

Now honour scorns the man who works. But then work was a patent of nobility, and luxury was the mark of mean men.

The bold youth pursues glory by robbing the cows of their mates, and offends the memory of Ceres.

An animal born for labour, and a symbol of jealousy to mortals, who was a disguise and a cloak to Jove;

Pudo sin miedo un español velloso
llamar a los tudescos «bacanales»,
y al holandés «hereje y alevoso».

Pudo acusar los celos desiguales
a la Italia; pero hoy de muchos modos
somos copias, si son originales.

Las descendencias gastan muchos godos,
todos blasonan, nadie los imita,
y no son sucesores, sino apodos.

Vino el betún precioso que vomita
la bellana, o la espuma de las olas,
que el vicio, no el olor, nos acredita.

Y quedaron las huestes españolas
bien perfumadas, pero mal regidas,
y alhajas las que fueron pieles solas.

Estaban las hazañas mal vestidas,
y aun no se hartaba de buriel y lana
la vanidad de fembras presumidas.

A la seda pomposa siciliana
que manchó ardiente múrice, el romano
y el oro hicieron áspera y tirana.

Nunca al duro español supo el gusano
persuadir que vistiese su mortaja,
intercediendo el Can por el verano.

Hoy desprecia el honor al que trabaja,
y entonces fue el trabajo ejecutoria,
y el vicio graduó la gente baja.

Pretende el alentado joven gloria
por dejar la vacada sin marido
y de Ceres ofende la memoria.

Un animal a la labor nacido
y símbolo celoso a los mortales,
que a Jove fue disfraz y fue vestido;

who once hardened royal hands, and behind whom consuls groaned, and who pastured in light in the celestial fields (transformed into the constellation of Taurus),

out of what hatred did they persuade themselves that to humble him was a great deed, and (thus) do such great harm to the harvest?

How shameful to see a grandee of Spain, crouching in the saddle with short stirrups, and wasting his mount on a cane lance!

I approve of children fighting a cock with such a weapon, but not grown men of mature age.

Let the youth display his strength at the head of squadrons, not with a holly-wood spear against the head of the useful beast.

Let the swift trumpet call him, imposing its force of law on the empty air, and let the army obey its sound.

How majestically does the pike fill the grasp, and the musket weigh down the shoulder of the man bold enough to be a true Castillian!

Disgustedly, I name among the foreigners one who immodestly desires rather to impress with his person than to strike terror.

The short stirrup and the cane lance are a Moorish infection. Let jousts and tourneys be held again, and let there be an end of cape-work against the bull.

Take us from play to spoils of victory: for only a great king and a good favourite can fulfil such a wish;

You who make a past century repeat itself by disembarrassing our persons and freeing our limbs from vexations;

que un tiempo endureció manos reales,
y detrás de él los cónsules gimieron,
y rumía luz en campos celestiales,

¿por cuál enemistad se persuadieron
a que su apocamiento fuese hazaña,
y a las mieses tan grande ofensa hicieron?

¡Qué cosa es ver un infanzón de España
abreviado en la silla a la jineta,
y gastar un caballo en una caña!

Que la niñez al gallo le acometa
con semejante munición apruebo;
mas no la edad madura y la perfeta.

Ejercite sus fuerzas el mancebo
en frentes de escuadrones; no en la frente
del útil bruto la asta del acebo.

El trompeta le llame diligente,
dando fuerza de ley al viento vano,
y al son esté el ejército obediente.

¡Con cuánta majestad llena la mano
la pica, y el mosquete carga el hombro,
de que se attreve a ser buen castellano!

Con asco entre las otras gentes nombro
al que de su persona, sin decoro,
más quiere nota dar que dar asombro.

Jineta y caña son contagio moro;
restitúyanse justas y torneos,
y hagan paces las capas con el toro.

Pasadnos vos de juegos a trofeos;
que sólo grande rey y buen privado
pueden ejecutar estos deseos.

Vos, que hacéis repetir siglo pasado
con desembarazarnos las personas
y sacar los miembros de cuidado;

you gave us liberty with the Walloon collar (in exchange for the ruff) so that heads might be courteous, ridding crowns of their cares.

And since you have reformed the outside, give medicine to the better part (the soul); let the theatres be turned back into fortresses.

For the courtly star which allows you to enjoy favour without designs or vengeances (of your own) – a miracle which throws envy into a passion –

has, as its one blessing, a fearful acknowledgement (of responsibility): no presumptuous or blind confidence.

And if your noble ancestor gave you shields full of arms and blasons, and glorious martyrdom for your crest,

let those (of your ancestors) who were good Guzmans be the better for you, and let this scornful pinnacle grudgingly give you a view only of quiet fields.

May you achieve such a happy age, my lord, and when banded and warlike assailants try our strength,

may the military, a brave discipline, have more followers than the bull-ring; may false cloth and fine cloth take their rest.

May the cuirass replace the Moorish robe, and unless the Corpus Christi dances require it, let gauzes and tinsel play no part (literally, take no tricks).

The man who divides (gauze and tinsel) into thirty ribbons performs feats at the expense of the bull, and the (tailor's) rod that measures out the ribbons performs other feats at his expense with the (tailor's) finger.*

See that this is so, and I can assure you that you will restore more than Pelayo did, for fear will do the work of armies and the heavens will see you wielding their thunderbolt.

* In other words, makes him look like a vain fool.

vos distes libertad con las valonas
para que sean corteses las cabezas,
desnudando el enfado a las coronas.

Y, pues vos enmendastes las cortezas,
dad a la mejor parte medicina:
vuélvanse los tablados fortalezas.

Que la cortés estrella que os inclina
a privar, sin intento y sin venganza,
milagro que a la invidia desatina,

tiene por sola bienaventuranza
el reconocimiento temeroso:
no presumida y ciega confianza.

Y si os dio el ascendiente generoso
escudos, de armas y blasones llenos,
y por timbre el martirio glorioso,

mejores sean por vos los que eran buenos
Guzmanes, y la cumbre desdeñosa
os muestre a su pesar campos serenos.

Lograd, señor, edad tan venturosa;
y cuando nuestras fuerzas examina
persecución unida y belicosa,

la militar, valiente disciplina
tenga más platicantes que la plaza;
descansen tela falsa y tela fina.

Suceda a la marlota la coraza,
y si el Corpus con danzas no los pide,
velillos y oropel no hagan baza.

El que en treinta lacayos los divide,
hace suerte en el toro, y con un dedo
la hace en él la vara que los mide.

Mandadlo ansí; que aseguraros puedo
que habéis de restaurar más que Pelayo,
pues valdrá por ejércitos el miedo,
y os verá el cielo administrar su rayo.

To Rome Buried in its Ruins

YOU look for Rome in Rome, oh traveller, and in Rome herself you do not find Rome: the walls that she boasted of are a corpse, and the Aventine is its own tomb.

The Palatine lies where it used to reign, and medals filed down by time appear more like the relics of ancient battles than the insignia of Rome.

Only the Tiber has remained, and its current, which washed her as a city now bewails her as a tomb with mournful sounds of woe.

Oh Rome, in your greatness and your beauty, what was firm has fled, and only the transient remains and lasts.

ADDITION to good fortune, and consolation in adversity, master key that by a secret of nature knows how to enclose two wills in one;

prop of human conduct; secure anchor for the unsteady ship of human life; mild law that keeps all that is beneath the moon at peace:

such is blessed friendship, a divine virtue that does not postpone the prize of its possession, for it is itself its own fruit;

to which nature is so kind that the most savage animal can admonish the man who can live without it.

A Roma sepultada en sus ruinas

BUSCAS en Roma a Roma ¡oh peregrino!
y en Roma misma a Roma no la hallas:
cadáver son las que ostentó murallas,
y, tumba de sí propio, el Aventino.

Yace, donde reinaba, el Palatino;
y limadas del tiempo las medallas,
más se muestran destrozo a las batallas
de las edades, que blasón latino.

Sólo el Tíber quedó; cuya corriente,
si ciudad la regó, ya sepultura
la llora con funesto son doliente.

¡Oh Roma!, en tu grandeza, en tu hermosura
huyó lo que era firme, y solamente
lo fugitivo permanece y dura.

JUAN RUIZ DE ALARCÓN

AUMENTO de la próspera fortuna
y alivio en la infeliz; maestra llave
que con un natural secreto sabe
dos voluntades encerrar en una;

del humano gobierno la coluna;
ancla segura de la incierta nave
de la vida mortal: fuero suave
que en paz mantiene cuanto ve la luna

es la santa amistad, virtud divina
que no dilata el premio de tenella,
pues ella misma es de sí misma el fruto;

a quien naturaleza tanto inclina
que al hombre que vivir sabe sin ella
sabe avisar el animal más bruto.

THE flowery hills on which the April bull pastured in the mountains are now hills of snow, and the cruel north-wind prevents the shepherds from entering and leaving their huts.

The days have found themselves so diminished that in their brief hours, when no work is possible, the pastures have hardly seen the light and the hill has seen little more than gleams.

All is becoming disturbed and angry, wrapped in snow and beneath the wind, the plantation groans and Manzanares swells.

The heavens fail to recognize their kingdom; sometimes it seems to them like a silver orb, at other times to be tumbling from its seat.

To the Tomb of Adonis

STRIP off the leaves from those shrines dedicated to the lamps of the sky, those scaly deities, the nereids, and let the gilded lyres show mute between the thorns.

Now that the springs are dry, let the meadows weep and the pinks cease to glow; and let the woods, today deserted by Love, lay bare the starkness of the ruins.

The god of our forests is dead, dead, and so is the song whose measured harmony stopped the birds in the air and stilled the wind.

DON FRANCISCO DE BORJA Y ACEVEDO, PRÍNCIPE DE ESQUILACHE

MONTES de nieve son los que de flores
pació el toro de abril en las montañas,
y el cierzo airado impide en sus cabañas
le entrada y la salida a los pastores.

Mirábanse los días tan menores
que en breves horas, al trabajo extrañas,
la luz apenas vieron las campañas
y el monte poco más que resplandores.

Todo se altera, todo se embravece,
y envueltos con la nieve y con el viento,
el soto gime y Manzanares crece.

Su imperio desconoce el firmamento
y orbe de plata a veces le parece,
y otras, que se trastorna de su asiento.

JUAN DE TASIS, CONDE DE VILLAMEDIANA

Al Sepulcro de Adonis

DESFRONDAD a los templos consagrados
a las del cielo lámparas Dorinas
escamosas deidades, y entre espinas,
mudos se dejen ver plectros dorados.

Las fuentes secas ya, lloren los prados
y dejen de flagrar las clavellinas,
indiquen el rigor de las rüinas
los hoy bosques de Amor desamparados.

Muerto es el dios de nuestras selvas, muerto,
y el canto cuya métrica armonía
las aves suspendió y enfrenó el viento.

Come then, Cyprian, when you have seen the gaping breast of bold Adonis, with due grief to pay tribute of flowers and tears to this movement (of sorrow).

To a Lady Singing

THE rare voice and the clear tone issuing from that sweet throat, with their soft affect on the ear, might well cause any pain to cease.

But the new rapture that I feel contains another mystery, which I do not understand. For when the sensation is at its height, the feelings find a cause for grief.

The effects are contradictory, because the same song, by the amazement with which it strikes, makes madness sane and reason mad.

And by a fresh miracle or fresh enchantment, when the voice sounds most sweetly, it touches the soul with echoes of grief.

THE man born in the sterile region of our age owes so little to time that, when guilt and deception have had their rewards, merit shrinks and is scorned.

To be a purposeless and hopeless yearning, and a natural resource to strangers, to announce insults by (showing) the injuries, to have to be grateful when injured.

Ambitious schemes and anger applauded, where the only true course is the proper fear of one who sees the mischief and retires;

violent adulation, skilful deception, with all faith broken, have given lying the force of law and the resemblance of courage.

Venga, pues, Cipria, visto el pecho abierto
el Adonis osado, en ansia pía
a dar flores y llanto al movimiento.

A una señora que cantaba

LA peregrina voz y el claro acento
por la dulce garganta despedido,
con el süave efecto del oído
bien pueden suspender cualquier tormento.

Mas el nuevo accidente que yo siento
otro misterio tiene no entendido,
pues en la mayor gloria del sentido,
halla causa de pena el sentimiento.

Efectos varios, porque el mismo canto
deja en la suspensión con que enajena
cuerdo el enloquecer, la razón loca.

Y por nuevo milagro o nuevo encanto,
cuando la voz más dulcemente suena,
con ecos de dolor el alma toca.

DEBE tan poco al tiempo el que ha nacido
en la estéril región de nuestros años,
que premiada la culpa y los engaños,
el mérito se encoge escarnecido.

Ser un inútil anhelar perdido,
y natural remedio a los extraños;
avisar las ofensas con los daños,
y haber de agradecer el ofendido.

Máquina de ambición, aplausos de ira
donde sólo es verdad el justo miedo
del que percibe el daño y se retira;

violenta adulación, mañoso enredo,
en fe violada han puesto a la mentira,
fuerza de ley y sombra de denuedo.

LET my desires cease now that they are disabused of their tiresome and persistent yearnings, and let my hopes, belied before they were formed, cease here.

Not mocked now but admonished, my cries will reach kind ears; my eyes will see a sun and some days, that are made up of uncorrupted hours.

The clear motion of these waves is a mirror which shows me my punishment in the purest glass of its shores,

All that is now left to rely on is the tribunal of the winds for my complaints and an obscure hope for my fortune.

A Loving Fancy Addressed to Silence

LEAVE your hidden abode, mute silence, for on the cold bank of this sacred river, and in this solitary and untilled valley, my heart awaits you. Enter into my heart and I will tell you fearfully what I tell to none and what Love can testify, though I hardly dare reveal it even to you. Come, faithful silence, and listen carefully, you alone and my silent thought.

You shall hear, but I should not wish the soft zephyr to hear me and to tell my words to Echo in some hollow tree, or for Guadalquivir, hidden in his

CESEN mis ansias ya desengañadas
del prolijo anhelar de mis porfías,
cesen aquí las esperanzas mías
desmentidas primero que formadas.

No escarnecidas ya, sino avisadas
mis voces lograrán orejas pías,
un sol verán mis ojos y unos días
que consten de horas nunca adulteradas.

De estas ondas el claro movimiento
espejo es que me muestra en el más puro
cristal de sus orillas mi escarmiento.

Quedándole ya sólo por seguro
a mi querella el tribunal del viento,
a mi fortuna un esperar oscuro.

JUAN DE JÁUREGUI

Afecto amoroso comunicado al silencio

DEJA tu albergue oculto,
mudo silencio; que en el margen frío
deste sagrado río,
y en este valle solitario inculto,
te aguarda el pecho mío.
Entra en mi pecho y te diré medroso,
lo que a ninguno digo,
de que es amor testigo,
y aun a ti revelarlo apenas oso.
Ven, ¡oh silencio fiel!, y escucha atento,
tú solo y mi callado pensamiento.

Sabrás, mas no querría
me oyese el blando céfiro, y al eco
en algún tronco hueco
comunicase la palabra mía,
o que en la agua fría

cold water, to overhear me. You must learn with what pleasing pains heaven ordains that Love's sweet flames shall burn me, and that when my heart is destroyed his fires must live on, satisfied with the torments they inflict.

I am delivered to the soft fires of a supreme passion and I ask for no relief, nor does she who must needs inflict them know my suffering, for my tongue is not bold enough (to trouble) her chaste ear; in short I expect no greater comfort than to know that the fire in which I suffer and burn is Heaven, and that the honour of this illustrious service is sufficient reward for my desires.

If such extremes amaze you, friendly Silence, do not, oh do not suppose that I am following the vain reasoning of lovers. I am not surprised that you should stand aghast, but I insist on your believing in the truth of what I say. Torture is my delight, the flame is my nourishment and on it my ideas are fed. With such gifts does the fair cause of my pains and fires inflame my heart.

I do not deny, Silence, that sometimes I should like boldly to try to make Lisarda hear how much the fire of seeing her burns me, and make her believe that I speak the truth. I burn in the pure air of bright day, and night sees me burning; I burn with a new ardour when night's dark shadow deflects the sun, and all objects are alike a burning flame to my eyes.

el Betis escondido me escuchase;
sabrás que el cielo ordena
con que alegre pena
en dulces llamas el amor me abrase,
y que su fuego, el corazón deshecho,
de sus tormentos viva satisfecho.

Al incendio süave
de un soberano ardor estoy rendido,
que ni remedio pido,
ni quien le me ha de dar penas sabe,
porque a su casto oído
no se atreve mi lengua; en fin, no aguardo
otro mayor consuelo,
sino saber que un cielo
es el incendio en que padezco y ardo,
y que el honor de tan ilustre empleo
es premio suficiente a mi deseo.

Si extremos semejantes
te maravillan, ¡oh silencio amigo!
no entiendas, no, que sigo
el vano razonar de los amantes.
No extraño que te espantes;
pretendo sí que mis verdades creas.
Mi gozo es el tormento,
el fuego mi sustento,
y deste me alimentan mis ideas.
Con tal regalo, el corazón me inflama
la causa bella de mi pena y llama.

Silencio, no te niego
que osado alguna vez tentar quisiera
que ya Lisarda oyera
cuánto me abrasa de su vista el fuego,
y mi verdad creyera.
Ardo en la pura luz del claro día,
veme la noche ardiendo;
en nuevo ardor me enciendo
cuando su oscura sombra el sol desvía,
y todos los objetos igualmente
son a mis ojos una llama ardiente.

But – with proper prudence – I shun her hearing you, whenever it comes to the point of my tongue informing her, and my bold voice finally offending her. Oh happy paradise, heaven forbid that a brief pang shall disturb the sweet calm of your serene beauty, even though the soul may suffer for a thousand centuries. Tell her, Silence, by mute signs, what she has never known and you do not doubt.

But, oh, do not tell her, for you will have to tell her in my presence and even though I am aware of your prudence and modesty, in the end you master me, and fear says to me in deliberate tones: 'You have been not a little bold in merely loving her; do not venture on any greater enterprise. Let it be enough that secret silence and your memory know the secret of your love'.

To a Ship Wrecked on the Sea-shore

THIS useless bark, dry and broken, now so despised by water and wind, looked with scorn on the vast movements of the stormy sea, of the east and the south winds.

Proud towards the deep, obedient to its pilot, and always thirsty for the rich metal, it brought the ores which it took aboard in the distant Indies to their Spanish destination.

Now it lies far from the dear woods in which it might have kept its green decoration better than it could cargoes of treasure.

So the man who follows miserly greed sometimes perishes miserably in a foreign land, lacking both consolation and wealth.

Mas huyo que te entienda
(¡justo recato!) si ha de ser preciso
le dé mi lengua aviso,
y mi atrevida voz al fin ofenda.
¡Oh alegre paraíso!
no quiera el cielo que la dulce calma
de tu beldad serena
turbe una breve pena,
aunque mil siglos la padezca el alma;
dile, silencio, tú, con señas mudas,
lo que ha ignorado siempre y tú no dudas.

Mas ¡ay! no se lo digas
que es forzoso decirlo en mi presencia,
y bien que la decencia
de tu recato advierto, al fin me obligas
y el temor ya me dice en voz expresa:
«No has sido poco osado
sólo en haberla amado:
no te abalances a mayor empresa;
basta que sepan tu amorosa historia
el secreto silencio y tu memoria.»

A un navío destrozado en la ribera del mar

ESTE bajel inútil, seco y roto,
tan despreciado ya del agua y viento,
vio con desprecio el vasto movimiento
del proceloso mar, del Euro y Noto.

Soberbio al golfo, humilde a su piloto,
y del rico metal siempre sediento,
trajo sus minas al ibero asiento
habidas en el índico remoto.

Ausente yace de la selva cara,
do el verde ornato conservar pudiera,
mejor que pudo cargas de tesoro.

Así quien sigue la codicia avara,
tal vez mezquino muere en extranjera
provincia, falto de consuelo y oro.

FRANCISCO DE RIOJA

To the Marvel of Peru

[the plant from which rouge is manufactured and which flowers only in the afternoon]

SAD hours and few the heavens gave you for life, and you, in disobedience to its eternal law, provoke it to no slight anger, and raise your tender head – bathed, shall I say, in flames or in purple? From the great shadow in the dark veil, parched and shrunken and wilting, you just survive to see the rosy white light of day. Speedy death is such a short way from your birth! If, then, it was decreed of old that you should pack the brief time of your life into the mere circle of one cold night, what good will it do you to flee, with the ambitious intention of adding moments to your life? Do not boldly disturb the deep seas' hoary breast, for they may, to your undoing, refuse a path to your serrated pine, and instead of the welcome that you have always found in the brown bosom of the hard earth, you may find a tomb in its waters. Tell me, what foolish passion urges you to see Apollo's splendid ray? What flower of all those that May spills in such plenty do its great fires not wither? Oh, what a vain mistake it is to weary oneself in order to see the splendours of a burning tyrant who unkindly robs flowers of their sheen, their odour, and their colours! And you, wonderful and inconstant, the night's sweet

FRANCISCO DE RIOJA

A la arrebolera

TRISTES horas y pocas
dio a tu vivir el cielo,
y tú, a su eterna ley mal obediente,
a no fáciles iras lo provocas;
alzas la tierna frente,
¿diré en llama o en púrpura bañada?
De la gran sombra en el oscuro velo,
y mustia y encogida y desmayada,
llegas a ver del día
la blanca luz rosada.
¡Tan poco se desvía
de tu nacer la muerte arrebatada!
Si es pues de alto decreto
que el tiempo breve de tu edad incluyas
en solo el cerco de una noche fría,
¿qué te valdrá que huyas
con ambicioso afeto
de acrecentarle instantes a la vida?
No inquietes atrevida
el cano seno a los profundos mares,
que por ventura negarán camino
en daño tuyo a tu serrado pino,
y en vez de la acogida
que en las pardas entrañas
hallaste siempre de la tierra dura,
hallarás en sus aguas sepultura.
Dime, ¿cuál necio ardor te solicita
por ver de Apolo el refulgente rayo?
¿Qúe flor de las que en larga copia el mayo
vierte, su grave incendio no marchita?
¡Oh, cómo es error vano
fatigarse por ver los resplandores
de un ardiente tirano
que impío roba a las flores
el lustre y el aliento y los colores!
Y tú, admirable y vaga,
dulce honor y cuidado de la noche,

ornament and care, if the sun's flame and colour are extinguished, what better fortune can be yours from whom the time of your existence flees so fast? The long course of the years is no more than one long succession of disasters. If the hours that you live are short, oh what glories you enjoy! You bind the divine temples of the silent, dark night, and not just once does the sleepy goddess offer the dye of your lovely colour to the dawns for their brows and hair. Leave the ambitious sea; for, despite your immense and prolonged wanderings, fortune will not add a single hour to your life, not even if you move to a place so far away that it is visited by another sun and another moon; and spend in leisure and fortunate peace the dark and brief time of your life, awaiting that ultimate swoon from which come your splendour and your purple.

On the Fleetness and Passage of Time

WITH what fleet steps you run by! Oh how you leave me, vain time! Oh tyrant over my fortune and my being, how continually I feel your lordly hand!

I thought that I could stop you, but you fled past; that I could follow you, but you went proudly away. I wasted you in seeking you, inhuman entity, and the more I sought you the more I lost you.

si la llama y color el sol se apaga,
¿cuál mayor dicha tuya
que el tiempo de tu edad tan veloz huya?
No es más el luengo curso de los años
que un espacioso número de daños.
Si vives breves horas,
¡oh cuántas glorias tienes!
Tú las divinas sienes
ciñes de la callada noche oscura,
y no una vez ofrece a las auroras
la soñolienta diosa
de tus colores bellos
tintas para su frente y sus cabellos.
Deja el mar ambiciosa;
que por tu errar inmenso y dilatado
no añadirá fortuna
hora a tu edad alguna,
ni por mudar lugar tan apartado,
que otro sol lo visite y otra luna;
y pasa en ocio y paz aventurada
de tu vivir el tiempo oscuro y breve,
esperando aquel último desmayo
a quien tu luz y púrpura se debe.

LUIS DE CARRILLO Y SOTOMAYOR

A la ligereza y pérdida del tiempo

¡CON qué ligeros pasos vas corriendo!
¡Oh cómo te me ausentas, tiempo vano!
¡Ay, de mi bien y de mi ser tirano,
cómo tu altivo brazo voy sintiendo!

Detenerte pensé, pasaste huyendo;
seguirte y ausentástete liviano.
Gastete a ti en buscarte, ¡oh inhumano!
mientras más te busqué te fui perdiendo.

Now I know your anger; now that I am brought low I am the spoils of your scythe, oh bitter disillusionment unconfessed!

I lived blind and was finally disabused. Made an Argus in my sorrow, with sad eyes I see you fly and see that I have lost you.

On the Duration of a Thought

YOUR proud forehead was not only the envy of the ground, not only envied by a star, oh gallant tower, as feared as you were beautiful, and as respected as you were feared.

Now overthrown – what does not Time lay low? – you increase Saguntum's tears; the ivy, a guest which embraces it (the tower) will not see it, or it (the tower) hides its affronts in it (the ivy).

Its strength did not give it faith. But what homage does stern Time leave that it does not throw to the winds, to rely on its own wings?

There is no brass that is secure against its strength. You, in your grief, seek eternity, valour and firmness, not in brass or in a tower, but in a thought.

The Friendship of a Brook Paid for in Tears

NOW the crystal of your lovely course, which is bright truth to the neighbouring flowers, unreservedly murmurs my love when I most tenderly complain.

Ya conozco tu furia, ya, humillado,
de tu guadaña pueblo los despojos,
¡oh amargo desengaño no admitido!

Ciego viví, y al fin desengañado.
Hecho Argos de mi mal, con tristes ojos
huir te veo, y veo te he perdido.

A la duración de un pensamiento

NO sólo envidia al suelo, no envidiada
sólo tu altiva frente de una estrella,
era, ¡oh gallarda torre, cuanto bella
temida y cuan temida respetada!

Ya – ¿qué no allana el tiempo? – derribada
creces llanto a Sagunto; niega vella
la hiedra, huésped que se abraza en ella,
o ella se esconde en ella, de afrentada.

No le prestó su fe su fortaleza.
Mas, ¿qué homenaje deja el tiempo duro
que en brazos de sus alas no dé al viento?

No hay bronce que a su fuerza esté seguro.
Tu, triste, eternidad, valor, firmeza
buscas, no a bronce o torre: a un pensamiento.

PEDRO SOTO DE ROJAS

Amistad de arroyo correspondida en llanto

YA los cristales de tu curso bello,
clara verdad de las vecinas flores,
murmuran sin recato mis amores:
cuando más tiernamente me querello.

Now it reveals the yoke round my neck, my cheeks furrowed with grief, the colours of their fields withered, and the mountains of the hair covered with snow.

You have shown me very plainly, friend brook, my wild lunacy – but, what matter? – if you instruct the trees of that meadow;

but today you will emulate the river with the payment I shall give you for your pains , in the streams of this, my weeping.

To a Linnet

OH how like is my sad life to yours! You are caged and I am caged, you sing and I sing, you are simple and I am senseless, I am in an eternal anxiety and you are restless. You give music to her that prevents your flight, and I give music, though to the accompaniment of tears, to her who holds me on a harsh chain. But the difference between your present state and mine is that you, linnet, live by singing, and I in singing die.

THAT sweetest of birds and this loveliest of flowers were scattering their gentlest love in songs and smooth mother-of-pearl,

Ya me descubren la coyunda al cuello,
mis mejillas surcadas con dolores,
marchitas de sus campos las colores
y nevados los montes del cabello.

Bien claro, amigo arroyo, me has mostrado,
(mas, ¡qué mucho!), mi loco desvarío
si doctrinas los troncos de aquel prado;

pues hoy harás emulación al río
con la paga que ofrezco a tu cuidado
en las corrientes deste llanto mío.

A un jilguero

¡OH cuánto es a la tuya parecida
ésta mi triste vida!
Tú preso estás, yo preso;
tú cantas, yo canto,
tú simple, yo sin seso,
yo en eterna inquietud, y tú travieso.
Música das a quien tu vuelo enfrena;
música doy (aunque a compás del llanto)
a quien me tiene en áspera cadena.
En lo que es diferente
nuestro estado presente
es en que tú, jilguero,
vives cantando, y yo cantando muero.

FRAY JERÓNIMO DE SAN JOSÉ

AQUELLA, la más dulce de las aves,
y ésta, la más hermosa de las flores,
esparcían blandísimos amores
en cánticos y nácares süaves,

when in suspense, between great troubles, a soul which was waiting for its perfection precipitately entrusted the keys of its heart to superior powers.

If here in life's desert, he said, a rose so exalts a nightingale, and its beauty and sweetness are so great, what will the promised woodland be? Oh sweet melody ever new! Oh ever bravely flowering beauty!

Ballad to Lesbia

TO the sound of the chestnuts leaping in the fire, pour out the wine, boy; drink, Lesbia, and let us play, even if Capricorn is hurling his spears of frost – a bad augury for the married, a good omen for bachelors; an enemy of Bacchus when he was on earth, destroying his vines and feeding on his vine-shoots, and not so docile today that he does not attempt to see us soaked by countless floods and frozen by countless frosts. I will swear, dear Lesbia, that if heaven were to give him power in his own right, he would make us barren.

cuando suspensa entre cuidados graves,
un alma, que atendía a sus primores,
arrebatada a objetos superiores,
les entregó del corazón las llaves.

Si aquí, dijo, en el yermo de esta vida,
tanto una rosa un ruiseñor eleva,
tan grande es su belleza y su dulzura,

¿cuál será la floresta prometida?
¡Oh dulce melodía siempre nueva!
¡Oh siempre floridísima hermosura!

ESTEBAN MANUEL DE VILLEGAS

Cantinela a Lesbia

AL son de las castañas
que saltan en el fuego,
echa vino, muchacho,
beba Lesbia y juguemos,
siquiera el Capricornio
tire lanzas de hielo,
mal agüero a casados,
buen auspicio a solteros;
enemigo de Baco
cuando estaba en el suelo,
destrozándole vides,
rumiándole sarmientos,
y agora no tan dócil
que no procure vernos
aguados con mil aguas
y helados con mil hielos.
Yo apostaré, mi Lesbia,
que si le diese el cielo
poder en causa propria,
que nos hiciese yermos.

And what an end the insolent fellow would put to the vine-country – and then into the Darro with all those who were thirsty! For more ills come to the body from drinking your waters, Tagus, than come from jumping into the waters of Ebro; but since the stars have not made it as bad as this, pour out the wine, boy; drink, Lesbia, and let us play.

THE ladies of today, Bras, are not content with graces; they love you dearly if you give them presents, and better if you give them more.

Today love is not child-like or blind, and he does not thank you for toys, because by tears and persistence snow glows in place of fire. He looks at the present and not the suit, and Venus turns to Pallas. They love you dearly, etc.

The most exalted plume flies from the danger of wax, and melts like the white foam on the shore; let no one who does not give presume, rather let him throw away his wings. They love you dearly, etc.

¡Oh cómo el insolente
diera fin al viñedo,
y juntamente en Darro
con todos los sedientos!
porque daños mayores
se le siguen al cuerpo
beber tus aguas, Tajo,
que echarse en las del Ebro;
pero ya que los astros
mejor que esto lo hicieron,
echa vino, muchacho,
beba Lesbia y juguemos.

FRANCISCO DE TRILLO Y FIGUEROA

LAS damas de ogaño, Bras,
no se contentan con galas;
querránte bien si regalas,
y más si regalas más.

Ya el amor no es niño y ciego,
ni agradece niñerías,
porque a llantos y porfías,
nieve enciende en vez de fuego.
La oferta mira, no el ruego,
volviéndose Venus Palas.
Querránte bien si regalas,
y más si regalas más.

La más levantada pluma
vuela ya riesgos de cera,
siendo como en la ribera,
deshecha la blanca espuma,
nada quien no da presuma,
antes arroje las alas.
Querránte bien si regalas,
y más si regalas más.

Now the best way to favour is the path of interest, and the bigger the bribe the bigger the compliment. There is no love except by this method, for it is in vain that you scale the heavens. They love you dearly, etc.

The most ingenious arguments have no force unless they give. There is no virtue that is not perverted by the stupid man who speaks in doubloons; he captivates hearts with his mettle and his fine clothes. They love you dearly, etc.

What happens if you see a shepherd talking and a noble citizen with him, if the former offers his (full) hand and the latter offers his love? They will give the shepherd the favour and fling pellets at the citizen. They love you dearly if you give them presents, and better if you give them more.

On the Portrait of a Lady Done in Wax, Alluding to the Inconstancy of Women

THE original is stone, the portrait wax; the first is ungrateful, the second a flatterer. Who joined hard marble with soft wax, when the latter is merciful, the former ungrateful?

Who but love could do so with his intriguing? Who but intrigue could do anything with love? As the sun and the moon in the upper sphere have an arrangement with the darkness and the light.

Ya para dar un favor
el mejor camino es
el paso del interés,
y mejor cuanto mejor.
No hay sin este medio amor,
porque en vano el cielo escalas.
Querránte bien si regalas,
y más si regalas más.

Las más discretas razones
si no dan, no tienen fuerza,
y no hay valor que no tuerza
el necio que habla en doblones;
cautiva los corazones
con su brío, con sus galas.
Querránte bien si regalas,
y más si regalas más.

¿Qué es ver hablar a un pastor
junto a un noble ciudadano,
si aquel extiende la mano,
y aqueste extiende el amor?
A aquel le dan el favor,
y a aqueste le arrojan balas.
Querránte bien si regalas,
y más si regalas más.

A un retrato de una dama, hecho de cera, aludiendo a la inconstancia de las mujeres

PIEDRA el original, cera el retrato,
aquel ingrato, aquesta lisonjera.
¿Quién mármol duro unió con blanda cera
si ésta es piadosa y aquél es ingrato?

¿Quién sino amor pudiera con su trato?
¿Quién sino el trato con amor pudiera?
Como el sol y la luna en la alta esfera
con la sombra y la luz tienen contrato.

It was well then that a murmuring bee offered his libation of flowers to Fili's portrait, for love turns hard marble to wax.

But, alas, she is wax in her inconstancy, and stone only in her cruelty. Who then is safe from her inconstancy?

THESE which were pomp and delight, waking at the first morning light, will be in the evening a vain object of compassion, sleeping in the arms of the cold night.

This blending of colours that challenges the heavens, a rainbow striped with gold, snow, and scarlet, will be an object lesson to human life. So much is attempted in the limits of a single day!

The roses got up early to flower and flowered to grow old; they found their cradle and their tomb in a bud.

Even so have men found their fortunes, in one day they have been born and expired; for when the centuries have passed they were but hours.

On the Deceptiveness of Human Life

WITHOUT any knowledge of my error, the years of so wasted a life – their terrible wound being incurable – were not years, but centuries of torment.

Bien, pues, de Fili abeja susurrante,
al retrato ofreció libadas flores,
pues amor vuelve cera el mármor duro.

Mas, ¡ay de mí! que es cera en lo inconstante,
y piedra solamente en los rigores.
¿Quién pues de su inconstancia está seguro?

PEDRO CALDERÓN DE LA BARCA

ÉSTAS que fueron pompa y alegría
despertando al albor de la mañana,
a la tarde serán lástima vana
durmiendo en brazos de la noche fría.

Este matiz que al cielo desafía,
iris listado de oro, nieve y grana,
será escarmiento de la vida humana:
¡tanto se emprende en término de un día!

A florecer las rosas madrugaron
y para envejecerse florecieron:
cuna y sepulcro en un botón hallaron.

Tales los hombres sus fortunas vieron,
en un día nacieron y espiraron;
que pasados los siglos, horas fueron.

ANTONIO ENRÍQUEZ GÓMEZ

Al engaño de la vida humana

SIN tener de mi error conocimiento,
los años de una vida tan perdida
(siendo incurable su terrible herida),
años no fueron, siglos de tormento.

I lived by dying. Oh mad thought! How can you choose to live, your brief life being your own life's murderer, an inner Hydra of blind understanding?

Live in order to die: and if you trust in the life you are leading, count your hurts, the external cause of your logical persistence (in your errors).

See that when you elect disillusion, you will be short of years and days, and you will have days and years too many.

The Orange-trees

THOSE lovely orange-trees whose flowers breathe amber on the meadows are pomanders in the sun's brazier: a perpetual and lovely emerald, in which the loquacious nightingale with harmonious voice tells us a thousand tales; among whose tender leaves the flowers which April shaped from short-lived stars of snow are fragrant clusters: the metamorphoses of time which will sweetly transform what are diamonds today into topazes tomorrow; to whose green liveries crystal twigs give handsome ornaments and a most

Viví muriendo; ¡oh loco pensamiento!
¿Cómo quieres vivir, siendo homicida
tu vida breve de tu propria vida,
hidra interior del ciego entendimiento?

Vive para morir; y si te fías
de la vida que traes, cuenta los daños,
causa exterior de lógicas porfías.

Mira que cuando quieras desengaños,
te faltarán los años y los días,
y sobrarán los días y los años.

SALVADOR JACINTO POLO DE MEDINA

Los naranjos

POMOS de olor son al prado
en el brasero del sol
estos naranjos hermosos
que ámbar exhala su flor.
Perpetua esmeralda bella
donde, en numerosa voz,
mil parlerías nos cuenta
el bachiller ruiseñor;
entre cuyas tiernas hojas
las flores que abril formó
de estrellas breves de nieve
racimos fragantes son.
Metamorfoseos del tiempo
que, en dulce transformación,
hará topacios mañana
los que son diamantes hoy;
a cuyas libreas verdes
dan vistosa guarnición
ramilletes de cristal,
fragantísimo candor.

fragrant whiteness. Rich mine of the valley where shy January gave us free gold and showy May free silver.

The Icarus
[a moth]

THROUGH seas of brightness you propel lights with soft oars, bold Icarus, you go to perish in the sun, moth; but a furious wave hurls you down on fire, oh plume of feathers, destroyed by the clouds for climbing to the golden ocean; and in your swift fall you return there, and with fiery wings seek to breast the winds of thirsty glass in the moist element; but the foam gives a soft burial to your flaming feathers.

Indian Pinks

SHORT-LIVED treasure, rich Indian flower, and sun curled into petals, flowered gold who deny your country, who despoil your East and settle in foreign valleys, and end up beneath the protection of laurels and rural oaks. For you, in his winged bark, the miser, the greedy and arrogant, passed courageously through coral forests, without the fatal destiny that attacks him presuming to raise its mountains of foam in its glassy valleys.

Rico mineral del valle,
adonde franco nos dio,
oro el enero encogido;
plata, el mayo ostentador.

El Ícaro

POR mares de esplendor navegas luces
con blandos remos, Ícaro atrevido,
a perderte en el sol vas, mariposa;
mas una ola furiosa
te despeña encendido,
penacho, destrozado por las nubes,
porque al dorado océano te subes;
y en veloz precipio vuelves luego,
y con alas de fuego
pretendes en el húmedo elemento
los vientos de cristal volar sediento;
pero dan las espumas
blando sepulcro a tus flamantes plumas.

Las clavellinas de Indias

BREVE tesoro, rica flor indiana,
y sol rizado en hojas,
oro florido que tu patria niegas,
que a tu oriente despojas
y en extranjeros valles te avecinas,
y a ser desvelo llegas
de laureles y rústicas encinas.
Por ti en alado pino,
por selvas de coral, pasó animoso
el avariento, el vano codicioso,
sin que el fatal destino
que le asalte, presuma
en valles de cristal, montes de espuma.

The Rose

THE snowy foot of a falcon, an experiment in mother-of-pearl, this rose, the coral answer to the cruel thorn's treacherous blow, to the blow of the bold and sacrilegious lancet, for when the punctured vein spilled ruby the tiniest drop proclaimed itself a flower: (rose) whose flowering beauty is the gold-crowned queen of the meadow, and an open ruff of rubies for majesty and honour, and on putting on the farthingale of its armour, lovely Venus wins the meadows' love, and without the hours counting her beauty, lives for ever immortal through centuries of dawns. At night fair flower of light in the sky, by day a mother-of-pearl star in the meadow.

THE eyes are large, the sight brief – or love cuts it short because it aims to wound – the brow is the bow, a glance the aim to which love owes its conquests.

On her cheek mother-of-pearl drinks mother-of-pearl, where in flames of coral a rose might have died, but its fire joins the white lily of tempered snow.

The art is excellent, but without art genius scores a certain hit, and not by luck; (her) step is measured and yet not studied.

Do not suspect acting in all her parts. She could be beautiful without beauty, and I in love without love.

La rosa

De un sacre pie de nieve,
experiencia de nácar, esta rosa,
respuesta de coral al golpe aleve
de espina rigorosa,
de lanceta sacrílega atrevida
que al derramar rubí la vena rota
se confesó flor por la menor gota:
cuya beldad florida
reina es del prado coronada de oro,
y por la majestad, por el decoro,
la lechuguilla abierta de rubíes,
y de sus armas puesto el verdugado
hermosa Venus enamora el prado,
y sin que cuenten su beldad las horas
vive siempre inmortal siglos de Auroras.
De noche, flor de luz al cielo bella;
de día, al prado nacarada estrella.

GABRIEL BOCÁNGEL Y UNZUETA

Grandes los ojos son, la vista breve,
(o amor la abrevia, porque a herir apunta)
arco es la ceja, y el mirar es punta,
a quien amor sus vencimientos debe.

A su mejilla el nácar, nácar bebe
adonde en llamas de coral, difunta
fuera la rosa, mas su incendio junta
a la azucena de templada nieve.

El arte es superior, pero sin arte
el ingenio es acierto, y no es ventura;
el andar es compás, y no es cuidado.

De tantas partes no presume parte,
hermosa pudo ser sin hermosura,
yo sin amor viviera enamorado.

On the Death of Rachel

JACOB weeps for his beloved Rachel's beauty, which has withered to an early end, which a powerful and mighty hand has cut off from the deceptive tree of life.

He sees the purple rose transformed to a livid colour, to empty dust, and the grace of the most elegant body brought to the earth and reduced to earth.

'Alas,' says he, 'how uncertain is joy! How vain is glory! How deceptive our pleasure! How insecure our condition! Who trusts in your green prime, inconstant life?

'For when she was at the height of her strength and charms, death robbed me in an instant of a possession that had cost me a weary time to win.'

Verses

against the inconsequence of men's taste and strictures, when they attack those qualities in women of which they are themselves the cause

STUPID men, who unreasonably attack women, without seeing that you are the cause of the very thing you blame;

if with unparalleled ardour you make love to their disdain, why do you expect them to act virtuously when you incite them to sin?

MIGUEL DE BARRIOS

A la muerte de Raquel

LLORA Jacob de su Raquel querida
la hermosura marchita en fin temprano,
que cortó poderosa y fuerte mano
del árbol engañoso de la vida.

Ve la purpúrea rosa convertida
en cárdeno color, en polvo vano,
y la gala del cuerpo más lozano
postrada en tierra, a tierra reducida.

«¡Ay!» dice, «¡gozo incierto! ¡gloria vana!
¡mentido gusto! ¡estado nunca fijo!
¿quién fía en tu verdor, vida inconstante?

Pues cuando más robusta y más lozana,
un bien que me costó tiempo prolijo
me lo quitó la muerte en un instante.»

SOR JUANA INÉS DE LA CRUZ

Redondillas

Arguye de inconsecuente el gusto y la censura de los hombres, que en las mujeres acusan lo que causan

HOMBRES necios, que acusáis
a la mujer sin razón,
sin ver que sois la ocasión
de lo mismo que culpáis;

si con ansia sin igual
solicitáis su desdén,
¿por qué queréis que obren bien
si las incitáis al mal!

You fight down their resistance, and then you solemnly say that what your persistence achieved was lightness on their part.

The audacity of your mad behaviour seems a deliberate imitation of the boy who sets up a bogey and is then frightened of it.

In your stupid presumption, you would like to find the woman you pursue a Thais when you woo her and a Lucrecia when won.

What behaviour could be stranger than that of the man who himself stupidly breathes on a mirror and is cross because it is not clear?

You set the same store on favours and on scorn, complaining if you are badly treated and mocking if you are loved.

No woman wins repute, for the most prudent woman is ungrateful if she does not admit you and loose if she does.

You always behave so stupidly that, with unjust impartiality, you blame one woman for being cruel, and another for being easy.

So how should the woman who seeks your love be constituted, if the ungrateful woman offends and the easy woman disgusts?

But between the disgust and pain that you are pleased to speak of, good luck to the woman who does not love you, complain as much as you will.

Combatís su resistencia,
y luego con gravedad
decís que fue liviandad
lo que hizo la diligencia.

Parecer quiere el denuedo
de vuestro parecer loco,
al niño que pone el coco,
y luego le tiene miedo.

Queréis con presunción necia
hallar a la que buscáis,
para pretendida, Thais,
y en posesión, Lucrecia.

¿Qué humor puede ser más raro,
que el que, falto de consejo,
él mismo empaña el espejo
y siente que no esté claro?

Con el favor y el desdén
tenéis condición igual,
quejándoos, si os tratan mal,
burlándoos, si os quieren bien.

Opinión ninguna gana,
pues la que más se recata,
si no os admite, es ingrata,
y si os admite, es liviana.

Siempre tan necios andáis,
que con desigual nivel,
a una culpáis por cruel,
y a otra por fácil culpáis.

¿Pues cómo ha de estar templada
la que vuestro amor pretende,
si la que es ingrata ofende
y la que es fácil enfada?

Mas entre el enfado y pena
que vuestro gusto refiere,
bien haya la que no os quiere
y quéjaos enhorabuena.

Your amorous teasing gives wing to their indiscretions, and after you have made the ladies wicked you want to find them very good.

Who is most to blame in a guilty passion, the woman who falls when she is begged, or the man who begs when he has fallen (on his knees)?

Or, which is most to blame, although both have done wrong, the woman who sins for payment, or the man who pays for the sin?

But why are you so astonished at what you are yourself to blame for? Like them as you make them, or make them as you would have them.

Stop pressing your suit, and then you will be more justified in blaming the fondness of the woman, who will have come to beg of you.

I have good reason for saying that your arrogance fights with many weapons, for with your promises and your insistence you band the devil, the flesh and the world together.

To a Linnet

CITHERN of carmine which at early dawn trilled a dirge for your beloved spouse and, feasting on the sweet perfume of the rose, stained your gold beak with coral.

Sweet linnet, sad little bird, who no sooner saw the lovely dawn than on the first note of a song you found death and lost the cadence.

Dan vuestras amantes penas
a sus libertades alas,
y después de hacerlas malas
las queréis hallar muy buenas.

¿Cuál mayor culpa ha tenido
en una pasión errada,
la que cae de rogada,
o el que ruega de caído?

O¿ cuál es más de culpar,
aunque cualquiera mal haga,
la que peca por la paga
o el que paga por pecar?

Pues¿ para qué os espantáis
de la culpa que tenéis?
Queredlas cual las hacéis
o hacedlas cual las buscáis.

Dejad de solicitar,
y después con más razón,
acusaréis la afición
de la que os fuere a rogar.

Bien con muchas armas fundo
que lidia vuestra arrogancia;
pues en promesa e instancia,
juntáis diablo, carne y mundo.

A un jilguero

CÍTARA de carmín que amaneciste
trinando endechas a tu amada esposa
y paciéndole el ámbar a la rosa
el pico de oro de coral teñiste.

Dulce jilguero, pajarillo triste,
que apenas el aurora viste hermosa,
cuando al tono primero de una glosa
la muerte hallaste y el compás perdiste.

There is in life no certain time for death, none: your own voice invites the huntsman, and guides the shot he fires to find its mark.

Oh fortune that man seeks and yet he fears! Who would have thought that your own life, from lack of silence, would have been the accomplice in your death?

To Hope

GREEN spell-binder of human existence, mad hope, gilded frenzy, what men dream of when they are awake, confused, as in a dream, worthless in her treasures;

soul of the world, flourishing senility, hope of a ripe old-age, the today desired by the lucky, and the unlucky man's tomorrow;

let them follow your name in search of your light, those who wear green spectacles and see everything painted as they desire it;

but I, wise in my fortune, keep both my eyes in my two hands and see only what I touch.

No hay en la vida, no, segura muerte;
tu misma voz al cazador convida,
para que el golpe cuando tira acierte.

¡Oh fortuna buscada, aunque temida!
¿Quién pensara que cómplice en tu muerte
fuera, por no callar, tu propia vida?

A la esperanza

VERDE embeleso de la vida humana,
loca esperanza, frenesí dorado,
sueño de los despiertos, intrincado,
como de sueños, de tesoros vana;

alma del mundo, senectud lozana,
decrépito verdor imaginado;
el hoy de los dichosos esperado
y de los desdichados el mañana:

sigan tu nombre en busca de tu día
los que, con verdes vidrios por anteojos,
todo lo ven pintado a su deseo;

que yo, más cuerda en la fortuna mía,
tengo en entrambas manos ambos ojos
y solamente lo que toco veo.

PART TWO

MODERN TIMES

GIANT waves that break with a roar on deserted and remote shores, carry me away with you, wrapped in a sheet of foam!

Hurricane gusts that bear off the withered leaves from the tall wood, dragging a whirlwind across the sky, carry me away with you!

Storm-clouds that the lightning breaks, and that decorate your torn fringes with fire, carry me away with you, dragged off among the dark mists!

Take me, out of pity, to that place where dizziness will take away my memory. Out of pity! . . . I am frightened to remain alone with my grief!

THE black swallows will return to hang their nests on your balcony, and once more, as they sport, to knock with their wings against its window-panes,

but those that stopped their flight to observe your beauty and my good fortune, those who learnt our names . . . they . . . will not return!

The thick honeysuckles of your garden will return to climb the walls, and will open their flowers in the evening once more, even more beautiful;

but those that were curded with dew, whose drops we saw tremble and fall, like day's tears . . . they . . . will not return!

GUSTAVO ADOLFO BÉCQUER

OLAS gigantes que os rompéis bramando
en las playas desiertas y remotas,
envuelto entre la sábana de espumas,
¡llevadme con vosotras!

Ráfagas de huracán, que arrebatáis
de alto bosque las marchitas hojas,
arrastrado en el cielo torbellino,
¡llevadme con vosotras!

Nubes de tempestad que rompe el rayo
y en fuego ornáis las desprendidas orlas,
arrebatado entre la niebla obscura,
¡llevadme con vosotras!

Llevadme, por piedad, adonde el vértigo
con la razón me arranque la memoria . . .
¡Por piedad! . . . ¡Tengo miedo de quedarme
con mi dolor a solas!

VOLVERÁN las oscuras golondrinas
en tu balcón sus nidos a colgar,
y otra vez con el ala a sus cristales
jugando llamarán;

pero aquellas que el vuelo refrenaban
tu hermosura y mi dicha al contemplar,
aquellas que aprendieron nuestros nombres . . .
ésas . . . ¡no volverán!

Volverán las tupidas madreselvas
de tu jardín las tapias a escalar,
y otra vez a la tarde, aun más hermosas,
sus flores se abrirán;

pero aquellas cuajadas de rocío,
cuyas gotas mirábamos temblar
y caer, como lágrimas de día . . .
ésas . . . ¡no volverán!

Burning words of love will sound once more in your ears; perhaps your heart will wake from its deep sleep:

but silent, absorbed and on their knees, as men worship God before his altar, as I have loved you . . . do not be deceived, you will not be loved like that!

I DID not sleep, but wandered in that limbo in which objects change shape, the mysterious tracts that separate waking from sleep.

Thoughts that revolved in their silent circuit about my brain gradually moved in their dance to slower time.

My lids veiled the reflection of the light that enters the soul through the eyes; but another light lit the world of visions from within.

At this point there echoed in my ears a sound like that which wavers confusedly in a church when the faithful are concluding their prayers with an amen.

And I seemed to hear a delicate and sad voice calling me from far away by my name, and I smelt the smell of snuffed candles, of dampness and incense.

Night came on and, in the arms of oblivion, I fell into her deep breast like a stone; I slept, and when I awoke I cried out: 'Someone whom I loved has died!'

Volverán del amor en tus oidos
las palabras ardientes a sonar;
tu corazón, de su profundo sueño
tal vez despertará;

pero mudo y absorto y de rodillas,
como se adora a Dios ante su altar,
como yo te he querido . . . desengáñate:
¡así no te querrán!

No dormía; vagaba en ese limbo
en que cambian de forma los objetos,
misteriosos espacios que separan
la vigilia del sueño.

Las ideas, que en ronda silenciosa
daban vueltas en torno a mi cerebro,
poco a poco en su danza se movían
con un compás más lento.

De la luz que entra al alma por los ojos
los párpados velaban el reflejo;
mas otra luz el mundo de visiones
alumbraba por dentro.

En este punto resonó en mi oído
un rumor semejante al que en el templo
vaga confuso, al terminar los fieles
con un amén sus rezos.

Y oí como una voz delgada y triste
que por mi nombre me llamó a lo lejos,
y sentí olor de cirios apagados,
de humedad y de incienso.

. . . .

Entró la noche y, del olvido en brazos,
caí, cual piedra, en su profundo seno:
dormí, y al despertar exclamé: «¡Alguno
que yo quería ha muerto!»

IN the imposing nave of the Byzantine church, I saw the Gothic tomb in the uncertain light that trembled in the painted windows.

Her hands on her breast, and in her hands a book, a beautiful woman lay on an urn, a miracle of carving.

Sinking beneath the sweet weight of her limp body, her granite bed was creased as if it were made of soft feathers and satin.

Her face preserved the divine brightness of her last smile, as the sky preserves the fleeting rays of the dying sun.

Sitting on the edge of her stone pillow, two angels with their fingers to their lips compelled silence all around.

She did not seem dead; she appeared to be sleeping in the shadow of the massive arches, and in her sleep to see paradise.

I approached that dark corner of the nave, like someone walking with silent steps up to a cradle in which a child is sleeping.

I looked at her for a moment, and at that soft brightness, and at that stone bed which offered another place, empty, beside the wall,

En la imponente nave
del templo bizantino,
vi la gótica tumba, a la indecisa
luz que temblaba en los pintados vidrios.

Las manos sobre el pecho,
y en las manos un libro,
una mujer hermosa reposaba
sobre la urna, del cincel prodigio.

Del cuerpo abandonado
al dulce peso hundido,
cual si de blanda pluma y raso fuera,
se plegaba su lecho de granito.

De la postrer sonrisa,
el resplandor divino
guardaba el rostro, como el cielo guarda
del sol que muere el rayo fugitivo.

Del cabezal de piedra
sentados en el filo
dos ángeles el dedo sobre el labio,
imponían silencio en el recinto.

No parecía muerta;
de los arcos macizos
parecía dormir en la penumbra,
y que en sueños veía el paraíso.

Me acerqué de la nave
al ángulo sombrío,
como quien llega con callada planta
junto a la cuna donde duerme un niño.

Le contemplé un momento,
y aquel resplandor tibio,
aquel lecho de piedra que ofrecía
próximo al muro otro lugar vacío,

and they revived in my soul its thirst for the infinite, a desire for that life in death for which the centuries are but a moment . . .

Weary of the battle which I fight as I live, I sometimes enviously remember that dark and hidden corner.

I remember that mute pale woman and say: 'Oh, what a silent love is the love of death! Oh, what a quiet sleep is the sleep of the grave!'

I DO not know what I am eternally seeking on earth, in the air, and in the sky: I do not know what I am seeking, but it is something that I lost I know not when, and that I do not find even when I dream that it invisibly pervades all that I touch and all that I see. Happiness, I shall never find you again on earth, in the air, or in the sky, even though I know that you exist and are not an empty dream.

AWAY from the regular sound of the waves and the moaning wind, from the uncertain reflection that lights wood and cloud; from the call of some passing bird, from the unknown rural smells that the west wind steals from

en el alma avivaron
la sed de lo infinito,
el ansia de esa vida de la muerte,
para la que un instante son los siglos . . .
. . . .

Cansado del combate
en que luchando vivo,
alguna vez recuerdo con envidia
aquel rincón oscuro y escondido.

De aquella muda y pálida
mujer, me acuerdo y digo:
«¡oh, qué amor tan callado el de la muerte!
¡Qué sueño el del sepulcro tan tranquilo!»

ROSALÍA CASTRO

Yo no sé lo que busco eternamente
en la tierra, en el aire y en el cielo;
yo no sé lo que busco; pero es algo
que perdí no sé cuando y que no encuentro,
aun cuando sueñe que invisible habita
en todo cuanto toco y cuanto veo.
¡Felicidad, no he de volver a hallarte
en la tierra, en el aire, ni en el cielo,
aun cuando sé que existes
y no eres vano sueño!

Del rumor cadencioso de la onda
y el viento que muge,
del incierto reflejo que alumbra
la selva y la nube;
del piar de alguna ave de paso,
del agreste ignorado perfume

valley or hill-top, there are worlds where souls sinking beneath the weight of the world find peace.

THE air is glowing with heat; the fox is exploring the deserted road; the crystalline water of the clear stream turns stagnant, and the pine waits motionless for the inconstant kisses of the breeze.

An imposing silence oppresses the countryside; only the humming of an insect can be heard in the vast, damp shade of the woods, monotonous and unceasing as a dull death rattle.

The midday hour in summer might well be called a night in which the imposing power of matter and the infinite anxieties of the soul tease more than ever man, weary of the struggle.

Return, oh nights of cold winter, our old loves of former days! Come back with your frosts and cruelties to refresh the blood, scorched by the unbearable and sad summer . . . Sad! . . . Full of vine-leaves and wheat!

Cold and heat, autumn or spring, where . . . where is happiness to be found? All seasons are beautiful for the man who carries happiness within him, but for the desolate and orphaned soul there is no smiling or favourable season.

que el céfiro roba
al valle o a la cumbre,
mundos hay donde encuentran asilo
las almas que al peso
del mundo sucumben.

CANDENTE está la atmósfera;
explora el zorro la desierta vía;
insalubre se torna
del limpio arroyo el agua cristalina,
y el pino aguarda inmóvil
los besos inconstantes de la brisa.

Imponente silencio
agobia la campiña;
sólo el zumbido del insecto se oye
en las extensas y húmedas umbrías;
monótono y constante
como el sordo estertor de la agonía.

Bien pudiera llamarse, en el estío,
la hora del mediodía,
noche en que al hombre de luchar cansado,
más que nunca le irritan
de la materia la imponente fuerza
y del alma las ansias infinitas.

Volved, ¡oh noches del invierno frío,
nuestras viejas amantes de otros días!
Tornad con vuestros hielos y crudezas
a refrescar la sangre enardecida
por el estío insoportable y triste . . .
¡Triste! . . . ¡Lleno de pámpanos y espigas!

Frío y calor, otoño o primavera,
¿dónde . . . dónde se encuentra la alegría?
Hermosas son las estaciones todas
para el mortal que en sí guarda la dicha;
mas para el alma desolada y huérfana,
no hay estación risueña ni propicia.

Beside Christ's Lake in Aldehuela de Yeltes, on a Night of Full Moon

WHITE night in which the glassy water sleeps quietly in its lake bed, over which watches a round full moon that leads its army of stars,

and a round holm-oak is reflected in the unrippling mirror, white night in which the water acts as cradle for the highest and most profound wisdom.

It is a tatter of sky that Nature holds clasped in her arms, it is a tatter of sky which has come down

and in the silence of the night prays the prayer of the lover resigned solely to love, which is his only riches.

In a Castilian Village Cemetery

SHEEP-FOLD of the dead, between poor walls made also of clay, poor sheep-fold in which the scythe does not reap, only a Cross in the deserted ground signifies your purpose.

Close to these walls the sheep take shelter from the lashing north wind, as they wander past in a flock, and on them (the walls) break the vain rumours of vain history like waves.

In June, the golden sea of the wheat which the breeze ripples encloses you like an island, and the lark sings its harvest song above you.

MIGUEL DE UNAMUNO

Junto a la laguna de Cristo en la Aldehuela de Yeltes, una noche de luna llena

NOCHE blanca en que el agua cristalina
duerme queda en su lecho de laguna
sobre la cual redonda llena luna
que ejército de estrellas encamina

vela, y se espeja una redonda encina
en el espejo sin rizada alguna,
noche blanca en que el agua hace de cuna
de la más alta y más honda doctrina.

Es un rasgón del cielo que abrazado
tiene en sus brazos la Naturaleza,
es un rasgón del cielo que ha posado

y en el silencio de la noche reza
la oración del amante resignado
sólo al amor que es su única riqueza.

En un cementerio de lugar castellano

CORRAL de muertos, entre pobres tapias,
hechas también de barro,
pobre corral donde la hoz no siega,
sólo una cruz, en el desierto campo
señala tu destino.

Junto a estas tapias buscan el amparo
del hostigo del cierzo las ovejas
al pasar trashumantes en rebaño,
y en ellas rompen de la vana historia,
como las olas, los rumores vanos.

Como un islote en junio,
te ciñe el mar dorado
de las espigas que a la brisa ondean,
y canta sobre ti la alondra el canto
de la cosecha.

When the sky falls down on the fields in rain, it falls too on the blessed grass of your corner, which the scythe never cuts, oh poor enclosure of the dead, and they feel in their bones the summons of the gushing waters of life!

Your rubble and clay walls save the winged seeds, or the birds dutifully bring them to you, and there grow hidden poppies, pinks, camomile, heather, and thistles among the tumbledown crosses, merely to serve as food for the ranging birds.

Sacred sheep-fold, they never dig your luxuriant weeds except to sow the grain of a soul who has suffered in the world, and then over this seed how long the ground lies fallow!

Beside you runs the road of the living, not surrounded by walls like you, not fenced, and along it they come and go, sometimes laughing and sometimes weeping, breaking the deathless silence of your enclosure with their laughter or their tears.

After the sun has slowly sunk to the earth, and the high tableland is mounting to the sky at the hour of remembrance, at the bell for prayers and rest, the rough stone cross on your clay walls remains as an unsleeping guardian, watching over the countryside's sleep.

Cuando baja en la lluvia el cielo al campo
baja también sobre la santa yerba
donde la hoz no corta,
de tu rincón ¡pobre corral de muertos!,
y sienten en sus huesos el reclamo
del riego de la vida.

Salvan tus cercas de mampuesto y barro
las aladas semillas,
o te las llevan con piedad los pájaros;
y crecen escondidas amapolas,
clavelinas, magarzas, brezos, cardos,
entre arrumbadas cruces,
no más que de las aves libres pasto.

Cavan tan sólo en tu maleza brava,
corral sagrado,
para de un alma que sufrió en el mundo
sembrar el grano;
luego, sobre esa siembra,
barbecho largo!

Cerca de ti el camino de los vivos,
no como tú, con tapias, no cercado,
por donde van y vienen,
ya riendo o llorando,
rompiendo con sus risas o sus lloros
el silencio inmortal de tu cercado!

Después que lento el sol tomó la tierra,
y sube al cielo el páramo
a la hora del recuerdo,
al toque de oraciones y descanso,
la tosca cruz de piedra
de tus tapias de barro
queda, como un guardián que nunca duerme,
de la campiña el sueño vigilando.

There is no Cross over the church of the living, around which the township sleeps: the Cross, like a faithful dog, protects the sleep of the dead, who are penned up in heaven. And from the night sky, Christ, the King of shepherds, with countless twinkling eyes counts the sheep of the flock!

Poor sheep-fold of the dead between walls made of the same clay, only a Cross marks your office in the deserted wastes of the country!

Symphony in Grey Major

THE sea like a vast quicksilver mirror reflects the metal sheet of a zinc sky; faraway flocks of birds stain the polished background of pale grey.

The sun like a round, opaque window-pane climbs to the zenith at a sick man's pace; the sea-wind rests in the shadows, using its black trumpet for a pillow.

The waves that move their leaden bellies seem to moan beneath the quay. Seated on a cable, smoking his pipe, is a sailor thinking of the beaches of a vague, faraway, misty land.

This sea-dog is an old man. The fiery beams of Brazilian suns have scorched his face; the violent typhoons of the China seas have seen him drinking his bottle of gin.

No hay cruz sobre la iglesia de los vivos,
en torno de la cual duerme el poblado;
la cruz, cual perro fiel, ampara el sueño
de los muertos al cielo acorralados.
Y desde el cielo de la noche, Cristo,
el Pastor Soberano,
con infinitos ojos centellantes
recuenta las ovejas del rebaño!

Pobre corral de muertos entre tapias
hechas del mismo barro,
sólo una cruz distingue tu destino
en la desierta soledad de campo!

∽

RUBÉN DARÍO

Sinfonía en gris mayor

EL mar como un vasto cristal azogado
refleja la lámina de un cielo de zinc;
lejanas bandadas de pájaros manchan
el fondo bruñido de pálido gris.

El sol como un vidrio redondo y opaco
con paso de enfermo camina al cenit;
el viento marino descansa en la sombra
teniendo de almohada su negro clarín.

Las ondas que mueven su vientre de plomo
debajo del muelle parecen gemir.
Sentado en un cable, fumando su pipa,
está un marinero pensando en las playas
de un vago, lejano, brumoso país.

Es viejo ese lobo. Tostaron su cara
los rayos de fuego del sol del Brasil;
los recios tifones del mar de la China
le han visto bebiendo su frasco de gin.

The foam that reeks of iodine and saltpetre has known from of old his red nose, his curly hair, and his athlete's biceps, his canvas cap and his drill blouse.

In the midst of the smoke-cloud that rises from his tobacco, the old man sees the faraway misty land for which one hot and golden evening his brigantine set out with all sails set . . .

The tropical siesta. The sea-dog sleeps. Now the scale of grey enfolds him complete. It is as if a soft and enormous charcoal pencil would rub out the line of the curved horizon.

The tropical siesta. The old cicada tries out his hoarse and ancient guitar, and the grasshopper strikes up a monotonous solo on the single string of his violin.

Anthem for the Death of Paul Verlaine

FATHER and master of magic, celestial lyre-bearer, who gave your enchanting music to the Olympic organ and the rustic pipe, the pipe of Pan, you yourself are Pan, who led choirs to the sacred temple columns that your sad soul loved, to the sound of the sistrum and the drum!

May Spring cover your tomb with flowers, may the rough snout of the wild beast be moistened with love if it passes that way, and may two-horned Pan visit these mournful precincts; and may fresh April adorn you with blood-red roses and carnations and rubies.

La espuma impregnada de yodo y salitre
ha tiempo conoce su roja nariz,
sus crespos cabellos, sus biceps de atleta,
su gorra de lona, su blusa de dril.

En medio del humo que forma el tabaco
ve el viejo el lejano, brumoso país,
adonde una tarde caliente y dorada
tendidas las velas partió el bergantín . . .

La siesta del trópico. El lobo se duerme.
Ya todo lo envuelve la gama del gris.
Parece que un suave y enorme esfumino
del curvo horizonte borrara el confín.

La siesta del trópico. La vieja cigarra
ensaya su ronca guitarra senil,
y el grillo preludia un solo monótono
en la única cuerda que está en su violín.

Responso
a la muerte de Paul Verlaine

PADRE y maestro mágico, liróforo celeste
que al instrumento olímpico y a la siringa agreste
    diste tu acento encantador;
¡Panida! Pan tú mismo, que coros condujiste
hacia el propíleo sacro que amaba tu alma triste,
    ¡al son del sistro y del tambor!

Que tu sepulcro cubra de flores Primavera,
que se humedezca el áspero hocico de la fiera
    de amor si pasa por allí;
que el fúnebre recinto visite Pan bicorne;
que de sangrientas rosas el fresco abril te adorne
    y de claveles y de rubí.

If the crow tries to perch on your tomb, may the sweet, crystalline song that Philomela pours over your sad bones, or the sweet music of laughter and kisses of the secret cult of the thickets, drive away that perverse bird's blackness.

May maidens bearing baskets offer you the acanthus, may tears never be shed on your tomb, but dew, wine, and honey: and may the vine-tendrils bud there, Cytherea's flowers, and may indistinct sighs of women be heard – beneath a symbolic laurel!

If a shepherd tries his pipe beneath a beech-tree, in days for love such as Virgil tells of, may he put your name in his song; and the virgin naiad, when she hears that name, struggle with desires and terrors in the flowing water, full of fear and passion.

At night in the mountains, in the black mountain of visions, may a strange and gigantic shade pass, the shade of a spectral Satyr: and may it shock the gloomy centaur by its size; may it accord the music of a superhuman flute to the harmony of the stars.

And may the troop of horses flee across the vast mountain; and may the chaste moon bathe your face beyond the tomb with compassionate and white light; and may the Satyr on a distant mountain gaze on a Cross that rises to cover the horizon – and a brightness on the Cross!

TOWERS of God! Poets! Celestial lightning-conductors that resist harsh storms like bare mountain-tops, like rough peaks, breakwaters against eternity!

Que si posarse quiere sobre la tumba el cuervo,
ahuyenten la negrura del pájaro protervo
el dulce canto de cristal
que Filomela vierta sobre tus tristes huesos,
o la harmonía dulce de risas y de besos
de culto oculto y florestal.

Que púberes canéforas te ofrenden el acanto,
que sobre tu sepulcro no se derrame el llanto,
sino rocío, vino, miel:
que el pámpano allí brote, las flores de Citeres,
y que se escuchen vagos suspiros de mujeres
¡bajo un simbólico laurel!

Que si un pastor su pífano bajo el frescor del haya,
en amorosos días, como en Virgilio, ensaya,
tu nombre ponga en la canción;
y que la virgen náyade, cuando ese nombre escuche,
con ansias y temores entre las linfas luche,
llena de miedo y de pasión.

De noche, en la montaña, en la negra montaña
de las Visiones, pase gigante sombra extraña,
sombra de un Sátiro espectral;
que ella al centauro adusto con su grandeza asuste;
de una extra-humana flauta la melodía ajuste
a la harmonía sideral.

Y huya el tropel equino por la montaña vasta;
tu rostro de ultratumba bañe la luna casta
de compasiva y blanca luz;
y el Sátiro contemple sobre un lejano monte
una cruz que se eleve cubriendo el horizonte
¡y un resplandor sobre la cruz!

¡Torres de Dios! ¡Poetas!
¡Pararrayos celestes,
que resistís las duras tempestades,
como crestas escuetas,
como picos agrestes,
rompeolas de las eternidades!

Magic hope proclaims a day on which the treacherous siren will expire on her rock of song. Hope, let us hope still!

Hope still. The bestial element consoles itself by its hatred of blessed poetry, and hurls insults from race to race.

The insurrection from below is directed against the élite. The cannibal covets his smoked meat with red gums and sharpened teeth.

Towers, put a smile on your flag. Place before this evil and this suspicion a proud suggestion of the breeze and a quietness of sea and sky . . .

Nocturne

YOU who listen to the heart of night, you who in persistent insomnia have heard the closing of a door, the rumble of a faraway carriage, a vague echo, a slight noise . . .

At the moments of mysterious silence, when the forgotten rise from their bonds, at the hour of the dead, at the hour of rest, you will know how to read these verses, impregnated with bitterness . . .

I pour into them as into a cup my griefs for faraway memories and sinister disasters, and the sad yearnings of my soul, drunk with flowers, and the sorrow of my heart, tired of merrymaking.

And repentance for not being what I might have been, the loss of the kingdom which was meant for me, and the thought that at one moment I might have avoided being born, and the dream that my life has been ever since I was born!

La mágica esperanza anuncia un día
en que sobre la roca de armonía
expirará la pérfida sirena.
¡Esperad, esperemos todavía!

Esperad todavía.
El bestial elemento se solaza
en el odio a la sacra poesía
y se arroja baldón de raza a raza.

La insurrección de abajo
tiende a los Excelentes.
El caníbal codicia su tasajo
con roja encía y afilados dientes.

Torres, poned al pabellón sonrisa.
Poned ante ese mal y ese recelo
una soberbia insinuación de brisa
y una tranquilidad de mar y cielo . . .

Nocturno

LOS que auscultásteis el corazón de la noche,
los que por el insomnio tenaz habéis oído
el cerrar de una puerta, el resonar de un coche
lejano, un eco vago, un ligero ruido . . .

¡En los instantes del silencio misterioso,
cuando surgen de su prisión los olvidados,
en la hora de los muertos, en la hora del reposo,
sabréis leer estos versos de amargor impregnados! . . .

Como en un vaso vierto en ellos mis dolores
de lejanos recuerdos y desgracias funestas,
y las tristes nostalgias de mi alma, ebria de flores,
y el duelo de mi corazón, triste de fiestas.

¡Y el pesar de no ser lo que yo hubiera sido,
la pérdida del reino que estaba para mí,
el pensar que un instante pude no haber nacido,
y el sueño que es mi vida desde que yo nací!

All this comes in the midst of the deep silence in which the night wraps the illusion of earth, and I seem to hear an echo from the world's heart that pierces and moves my own.

Fatality

HAPPY the tree that can scarcely feel, and happier the hard stone because it does not feel at all, for there is no greater grief than the grief of being alive, and no greater affliction than conscious life.

To be and to know nothing, and to have no fixed course, and the fear of what was and a terror of the future . . . and the certain terror of being dead tomorrow, and to suffer for life and the shadow (of death) and for

what we do not know and hardly suspect, and for the flesh that tempts with its fresh grapes and the tomb that waits with its funeral branches, and not to know whither we go or whence we come . . .

Autumn Verses

WHEN my thought goes out towards you it smells sweet; your look is so sweet that my thought becomes deep. Beneath your naked feet there is still the whiteness of foam, and in your lips you contain the world's happiness.

Passing love has a brief enchantment, and offers a similar end to joy and grief. An hour ago I cut a name in the snow; a minute ago I proclaimed my love on the sand.

The yellow leaves fall in the poplar-grove in which so many loving couples wander. And in autumn's cup there remains a cloudy wine, into which your roses, Spring, must shed their petals.

Todo esto viene en medio del silencio profundo
en que la noche envuelve la terrena ilusión,
y siento como un eco del corazón del mundo
que penetra y conmueve mi propio corazón.

Lo fatal

DICHOSO el árbol, que es apenas sensitivo,
y más la piedra dura porque ésa ya no siente,
pues no hay dolor más grande que el dolor de ser vivo,
ni mayor pesadumbre que la vida consciente.

Ser, y no saber nada, y ser sin rumbo cierto,
y el temor de haber sido y un futuro terror . . .
¡Y el espanto seguro de estar mañana muerto,
y sufrir por la vida y por la sombra y por

lo que no conocemos y apenas sospechamos,
y la carne que tienta con sus frescos racimos,
y la tumba que aguarda con sus fúnebres ramos,
y no saber adónde vamos,
ni de dónde venimos! . . .

Versos de Otoño

CUANDO mi pensamiento va hacia ti, se perfuma;
tu mirar es tan dulce, que se torna profundo.
Bajos tus pies desnudos aún hay blancor de espuma,
y en tus labios compendias la alegría del mundo.

El amor pasajero tiene el encanto breve,
y ofrece un igual término para el gozo y la pena.
Hace una hora que un nombre grabé sobre la nieve;
hace un minuto dije mi amor sobre la arena.

Las hojas amarillas caen en la alameda,
en donde vagan tantas parejas amorosas.
Y en la copa de Otoño un vago vino queda
en que han de deshojarse, Primavera, tus rosas.

From the Road

THE clock struck twelve . . . it was twelve blows of the spade on the earth. 'My hour!' I cried. But silence answered me: 'Have no fear. You shall not see the last drop fall that is trembling in the water-clock. You will sleep many hours yet on the familiar shore, and one fine morning you will wake to find your boat made fast to the further shore.'

OVER the bitter earth sleep has her mazy tracks, tortuous paths, parks in flower and in shade and in silence; deep crypts and ladders to the stars; puppet plays of hopes and memories. Little figures pass and smile – the melancholy playthings of the old –; friendly forms at the flowery turn of the path and rosy visions which point the road . . . in the distance.

THE embers of a violet dusk are smoking behind the cypress-grove. In the shadowy columned arbour is the fountain with its winged and naked stone Cupid, who dreams in silence. In the marble basin lies the dead water.

ANTONIO MACHADO

Del camino

DABA el reloj las doce . . . y eran doce
golpes de azada en tierra . . .
. . . ¡Mi hora! – grité – . . . El silencio
me respondió: – No temas;
tú no verás caer la última gota
que en la clepsidra tiembla.

Dormirás muchas horas todavía
sobre la orilla vieja,
y encontrarás una mañana pura
amarrada tu barca a otra ribera.

SOBRE la tierra amarga,
caminos tiene el sueño
laberínticos, sendas tortuosas,
parques en flor y en sombra y en silencio;
    criptas hondas, escalas sobre estrellas;
retablos de esperanzas y recuerdos.
Figurillas que pasan y sonríen
– juguetes melancólicos de viejo – ;
    imágenes amigas,
a la vuelta florida del sendero,
y quimeras rosadas
que hacen camino . . . lejos . . .

LAS ascuas de un crepúsculo morado
detrás del negro cipresal humean . . .
En la glorieta en sombra está la fuente
con su alado y desnudo Amor de piedra,
que sueña mudo. En la marmórea taza
reposa el agua muerta.

Corridors

THE cloud was rent apart, the rainbow was already bright in the sky, and the fields framed in a glass case of rain and sun. I awoke. Who was clouding the magic windows of my dream? My heart was thumping with astonishment and fright . . . The lemon tree in blossom, the cypress clump in the garden, the green fields, the sun, the wet, and the rainbow . . . the wet drops in your hair. And all this was fading in memory, like a soap-bubble on the breeze.

AND it was the demon of my dream, the loveliest angel. His triumphant eyes shone like steel, and the bleeding flames of his torch lit the deep crypt of my soul.

'Will you come with me?' 'No, never. Tombs and the dead frighten me.'

But his iron hand clutched my right hand. 'You will come with me.' And I went forward in my dream, blinded by the red light before the altar. And in the crypt I heard the clink of chains and the stirring of caged beasts.

Galerías

DESGARRADA la nube; el arco iris
brillando ya en el cielo,
y en un fanal de lluvia
y sol el campo envuelto.

Desperté. ¿Quién enturbia
los mágicos cristales de mi sueño?
Mi corazón latía
atónito y disperso.

. . . ¡El limonar florido,
el cipresal del huerto,
el prado verde, el sol, el agua, el iris . . .,
¡el agua en tus cabellos! . . .

Y todo en la memoria se perdía
como una pompa de jabón al viento.

YERA el demonio de mi sueño, el ángel
más hermoso. Brillaban
como aceros los ojos victoriosos,
a las sangrientas llamas
de su antorcha alumbraron
la honda cripta del alma.

– ¿Vendrás conmigo? – No, jamás; las tumbas
y los muertos me espantan.
Pero la férrea mano
mi diestra atenazaba.

– Vendrás conmigo . . . Y avancé en mi sueño,
cegado por la roja luminaria.
Y en la cripta sentí sonar cadenas,
y rebullir de fieras enjauladas.

FROM the threshold of a dream they called me. It was the good voice, the beloved voice. 'Tell me, will you come with me to see the soul?' A caress reached my heart.

'With you, always.' And I went forward in my dream along a long empty corridor, hearing the rustle of her pure robe and feeling the soft pulse of her friendly hand.

ONE fine day the wind summoned my heart with a scent of jasmine. 'In exchange for this aroma, I should like all the aroma of your roses.' 'I have no roses; there are no flowers in my garden; they have all died.' 'I will take away the weeping of the fountains, the yellow leaves, and the withered petals.' And the wind fled . . . My heart was bleeding . . . Soul, what have you done with your poor garden?

PERHAPS, in dreams, the hand which sows the stars made the forgotten music sound like a note of the immense lyre, and the humble wave of a few words of truth came to our lips.

THE bench of greenish stone under the laurel is damp: on the white wall the rain has washed the dusty leaves of the ivy.

DESDE el umbral de un sueño me llamaron . . .
Era la buena voz, la voz querida.
– Dime: ¿vendrás conmigo a ver el alma? . . .
Llegó a mi corazón una caricia.

– Contigo siempre . . . Y avancé en mi sueño
por una larga, escueta galería,
sintiendo el roce de la vesta pura
y el palpitar suave de la mano amiga.

LLAMÓ a mi corazón, un claro día,
con un perfume de jazmín, el viento.

– A cambio de este aroma,
todo el aroma de tus rosas quiero.

– No tengo rosas; flores
en mi jardín no hay: todas han muerto.
– Me llevaré los llantos de las fuentes,
las hojas amarillas y los mustios pétalos.
Y el viento huyó . . . Mi corazón sangraba . . .
Alma ¿qué has hecho de tu pobre huerto?

TAL vez la mano, en sueños,
del sembrador de estrellas,
hizo sonar la música olvidada
como una nota de la lira inmensa,
y la ola humilde a nuestros labios vino
de unas pocas palabras verdaderas.

HÚMEDO está, bajo el laurel, el banco
de verdinosa piedra;
lavó la lluvia, sobre el muro blanco,
las empolvadas hojas de la hiedra.

The warm breath of the autumn wind ripples the lawns, and the poplar grove talks with the wind . . . the evening wind in the shrubbery. Whilst the sun is resplendent in its setting, which refreshes the grape-bunches on the vine, and the good bourgeois on his balcony lights his stoical pipe from which his tobacco smokes, I go on remembering juvenile verses . . . What has become of that singing heart of mine? Is it true that you will depart, charming shadows, flying off between the golden trees?

For Don Francisco Giner de los Ríos

WHEN the master went the light of the morning said to me: 'It is three days now since my brother Francisco has done any work. Is he dead?' We only know that he departed from us along a shining path, saying to us: 'Make your mourning for me in work and hopes. Be good and nothing more, be what I have been amongst you: a soul. Live, for life goes on; the dead die and shadows pass; the man who leaves (something behind) takes something with him, and it is he who has lived that lives. Ring out, anvils: church bells be silent!'

And the brother of the dawn-light departed from the sun of his labours towards another, purer light, the happy old man who had lived a saintly life. Oh, bear his body to the mountains, friends, to the blue mountains of the broad Guadarrama. There are deep gorges with green pines, in which the

Del viento del otoño el tibio aliento
los céspedes undula, y la alameda
conversa con el viento. . .
¡el viento de la tarde en la arboleda!

Mientras el sol en el ocaso esplende
que los racimos de la vid orea,
y el buen burgués, en su balcón, enciende
la estoica pipa en que el tabaco humea,

voy recordando versos juveniles . . .
¿Qué fue de aquél mi corazón sonoro?
¿Será cierto que os vais, sombras gentiles,
huyendo entre los árboles de oro?

A Don Francisco Giner de los Ríos

COMO se fue el maestro,
la luz de esta mañana
me dijo: Van tres días
que mi hermano Francisco no trabaja.
¿Murió? . . . Sólo sabemos
que se nos fue por una senda clara,
diciéndonos: Hacedme
un duelo de labores y esperanzas.
Sed buenos y no más, sed lo que he sido
entre vosotros: alma.
Vivid, la vida sigue,
los muertos mueren y las sombras pasan;
lleva quien deja y vive el que ha vivido.
¡Yunques, sonad; enmudeced, campanas!

Y hacia otra luz más pura
partió el hermano de la luz del alba,
del sol de los talleres,
el viejo alegre de la vida santa.
. . . Oh, sí, llevad, amigos,
su cuerpo a la montaña,
a los azules montes
del ancho Guadarrama.

wind sings. Let his heart lie beneath a modest holm-oak in a thyme field, where the gilded butterflies play. There one day the Master dreamed of a new flowering for Spain.

Siesta
In Memory of Abel Martín

WHILST the fiery fish traces his arc beside the cypress, beneath the highest blue, and the blind boy disappears into white stone, and in the elm the ivory verse of the green cicada beats and booms, let us honour the Lord – the black imprint of his kindly hand – who has compelled silence among the clamour.

To the God of distance and absence, of the anchor in the sea, the sea at high tide . . . He frees us from the world – from the omnipresent – and opens us up a path to travel.

With a cup overflowing with shadow and with this never filled heart, let us honour the Lord who made Non-existence and sculpted our reason out of faith.

Return

THE world's thousand towers against a golden sunset, raise their beauty before my mind. An ecstasy of stone in a thousand shapes is a dazzlement, and carries me away mute and blind.

Allí hay barancos hondos
de pinos verdes donde el viento canta.
Su corazón repose
bajo una encina casta,
en tierra de tomillos, donde juegan
mariposas doradas . . .
Allí el maestro un día
soñaba un nuevo florecer de España.

Siesta

En memoria de Abel Martín

MIENTRAS traza su curva el pez de fuego,
junto al ciprés, bajo el supremo añil,
y vuela en blanca piedra el niño ciego,
y en el olmo la copla de marfil
de la verde cigarra late y suena,
honremos al Señor
– la negra estampa de su mano buena –
que ha dictado el silencio en el clamor.

Al Dios de la distancia y de la ausencia,
del áncora en la mar, la plena mar . . .
Él nos libra del mundo – omnipresencia –,
nos abre senda para caminar.

Con la copa de sombra bien colmada,
con este nunca lleno corazón,
honremos al Señor que hizo la Nada
y ha esculpido en la fe nuestra razón.

JUAN RAMÓN JIMÉNEZ

Retorno

LAS mil torres del mundo, contra un ocaso de oro,
levantan su hermosura frente a mi pensamiento.
Un éstasis de piedra de mil arquitecturas,
en un deslumbramiento, me lleva, mudo y ciego.

The sun sets behind me, red and scorching. The world is deserted, silence is king over me. And I walk step by step over high sands towards the brightness of an eternal horizon.

And . . . a confused scent of dates and figures is enveloping me strangely between light and darkness . . . The evening has fallen . . . of today . . . Monday . . . of August . . . and there weeps . . . humble and poor . . . an Angelus . . . from the village.

Tenebrae

THE whole West is a lemon yellow. At the barred zenith, beneath the silent clouds, black flocks of melancholy birds continually streak the false sky like rain.

About the garden, gloomy with its leaden haloes, the roses have been touched with a violet wash, and the uncertain dusk, which makes truth lies, drops I know not what damp vapours into all that it brushes.

Livid, dazzled by the yellow and leaden-grim, like a horse-fly there hums in my ears a monotonous catch, which comes from I know not where . . . which leaves tears . . . which says: 'Never . . . never . . .'

Fleeting Return

HOW was it, my Lord, how was it? – Oh fallacious heart, irresolute mind! – Was it like the passing of the breeze? Like the fleeting of the Spring?

As light, as fickle, as airy as summer thistledown . . . Yes, as unformed as a smile that passes into a laugh . . . Proud on the air, like a flag.

A flag, a smile, thistledown, the winged Spring in June, a pure breeze. How mad your carnival was, and how sad!

El sol, detrás de mí, se pone, grana y cálido.
Está desierto el orbe, mi rey es el silencio.
Y por arenas altas, paso a paso, camino
hacia la claridad de un horizonte eterno.

Y . . . un aroma confuso de fechas y de cifras,
me va, entre luz y sombra, raramente envolviendo . . .
Ha caído la tarde . . . de hoy . . ., lunes . . . de agosto . . .,
y llora . . ., bajo y pobre . . ., un Ángelus . . . de pueblo.

Tenebrae

TODO el ocaso es amarillo limón.
En el cenit cerrado, bajo las nubes mudas,
bandadas negras de pájaros melancólicos
rayan, constantes, el falso cielo de lluvia.

Por el jardín, sombrío de los plúmbeos nimbos,
las rosas tienen una morada veladura,
y el crepúsculo vago, que cambia las verdades,
pone en todo, al rozarlo, no sé qué gasas húmedas.

Lívido, deslumbrado del amarillo, torvo
del plomo, en mis oídos, como un moscardón zumba
una ronda monótona, que yo no sé de donde
viene, . . . que deja lágrimas, . . . que dice: «Nunca, . . . Nunca . . .»

Retorno fugaz

¿CÓMO era, Dios mío, cómo era?
– ¡Oh corazón falaz, mente indecisa! –
¿Era como el pasaje de la brisa?
¿Como la huida de la primavera?

Tan leve, tan voluble, tan lijera
cual estival vilano . . .¡ Sí! Imprecisa
como sonrisa que se pierde en risa . . .
¡Vana en el aire, igual que una bandera!

¡Bandera, sonreír, vilano, alada
primavera de junio, brisa pura . . .
¿Qué loco fue tu carnaval, qué triste!

All your change was transformed into nothing – Memory, a blind and bitter bee – I do not know what form you took, I who know that you were.

Sleep

HIGH and tender image of consolation, dawn on my seas of sadness, lily of peace with the scent of purity, divine reward for my long mourning!

Like the stem of the flower of heaven, your height is forgotten in your beauty . . . when you turned your head towards me, I believed that I was being raised from this earth.

Now, in the chaste dawn of your arms, gathered to your transparent breast, how light my chains become for me!

How my shattered heart is grateful for the pain, for the burning kiss with which you smilingly mend it!

INTELLIGENCE, give me the precise name of things . . . Let my word be the thing itself, newly created by my soul. Through me let all those who do not know things approach them; through me let all those who are now forgetting things, approach them; through me let all those who love things approach them.

Intelligence, give me the exact name and your name and their name and my name for things.

Todo tu cambiar trocóse en nada
– ¡memoria, ciega abeja de amargura! –
¡No sé cómo eras, yo que sé que fuiste!

Sueño

ÍMAJEN alta y tierna del consuelo,
aurora de mis mares de tristeza,
lis de paz con olores de pureza,
¡premio divino de mi largo duelo!

Igual que el tallo de la flor del cielo,
tu alteza se perdía en su belleza . . .
Cuando hacia mí volviste la cabeza,
creí que me elevaban de este suelo.

Ahora, en el alba casta de tus brazos,
acojido a tu pecho trasparente,
¡cuán claras a mí tornan mis prisiones!

¡Cómo mi corazón hecho pedazos
agradece el dolor, al beso ardiente
con que tú, sonriendo lo compones!

¡INTELIJENCIA, dáme
el nombre exacto de las cosas!
. . . Que mi palabra sea
la cosa misma,
creada por mi alma nuevamente.
Que por mí vayan todos
los que no las conocen, a las cosas;
que por mí vayan todos
los que ya las olvidan, a las cosas;
que por mí vayan todos
los mismos que las aman, a las cosas . . .
¡Intelijencia, dáme
el nombre exacto y tuyo,
y suyo, y mío, de las cosas!

LEAVE the doors open tonight, in case he who is dead wishes to come tonight.

Let all be open to see if we look like his body; to see if we are something of his soul, being delivered over to space; to see if the great infinite will throw us something, infusing us with ourselves; if we may die a little here, and live a little there, in him.

Let the whole house be open, as if his body were laid out in the blue night, with us like blood and with the stars for flowers.

HOW should I be afraid of you, Death? Are you not here, working with me? Do I not touch you in my eyes; do you not tell me that you know nothing about anything, that you are hollow, unconscious, and peaceful? Do you not enjoy everything with me: glory, solitude, love, to your very quick? Are you not standing there, enduring my life? Do I not lead you up and down, blind Death, like your guide? Do you not repeat with your passive lips what I want you to say? Do you not, like a slave, put up with the kindness with which I compel your favours? What will you see, what will you say, where will you go without me? Shall I not be, Death, your death whom you, Death, must fear, pamper, and love?

DEJAD las puertas abiertas
esta noche, por si él
quiere, esta noche, venir,
que está muerto.
Abierto todo,
a ver si nos parecemos
a su cuerpo; a ver si somos
algo de su alma, estando
entregados al espacio;
a ver si el gran infinito
nos echa un poco, invadiéndonos
de nosotros; si morimos
un poco aquí; y allí, en él
vivimos un poco.
¡Abierta
toda la casa, lo mismo
que si estuviera de cuerpo
presente en la noche azul,
con nosotros como sangre,
con las estrellas por flores!

¿CÓMO, muerte, tenerte
miedo? ¿No estás aquí conmigo trabajando?
¿No te toco en mis ojos; no me dices
que no sabes de nada, que eres hueca,
inconsciente y pacífica? ¿No gozas
conmigo, todo: gloria, soledad,
amor, hasta tus tuétanos?
¿No me estás aguantando,
muerte, de pie, la vida?
¿No te traigo y te llevo, ciega,
como tu lazarillo? No repites
con tu boca pasiva
lo que quiero que digas? No soportas,
esclava, la bondad con que te obligo?
¿Qué verás, qué dirás, adónde irás
sin mí? ¿No seré yo,
muerte, tu muerte, a quien tú, muerte,
debes temer, mimar, amar?

Fortunate Creature

YOU go singing and laughing through the water, you go whistling and laughing through the air in a circle of blue and gold, of silver and green, happy to pass and repass among the red first budding of April, a separate form with momentary similarities in light, life, and colour to ourselves, your fiery shores!

How happy you are, being, with what an eternal and universal happiness! Gaily you break the waves of the air, you row against the undulations of the water. Do you not have to eat or sleep? Is all the Spring your home? Is all the green, all the blue, all the blossoming yours? There is no fear mingled with your splendour; your fate is to return, to return, to return in a silver and green, a blue and gold circle for an eternity of eternities!

You give us your hand in a moment of possible closeness, of sudden love, of radiant yielding, and at your glowing touch, with a mad tremor in body and soul, we burn with music and when we are renewed we forget it; for a moment, in our happiness, we shine like gold. It seems for a moment that we too are going to be, like you, eternal, that we are going to fly from sea to mountain, that we are going to jump from heaven to the sea, that we are going to return, return, return, for an eternity of eternities. And we sing, we laugh in the air, we laugh and whistle in the water!

Criatura afortunada

CANTANDO vas, riendo por el agua,
por el aire silbando vas, riendo,
en ronda azul y oro, plata y verde,
dichoso de pasar y repasar
entre el rojo primer brotar de abril,
¡forma distinta, de instantáneas
igualdades de luz, vida, color,
con nosotros, orillas inflamadas!

¡Qué alegre eres tú, ser,
con qué alegría universal eterna!
¡Rompes feliz el ondear del aire,
bogas contrario al ondular del agua!
¿Ni tienes que comer ni que dormir?
¿Toda la primavera es tu lugar?
¿Lo verde todo, lo azul todo,
lo floreciente todo es tuyo?
¡No hay temor en tu gloria;
tu destino es volver, volver, volver,
en ronda plata y verde, azul y oro,
por una eternidad de eternidades!

Nos das la mano, en un momento
de afinidad posible, de amor súbito,
de concesión radiante;
y a tu contacto cálido,
en loca vibración de carne y alma,
nos encendemos de armonía,
nos olvidamos, nuevos, de lo mismo,
lucimos, un instante, alegres de oro.
¡Parece que también vamos a ser
perenes como tú,
que vamos a volar del mar al monte,
que vamos a saltar del cielo al mar,
que vamos a volver, volver, volver
por una eternidad de eternidades!
¡Y cantamos, reímos por el aire,
por el agua reímos y silbamos!

But you do not have to forget, you are a perpetual and accidental presence, you are the fortunate creature, the unique and magic being, the never dark, beloved for your warmth and grace, the free, the intoxicating thief, who in a blue and gold, a silver and green circle, go laughing, whistling through the air, go singing, laughing through the water!

DO souls keep you company? Do you sense them? Or are what keep you company tiny thimbles of glass, imprisoning the pink tips and flights of the fingers?

Do desires keep you company? Those 'Mores', do not those 'Mores' keep you company? Or do you have beside you only music, so martyred and shattered from colliding with all the world's corners, the music that spectres play, in despair and without a kiss, over the wireless?

Do wings keep you company or are they far off? And tell me, does that immense longing to be with yourself, which is called love or a telegram – does that keep you company?

Or are you alone, with no other company but looking very gently, with your eyes brimming with tears, at old prints of ancient fashions and feeling yourself naked, alone, with a nakedness that holds a promise?

¡Pero tú no tienes que olvidar,
tú eres presencia casual perpetua,
eres la criatura afortunada,
el májico ser solo, el ser insombre,
el adorado por calor y gracia,
el libre, el embriagante robador,
que, en ronda azul y oro, plata y verde,
riendo vas, silbando por el aire,
por el agua cantando vas, riendo!

PEDRO SALINAS

¿ACOMPAÑAN las almas? ¿Se las siente?
¿O lo que te acompañan son dedales
minúsculos, de vidrio,
cárceles de las puntas, de las fugas,
rosadas, de los dedos?

¿Acompañan las ansias? ¿Y los «más»,
los «más», los «más», no te acompañan?
¿O tienes junto a ti sólo la música
tan mártir, destrozada
de chocar contra todas las esquinas
del mundo, la que tocan
desesperadamente, sin besar,
espectros, por la radio?

¿Acompañan las alas, o están lejos?
Y dime ¿te acompaña
ese inmenso querer estar contigo
que se llama el amor o el telegrama?

¿O estás sola, sin otra compañía
que mirar muy despacio, con los ojos
arrasados de llanto, estampas viejas
de modas anticuadas, y sentirte desnuda,
sola, con desnudo prometido?

IF the voice could be sensed by the eyes, oh how I should see you! Your voice has a light that shines upon me, the light of hearing. When you speak, space catches fire with the sound, and the great darkness which is silence is broken. Your words have the look of whiteness, of the young dawn, every day when they come to me afresh. When you make a statement a vertical joy, a midday reigns, yet without the means of the eye. There is no night if you talk to me in the night, no solitude here alone in my room if your voice comes so bodiless and light. For your voice creates its body. In empty space arise innumerable shapes, the delicate possible shapes of your voice's body. The lips and arms that seek you are almost deceived. And souls of the lips, souls of the arms, seek all about them the divine creatures, brought to birth by your voice, the invention of your speech. And in the light of the ear, in that sphere that the eyes do not see, those two – all radiant – kiss for us, lovers who have no other day or night than your starry voice or your sun.

Si la voz se sintiera con los ojos
¡ay, cómo te vería!
Tu voz tiene una luz que me ilumina,
luz de oír.
Al hablar,
se encienden los espacios del sonido,
se le quiebra al silencio
la gran oscuridad que es. Tu palabra
tiene visos de albor, de aurora joven,
cada día, al venir a mí de nuevo.
Cuando afirmas,
un gozo cenital, un mediodía,
impera, ya sin arte de los ojos.
Noche no hay si me hablas por la noche.
Ni soledad, aquí solo en mi cuarto
si tu voz llega, tan sin cuerpo, leve.
Porque tu voz crea su cuerpo. Nacen
en el vacio espacio, innumerables,
las formas delicadas y posibles
del cuerpo de tu voz. Casi se engañan
los labios y los brazos que te buscan.
Y almas de labios, almas de los brazos,
buscan alrededor las, por tu voz
hechas nacer, divinas criaturas,
invento de tu hablar.
Y a la luz del oír, en ese ámbito
que los ojos no ven, todo radiante,
se besan por nosotros
los dos enamorados que no tienen
más día ni más noche
que tu voz estrellada, o que tu sol.

Nude

WHITES, pinks. Blues, almost in veins, fugitive, of the mind. Points of latent light give signs of a hidden shadow.

But the colour, disloyal to the half-shadow, consolidates itself into a mass. Lying in the house's summer, a form lights up.

Brightness sharpened between contours so pure and quiet that with their edges they cut and annihilate base confusions.

The flesh is naked. Its blatancy is resolved into repose. Its monotony is exactly lit, a complete, prodigious assertion of its presence.

Fullness complete in the present moment, without environment, of the female body. No contrived beauty; nor voice nor flower. Fate? Oh, absolute present!

I CLOSE my eyes, and the darkness tells me that it is not quite black, and lights up some sparks to inform me that they are really shouts of joy in the background of our destiny,

that unknown thing in the night, so strong already that it succeeds in breaking its seals in my presence, and bringing up from the abyss the finest of the splendours that fight death.

I close my eyes. And there is still a world so great that it dazzles me, though empty of this world's tumultuous depths.

JORGE GUILLÉN

Desnudo

BLANCOS, rosas. Azules casi en veta,
Retraídos, mentales.
Puntos de luz latente dan señales
De una sombra secreta.

Pero el color, infiel a la penumbra,
Se consolida en masa.
Yacente en el verano de la casa,
Una forma se alumbra.

Claridad aguzada entre perfiles,
De tan puros tranquilos,
Que cortan y aniquilan con sus filos
Las confusiones viles.

Desnuda está la carne. Su evidencia
Se resuelve en reposo.
Monotonía justa, prodigioso
Colmo de la presencia.

¡Plenitud inmediata, sin ambiente,
Del cuerpo femenino!
Ningún primor: ni voz ni flor. ¿Destino?
¡Oh absoluto Presente!

CIERRO los ojos y el negror me advierte
Que no es negror, y alumbra unos destellos
Para darme a entender que sí son ellos
El fondo en algazara en la suerte,

Incógnita nocturna ya tan fuerte
Que consigue ante mí romper sus sellos
Y sacar del abismo los más bellos
Resplandores hostiles a la muerte.

Cierro los ojos. Y persiste un mundo
Grande que me deslumbra así, vacío
De su profundidad tumultuosa.

I found my certainty upon the dark; the lightning is more mine when darkened, and in the blackness rises even a rose.

Poplars with river

IN front of the whitish grey of the bluff, level with the river, the road descries with longing poplars, the profile of the rain.

Beside their tremulous leaves someone who is never solitary is talking alone to the river. Are they the breeze's and the Muse's poplars?

Gently the river draws out its pleasure, curve by curve, whilst the poplars sketch themselves with a light and trembling line,

and as green as the river, leafage by leafage, poplars that are almost music coo to him who is lucky enough to hear.

Lucky on the bank is the man who follows the river, which sharpens the (reflections of the) company in the water and in the poplars put to flight!

From the Domain of Memory

A MEMORY – delightful past – assaults me and so overpowers me, that an inner Spring pursues me.

That love still vibrates under the impulse of an image, a mere phantom. I beg, I desire. A magnet takes control of me, fibre by fibre.

Mi certidumbre en la tiniebla fundo,
Tenebroso el relámpago es más mío,
En lo negro se yergue hasta una rosa.

Álamos con río

FRENTE al blanco gris del cerro,
A par del río, la ruta
Divisa con ansiedad
Álamos, perfil de lluvia.

Junto a las trémulas hojas
Alguien, solitario nunca,
Habla a solas con el río.
¿Álamos de brisa y musa?

Mansamente el río traza
Su recreo curva a curva
Mientras en leve temblor
Los álamos se dibujan,

Y tan verdes como el río
Follaje a follaje arrullan
Al dichoso de escuchar
Álamos de casi música.

¡Dichoso por la ribera
Quien sigue el río que aguza
La compañía en el agua,
En los álamos la fuga!

Dominio del recuerdo

UN recuerdo – Pasado deleitoso –
Me ataca y se apodera
Tanto de mí que interna primavera
Me somete a su acoso.

Aquel amor aún vibra
Bajo el impulso de una imagen, mero
Fantasma. Pido, quiero.
Un imán se me impone fibra a fibra.

The spirit invades my existence with sovereign power. Spirit now is form. Who witnesses such a fusion, such a secret?

Love, that was so strong during that concluded minute, emerging from its mental nest, is transformed into feeling before me.

My memory now is flesh. Now it revives a pleasure – dreamed about – and fuses with the truth of my existence. Soul, body? My being.

Epiphany

THE Magi come to the archway, Melchior, Gaspar and Balthasar, they bow down with their splendid offerings and adore the Child without song.

God is not king, nor looks like a king, God is not sumptuous or rich. God bears within him the human flock and all its immense pin-cushion.*

The starry sky gravitates over Bethlehem, and this archway welcomes all men in brotherly invitation.

God has taken on a new form and comes to a family of workers, member of a woodworkers' union. The humble man is the true one.

Beside the donkey, beside the ox, the feeble baby silently says: 'I am not king, I am the way, the truth and the life.'

* This seems to imply that humanity is subject to the many pin-pricks of misfortune.

El espíritu invade mi existencia
Con poder soberano.
Espíritu ya es cuerpo. ¿Quién presencia
Tal fusión, tal arcano?

Amor, que fue tan fuerte
Durante aquel minuto fenecido,
Saliendo de su nido
Mental en sensación se me convierte.

Mi memoria ya es carne, ya un placer
– Soñado – resucita,
Y a la verdad de mi vivir da cita.
¿Alma, cuerpo? Mi ser.

Epifanía

LLEGAN al portal los Mayores,
Melchor, Gaspar y Baltasar,
Se inclinan con sus esplendores
Y al Niño adoran sin cantar.

Dios no es rey ni parece rey,
Dios no es suntuoso ni rico.
Dios lleva en sí la humana grey
Y todo su inmenso acerico.

El cielo estrellado gravita
Sobre Belén, y ese portal
A todos los hombres da cita
Por invitación fraternal.

Dios está de nueva manera,
Y viene a familia de obrero,
Sindicato de la madera.
El humilde es el verdadero.

Junto al borrico, junto al buey,
La criatura desvalida
Dice en silencio: No soy rey,
Soy camino, verdad y vida.

Mediterranean

ON the beach at midday, sand or light with dense waves, a defenceless, half naked body seeks and entrusts itself to the sun, which is now cruel.

The lady then offers her blend of health and beauty as an offering in the worship of the solar deity. (And meanwhile I wonder how I should respond to such faith.)

Forever happy, her body shows signs of the intense concentration the rays from the zenith are consecrating to the beautiful woman.

Motionless, she accepts the brutal caresses of that sky as manifestations of a mythological love for a goddess.

Susanna and the Elders

FURTIVE, silent, tense, watchful, they slip, peer, and parting the branches, extend their gaze to the scene of the drama: the shock of a naked body against their previous dreams.

Alone and dreaming, they have already been the possible lovers of the lady, intended in dreams. Such real nakedness now inflames them for the old men take quick looks like timid students.

Are they old men? So they say. That is the official reckoning. In their flesh they feel and confirm themselves young. For so they are. Susanna rises up before their desire, which still has the pure impulse of a torrent. There are autumns with the peaks and gusts of Aprils. – Oh, Susanna. – How terrible! – Forgive me. I can see you!

Mediterráneo

(VERSILIA)

SOBRE la playa de este mediodía,
Arena o luz con oleaje denso,
Al sol que es ya cruel un indefenso
Casi-desnudo busca y se confía.

La dama ofrece entonces su armonía
De salud y hermosura en un incienso
De culto al dios solar. (Y mientras, pienso
Cómo yo a tanta fe respondería.)

Siempre feliz, el cuerpo da señales
De la atención muy tensa que los rayos
Desde el cenit consagran a la hermosa.

Inmóvil, ella acepta las brutales
Caricias de este cielo como ensayos
De un amor mitológico a una diosa.

Susana y los viejos

FURTIVOS, silenciosos, tensos, avizorantes,
Se deslizan, escrutan y apartando la rama
Alargan sus miradas hasta el lugar del drama:
El choque de un desnudo con los sueños de antes.

A solas y soñando ya han sido los amantes
Posibles, inminentes, en visión, de la dama.
Tal desnudez real ahora los inflama
Que los viejos se asoman, tímidos estudiantes.

¿Son viejos? Eso cuentan. Es cómputo oficial.
En su carne se sienten, se afirman juveniles
Porque lo son. Susana surge ante su deseo,

Que conserva un impulso cándido de caudal.
Otoños hay con cimas y ráfagas de abriles.
– Ah, Susana. – ¡Qué horror! – Perdóname. ¡Te veo!

The Eagles

THE world contains the truth of life, though the blood may lie sadly when, like a calm sea at evening, it feels the wing beats of the free eagles up above.

The metal feathers, the powerful claws, that impulse towards love or death, that desire to drink from the eyes with iron beak, to be able finally to kiss the earth's crust, flies like desire, like the clouds that oppose nothing, like the radiant blue, heart now on the outside, where freedom has opened up to the world.

The calm eagles will never be skiffs, will not be a dream or a bird, will not be a box in which to leave forgotten what is sad, in which to keep emeralds or opals.

The sun which thickens the pupils, which looks freely into the pupils is an everlasting bird, vanquisher of breasts, in which to sink its fury against a captive body.

The violent wings that brush faces like eclipses, that pierce veins of dead sapphire, that sever the coagulated blood, break the wind into a thousand pieces, marble or impenetrable space in which a dead and halted hand is the brightness that glows in the night.

VICENTE ALEIXANDRE

Las águilas

El mundo encierra la verdad de la vida,
aunque la sangre mienta melancólicamente
cuando como mar sereno en la tarde
siente arriba el batir de las águilas libres.

Las plumas de metal,
las garras poderosas,
ese afán del amor o la muerte,
ese deseo de beber en los ojos con un pico de hierro,
de poder al fin besar lo exterior de la tierra,
vuela como el deseo,
como las nubes que a nada se oponen,
como el azul radiante, corazón ya de afuera
en que la libertad se ha abierto para el mundo.

Las águilas serenas
no serán nunca esquifes,
no serán sueño o pájaro,
no serán caja donde olvidar lo triste,
donde tener guardado esmeraldas u ópalos.

El sol que cuaja en las pupilas,
que a las pupilas mira libremente,
es ave inmarcesible, vencedor de los pechos
donde hundir su furor contra un cuerpo amarrado.

Las violentas alas
que azotan rostros como eclipses,
que parten venas de zafiro muerto,
que seccionan la sangre coagulada,
rompen el viento en mil pedazos,
mármol o espacio impenetrable
donde una mano muerta detenida
es el claror que en la noche fulgura.

Eagles, like abysses, like mountain peaks, overthrow kingships, crumbling lineages, that green ivy that on the thighs imitates the almost living vegetable tongue.

The moment is approaching when fortune may lie in stripping human bodies of their skin, when a victorious heavenly eye may alone see earth as revolving blood.

Eagles of most sonorous metal, furious harps with their almost human voice, sing the anger of loving hearts, of loving them with claws and crushing them to death.

City of Paradise

MY eyes always see you, city of my days by the sea. Hanging from the powerless mountain, scarcely supported up in your headlong fall to the blue waves, you seem to reign beneath the sky, over the waters, half-way up in the air, as if a lucky hand had held you for one glorious moment before sinking you for ever in the waves that love you.

But you stay, you never fall, and the sea sighs or roars for you, city of my happy times, my mother city most white, where once I lived, and I remember, angelic city, that taller than the sea you preside over its foam.

Streets hardly, so light and musical. Gardens in which its stout young palms raise tropical flowers. Palms of light that overhead, winged, rock the brilliance of the breeze and hold poised for a moment celestial lips that cross, bound for the farthest, magic islands, which sail at liberty there in the indigo deep.

I lived there also, there, gracious city, profound city. There where the young skim over the lovely stone, and where the shining walls always kiss the habitual passers, the seething crowds, with brilliance.

Águilas como abismos,
como montes altísimos,
derriban majestades, troncos polvorientos,
esa verde hiedra que en los muslos
finge la lengua vegetal casi viva.

Se aproxima el momento en que la dicha consista
en desvestir de piel a los cuerpos humanos,
en que el celeste ojo victorioso
vea sólo a la tierra como sangre que gira.

Águilas de metal sonorísimo,
arpas furiosas con su voz casi humana,
cantan la ira de amar los corazones,
amarlos con las garras estrujando su muerte.

Ciudad del Paraíso

SIEMPRE te ven mis ojos, ciudad de mis días marinos.
Colgada del impotente monte, apenas detenida
en tu vertical caída a las ondas azules,
pareces reinar bajo el cielo, sobre las aguas,
intermedia en los aires, como si una mano dichosa
te hubiera retenido, un momento de gloria, antes de hundirte para
siempre en las olas amantes.

Pero tú duras, nunca desciendes, y el mar suspira
o brama, por ti, ciudad de mis días alegres,
ciudad madre y blanquísima donde viví, y recuerdo
angélica ciudad que, más alta que el mar, presides sus espumas.

Calles apenas, leves, musicales. Jardines
donde flores tropicales elevan sus juveniles palmas gruesas.
Palmas de luz que sobre las cabezas, aladas,
mecen el brillo de la brisa y suspenden
por un instante labios celestiales que cruzan
con destino a las islas remotísimas, mágicas,
que allá en el azul índigo, libertadas, navegan.

Allí también viví, allí, ciudad graciosa, ciudad honda.
Allí donde los jóvenes resbalan sobre la piedra amable,
y donde las rutilantes paredes besan siempre
a quienes siempre cruzan, hervideros, en brillos.

There I was led by a mother's hand. Perhaps from behind flowery bars a melancholy guitar struck up its sudden tune, suspended in time; quiet was the night and quieter the lover, beneath the eternal moon that moves on in a moment.

A breath of eternity could destroy you, magical city, the moment you emerged into the mind of a God. Men have lived and died for a dream, for ever resplendent like a divine breath.

Gardens, flowers. A sea brave as an arm that reaches out for the city flying between mountain and abyss, white in the air with the look of a poised bird that never arrives. Oh city not on this earth!

By that mother's hand I was led lightly through your featherlight streets. Barefoot by day. Barefoot by night. Full moon. Clear sun. There you were the sky, oh city that dwelt in the sky. City that used to fly through the sky with your wings outspread.

The Old Man and the Sun

HE had lived long. He used to lean there, an old man, on a trunk, on a very thick trunk, on many evenings when the sun was setting. I used to pass there at that hour and stopped to observe him. He was old and had a wrinkled face, and eyes more quenched than sad. He leant on the trunk, and the sun reached him first, softly biting his feet, and stayed there for a few moments as if huddled up. Then it climbed higher, and went on submerging him, drowning him, pulling softly at him, unifying him in its sweet light. Oh, how that oldness living and surviving dissolved! All the eagerness, the story of his sad life, the remains of the wrinkles, the poverty of his corroded skin, how it slowly departed, filing itself away, vanishing! Like a rock that disappears in the destructive torrent softly crumbling away, surrendering to a loudly resounding love, so, in that silence, the old man slowly became

Allí fui conducido por una mano materna.
Acaso de una reja florida una guitarra triste
cantaba la súbita canción suspendida en el tiempo;
quieta la noche, más quieto el amante,
bajo la luna eterna que instantánea transcurre.

Un soplo de eternidad pudo destruirte,
ciudad prodigiosa, momento que en la mente de un Dios emergiste.
Los hombres por un sueño vivieron, no vivieron,
eternamente fúlgidos como un soplo divino.

Jardines, flores. Mar alentado como un brazo que anhela
a la ciudad voladora entre monte y abismo,
blanca en los aires, con calidad de pájaro suspenso
que nunca arriba. ¡Oh ciudad no en la tierra!

Por aquello mano materna fui llevado ligero
por tus calles ingrávidas. Pie desnudo en el día.
Pie desnudo en la noche. Luna grande. Sol puro.
Allí el cielo eras tú, ciudad que en él morabas.
Ciudad que en él volabas con tus alas abiertas.

El viejo y el sol

HABÍA vivido mucho.
Se apoyaba allí, viejo, en un tronco, en un gruesísimo tronco,
    muchas tardes cuando el sol caía.
Yo pasaba por allí a aquellas horas y me detenía a observarle.
Era viejo y tenía la faz arrugada, apagados, más que tristes, los ojos.
Se apoyaba en el tronco, y el sol se le acercaba primero, le mordía
    suavemente los pies
y allí se quedaba unos momentos como acurrucado.
Después ascendía e iba sumergiéndole, anegándole,
tirando suavemente de él, unificándole en su dulce luz.
¡Oh el viejo vivir, el viejo quedar, cómo se desleía!
Toda la quemazón, la historia de la tristeza, el resto de las arrugas, la
    miseria de la piel roída,
¡cómo iba lentamente limándose, deshaciéndose!
Como una roca que en el torrente devastador se va dulcemente
    desmoronando,
rindiéndose a un amor sonorísimo,

nothing, slowly surrendered himself. And I saw the mighty sun slowly bite him with great love and put him to sleep, in order thus to take him little by little, in order thus to dissolve him very little by little in its light, like a mother that very softly restores her child to her breast.

I passed by and saw it. But sometimes I only saw very slight remains. Hardly so much as a very frail thread of his being. What remained after the loving old man, the sweet old man, had already turned into light, and was very slowly borne off in the sun's last rays, like so many other invisible things in the world.

The Poet Sings for All

I

THERE they all are, and you are watching them pass. Oh, how much you would like to mix with them there and recognize yourself!

The furious whirlwind within your heart maddens you. A frenzied mass of grief, spattered against those mute interior walls of flesh. And then with an ultimate effort you decide. Yes, they pass. All are passing. There are children, women. Grave men. Evident mourning, glances. And one mass only, a single being, files concentratedly by. And you, with your heart distressed, convulsed by your solitary grief, with a final effort submerge yourself.

Finally, then, you meet and discover yourself indeed! There calmly you give yourself to the wave. Quietly you drift. And you are pushed forward with a rocking motion, as if tossed and soothed. And you hear a confused noise, like a muted psalm. It is thousands of hearts, forming a single heart, that carry you.

así, en aquel silencio, el viejo se iba lentamente anulando, lentamente entregando.
Y yo veía el poderoso sol lentamente morderle con mucho amor y adormirle
para así poco a poco tomarle, para así poquito a poco disolverle en su luz,
como una madre que a su niño suavísimamente en su seno lo reinstalase.
Yo pasaba y lo veía. Pero a veces no veía sino un sutilísimo resto. Apenas un levísimo encaje del ser.
Lo que quedaba después que el viejo amoroso, el viejo dulce, había pasado ya a ser la luz
y despaciosísimamente era arrastrado en los rayos postreros del sol,
como tantas otras invisibles cosas del mundo.

El poeta canta por todos

I

ALLÍ están todos, y tú los estás mirando pasar.
¡Ah, sí, allí, cómo quisiera mezclarte y reconocerte!

El furioso torbellino dentro del corazón te enloquece.
Masa frenética de dolor, salpicada
contra aquellas mudas paredes interiores de carne.
Y entonces en un último esfuerzo te decides. Sí, pasan.
Todos están pasando. Hay niños, mujeres. Hombres serios. Luto cierto, miradas.
Y una masa sola, un único ser, reconcentradamente desfila.
Y tú, con el corazón apretado, convulso de tu solitario dolor, en un último esfuerzo te sumes.
Sí, al fin, ¡cómo te encuentras y hallas!
Allí serenamente en la ola te entregas. Quedamente derivas.
Y vas acunadamente empujado, como mecido, ablandado.
Y oyes un rumor denso, como un cántico ensordecido.
Son miles de corazones que hacen un único corazón que te lleva.

II

A single heart that carries you. Give up your own grief. Distend your own contracted heart. A single heart runs through you, a single heartbeat rises to your eyes, powerfully invades your body, raises your breast, makes you wave your hands as you now advance. And if you get up for a moment, if for a moment you raise your voice, I know very well what you sing. That which has united and flashed like lightning from an almost infinity of dark bodies, which suddenly through bodies and souls liberates itself in your cry, is the voice of those that carry you away, the true raised voice in which you can hear yourself, in which with astonishment you recognize yourself. The voice that through your throat, from all those scattered hearts, arises pure in the air.

III

And for all ears. Yes. Watch them listening to you. They are listening to themselves. They are listening to a single voice that is singing to them. A very mass of song, they move like a wave. And you, overwhelmed, almost dissolved, recognize yourself as a lump of their being. The voice that bears them sounds. It lies down like a road. All feet are treading it. They are treading it beautifully, they are cutting it with their flesh. And it unfolds and offers itself, and the whole mass gravely files past. It rises like a mountain. On the path of the marchers. And ascends to the clear summit. And the sun comes out above their brows. And at the top, in their greatness, now they are all singing. And it is your voice that gives them expression. Your collective voice upraised. And a heaven of power, completely existent, now majestically returns the whole echo of man.

II

Un único corazón que te lleva.
Abdica de tu propio dolor. Distiende tu propio corazón contraído.
Un único corazón te recorre, un único latido sube a tus ojos,
poderosamente invade tu cuerpo, levanta tu pecho, te hace agitar
las manos cuando ahora avanzas.
Y si te yergues un instante, si un instante levantas la voz, yo sé bien
lo que cantas.
Eso que desde todos los oscuros cuerpos casi infinitos se ha unido y
relampagueado,
que a través de cuerpos y almas se liberta de pronto en tu grito,
es la voz de los que te llevan, la voz verdadera y alzada
donde tú puedes escucharte, donde tú, con asombro, te reconoces.
La voz que por tu garganta, desde todos los corazones esparcidos,
se alza limpiamente en el aire.

III

Y para todos los oídos. Sí. Mírales cómo te oyen.
Se están escuchando a sí mismos. Están escuchando una única voz
que los canta.
Masa misma del canto, se mueven como una onda.
Y tú sumido, casi disuelto, como un nudo de su ser te conoces.
Suena la voz que los lleva. Se acuesta como un camino.
Todas las plantas están pisándola.
Están pisándola hermosamente, están grabándola con su carne.
Y ella se despliega y ofrece, y toda la masa gravemente desfila.
Como una montaña sube. En la senda de los que marchan.
Y asciende hasta el pico claro. Y el sol se abre sobre las frentes.
Y en la cumbre, con su grandeza, están todos ya cantando.
Y es tu voz la que les expresa. Tu voz colectiva y alzada.
Y un cielo de poderío, completamente existente,
hace ahora con majestad el eco entero del hombre.

The Past: 'Villa Pura'

HERE in the little house, three trees in front, the door still standing, the sound of the bell: everything persists, or is dead when I go in. I remember: 'Villa Pura'. Pure of what; of the wind. Here that boy started trembling. Here he looked at the dead sand, the clay like a glove, the light like his pale cheeks, the old gold giving his hair a kiss, without yesterday. Today, tomorrow. The leaves have fallen, or have climbed today from the earth to the tree, and still feign passion, being, sound. And I go in and they give no shade, since they are. And there is no smoke.

Face through the Glass
(An Old Man Gazes)

EITHER late or soon or never. But here through the glass the face insists. Beside some natural flowers the flower itself appears in the form of colour, cheek, rose. Through the glass the rose is always a rose. But it has no scent. Distant youth is itself. But here it is not heard.

Only light passes through the virgin glass.

El Pasado: «Villa Pura»

AQUÍ en la casa chica,
tres árboles delante, la puerta en pie, el sonido:
todo persiste, o muerto,
cuando cruzo. Me acuerdo: «Villa Pura».
Pura ¿de qué? del viento.
Aquí ese niño puso
en pie el temblor. Aquí miró la arena
muerta,
el barro como un guante,
la luz como sus pálidas mejillas
y el oro viejo dando
en el cabello un beso
sin ayer. Hoy, mañana.
Las hojas han caído, o de la tierra al árbol
subieron hoy
y aún fingen
pasión, estar, rumor. Y cruzo
y no dan sombra,
pues que son. Y no hay humo.

Rostro tras el cristal
(Mirada del viejo)

O TARDE o pronto o nunca.
Pero ahí tras el cristal el rostro insiste.
Junto a unas flores naturales la misma flor se muestra
en forma de color, mejilla, rosa.
Tras el cristal la rosa es siempre rosa.
Pero no huele.
La juventud distante es ella misma.
Pero aquí no se oye.

Sólo la luz traspasa el cristal virgen.

Without Faith

YOU have dark eyes. Gleams there that promise darkness. Oh, how certain is your night, how uncertain my doubt. I see the light in the depths, and alone, I believe.

Alone then you exist. To exist is to live with knowledge blindly. For you approach darkly and in my eyes more lights are felt without my observing that they are shining in them.

They do not shine, for they were aware. Is awareness knowledge? I do not know you and was aware. To be aware is to breathe with open eyes. To doubt? . . . One who doubts exists. Only death is knowledge.

Yesterday

THAT curtain of yellow silks that a sun still gilds and a sigh ripples. In one breath yesterday sways and rustles. In space it still exists but conceives itself or sees itself. Asleep, whoever looks at it does not reply, for he sees a silence, or is a sleeping love.

To sleep, to live, to die. Slowly the silk rustles, tiny, very fine, dreamed of, regal. Whoever is, is a sign, an image of one who thought, and there it remains. A weft into which living slowly wove itself and was left thread by thread, for the breath in which it is still moving.

Not to know is life. To know is to kill it.

Sin fe

TIENES ojos oscuros.
Brillos allí que oscuridad prometen.
Ah, cuán cierta es tu noche,
cuán incierta mi duda.
Miro al fondo la luz, y creo a solas.

A solas pues que existes. Existir es vivir con ciencia a ciegas.
Pues oscura te acercas
y en mis ojos más luces
siéntense sin mirar que en ellos brillen.

No brillan, pues supieron.
¿Saber es conocer? No te conozco y supe.
Saber es alentar con los ojos abiertos.
¿Dudar . . .? Quien duda existe. Sólo morir es ciencia.

Ayer

ESE telón de sedas amarillas
que un sol aún dora y un suspiro ondea.
En un soplo el ayer vacila, y cruje.
En el espacio aún es, pero se piensa
o se ve. Dormido quien lo mira no responde,
pues ve un silencio, o es un amor dormido.

Dormir, vivir, morir. Lenta la seda cruje diminuta,
finísima, soñada: real. Quien es es signo:
una imagen de quien pensó, y ahí queda.
Trama donde el vivir se urdió despacio, y hebra a hebra
quedó, para el aliento en que aún se agita.

Ignorar es vivir. Saber, morirlo.

The Moon Peeps Out

WHEN the moon comes out, the bells are lost and the impenetrable paths appear.

When the moon comes out sea covers the earth, and the heart feels itself an island in the infinite.

No one eats oranges beneath a full moon. It is proper to eat green and icy fruit.

When the moon comes out with a hundred identical faces, silver money sobs in the purse.

The Rider's Song

CÓRDOBA. Faraway and lonely.

Small black horse and great moon, and olives in my saddle-bag. Although I know the roads, I shall never reach Córdoba.

Over the plain, through the wind, small black horse, red moon. Death is staring at me from the towers of Córdoba.

FEDERICO GARCÍA LORCA

La luna asoma

CUANDO sale la luna
se pierden las campanas
y aparecen las sendas
impenetrables.

Cuando sale la luna,
el mar cubre la tierra
y el corazón se siente
isla en el infinito.

Nadie come naranjas
bajo la luna llena.
Es preciso comer
fruta verde y helada.

Cuando sale la luna
de cien rostros iguales,
la moneda de plata
solloza en el bolsillo.

Canción de jinete

CÓRDOBA.
Lejana y sola.

Jaca negra, luna grande,
y aceitunas en mi alforja.
Aunque sepa los caminos
yo nunca llegaré a Córdoba.

Por el llano, por el viento,
jaca negra, luna roja.
La muerte me está mirando
desde las torres de Córdoba.

Oh how long the road is! Oh how brave is my little horse! Alas that death is expecting me before I reach Córdoba!

Córdoba, faraway and lonely.

Somnambular Ballad

GREEN, how much I want you green.* Green wind. Green boughs. The ship on the sea and the horse on the mountain. With the shadow at her waist, she dreams on her balcony, green flesh, green hair, with eyes of cold silver. Green, how much I want you green. Beneath the gipsy moon, things are looking at her, but she cannot look at them.

Green, how much I want you green. Great stars of white frost come with the fish of darkness, which opens a way for the dawn. The fig-tree rubs its wind with the sandpaper of its branches, and the mountain, like a thieving cat, bristles its (fur like) bitter aloes.† But who is coming? And from where? She stays on her balcony, green flesh, green hair, dreaming in the bitter sea.

'Friend, I should like to change my horse for your house, my saddle for your mirror, my knife for your blanket. Friend, I have come bleeding from

* There is a secondary meaning that suits the line better: 'Green, how very deeply green.'

† The agave plant, a bitter succulent.

¡Ay qué camino tan largo!
¡Ay mi jaca valerosa!
¡Ay que la muerte me espera,
antes de llegar a Córdoba!

Córdoba.
Lejana y sola.

Romance sonámbulo

VERDE que te quiero verde.
Verde viento. Verdes ramas.
El barco sobre la mar
y el caballo en la montaña.
Con la sombra en la cintura
ella sueña en su baranda,
verde carne, pelo verde,
con ojos de fría plata.
Verde que te quiero verde.
Bajo la luna gitana,
las cosas le están mirando
y ella no puede mirarlas.

Verde que te quiero verde.
Grandes estrellas de escarcha
vienen con el pez de sombra
que abre el camino del alba.
La higuera frota su viento
con la lija de sus ramas,
y el monte, gato garduño,
eriza sus pitas agrias.
Pero ¿quién vendrá? ¿Y por dónde . . .?
Ella sigue en su baranda,
verde carne, pelo verde,
soñando en la mar amarga.

«Compadre quiero cambiar
mi caballo por su casa,
mi montura por su espejo,
mi cuchillo por su manta.

the passes of Cabra.'

'If I could, young man, this deal should be clinched, but now I am not myself, nor is my house now my own.'

'Friend, I should like to die decently in my bed. An iron one, if it may be, with holland sheets. Do you not see the wound I have from my breast to my throat?'

'Your white shirt bears three hundred red roses. Your blood oozes and smells around your sash. But now I am not myself, nor is my house now my own.'

'At least let me climb up to your high balconies. Let me climb up, let me come to your green balconies. Balconies of the moon where the water echoes.'

Now the two friends climb up to the tall balconies. Leaving a trail of blood, leaving a trail of tears. Little tin lanterns were trembling on the roofs. A thousand glass tambourines were wounding the dawn.

Green, how much I want you green, green wind, green boughs. The two friends climbed up. The great wind was leaving a strange taste in the mouth, of gall and mint and sweet-basil.

Compadre, vengo sangrando,
desde los puertos de Cabra.»
«Si yo pudiera, mocito,
este trato se cerraba.
Pero yo ya no soy yo,
ni mi casa es ya mi casa.»
«Compadre, quiero morir
decentemente en mi cama.
De acero, si puede ser,
con las sábanas de holanda.
¿No ves la herida que tengo
desde el pecho a la garganta?»
«Trescientas rosas morenas
lleva tu pechera blanca.
Tu sangre rezuma y huele
alrededor de tu faja.
Pero yo ya no soy yo,
ni mi casa es ya mi casa»

«Dejadme subir al menos
hasta las altas barandas;
¡dejadme subir!, dejadme,
hasta las verdes barandas.
Barandales de la luna
por donde retumba el agua.

Ya suben los dos compadres
hacia las altas barandas.
Dejando un rastro de sangre.
Dejando un rastro de lágrimas.
Temblaban en los tejados
farolillos de hojalata.
Mil panderos de cristal
herían la madrugada.

Verde que te quiero verde,
verde viento, verdes ramas.
Los dos compadres subieron.
El largo viento dejaba
en la boca un raro gusto
de hiel, de menta y de albahaca.

Friend, where is she, tell me, where is your bitter girl? How many times she waited for you! How many times she must have waited for you, cool face, black hair, on this green balcony!'

On the face of the water-tank the gipsy-girl was rocking. Green flesh, green hair, with eyes of cold silver. An icicle of moon keeps her above the water. The night became as intimate as a little square. Drunken Civil Guards were knocking at the door. Green, how much I want you green. Green wind. Green boughs. The ship on the sea. And the horse on the mountain.

Lament for Ignacio Sánchez Mejías

1. THE TOSSING AND THE DEATH

AT five in the afternoon. It was exactly five in the afternoon. A boy brought the white sheet *at five in the afternoon.* A basket of lime ready prepared *at five in the afternoon.* The rest was death and death only *at five in the afternoon.*

The wind blew away the cotton-wool *at five in the afternoon.* And the chloride scattered glass and nickel, *at five in the afternoon.* Now the dove and the leopard are struggling, *at five in the afternoon.* And a thigh with a desolate

¡Compadre! ¿Dónde está, dime,
dónde está tu niña amarga?
¡Cuántas veces te esperó!
¡Cuántas veces te esperara,
cara fresca, negro pelo,
en esta verde baranda!

Sobre el rostro del aljibe
se mecía la gitana.
Verde carne, pelo verde,
con ojos de fría plata.
Un carámbano de luna
la sostiene sobre el agua.
La noche se puso íntima
como una pequeña plaza.
Guardias civiles borrachos
en la puerta golpeaban.
Verde que te quiero verde.
Verde viento. Verdes ramas.
El barco sobre la mar.
Y el caballo en la montaña.

Llanto por Ignacio Sánchez Mejías

1. LA COGIDA Y LA MUERTE

A LAS cinco de la tarde.
Eran las cinco en punto de la tarde.
Un niño trajo la blanca sábana
a las cinco de la tarde.
Una espuerta de cal ya prevenida
a las cinco de la tarde.
Lo demás era muerte y sólo muerte
a las cinco de la tarde.

El viento se llevó los algodones
a las cinco de la tarde.
Y el óxido sembró cristal y níquel
a las cinco de la tarde.
Ya luchan la paloma y el leopardo
a las cinco de la tarde.

horn, *at five in the afternoon.* The base notes struck up, *at five in the afternoon.* Arsenic bells and smoke, *at five in the afternoon.* Silent groups in the corners, *at five in the afternoon.* And the bull alone holding his head high, *at five in the afternoon.* When the sweat of snow was arriving, *at five in the afternoon*, when the bull-ring was covered with iodine, *at five in the afternoon*, death laid eggs in the wound, *at five in the afternoon. At five in the afternoon. At exactly five in the afternoon.*

A coffin on wheels is his bed *at five in the afternoon.* Bones and flutes sound in his ears, *at five in the afternoon.* Now the bull was bellowing close to his forehead, *at five in the afternoon.* The room was rainbowed with agony, *at five in the afternoon.* Now in the distance gangrene is approaching, *at five in the afternoon.* A lily trumpet in his green groins, *at five in the afternoon.* The wounds burned like suns, *at five in the afternoon*, and the crowd was breaking the windows, *at five in the afternoon.* At five in the afternoon. Oh that terrible five in the afternoon! It was five on all the clocks! It was five in the shade of the afternoon.

Y un muslo con una asta desolada
a las cinco de la tarde.
Comenzaron los sones de bordón
a las cinco de la tarde.
Las campanas de arsénico y humo
a las cinco de la tarde.
En las esquinas grupos de silencio
a las cinco de la tarde.
¡Y el toro solo corazón arriba!
a las cinco de la tarde.
Cuando el sudor de nieve fue llegando
a las cinco de la tarde,
cuando la plaza se cubrió de yodo
a las cinco de la tarde,
la muerte puso huevos en la herida
a las cinco de la tarde.
A las cinco de la tarde.
A las cinco en punto de la tarde.

Un ataúd con ruedas es la cama
a las cinco de la tarde.
Huesos y flautas suenan en su oído
a las cinco de la tarde.
El toro ya mugía por su frente
a las cinco de la tarde.
El cuarto se irisaba de agonía
a las cinco de la tarde.
A lo lejos ya viene la gangrena
a las cinco de la tarde.
Trompa de lirio por las verdes ingles
a las cinco de la tarde.
Las heridas quemaban como soles
a las cinco de la tarde,
y el gentío rompía las ventanas
a las cinco de la tarde.
A las cinco de la tarde.
¡Ay, qué terribles cinco de la tarde!
¡Eran las cinco en todos los relojes!
¡Eran las cinco en sombra de la tarde!

2. THE SPILT BLOOD

I DO not want to see it! Tell the moon to come, for I do not want to see Ignacio's blood on the sand. I do not want to see it!

The great wide moon. Horse of the still clouds and the grey bull-ring of dreams, with willows on its barriers. I do not want to see it! For my memory is burning. Tell this to the jasmines with their minute whiteness! I do not want to see it!

The cow of the ancient world passed her sad tongue over a snout red with all the blood spilt on the sand, and the bulls of Guisando, formed half of death and half of stone, bellowed like two centuries glutted with treading the earth. No. I do not want to see it!

Ignacio ascends the tiers with all his death on his shoulders. He was seeking the dawn, and there was no dawn. He seeks his firm profile, and the dream makes him lose his way. He was seeking his handsome body, and he found his blood opened up. Do not tell me to see it. I do not want to feel it spurt, with less strength every time; that spurt that lights the seats and spills over

2. LA SANGRE DERRAMADA

¡QUE no quiero verla!

Díle a la luna que venga,
que no quiero ver la sangre
de Ignacio sobre la arena.

¡Que no quiero verla!

La luna de par en par.
Caballo de nubes quietas,
y la plaza gris de sueño
con sauces en las barreras.
¡Que no quiero verla!
Que mi recuerdo se quema.
¡Avisad a los jazmines
con su blancura pequeña!

¡Que no quiero verla!

La vaca del viejo mundo
pasaba su triste lengua
sobre un hocico de sangres
derramadas en la arena,
y los toros de Guisando,
casi muerte y casi piedra,
mugieron como dos siglos
hartos de pisar la tierra.
No.
¡Que no quiero verla!

Por las gradas sube Ignacio
con toda su muerte a cuestas.
Buscaba el amanecer,
y el amanecer no era.
Busca su perfil seguro,
y el sueño lo desorienta.
Buscaba su hermoso cuerpo
y encontró su sangre abierta.
¡No me digáis que la vea!
No quiero sentir el chorro
cada vez con menos fuerza;

the corduroy and leather of a thirsty crowd. Who shouts to me to have a look? Do not ask me to look at it.

His eyes did not shut when he saw the horns near, but the terrible mothers lifted their heads, and over the ranches rose a breeze of secret voices, the herdsmen of pale mist calling to the bulls of heaven. There was no prince in Seville to compare to him, no sword like his sword, and no heart so true. His marvellous strength was like a stream of lions, and his exemplary caution like a marble torso. Airs of Andalusian Rome gilded his head, whereon his smile was a spikenard of wit and intelligence. What a great fighter in the ring! What a good highlander in the mountains! How gentle with the wheat! How tough with the spurs! How tender with the dew! How dazzling on fair-days! How tremendous with the final darts* of darkness.

But now he sleeps for ever. Now the moss and the grass with sure fingers open the flower of his skull. And now his blood comes singing, singing

* The *banderillas* are thrown to provoke a blind charge.

ese chorro que ilumina
los tendidos y se vuelca
sobre la pana y el cuero
de muchedumbre sedienta.
¡Quién me grita que me asome!
¡No me digáis que la vea!

No se cerraron sus ojos
cuando vio los cuernos cerca,
pero las madres terribles
levantaron la cabeza.
Y a través de las ganaderías,
hubo un aire de voces secretas
que gritaban a toros celestes,
mayorales de pálida niebla.
No hubo príncipe en Sevilla
que compararsele pueda,
ni espada como su espada
ni corazón tan de veras.
Como un río de leones
su maravillosa fuerza,
y como un torso de mármol
su dibujada prudencia.
Aire de Roma andaluza
le doraba la cabeza
donde su risa era un nardo
de sal y de inteligencia.
¡Qué gran torero en la plaza!
¡Qué buen serrano en la sierra!
¡Qué blando con las espigas!
¡Qué duro con las espuelas!
¡Qué tierno con el rocío!
¡Qué deslumbrante en la feria!
¡Qué tremendo con las últimas
banderillas de tiniebla!

Pero ya duerme sin fin.
Ya los musgos y la hierba
abren con dedos seguros
la flor de su calavera.
Y su sangre ya viene cantando:

through marshes and meadows, sliding on horns stiff with cold, wavering without a soul in the mist, meeting with thousands of hoofs, like a long, dark, sad tongue to form a pool of agony beside the starry Guadalquivir. Oh white wall of Spain! Oh black bull of sorrow! Oh congealed blood of Ignacio! Oh nightingale of his veins! No. I do not want to see it! For there is no chalice that can contain it, no swallows that can drink it, no white frost of the light that can cool it, no song nor flood of white lilies, nor glass to cover it with silver. No. I will not see it!

3. LYING IN STATE

STONE is a brow where dreams groan, lacking curves of water and frozen cypresses. Stone is a shoulder to carry Time, with trees of tears and ribbons and planets.

I have seen grey showers running towards the waves, raising their tender, riddled arms, so as not to be caught by the outstretched stone, which relaxes their limbs without soaking up the blood.

For stone gathers seeds and clouds, skeletons of larks and wolves of the half-dark; but it gives no sound, nor crystal, nor fire, only bull-rings and bull-rings and more bull-rings without walls.

Now Ignacio the well-born is lying on stone. Now it is all over. What is happening? Gaze upon his face. Death has covered him with pale sulphur and put the head of a dark minotaur upon him.

cantando por marismas y praderas,
resbalando por cuernos ateridos,
vacilando sin alma por la niebla,
tropezando con miles de pezuñas
como una larga, oscura, triste lengua,
para formar un charco de agonía
junto al Guadalquivir de las estrellas.
¡Oh blanco muro de España!
¡Oh negro toro de pena!
¡Oh sangre dura de Ignacio!
¡Oh ruiseñor de sus venas!
No.
¡Que no quiero verla!
Que no hay cáliz que la contenga,
que no hay golondrinas que se la beban,
no hay escarcha de luz que la enfríe,
no hay canto ni diluvio de azucenas,
no hay cristal que la cubra de plata.
No.
¡¡Yo no quiero verla!!

3. CUERPO PRESENTE

LA piedra es una frente donde los sueños gimen
sin tener agua curva ni cipreses helados.
La piedra es una espalda para llevar al tiempo
con árboles de lágrimas y cintas y planetas.

Yo he visto lluvias grises correr hacia las olas,
levantando sus tiernos brazos acribillados,
para no ser cazadas por la piedra tendida
que desata sus miembros sin empapar la sangre.

Porque la piedra coge simientes y nublados,
esqueletos de alondras y lobos de penumbra;
pero no da sonidos, ni cristales, ni fuego,
sino plazas y plazas y otras plazas sin muros.

Ya está sobre la piedra Ignacio el bien nacido.
Ya se acabó; ¿qué pasa? Contemplad su figura:
la muerte le ha cubierto de pálidos azufres
y le ha puesto cabeza de oscuro minotauro.

Now it is all over. The rain seeps in through his mouth. The air, as though crazy, leaves his sunken chest, and Love, soaked with snowy tears, warms himself on the heights of the ranches.

What are they saying? A stenching silence settles down. We are here with a body present (laid-out) which is vanishing, with a pure shape that held nightingales and we see it being filled with bottomless holes.

Who is creasing the shroud! What he is saying is not true! Nobody is singing here or weeping in the corner, or pricking his spurs, or frightening the snake. Here I want nothing more than round eyes to see this body without a possibility of rest.

I want to see here those men of hard voice. Those who break horses and master rivers: the men whose skeletons thunder and who sing with their mouths full of sun and flints.

I want to see them here. Facing the stone. Facing this body with broken reins. I want them to show where there is a way out for this captain tied down by death.

I want them to teach me a dirge like a river, which will have sweet mists and steep banks, to bear Ignacio's body, that it may lose itself out of earshot of the bulls' double snort.

That it may lose itself in the round bull-ring of the moon, who pretends when she is a girl to be a sad, still beast; that it may lose itself in the night without the song of fishes and in the white thicket of frozen vapour.

I do not want them to cover his face with handkerchiefs to accustom him to the death he carries. Go, Ignacio. Do not feel the hot bellowing. Sleep, fly away, rest. Even the sea dies!

Ya se acabó. La lluvia penetra por su boca.
El aire como loco deja su pecho hundido,
y el Amor, empapado con lágrimas de nieve,
se calienta en la cumbre de las ganaderías.

¿Qué dicen? Un silencio con hedores reposa.
Estamos con un cuerpo presente que se esfuma,
con una forma clara que tuvo ruiseñores
y la vemos llenarse de agujeros sin fondo.

¿Quién arruga el sudario? ¡No es verdad lo que dice!
Aquí no canta nadie, ni llora en el rincón,
ni pica las espuelas, ni espanta la serpiente:
aquí no quiero más que los ojos redondos
para ver ese cuerpo sin posible descanso.

Yo quiero ver aquí los hombres de voz dura.
Los que doman caballos y dominan los ríos:
los hombres que les suena el esqueleto y cantan
con una boca llena de sol y pedernales.

Aquí quiero yo verlos. Delante de la piedra.
Delante de este cuerpo con las riendas quebradas.
Yo quiero que me enseñen dónde está la salida
para este capitán atado por la muerte.

Yo quiero que me enseñen un llanto como un río
que tenga dulces nieblas y profundas orillas,
para llevar el cuerpo de Ignacio y que se pierda
sin escuchar el doble resuello de los toros.

Que se pierda en la plaza redonda de la luna
que finge cuando niña doliente res inmóvil;
que se pierda en la noche sin canto de los peces
y en la maleza blanca del humo congelado.

No quiero que le tapen la cara con pañuelos
para que se acostumbre con la muerte que lleva.
Vete, Ignacio: No sientas el caliento bramido.
Duerme, vuela, reposa: ¡También se muere el mar!

4. THE SOUL IS ABSENT

THE bull does not know you nor the fig-tree, nor the horses nor the ants of your house. The child does not know you nor the afternoon, because you have died for ever.

The stones' back does not know you, nor the black satin in which you are crumbling. Your silent memory does not know you, because you have died for ever.

Autumn will come with its conches,* its misted grapes and clustered hills, but no one will want to look into your eyes because you have died for ever.

Because you have died for ever, like all the Earth's dead, like all the dead who are forgotten in a pile of snuffed-out dogs.

Nobody knows you. No. But I sing of you. I sing for posterity of your profile and your grace; of the signal maturity of your understanding; of your appetite for death and the taste of its mouth, of the sorrow that was in your valiant gaiety.

It will be a long time before there is born, if ever, an Andalusian so distinguished and rich in adventure. I sing of his elegance in words that moan, and remember a sad breeze among the olive-trees.

IF my voice should die on earth, take it to sea-level and leave it on the shore.

* Horns blown by the shepherds on the hills.

4. ALMA AUSENTE

No te conoce el toro ni la higuera,
ni caballos ni hormigas de tu casa.
No te conoce el niño ni la tarde
porque te has muerto para siempre.

No te conoce el lomo de la piedra,
ni el raso negro donde te destrozas.
No te conoce tu recuerdo mudo
porque te has muerto para siempre.

El otoño vendrá con caracolas,
uva de niebla y montes agrupados,
pero nadie querrá mirar tus ojos
porque te has muerto para siempre.

Porque te has muerto para siempre,
como todos los muertos de la Tierra,
como todos los muertos que se olvidan
en un montón de perros apagados.

No te conoce nadie. No. Pero yo te canto.
Yo canto para luego tu perfil y tu gracia.
La madurez insigne de tu conocimiento.
Tu apetencia de muerte y el gusto de su boca.
La tristeza que tuvo tu valiente alegría.

Tardará mucho tiempo en nacer, si es que nace,
un andaluz tan claro, tan rico de aventura.
Yo canto su elegancia con palabras que gimen
y recuerdo una brisa triste por los olivos.

RAFAEL ALBERTI

Si mi voz muriera en tierra,
llevadla al nivel del mar
y dejadla en la ribera.

Take it to sea-level, and make it captain of a white ship of war. Oh my voice decorated with sailor's badges, on the heart an anchor, and on the anchor a star, and on the star the wind and on the wind the sail!

To a Ship's Captain

ON your ship – a green ledge of seaweeds, molluscs, shells, and the starry emerald – captain of the winds and the swallows, you were invested by the sea's accolade.

For you the serpentine-edged sea-coasts unroll a song in time with your ploughing. Sailor, free man who goes down the seas, tell us the radio-messages of the Pole Star.

Good sailor, son of the North's weeping, lemon of the noon (or South), banner of the water's foaming court, chaser of sirens;

we, all the moored shores of the world, beg you to take us in your ship's deep wake, to the sea, with our chains broken.

Aracelli

IF it is not from the two sails of a melancholy archangel that the snowflakes have fallen on you. At least it is from the sad jasmine that they come, slipping along the wake of soft and heavenly eyes.

Llevadla al nivel del mar
y nombradla capitana
de un blanco bajel de guerra.

¡Oh mi voz condecorada
con la insignia marinera:

sobre el corazón un ancla
y sobre el ancla un estrella
y sobre la estrella el viento
y sobre el viento la vela!

A un capitán de navío

Homme libre, toujours tu chériras la mer!
C. Baudelaire

Sobre tu nave – un plinto verde de algas marinas,
de moluscos, de conchas, de esmeralda estelar –,
capitán de los vientos y de las golondrinas,
fuiste condecorado por un golpe de mar.

Por ti los litorales de frentes serpentinas
desenrollan al paso de tu arado un cantar:
– Marinero, hombre libre, que las mares declinas,
dínos los radiogramas de tu Estrella Polar.

Buen marinero, hijo de los llantos del norte,
limón del mediodía, bandera de la corte
espumosa del agua, cazador de sirenas;

todos los litorales amarrados del mundo,
pedimos que nos lleves en el surco profundo
de tu nave, a la mar, rotas nuestras cadenas.

Aracelli

No si de arcángel triste, ya nevados
los copos, sobre ti, de sus dos velas.
Si de serios jazmines, por estelas
de ojos dulces, celestes, resbalados.

Not from swans that have curded above you, caravels pressed out of glass. But from moon speechless at your flight, from silent and melted marble.

Altar of heaven, tell me of what you are made, if you are of archangel's feathers and jasmine, if you are of the liquid marble of dawn and feather.

You are born ivory, and ivory you die, imprisoned and brought to flower in lakeside gardens of gold and green foam.

The Good Angel

ONE year when I was sleeping, someone I did not expect stopped at my window. 'Rise up!' he cried, and my eyes saw feathers and swords. Behind, mountains and seas, clouds, peaks and wings, the sunsets, the dawns. 'Look on her there, with nothing to dream of.'

'Oh, deep desire, firm marble, firm light, firm, shifting waters of my soul!'

Someone said: 'Rise up!', and I found myself where you were.

The Revengeful Angels

NO, they did not know you, the souls you knew. But mine did.

Who are you, tell us, for we do not remember you either on earth or in heaven?

No si de cisnes sobre ti cuajados,
del cristal exprimidas carabelas.
Si de luna sin habla cuando vuelas,
si de mármoles mudos, deshelados.

Ara del cielo, dime de qué eres,
si de pluma de arcángel y jazmines,
si de líquido mármol de alba y pluma.

De marfil naces y de marfil mueres,
confinada y florida de jardines
lacustres de dorada y verde espuma.

El Ángel bueno

UN año, ya dormido,
alguien que no esperaba
se paró en mi ventana.

– ¡Levántate! Y mis ojos
vieron plumas y espadas.

Atrás, montes y mares,
nubes, picos y alas,
los ocasos, las albas.

– ¡Mírala ahí! Su sueño
pendiente de la nada.

– ¡Oh anhelo, fijo mármol,
fija luz, fijas aguas
movibles de mi alma!

Alguien dijo: ¡Levántate!
Y me encontré en tu estancia.

Los Ángeles vengativos

NO, no te conocieron
las almas conocidas.
Sí la mía.

¿Quién eres tú, dínos, que no te recordamos
ni de la tierra ni del cielo?

Tell us, of what dimension is your shadow? Speak, what light extended it into our kingdom?

Where do you come from, tell us, wordless shadow, for we do not remember you? Who has sent you? If you were a lightning flash in any dream, lightning is forgotten once it is quenched.

And since you were unknown (to them), the souls you knew have killed you. But not mine.

The Covetous Angel

PEOPLE of the street corners of towns and nations that are not on the map were making remarks.

That man is dead and does not know it. He wants to storm the bank, steal clouds, stars, golden comets, and to buy what is most difficult: the sky. And that man is dead.

Subterranean tremors shake his brow. Falls of loose earth, delirious echoes, confused sounds of picks and shovels, his ears. His eyes, acetylene flares, damp, golden corridors. His heart, explosions of stone, bursts of glee, dynamite.

He dreams of mines.

Tu sombra, dínos, ¿de qué espacio?
¿Qué luz la prolongó, habla,
hasta nuestro reinado?

¿De dónde vienes, dínos,
sombra sin palabras,
que no te recordamos?
¿Quién te manda?
Si relámpago fuiste en algún sueño,
relámpagos se olvidan, apagados.

Y por desconocida,
las almas conocidas te mataron.
No la mía.

El Ángel avaro

GENTES de las esquinas
de pueblos y naciones que no están en el mapa,
comentaban.

Ese hombre está muerto
y no lo sabe.
Quiere asaltar la banca,
robar nubes, estrellas, cometas de oro,
comprar lo más defícil:
el cielo.
Y ese hombre está muerto.

Temblores subterráneos le sacuden la frente.
Tumbos de tierra desprendida,
ecos desvariados,
sones confusos de piquetas y azadas,
los oídos.
Los ojos,
luces de acetileno,
húmedas, áureas galerías.
El corazón,
explosiones de piedras, júbilos, dinamita.

Sueña con las minas.

Monte de el Pardo

SO much sun on the war, suddenly so much light spread in cartloads over the valleys and hills, such furious silence, such savage calm, coming down like a crime from heaven on to the holm-oaks;

this ignoring of death, which, in concert with the fields, attempts such dazzling light; the snow that goes far off in ecstasy, the hours that do not affect them at all as they pass;

all this gnaws at me, undermines me, and takes the lightness from my eyes, mists them over, and places a load of tears and dynamite on my mind. Solitude echoes and the sun decays.

Poem from Exile

WHO are you that voicelessly call me from afar with such a terrified thought, and silently pronounce my name on the appalled and silent wind?

Who are you, and what do you ask, and what do you cry, and what is dying in such distant sounds; who are you that with such hushed calling wrench my bones from my skin?

My teeth taste of a frozen word, my dead tongue of a fear that has died, and my heart of a silenced beating.

The bull's skin flows in blood, the seas flow a dry sea of tears . . . and those who called me have already gone away.

Monte de el Pardo

TANTO sol en la guerra, de pronto, tanta lumbre
desparramada a carros por valles y colinas;
tan rabioso silencio, tan fiera mansedumbre
bajando como un crimen del cielo a las encinas;

este desentenderse de la muerte que intenta,
de acuerdo con el campo, tanta luz deslumbrada;
la nieve que a lo lejos en éxtasis se ausenta,
las horas que pasando no les preocupa nada;

todo esto me remuerde, me socava, me quita
ligereza a los ojos, me los nubla y me pone
la conciencia cargada de llanto y dinamita.
La soledad retumba y el sol se descompone.

Poema del destierro

¿QUIÉNES sin voz de lejos me llamáis
con tan despavorido pensamiento
y en aterrado y silencioso viento
sin sonido mi nombre pronunciáis?

¿Quiénes y qué pedís y qué gritáis
y qué se muere en tan remoto acento;
quiénes con tan collado llamamiento
los huesos de la piel me desclaváis?

Saben los dientes a palabra helada,
la lengua muerta a fallecido espanto
y el corazón a pulso enmudecido.

La piel de toro fluye ensangrentada,
fluye la mar un seco mar de llanto . . .
. . . y quienes me llamaban ya se han ido.

Memories of Love in Landscapes that are Alive

WE believe, my love, that those landscapes have remained asleep or dead with ourselves at the age and in the time when we inhabited them; that trees lose their memory and nights depart, giving to oblivion what made them beautiful and perhaps immortal. But the slightest stirring of a leaf is enough, the sudden breathing of an obliterated star, to see us the same happy beings, filling the places that were ours together. And so, my love, you wake up today at my side among the currant bushes and the hidden strawberries, protected by the firm heart of the woods. There is the caress damp with dew, the delicate threads that refresh your bed, the sylphs delighted to decorate your hair, and the high mysterious squirrels that rain the small green of the branches on your sleep.

Be happy, leaf, for ever; may you never know autumn, leaf that has brought me with your slight stirring the aroma of such blind, luminous years. And you, tiny lost star that opens to me the intimate windows of my more youthful nights, never turn off your light above all those bedrooms where we slept at dawn, and from that library in moonlight, and those books in sweet disorder, and the wakeful mountains outside singing to us.

Retornos del amor en los vívidos paisajes

CREEMOS, amor mío, que aquellos paisajes
se quedaron dormidos o muertos con nosotros
en la edad, en el día en que los habitamos;
que los árboles pierden la memoria
y las noches se van, dando al olvido
lo que las hizo hermosas y tal vez inmortales.
Pero basta el más leve palpitar de una hoja,
una estrella borrada que respira de pronto
para vernos los mismos alegres que llenamos
los lugares que juntos nos tuvieron.
Y así despiertas hoy, mi amor, a mi costado,
entre los groselleros y las fresas ocultas
al amparo del firme corazón de los bosques.
Allí está la caricia mojada de rocío,
las briznas delicadas que refrescan tu lecho,
los silfos encantados de ornar tu cabellera
y las altas ardillas misteriosas que llueven
sobre tu sueño el verde menudo de las ramas.

Sé feliz, hoja, siempre: nunca tengas otoño,
hoja que me has traído
con tu temblor pequeño
el aroma de tanta ciega edad luminosa.
Y tú, mínima estrella perdida que me abres
las íntimas ventanas de mis noches más jóvenes,
nunca cierres tu lumbre
sobre tantas alcobas que al alba nos durmieron
y aquella biblioteca con la luna
y los libros aquellos dulcemente caídos
y los montes afuera desvelados cantándonos.

Pictures, rivers, trains, planes . . .

IN melancholy mood, sadly. Why? I know. Shall I tell? I will not tell . . .

English painting, Stubbs, Gainsborough, Reynolds . . . What cold boredom. A train – Turner (Better!) – passes between the rails of my river-view balcony.

Chardin. Musical instruments. Silent clocks. Pipes and events. A hare beside a copper kettle. How still, how sweet the world of these living inanimate things! I look. The street, the sky, the smoke of the factories, the braking of a car . . . my world. Amidst the clouds and the soot, shining, a rare insect, I tell you, a helicopter. Liotard, Nattier, Rowlandson, Watts . . . I prefer a tiny sailing-craft, far off, among the cranes – good-bye! – like a handkerchief.

Mythological scenes. High architraves. Roofs. Great open skies. Real clouds mingling in my mind with the wonderful clouds of Giovanni Batista Tiepolo. Nymph and dolphin. Oh Venetian grace! Where is grace today? Where the grace of those verses I receive every day? I live in the realm of lead, of heavy anguish, of the sinister distortion of forms, of the facile, the destroyed. Where is the lightness, my feet, what do I need you for? Give me wings! Quickly! To fly, to fly! What blind hunter shot me! My wings are clipped. My left shoulder pains me. The Rio de la Plata, blue today, at afternoon.

Cuadros, ríos, trenes, aviones . . .

MELANCÓLICAMENTE, tristemente.
¿Por qué? Lo sé. ¿Lo digo? No lo digo . . .

Pintura inglesa: Stubbs, Gainsborough, Reynolds . . .
¡Qué aburrimiento frío!
Un tren – Turner (¡Mejor!) – pasa entre las barandas
de mi balcón de-mira-al-rió.

Chardin. Los instrumentos
musicales. Relojes, sin sonido.
Pipas y casos. Liebre
junto a un perol de cobre. ¡Qué tranquilo,
qué dulce el mundo de estas vivas cosas
inanimadas! Miro.
La calle, el cielo, el humo de las fábricas . . .
el frenazo del auto . . . el mundo mío.
Entre las nubes y el hollín, brillante,
un raro insecto, digo, un autogiro . . .
Liotard, Nattier, Rowlandson, Watts . . . Prefiero
un mínimo velero,
lejano, entre las grúas – ¡adiós! – , como un pañuelo.

Escenas mitológicas.
Plafones altos. Techos.
Grandes cielos abiertos.
Las nubes de verdad pasan cruzándome
con las maravillosas de Juan Bautista Tiépolo.
Ninfa y delfín. ¡Oh gracia veneciana!
¿Dónde la gracia hoy? ¿Dónde la de los versos
que recibo a diario? Vivo el reino
del plomo, de la angustia
pesada, del siniestro
desquicio de las formas,
de lo fácil, deshecho.
¿Dónde la ligereza, los pies para qué os quiero?
¡Dadme alas! ¡De prisa!
¡Volar, volar! ¡Qué ciego
cazador me dio un tiro! Alicortado estoy.
Me duele el hombro izquierdo.
El Río de la Plata, azul hoy, en la tarde.

Antonio Canaletto. Venice again! A gondola. The port is full of foreign ships. A flag, foreign here. Spain. And a foreigner on a balcony, hearing how the pictures in this book pass, how time passes slipping by. Are you dead? Wake up! Still, because I am looking, writing and listening, I am not dead.

Town Cemetery
[written in Glasgow]

BEHIND the open railings, there within the walls, the black earth without trees or grass, with wooden benches where in the afternoons a few old people sit in silence. Around are the houses, and nearby are shops. Streets in which children play and the trains pass beside the tombs. It is a poor suburb.

Like patches on the grey façades, rags, damp with rain, hang in the windows. The inscriptions are already worn away from these gravestones with their two-centuries-old dead, who have no friends to forget them, the secret dead. But when the sun shines on certain days towards June, the old bones must feel something down there.

Not a leaf nor a bird. Nothing but stone. The earth. Is hell like this? Here is pain without oblivion, with noise and misery, wide and hopeless cold. Death's silent sleep has no existence here, for life is always stirring among these graves, like a prostitute pursuing her trade beneath the unmoving night.

Antonio Canaletto.
¡Ay, Venecia otra vez!
Una góndola. El puerto
está lleno de barcos extranjeros.
Una bandera, aquí extranjera. España.
Y un extranjero en un balcón, oyendo
cómo pasan los cuadros de este libro
y cómo pasa, resbalando, el tiempo.
¿Estás muerto? ¡Despierta! Todavía,
puesto que miro, escribo y escucho no estoy muerto.

LUIS CERNUDA

Cementerio de la ciudad

TRAS de la reja abierta entre los muros,
La tierra negra sin árboles ni hierba,
Con bancos de madera donde allá a la tarde
Se sientan silenciosos unos viejos.
En torno están las casas, cerca hay tiendas,
Calles por las que juegan niños, y los trenes
Pasan al lado de las tumbas. Es un barrio pobre.

Tal remiendos de las fachadas grises,
Cuelgan en las ventanas trapos húmedos de lluvia.
Borradas están ya las inscripciones
De las losas con muertos de dos siglos,
Sin amigos que los olviden, muertos
Clandestinos. Mas cuando el sol brilla algunos días hacia junio,
En lo hondo algo deben sentir los huesos viejos.

Ni una hoja ni un pájaro. La piedra nada más. La tierra.
¿Es el infierno así? Hay dolor sin olvido,
Con ruido y miseria, frío largo y sin esperanza.
Aquí no existe el sueño silencioso
De la muerte, que todavía la vida
Se agita entre estas tumbas, como una prostituta
Prosigue su negocio bajo la noche inmóvil.

When the shadows fall from the clouded sky and the smoke of the factories settles as grey dust, voices come from the pub, and then a passing train shakes its long echoes like a wrathful trumpet.

It is not the judgement yet, oh nameless dead. Be calm and sleep; sleep if sleep you can. Perhaps God also is forgetting you.

Spring of Long Ago

NOW in the purple sunset of evening, with the magnolias wet with dew already in flower, to pass through those streets while the moon grows large in the sky will be a waking dream.

The flocks of swallows will make the sky vaster with their lament; the water in a fountain will release the deep voice of the earth in its purity; immediately the sky and the earth will fall silent.

In a corner of some cloister, alone with your head in your hand, like a revenant ghost you will be weeping as you think how beautiful life was and how useless.

The Harp

CAGE of an invisible bird, sister of the water and the air, whose song the slow and smooth hand begs for.

Like the water, imprisoned in the jet, it trembles and rises in a rainbow spurt, which is a lesson to the spirit.

Like the breeze, between the leaves, it talks so vaguely and with such purity of things remembered and forgotten which have become legendary with time.

Cuando la sombra cae desde el cielo nublado
Y el humo de las fábricas se aquieta
En polvo gris, vienen de la taberna voces,
Y luego un tren que pasa
Agita largos ecos como un bronce iracundo.

No es el juicio aun, muertos anónimos.
Sosegáos, dormir; dormir si es que podéis.
Acaso Dios también se olvida de vosotros.

Primavera vieja

AHORA, al poniente morado de la tarde,
En flor ya los magnolios mojados de rocío,
Pasar aquellas calles, mientras crece
La luna por el aire, será soñar despierto.

El cielo con su queja harán más vasto
Bandos de golondrinas; el agua en una fuente
Librará puramente la honda voz de la tierra;
Luego el cielo y la tierra quedarán silenciosos.

En el rincón de algún compás, a solas
Con la frente en la mano, tal fantasma
Que vuelve, llorarías pensando
Cuán bella fue la vida y cuán inútil.

El arpa

JAULA de un ave invisible,
Del agua hermana y del aire,
A cuya voz solicita
Pausada y blanda la mano.

Como el agua prisionera
Del surtidor, tiembla, sube
En una fuga irisada,
Las almas adoctrinando.

Como el aire entre las hojas,
Habla tan vaga, tan pura,
De memorias y de olvidos
Hechos leyenda en el tiempo.

What paradisaical fruits, what heavenly cisterns feed your voice? Tell me, sing, bird in the harp, oh lyre.

The Sirens

NO one has known the language in which the sirens sing, and they are few who perhaps, hearing some song at midnight (not in the sea, but inland, on the waters of a lake), believed they saw a chilly and sad one rise like a phantom and intone to them that same song that Ulysses withstood.

When night ends and there is no longer time for what was hoped for in the hours of a day, they return, who saw them; but the song remained, a philtre, a potion of tears, immersed in their spirit, and they felt within them together with a deep resonance the enchantment in the song of the siren grown old.

After listening so intently and hearing with such passion, they were no longer the same and sought another way of life, possessed by the philtre which fevered their blood. Can one song alone thus change a life? The song had ceased, the sirens fallen silent and their echoes. A man who once hears them remains widowed and desolate for ever.

From the Other Side

THEY went through the same places: the cloister, the beautiful, vast courtyard where the clock went on measuring the time for others, the passage, the little garden and, entering the house, they climbed the stairs that he had trodden. The two were talking of him.

¿Qué frutas del paraíso,
Cuáles aljibes del cielo
Nutren tu voz? Díme, canta,
Pájaro del arpa, oh lira.

Las sirenas

NINGUNO ha conocido la lengua en la que cantan las sirenas
Y poco los que acaso, al oír algún canto a medianoche
(No en el mar, tierra adentro, entre las aguas
De un lago), creyeron ver a una friolenta
Y triste surgir, como fantasma y entonarles
Aquella canción misma que resistiera Ulises.

Cuando la noche acaba y tiempo ya no hay
A cuanto se esperó en las horas de un día,
Vuelven los que las vieron; mas la canción quedaba,
Filtro, poción de lágrimas, embebida en su espíritu,
Y sentían en sí con resonancia honda
El encanto en el canto de la sirena envejecida.

Escuchado tan bien y con pasión tanta oído,
Ya no eran los mismos y otro vivir buscaron,
Posesos por el filtro que enfebreció su sangre.
¿Una sola canción puede cambiar así una vida?
El canto había cesado, las sirenas callado, y sus ecos.
El que una vez las oye viudo y desolado queda para siempre.

Del otro lado

FUERON por los mismos lugares:
El claustro, el vasto patio hermoso
Donde el reloj seguía midiendo a otros el tiempo,
El corredor, el jardinillo
Y, entrados en la casa,
Subieron los peldaños que él pisara.
De él los dos iban hablando.

If he could have heard them, he would not have recognized himself in anything; strange within the place, his actions and his life commented on, still no less strange. The words of others involuntarily weave the myth of an existence when it is now absent or gone.

Though totally strange, perhaps his existence could also be said to be less hard, as if it were now endowed with that fate, easy for many, which he once envied them, despite his rarer good fortune, of enjoying the sunny hours.

Arriving at the door of what had been his room, occupied by another, pausing a moment, silent a moment, they appeared to listen, as if the absent one, although he was now extinguished, without consciousness, in the safe place where in the end friends take rest, might be about to speak to them.

Toast

LEAVE the wine on the table. See how a new winter of profound distances – brushwood and clouds, dryness and cold – appears unfathomable and fantastic. Let us drink again. So that our souls may be of ash and gauze to cut through the infinite thicket of death. So that they may enter into the winter of the thorn, so that the spiders' webs may be torn through, so that the white and quiet smoke may divide. Let our deserted flesh be forgotten, and fall insensibly to dust because we are subject to these grey penances for ever.

Si él pudiera oírles, no se reconociera
En nada: extraño en el paraje,
Sus actos y su vida, comentados,
Aún no menos extraños. Las palabras de otros
El mito involuntarias tejen
De un existir cuando ya ausente o ido.

Si extraño todo, también acaso menos duro
Su existir se diría, como si ya dotado
De aquella suerte fácil para muchos
Que antes les envidió, a pesar de su dicha
Más rara en disfrutar de las horas soleadas.

Llegados a la puerta del que fuera su cuarto,
Ocupado por otro, detenidos un punto,
Silenciosos un punto, escuchar parecían
Como si fuera a hablarles el ausente,
Aunque estuviera ya, apaciguado, sin conciencia,
En el seguro adonde al fin reposan los amigos.

MANUEL ALTOLAGUIRRE

Brindis

DEJA el vino en la mesa. Mira como
un nuevo invierno de honda lejanía
– leñas y nubes, sequedad y frío –
insondable y fantástico aparece.
Bebamos más. Que nuestras almas sean
de cenizas y tul las que separen
la infinita maraña de la muerte.
Que entren en el invierno de la espina,
que las telas de araña se desgarren,
que el humo blanco y quieto se divida.
Nuestra carne desierta sea olvidada
y se pudra insensible porque estemos
en los grises castigos para siempre.

Drink, for the air is blind. Drink, and see the deep and cruel winter expand, held in submission by its clouded lights.

Condemned, I bury myself. My future a winter fathomless, dry, and cold.

In Every Way
To Goethe and his Faust

WHILST one is in the world, one has full life. Whilst one is in the world of death, one has a full longing to live. It is known that life is a flux that uses us like a faithful riverbed to light up its irresistible enterprise: the eternal flame.

Whilst one is in the world of life one is used as replacement or fresh wood for the endless bonfire.

Man is like straw consumed by growing life.

Someone consumes the whole of the species, like a sacred fire. Someone springs to life every time we sink contorted into the unknown dark night.

Whilst we are in the world, we know ourselves to be a body that carries in its heart the onyx of immortality, the living embers from which the thirsty universe is endlessly nourished. We know it.

Bebe, que el aire es ciego. Bebe y mira
en hondo y crudo invierno dilatarse
a sus nubladas luces sometido.

Condenado me entierro. Mi futuro
un invierno insondable, seco y frío.

JUAN GIL-ALBERT

Omnimodo

A Goethe y su Fausto

MIENTRAS se está en el mundo
se tiene plena vida.
Mientras se está en el mundo de la muerte
se tiene plenas ganas de vivir.
Se sabe que la vida es un efluvio
que como un cauce fiel nos utiliza
para alumbrar su empresa irresistible:
la llama eterna.

Mientras se está en el mundo de la vida
se sirve de recambio o leña fresca
a la hoguera sin fin.

El hombre es como paja consumido
por la vida creciente.

Alguien consume el todo de la especie
como un fuego sagrado. Alguien retoña
cada vez que, crispados, nos sumimos
en la desconocida noche oscura.

Mientras se está en el mundo nos sabemos
cuerpo que en las entrañas lleva el ónix
de la inmortalidad, el ascua viva
de la que inagotable se alimenta
el sediento universo. Lo sabemos.

And it is in that knowledge that our human deeds are given life. Only man knows what it is to live, feels death like an inevitable transcendence. He knows that he lives only fleetingly, that like the passing cloud that abounds in blond wheat, so his shadow is the sweet carrier of the secret that, like a god, never reveals itself.

While the earth floats, and the mute abyss of fear does not know what nothingness is, only man sitting at his table with his books open, and the morning-star shining on him through his window, seems to control with his smile the fearful truce.

Refinement of the Country

STONES placed upon stones, and above that primitive wall the odd white olive tree. I do not know why it is that certain things that say hardly anything, that well considered are not things that are worthy of anything, exert on my mind an influence of inextinguishable peace. It might be said that I feel my roots within those purified outlines that are nothing, within that old age of so firm a humility, as if a very familiar incitement were keeping me there. Something like a voice saying to me from within myself: this enchanting faith is poverty.

Y es en ese saber donde se animan
nuestros rasgos humanos. Sólo el hombre
sabe lo que es vivir, siente la muerte
como una inevitable trascendencia.
Sabe que sólo vive lo fugaz
y que como la nube pasajera
que abunda en rubio trigo así su sombra
es portadora dulce del secreto
que nunca, como un dios, se exterioriza.

Mientras la tierra flota y el abismo
mudo de espanto ignora lo que es nada
sólo el hombre sentado ante su mesa,
con sus libros abiertos y el lucero
brillándole a través de su ventana,
parece dominar con su sonrisa
la tregua pavorosa.

Refinamiento del campo

LAS piedras colocadas sobre piedras
y encima de ese muro primitivo
algún olivo blanco.
No sé porqué será que ciertas cosas
que apenas dicen nada,
que bien analizadas no son cosa
digna de nada,
causan sobre mi ánimo un influjo
de inextinguible paz.
Se diría que siento mis raíces
dentro de esos contornos depurados
que no son nada
dentro de esa vejez
de una humildad tan firme
cual si una incitación muy familiar
me retuviera allí.
Algo como una voz que me dijera
de dentro de mí mismo:
esta fe encantadora
es la pobreza.

The Siesta
To Antonio Díaz Zamora

IF anyone should ask me when one day I reach the secret confine: what is the earth? I should say a place where it is cold, where the strong man oppresses and the weak man weeps, and where, like a shadow, injustice goes with open cloak, gathering the rich man's half-penny and the tragedy of those past all hope, a craggy place. But I should also say that at other times in clear, alternating situations when summer arrives and countries seem to give out the somnolence of not knowing why one is tired, while a blue sky pulsates above, hallucinatory, and fruit succeeds fruit on the white tables, and the great windows, set ajar, cool in the half-light, we seek a corner where we can surrender to the sweet heaviness, then indeed I should say that the earth is an irreplaceable good, a happy flowing, an inward prompting. Like an unprecedented temptation, composed both of ardour and renunciation. A pleasant immersion, a slow love-potion.

LIKE the bull, I was born for mourning and grief, like the bull I am marked by a hellish brand on my side, and as a man by a seed in my groin.

La siesta

A Antonio Díaz Zamora

SI alguien me preguntara cuando un día
llegue al confín secreto: ¿Qué es la tierra?
Diría que un lugar en que hace frío.
En el que el fuerte oprime, el débil llora,
y en el que como sombra, la injusticia
va con su capa abierta recogiendo
el óbolo del rico y la tragedia
del desahuciado: un sitio abrupto.
Pero también diría que otras veces,
en claras situaciones alternantes,
cuando llega el estío y los países
parecen dispensar la somnolencia
de un no saber porqué se está cansado,
mientras vibra en lo alto, alucinante,
un cielo azul, los frutos se suceden
sobre las mesas blancas, y entornados
los ventanales, frescos de penumbra,
buscamos un rincón donde rendirnos
al dulce peso, entonces sí, diría
que la tierra es un bien irreemplazable,
un fluido feliz, un toque absorto.
Como una tentación sin precedentes
hecha a la vez de ardor y de renuncia.
Una inmersión gustosa, un filtro lento.

MIGUEL HERNÁNDEZ

COMO el toro he nacido para el luto
y el dolor, como el toro estoy marcado
por un hierro infernal en el costado
y por varón en el ingle con un fruto.

Like the bull, I find all my immeasurable heart too small, and with face in love with a kiss, I fight for your love like the bull.

Like the bull, I grow under punishment, I have my tongue bathed in my heart, and wear a loud west wind on my neck.

Like the bull, I follow and chase you, and you leave my desire on a sword, mocked like the bull, like the bull.

DEATH, all full of holes and of the horns of its own catastrophe, clad in a bull-skin, treads and feeds on a bullfighters' shining meadow.

With sudden blaze he gives volcanic roars and steams with general love for all that is born, and all the time he kills the quiet ranchers.

Now, loving, cruel, and hungry beast, you may pasture on my heart, on tragic grass, if its bitter preoccupation pleases you.

A love for everything tortures me, as it does you, and my heart in a dead man's disguise spills out towards everything.

LOVE ascended between us, like the moon between two palm-trees that have never embraced.

The street sounds of our two bodies surged towards a lullaby, but the hoarse music was tortured. The lips were hard as stone.

Como el toro lo encuentro diminuto
todo mi corazón desmesurado,
y del rostro del beso enamorado,
como el toro a tu amor se lo disputo.

Como el toro me crezco en el castigo,
la lengua en corazón tengo bañada
y llevo al cuello un vendaval sonoro.

Como el toro te sigo y te persigo,
y dejas mi deseo en una espada,
como el toro burlado, como el toro.

LA muerte, toda llena de agujeros
y cuernos de su mismo desenlace,
bajo una piel de toro pisa y pace
un luminoso prado de toreros.

Volcánicos bramidos, humos fieros
de general amor por cuanto nace,
a llamaradas echa mientras hace
morir a los tranquilos ganaderos.

Ya puedes, amorosa fiera hambrienta,
pastar mi corazón, trágica grama,
si te gusta lo amargo de su asunto.

Un amor hacia todo me atormenta
como a ti, y hacia todo se derrama
mi corazón vestido de difunto.

EL amor ascendía entre nosotros
como la luna entre las dos palmeras
que nunca se abrazaron.

El amor íntimo rumor de los dos cuerpos
hacia el arrullo un oleaje trajo,
pero la ronca voz fue atenazada.
Fueron pétreos los labios.

The longing to clasp moved the flesh, it lit up the kindled bones, but when the arms tried to stretch out they died as they met.

Love passed like a moon between us and ate our solitary bodies. And we are two ghosts who seek one another and meet afar off.

IT is to the great majority, leafage of troubled brows and suffering breasts, to those who struggle with God, and are destroyed at a single blow in His deep darkness.

To you, and to you, and to you, round wall of a thirsty sun, hungry fallowlands, to all, oh, yes, to all, these poems go straight that have become flesh and serenade.

Listen to them as to the sea. They bite the hand of whoever passes it over their burning backs

and they throw themselves down headlong like a leaden sea. Alas, this fiercely human angel runs to save you and does not know how!

Shadows Warned Him

EACH kiss I give, like a thud in the void, is flesh of God that I scent, hunger for God, thirst kindled in the dancing bonfire of an embrace.

El ansia de ceñir movió la carne,
esclareció los huesos inflamados,
pero los brazos al querer tenderse
murieron en los brazos.

Pasó el amor, la luna, entre nosotros
y devoró los cuerpos solitarios.
Y somos dos fantasmas que se buscan
y se encuentran lejanos.

BLAS DE OTERO

ES a la inmensa mayoría, fronda
de turbias frentes y sufrientes pechos,
a los que luchan contra Dios, deshechos
de un solo golpe en su tiniebla honda.

A ti, y a ti, y a ti, tapia redonda
de un sol con sed, famélicos barbechos,
a todos, oh sí, a todos van derechos,
estos poemas hechos carne y ronda.

Oídlos cual al mar. Muerden la mano
de quien la pasa por su hirviente lomo.
Restalla al margen su bramar cercano

y se derrumban como un mar de plomo.
¡Ay, ese ángel fieramente humano
corre a salvaros, y no sabe cómo!

Sombras le avisaron

CADA beso que doy, como un zarpazo
en el vacío, es carne olfateada
de Dios, hambre de Dios, sed abrasada
en la trenzada hoguera de un abrazo.

I cling to you, I stretch in your lap like a dreadful shipwrecked man who groans as he swims, I swallow gulps of sea and rosewater, breasts are the waves and their breaking is gentle.

Your eyes and your life break. You weep God's blood through a wound through which is born the death of love.

And it is useless to think that we are united. It is madness to believe that I can see you, God, clearing the mud, in the darkness.

Psalm for Contemporary Man

SAVE man, oh Lord, in this dreadful hour of tragic destiny; he does not know where he is going or whence has come so much pain that it weeps like a broken willow.

Raise him to his feet, oh Lord, nail your dawn to his side, and let him know that he is a divine spoil, wandering dust on the road, but that your light makes him immortal and glorifies him.

See, oh Lord, that so much weeping up there, at high water, giving extreme unction as it drifts, threatens to overlay us with nothingness.

Raise us, Oh Lord, above death. Extend and support our gaze so that it may learn henceforth to see you.

St James's Daughter

HERE, the prow of Europe pregnantly pointed; here the bleeding heel of the barbarous West, asp of living stone that the sea scatters and joins, Panic Iberia, granary of the sun, rustling arable field.

Me pego a ti, me tiendo en tu regazo
como un náufrago atroz que gime y nada,
trago trozos de mar y agua rosada:
senos las olas son, suave el bandazo.

Se te quiebran los ojos y la vida.
Lloras sangre de Dios por una herida
que hace nacer, para el amor, la muerte.

Y es inútil soñar que nos unimos.
Es locura creer que pueda verte,
oh Dios, abriendo, entre la sombra, limos.

Salmo por el hombre de hoy

SALVA al hombre, Señor, en esta hora
horrorosa, de trágico destino;
no sabe adónde va, de dónde vino
tanto dolor, que en sauce roto llora.

Ponlo de pie, Señor, clava tu aurora
en su costado, y sepa que es divino
despojo, polvo errante en el camino:
mas que Tu luz lo inmortaliza y dora.

Mira, Señor, que tanto llanto, arriba,
en pleamar, oleando a la deriva,
amenaza cubrirnos con la Nada.

¡Ponnos, Señor, encima de la muerte!
¡Agiganta, sostén, nuestra mirada
para que aprenda, desde ahora, a verte!

Hija de Yago

AQUÍ, proa de Europa preñadamente en punta;
aquí, talón sangrante del bárbaro Occidente;
áspid en piedra viva, que el mar dispersa y junta;
pánica Iberia, silo del sol, haza crujiente.

The tremor of death, the eternal tremor made flesh, avidly turned the prow into the wind towards another life, whilst the heel, caught in the earth, horribly trod the face of a torpid America.

St James, and close with them, Spain! With their nails they tear faces and with their teeth pray to a God of hell with their lances in the rest, they raise their dead to heaven, they bury their hoofs in the most difficult history recorded by History.

Angels* and archangels unite against man, and hunger seizes its prey, the tombs of their harvest. Three years and a hundred spouts of the blood of nameless Abels . . . (Unbearably terrible is their relish for it.)

Mother and my guide, sad and vast Spain. Here is your son. Anoint us, mother. Make your borders habitable. Your strange peace breathable. For man. Peace. For the air. Mother, peace.

And the Poem Was Made Man

I

I SPEAK of what I have seen; of the table and the glass; of the man and his two deaths; I write at the top of my voice, I use strong words, and even God understands. That is the way to speak.

Come and see my verse in the street. My voice naked beneath the dog-star. Poets that like weighted dolls always bob up again, absurd creatures. Back with that rabble! Let them keep quiet!

I speak as if in prison, taking liberties with the language, making a trumpet of my hands. 'Tachia, what do you say? How? Where? When?'

I write as I spit. On the ground (oh those genteel poets, with a mute, their daddy's sons) and into the sky.

* The word is of the poet's own coining, and suggests winged angels (*ala* + *ángeles*).

Tremor de muerte, eterno tremor encarnecido,
ávidamente orzaba la proa hacia otra vida,
en tanto que el talón, en tierra entrometido,
pisaba, horrible, el rostro de América adormida.

¡Santiago, y cierra, España! Derrostran con las uñas
y con los dientes rezan a un Dios de infierno en ristre,
encielan a sus muertos, entierran las pezuñas
en la más ardua historia que la Historia registre.

Alángeles y arcángeles se juntan contra el hombre.
Y el hambre hace su presa, los túmulos su agosto.
Tres años y cien caños de sangre abel, sin nombre . . .
(Insoportablemente terrible es su arregosto.)

Madre y maestra mía, triste, espaciosa España.
He aquí a tu hijo. Úngenos, madre. Haz
habitable tu ámbito. Respirable tu extraña
paz. Para el hombre. Paz. Para el aire. Madre, paz.

Y el verso so hizo hombre

I

HABLO de lo que he visto: de la tabla
y el vaso; del varón y sus dos muertes;
escribo a gritos, digo cosas fuertes
y se entera hasta dios. Así se habla.

Venid a ver mi verso por la calle.
Mi voz en cueros bajo la canícula.
Poetas tentempié, gente ridícula.
¡Atrás, esa canalla! ¡Que se calle!

Hablo como en la cárcel: descarando
la lengua, con las manos en bocina:
«¡Tachia! ¡qué dices! ¡cómo! ¡dónde! ¡cuándo!»

Escribo como escupo. Contra el suelo
(Oh esos poetas cursis, con sordina,
hijos de sus papás) y contra el cielo.

II

I go about seeking a poem that would stop a man in the middle of the street, a poem on its feet – that is the specification – that could even shake hands and spit.

Poets, pursue that poem, catch hold of it, flourish it, and let it crack (like a whip) on a level with man – plough and sickle and scythe – whoever falls, look out, and whatever anyone says.

We are the dross, the wind's carnival, the absurd embankment, with our buttocks exposed and our shirt waving.

I go about looking for a poem that feels itself in the midst of men. And so rude that it will look insolently at Tachia.

Between Papers and Realities

ALL my life among papers. But transparent papers. In life I plunged, I buried my pen, revived under my name, blas de otero.

Having to write, what I prefer is the torn-up page, relived, not the blank page, oh no, which is wasted like the shadow of a cloud on the hillock.

All my life. Always travelling through villages and countries and cities: they become familiar-sounding under my hand.

All my life among papers. But between papers and realities, it is reality I prefer.

II

Ando buscando un verso que supiese
parar a un hombre en medio de la calle,
un verso en pie – ahí está el detalle –
que hasta diese la mano y escupiese.

Poetas: perseguid al verso ese,
asidlo bien, blandidlo, y que restalle
a ras del hombre – arado, y hoz, y dalle –
caiga quien caiga, ¡ahé!, pese a quien pese.

Somos la escoria, el carnaval del viento,
el terraplén ridículo, y el culo
al aire y la camisa en movimiento.

Ando buscando un verso que se siente
en medio de los hombres. Y tan chulo
que mira a Tachia descaradamente.

Entre papeles y realidades

TODA la vida entre papeles. Pero
papeles transparentes. En la vida
hundí, enterré la pluma, removida
debajo de mi nombre, blas de otero.

De tener que escribir, lo que prefiero
es la página rota, revivida,
no la blanca qué va que va perdida
como sombra de nube en el otero.

Toda la vida. Siempre caminando
aldeas y países y ciudades:
debajo de mi mano están sonando.

Toda la vida entre papeles. Pero
entre papeles y realidades,
es la realidad lo que prefiero.

Ianother

SO ends the first part. How many sheets for what. Five hundred. Five hundred odd to the four winds and – alone – one man against the whole of Art.

Is it ending? It is being born. Conclusive, set aside. Forty ashen Marches, damp, and in the end a fire in which to phoenix yourself.

A man. Alone? With his soluble ego in you, in you and in you. A round mud wall? Oh no. Us. A broad sea. Hear us.

And when the red rock mists over, another, another and another will link its green leafage. It is the wood. It is the sea. Follow us.

Death

LORD: you have all things, a dark zone, and another of light, celestial and clear. But tell me, Lord, those that have died, is it night or day that they come to?

We are your sons, yes, those whom you bore, and who naked in our human flesh offer ourselves like sad fields to the hatred or love of your two claws.

A terrible noise of struggle sounds always obscurely within us, because you are fighting there and do not conquer yourself, leaving us the ground stained with blood.

Yotro

ASÍ termina la primera parte.
Cuántos papeles para qué. Quinientos.
Quinientos tantos a los cuatro vientos
y – solo – un hombre contra todo el Arte.

¿Termina? Nace. Terminante, aparte.
Cuarenta marzos cenicientos,
lientos,
y al fin un fuego donde enfenixarte.

Un hombre. ¿Solo? Con su yo soluble
en ti, en ti, y en ti. ¿Tapia redonda?
Oh no. Nosotros. Ancho mar. Oídnos.

Y cuando el rojo farellón se anuble,
otro, otro y otro entroncarán su fronda
verde. Es el bosque. Y es el mar. Seguidnos.

JOSÉ LUIS HIDALGO

Muerte

SEÑOR: lo tienes todo; una zona sombría
y otra de luz, celeste y clara.
Mas, dime Tú, Señor, ¿los que se han muerto,
es la noche o el día lo que alcanzan?

Somos tus hijos, sí, los que naciste,
los que desnudos en su carne humana
nos ofrecemos como tristes campos
al odio o al amor de tus dos garras.

Un terrible fragor de lucha, siempre
nos suena oscuramente en las entrañas,
porque en ellas Tú luchas sin vencerte,
dejándonos su tierra ensangrentada.

Tell me, tell me, Lord, why did you choose us for your battle? And afterwards, in death, what do we gain, eternal peace or eternal storms?

I Am Ripe

THE sun has warmed me for so many years now that I think I am ripe within, and you will come down, Lord, to pluck me with your huge, naked hands.

I am full and golden for your dream, I will sail through it like a moon that travels shining brilliantly, a star like a fruit on your pure light.

A cloud will come and perhaps blot out my light for the living, and in the rain, your sweet juice, the sap of my being will fall to you like music.

Then I shall be dead and delivered once more to the earth of the tombs. But, immortal blood, your future light will once more burn my red bowels.

For an Aesthete

YOU who smell the flower of fine words may perhaps not understand mine, that have no scent. You who seek the water that runs clear, should not drink my red waters.

You who follow the flight of beauty, have perhaps never thought how death prowls, or how life and death – water and fire – in partnership, are undermining our rock.

Dime, dime, Señor: ¿Por qué a nosotros
nos elegiste para tu batalla?
Y después, con la muerte, ¿qué ganamos,
la eterna paz o la eterna borrasca?

Estoy maduro

ME ha calentado el sol ya tantos años
que pienso que mi entraña está madura
y has de bajar, Señor, para arrancarme
con tus manos inmensas y desnudas.

Pleno y dorado estoy para tu sueño,
por él navegaré como una luna
que irá brillando silenciosamente,
astro frutal sobre tu noche pura.

Una nube vendrá y acaso borre
mi luz para los vivos y, entre lluvia,
zumo dulce de Ti, te irá cayendo
la savia de mi ser, como una música.

Será que estaré muerto y entregado
otra vez a la tierra de las tumbas.
Pero, sangre inmortal, mi roja entraña
de nuevo quemará tu luz futura.

JOSÉ HIERRO

Para un esteta

TÚ, que hueles la flor de la bella palabra,
acaso no comprendas las mías, sin aroma.
Tú que buscas el agua que corre transparente,
no has de beber mis aguas rojas.

Tú, que sigues el vuelo de la belleza, acaso
nunca jamás pensaste cómo la muerte ronda,
ni cómo vida y muerte – agua y fuego –, hermanadas,
van socavando nuestra roca.

Perfection of life, that cuts us down and prepares us for the perfection of faraway death. And the rest, words, words and words; oh, marvellous words!

You who drink wine from your silver cup do not know the road to the spring that bubbles out of the stone. You do not quench your thirst with its pure water, using your two hands as a cup.

You have forgotten everything because you know everything. You think yourself the master, not the younger brother of everything you name. And you forget the roots ('My Work,' you say); you forget that life and death are your work.

You did not come on earth to impose dikes and order on the marvellous disorder of things. You came to name them, to communicate with them without raising barricades to their glory.

Nothing belongs to you. Everything is abundant, a stream. Its waters flow out into your temporal bed. And transformed into a single river, you spill into the sea 'which is death', as the coplas say.

You did not come to impose order, a dike. You came to make the mill-wheel grind with your transitory water. Your end is not in yourself ('My Work,' you say), you forget that life and death are your work.

And that the song you sing today will one day be silenced by the music of other waves.

The Poem without Music

WHEREVER you are, you will know why I say what I am now saying. Only you can understand it, interpret it. My message is quite simple: purity, a little life, a little truth are never forgotten; although life, truth, and purity

Perfección de la vida que nos talla y dispone
para la perfección de la muerte remota.
Y lo demás, palabras, palabras y palabras;
¡ay!, palabras maravillosas.

Tú, que bebes el vino en la copa de plata,
ignoras el camino de la fuente que brota
de la piedra. No sacias tu sed en su agua pura
con tus dos manos como copa.

Lo has olvidado todo porque lo sabes todo.
Te crees dueño, no hermano menor de cuanto nombras.
Y olvidas las raíces («Mi Obra» – dices –); olvidas
que vida y muerta son tu obra.

No has venido a la tierra a poner diques y orden
en el maravilloso desorden de las cosas.
Has venido a nombrarlas, a comulgar con ellas
sin alzar vallas a su gloria.

Nada te pertenece. Todo es afluente, arroyo.
Sus aguas en tu cauce temporal desembocan.
Y hechos un solo río, os vertéis en el mar
«que es el morir», dicen las coplas.

No has venido a poner orden, dique. Has venido
a hacer moler la muela con tu agua transitoria.
Tu fin no está en ti mismo («Mi Obra» – dices –), olvidas
que vida y muerte son tu obra.

Y que el cantar que hoy cantas será apagado un día
por la música de otras olas.

El poema sin música

DONDEQUIERA que estés, sabrás
por qué digo lo que ahora digo.
Sólo tú puedes comprenderlo,
interpretarlo. Mi mensaje
es bien sencillo: la pureza,
un poco de vida, un poco
de verdad, no se olvidan nunca;

disappear from our hands. Listen, these words could only be said for you. Only you will be able to understand them. One day like this clear winter day of 1953, beneath the pines, you will read these verses. Then they will call to life for you a vanished moment. And these verses will have fulfilled their purpose. When the moment that provokes them is buried beneath a cloak of custom, of small happiness, you will read these verses, this obscure chronicle. And since the words give no information, as they only hint at what we two know without stating it, you will throw the book aside, beside the skein of wool with which you will be knitting a coat for the son who is coming to you. And you will laugh at what dreams and words (inexperienced youth, you will say) once raised in your soul. I wrote confusedly, in allusions, so that no one should penetrate the secret. Because if you feel that the moment has died, no one ought to hear the sound in his heart. When you die, the poem will have died. When you forget, the poem

aunque la vida, la verdad
y la pureza se nos vayan
de las manos.

Escucha. Sólo
para ti podrían decirse
estas palabras. Sólo tú
las podrás entender.

Un día,
como este claro del invierno
de mil novecientos cincuenta
y tres, debajo de los pinos,
leerás estos versos. Entonces
vivirán ellos para ti
el momento desvanecido.
Y estos versos habrán cumplido
su misión. Cuando ya el instante
que los provoca esté enterrado
bajo una capa de costumbre,
de pequeña felicidad,
leerás estos versos, esta
crónica oscura. Y pues de nada
informan las palabras, como
sólo apuntan lo que nosotros
dos sabemos, sin expresarlo,
arrojarás el libro a un lado,
junto a la madeja de lana
con la que tejes una prenda
para el hijo que ha de llegarte.
Y reirás de lo que sueños
y palabras (la juventud
inexperta, dirás) alzaron
en tu alma.

Escribí confuso,
aludiendo, para que nadie
desentrañe el secreto. Porque
si tú sientes que ya el instante
ha muerto, nadie debe oír
el rumor en su corazón.

will have died. It is like a note written on an agenda, a key that you must understand so long as the happiness I dreamt of for you has not fallen into your lap. In this way you will understand that this moment must be swept away by oblivion.

If there is an underground poetry in my words, only you know it. It has to end in you because you were its beginning. The others neither can nor should even remotely understand what this means. It is all I had to tell you.

Dublin Hallucination

A MOMENT empty of action may be filled only with nostalgia or with wine. There is one who fills it with live words, with poetry (the action of spectres, wine with remorse).

When life stops, the past or the impossible is written, so that others may experience what the poet once experienced (or did not experience). He cannot give wine or nostalgia to others: only words. If he could give them action . . .

Cuando tú mueras, el poema
habrá muerto. Cuando tú olvides,
el poema habrá muerto. Es como
una nota escrita en la agenda,
una clave que has de entender
mientras no llegue a tu regazo
la felicidad que soñé
para ti.
Así comprenderás
que este instante debía ser
arrastrado por el olvido.

Si hay poesía subterránea
en mis palabras, sólo tú
lo sabes. En ti ha de acabar,
puesto que fuiste tú su origen.

Los demás, no pueden ni deben
entender, aun remotamente,
lo que esto significa.
Es todo
cuanto tenía que decirte.

Alucinación de Dublin

UN instante vacío
de acción puede poblarse solamente
de nostalgia o de vino.
Hay quien lo llena de palabras vivas,
de poesía (acción
de espectros, vino con remordimiento).

Cuando la vida se detiene,
se escribe lo pasado o lo imposible
para que los demás vivan aquello
que ya vivió (o que no vivió) el poeta.
El no puede dar vino,
nostalgia a los demás: sólo palabras.
Si les pudiese dar acción . . .

Poetry is like the wind, or like fire, or like the sea. It makes trees, clothes shake, sets light to blades of corn, dry leaves, rocks on its waves things that are sleeping on the beach. Poetry is like the wind, or like fire, or like the sea: it gives the appearance of life to the motionless, to the paralysed. And the firewood that burns, the shells that the waves bring or carry, the paper which the wind snatches away sparkle with momentary life between two things that do not move.

But those that are living, those filled with action, those palpitating with nostalgia or wine, those . . . happy, fortunate, because they do not need words, as the horse runs, although the wind may not be blowing, and the gull flies, although the sea may be dry, and man weeps, and sings, plans and builds, even without fire.

The Sun Sets

FORGIVE me. It will not occur again. Now I should like to meditate, to recollect myself, to forget: to be a leaf of oblivion and solitude. The wind that scatters the detritus of autumn with sound and colour would have been needed. The wind would have been needed.

I speak with the humility, with the disillusion, with the gratitude of one who lived on the alms of life. With the sadness of one who seeks a poor truth

La poesía es como el viento,
o como el fuego, o como el mar.
Hace vibrar árboles, ropas,
abrasa espigas, hojas secas,
acuna en su oleaje los objetos
que duermen en la playa.
La poesía es como el viento,
o como el fuego, o como el mar:
da apariencia de vida
a lo inmóvil, a lo paralizado.
Y el leño que arde,
las conchas que las olas traen o llevan,
el papel que arrebata el viento,
destellan una vida momentánea
entre dos inmovilidades.

Pero los que están vivos,
los henchidos de acción,
los palpitantes de nostalgia o vino,
esos . . . felices, bienaventurados,
porque no necesitan las palabras,
como el caballo corre, aunque no sople el viento,
y vuela la gaviota, aunque esté seco el mar,
y el hombre llora, y canta,
proyecta y edifica, aun sin el fuego.

Cae el sol

PERDÓNAME. No volverá a ocurrir.
Ahora quisiera
meditar, recogerme, olvidar: ser
hoja de olvido y soledad.
Hubiera sido necesario el viento
que esparce las escamas del otoño
con rumor y color.
Hubiera sido necesario el viento.

Hablo con la humildad,
con la desilusión, la gratitud
de quien vivió de la limosna de la vida.

on which to support himself and rest. The alms were beautiful – beings, dreams, events, love – a free gift, since I deserved nothing.

And truth! And truth! Sought violently in beings, wounding them and wounding me; provoked in words, dug out of the depths of deeds – the smallest, the gigantic, what difference does it make: after all, nobody knows what is small, what is great: a cherry might be called great ('only cherries are falling today', I was told one day, and I know why it was), small may be a mountain, the universe, love –

Something that happened has escaped my memory. Something that I was sorry for, or, perhaps, I gloried in. Something that should have been different. Something that was important, because it belonged to my life: was my life. (Forgive me if I consider my life important: it is all I have, all I had; a long time ago I must have lived it in the dark, without a voice, without hearing, without hands, hanging in the void, without hope.)

But history has been expunged for me (nostalgia) and I have no plans for tomorrow, nor do I even believe that tomorrow exists (hope). I go through the present and I do not live the present (fullness in pain and joy). I am like an

Con la tristeza de quien busca
una pobre verdad en qué apoyarse y descansar.
La limosna fue hermosa – seres, sueños, sucesos, amor –
don gratuito, porque nada merecí.

¡Y la verdad! ¡Y la verdad!
Buscada a golpes, en los seres,
hiriéndolos e hiriéndome;
hurgada en las palabras;
cavada en lo profundo de los hechos
– mínimos, gigantescos, qué más da:
después de todo, nadie sabe
qué es lo pequeño y qué lo enorme;
grande puede llarmarse a una cereza
(«hoy se caen solas las cerezas»,
me dijeron un día, y yo sé por qué fué),
pequeño puede ser un monte,
el universo y el amor – .

Se me ha olvidado algo
que había sucedido.
Algo de lo que yo me arrepentía
o, tal vez, me jactaba.
Algo que debió ser de otra manera.
Algo que era importante
porque pertenecía a mi vida: era mi vida.
(Perdóname si considero importante mi vida:
es todo lo que tengo, lo que tuve;
hace ya mucho tiempo yo la habría vivido
a oscuras, sin lengua, sin oídos, sin manos,
colgado en el vacío,
sin esperanza.)

Pero se me ha borrado
la historia (la nostalgia)
y no tengo proyectos
para mañana, ni siquiera creo
que exista ese mañana (la esperanza).
Ando por el presente
y no vivo el presente
(la plenitud en el dolor y la alegría).

exile who has forgotten even the name of his country, its exact position, the roads that lead there. Forgive me that I should need to make sure of its exact position.

And when I know where I lost it, I wish to offer you my exile, which is worth as much as life to me, which is its meaning. And then, sad but steadfast, forgive me, I shall offer you a life now without a devil or hallucinations.

Night of the Senses

THE nose does not smell, the eye does not see. Nor does the tongue taste, or the brain recognize. This we know, aspiring heart. Only so much.

Who could glance as lightly as you at this hill that peace has just captured: could see the field with love, in snow: could call it fresh light, a dove.

Who could, like you, touch your hand, know that it is a hand, and know your destiny, know your wearied, human bone, and think of the wind that came in the night . . .

Know what that noise is, that nil, that shout that springs from an abyss, from a sadness as disconsolate as the love that rises out of you.

Parezco un desterrado
que ha olvidado haste el nombre de su patria,
su situación precisa, los caminos
que conducen a ella.
Perdóname que necesite
averiguar su sitio exacto.

Y cuando sepa dónde la perdí,
quiero ofrecerte mi destierro, lo que vale
tanto como la vida para mí, que es su sentido.
Y entonces triste, pero firme,
perdóname, te ofreceré una vida
ya sin demonio ni alucinaciones.

CARLOS BOUSOÑO

Noche del sentido

El olfato no huele, ojo no mira.
Ni gusta lengua ni conoce el seso.
Eso sabemos, corazón que aspira.
Tan sólo eso.

Quién pudiera cual tú mirar tan leve
esta colina que una paz ya toma:
mirar el campo con amor, con nieve:
poder llamarlo fresca luz, paloma.

Quién pudiera cual tú tocar tu mano,
saber que es mano y conocer tu sino,
saber tu hueso fatigado, humano,
pensar el viento que en la noche vino . . .

Saber qué es este ruido, esta nonada,
este grito que nace de un abismo,
de una tristeza tan desconsolada
como el amor que surge de ti mismo.

Know the light and know that it is beautiful, look at a body and know its vigour, look at the night that rests in peace, a fountain sealed to my thought . . .

To look at yourself, to look at your tenderness when you contemplate my human grief and ease me in the pure night with the caress of your white hand . . .

Who could speak to you of love, protection of my life, and in a slow litany call you light, call you the friendly wind, a happy field and harmonious sky.

The Door
(Plaza Mayor, Madrid)

WE are still on the street. Afterwards, perhaps, we climb a stone staircase, worn by other stubborn, confident steps away in the dark depths of a remote past. And we knock anxiously, disguising our distress, on this stout door of heavy wood that endures, that has endured, that has impassively and silently watched with the rough pride or insensibility of its material hand after hand thump its very heavy iron knocker. It has allowed itself to be worn away very gently by the hasty brushing of fingers. It has seen the human countenance grow very gradually old, so gradually that no one fixed his distracted attention on the slight detail of an incipient wrinkle. This door is here as it was then. The traffic has grown quiet. The horsemen have disappeared from the square in front. The horses are not here. The badges of the horsemen on the afternoons of bullfights, the proud majesty of some

Saber la luz y conocerla hermosa,
mirar el cuerpo y conocer su brío,
mirar la noche que en la paz reposa,
fuente sellada al pensamiento mío . . .

Mirarte a ti, mirar a tu ternura
cuando contemplas mi dolor humano
y me suavizas en la noche pura
con la caricia de tu blanca mano . . .

Quién pudiera decirte amor, abrigo
de mi vivir, y en lenta letanía
llamarte luz, nombrarte viento amigo,
campo feliz y cielo de armonía.

La puerta

(Plaza Mayor, de Madrid)

SOBRE la calle estamos
aún. Después acaso
subimos una escalera de piedra, gastada
por otros pasos tercos, confiados,
allá en el fondo oscuro de un pasado remoto. Y tocamos,
tocamos con ansiedad, con disimulada agonía
esta gruesa puerta de madera pesada,
que dura, que ha durado, que ha contemplado con impasibilidad y
silencio
desde su abrupta altivez o insensibilidad de materia,
unas manos tras otras golpear en el pesadísimo picaporte de hierro.
Se ha dejado gastar muy levemente
por el roce presuroso de unos dedos. Ha visto
envejecer el rostro humano muy poco a poco,
tan poco a poco que nadie fijaba su atención distraída
en el menudo pormenor de una arruga incipiente.
Esta puerta está aquí como entonces.
Se ha acallado el tráfago.
Los caballeros han desaparecido de la plaza frontera.
Los caballos no están.
Las divisas de los jinetes en la tarde de toros,
la altiva majestad de algun rey contemplando

king gazing on the square, the dark gravity of court-dress, the indifference of a distracted glance, the slow hours announced by a clock, the slow, deliberate clouds that sometimes cover the blue.

I do not know, I could not tell who these others are, this crowded audience looking at something, something that absorbs them for a moment in the summer afternoon.

What a silence has suddenly fallen! What a very strange quiet has fallen on the festival! The square is left deserted. Now all is dispelled like a smoke. A clock strikes the hour slowly. My heart suddenly strikes the hour. And I before this door, before this heavy door, ask. With no intention of offending you, Lord, with no intention of insulting you, I ask. I should like to examine, I want to investigate the fact itself that I am now contemplating, the very small fact of this door which exists, with its iron lock. This implacable door that the woodworm has spared. And here it is secure, and firmly locked, implacable in its dreamlessness, its material that has survived, its matter that is resolved to live. And here is the human sadness of eyes that look but do not know, that investigate and examine slowly each portion of the material, asking themselves how it has been possible, how it has reached us with certainty, how it has reached us undamaged, complete, without fraud, this door that I gaze on and make known, this closed door that I should like to see opening in the course of the night, turning slowly, opening amidst the silence, opening secretly and very delicately, amidst the silence, opening pure.

la plaza, el señorío opaco de un atuendo,
la indiferencia de una mirada distraída,
las lentas horas que un reloj anuncia,
las nubes lentas, pausadas que a ratos cubren el azul . . .
No sé, no sabría decir quiénes son esos otros,
ese público denso que algo mira,
algo que les absorbe en la tarde de estío
un momento.
¡Qué silencio se ha hecho de pronto!
¡Qué quietud tan extraña en la fiesta!
Desierta ha quedado la plaza.
Ya todo como un vapor se ha extinguido.
Un reloj da las horas
despacio. Mi corazón de pronto da las horas.
Y yo delante de esta puerta,
de esta pesada puerta,
pregunto.
Sin intención de ofenderte, Señor, sin pretender injuriarte
pregunto. Yo quisiera inquirir, yo desearía indagar el hecho mismo
que ahora contemplo,
el hecho mínimo de esta puerta que existe,
con su cerradura de hierro.
Esta implacable puerta que la carcoma ha respetado.
Y aquí está, segura, cerradísima,
implacable en su sin soñar,
su materia sobrevivida, su materia resuelta a vivir.
Y he aquí la humana tristeza de unos ojos que miran,
que no saben, que inquieren, que examinan con lentitud cada
porción de materia,
preguntándose cómo ha sido posible,
cómo ha llegado hasta nosotros cierta,
cómo ha llegado sin detrimento, con integridad, sin falacia,
esta puerta que miro y señalo,
esta puerta cerrada que yo quisiera ver entre la noche abrirse,
girar despacio,
abrirse en medio del silencio,
abrirse sigilosa y finísima,
en medio del silencio, abrirse pura.

Come in

HERE are the fields of the beautiful country of the eye, life imprisoned in stone, mountain, valley, moon and that hill which drops lazily down.

Set me free, rippling stream, fountains of the world, unceasing life with its darkness or its imprisoned sweetness, enter dark sunset, pink evening!

Come in, come in, the soul is waking. It wants life with its certain night, its terrible and certain menace; Come in!

Come in, come in, loves, disenchantments, moon, half-light, days, months, years, dark fear and black solitude!

The River of the Hours

(Time in Things)

'Time is in things, in your fingers, in that walnut table.' C.B.

AS if evil really existed, like an object, a tool or a hard and tenacious shape, tangible and embraceable;

like this, but all solidity or dark sensation removed, quietly fluid, but not like water and much more than wind, dark, without being ash exactly, far more transparent than glass, irreversible as a thorn, it advances in the night, this implacable river.

Entrad

HE aquí los campos de la patria hermosa
de la mirada, vida que se apresa
en piedra, en monte, en valle, en luna, en esa
colina que desciende perezosa.

Dadme la libertad, corriente undosa,
fuentes del mundo, vida que no cesa.
Con su tiniebla o su dulzura presa,
¡entrad, poniente oscuro, tarde rosa!

Entrad, entrad, el alma se despierta.
Quiere la vida con su noche cierta,
su amenaza terrible y cierta: ¡entrad!

¡Entrad, entrad, amores, desengaños,
luna, penumbra, días, meses, años,
pavor oscuro y negra soledad!

El río de las horas

(TIEMPO EN LAS COSAS)

«El tiempo está en las cosas, en tus dedos,
en esa mesa de nogal. . .»

C. B.

COMO si la maldad físicamente existiese,
tal un objeto, un útil, o una forma
dura y tenaz,
tocable y abarcable;

así, pero quitada toda solidez
o tenebrosa sensación,
quietamente fluido, pero no como el agua y mucho más que el viento,
oscuro, sin ser exactamente la ceniza,
transparente más allá del cristal,
irreversible como una espina,
avanza
en la noche,
implacable, este río.

It advances silent and imperceptible between my fingers, simulating its shape precisely as if it were fingers; astutely disguised as a cupboard, it advances across the room, advances motionless as a coffin; it pretends to be a coffin, archiepiscopal repose, a motionless constellation, a burning flame and a frenzy . . . Motionless it hurls itself headlong or ends up as an oak bed in the ambiguous silence and the immobility of the white sheet; it pretends to be dying and then dies in it, as if it had died, and goes on its way . . .

Nothing is the Same

THE tear was spoken.

Let us forget the weeping and begin anew, with patience, observing things till we find the minute difference that divides them from their significance of yesterday, and that defines the passage of time and its efficacy.

Why weep for the fallen fruit, for the collapse of that profound desire, compact as a seed-grain?

Avanza silencioso, imperceptible
entre mis dedos, simulando su forma,
precisamente cual si fuesen dedos;
con astucia, disfrazado de armario,
avanza por la habitación,
avanza inmóvil como un ataúd;
finge ser ataúd, arzobispal
reposo, quieta constelación,
ardiente llama y frenesí . . .
Inmóvilmente se arroja o determina
como cama de roble en el silencio ambiguo y la inmovilidad de la
    sábana blanca;
finge ser moribundo y luego muere en él,
como si hubiese muerto, y sigue andando . . .

ÁNGEL GONZÁLEZ

Nada es lo mismo

LA lágrima fue dicha.

Olvidemos
el llanto
y empecemos de nuevo,
con paciencia,
observando a las cosas
hasta hallar la menuda diferencia
que las separa
de su entidad de ayer
y que define
el transcurso del tiempo y su eficacia.

¿A qué llorar por el caído
fruto,
por el fracaso
de ese deseo hondo,
compacto como un grano de simiente?

It is not good to repeat what has been said. After having spoken and shed tears, be silent and smile:

nothing is the same. There will be new words for the new story, and it is essential to find them before it is too late.

Interval

THE story does not stop here. This is just a little pause for us to rest. The tension is so great, the emotion that is released by the plot is so intense that everybody, dancers and actors, acrobats and distinguished public, all of us welcome the conventional truce of the interval, and confirm with pleasure that it was all a deception, while the musicians tune their violins. Up to now we have seen several rapid scenes that preluded death, we know the faces of certain characters, and we know something which even many of them do not know: the motive for the betrayal and the name of the betrayer.

Nothing definitive has yet occurred, but desperation is clearly outlined, and the actors are bent on avoiding the harshness of destiny, putting too much warmth into their exuberant gestures, too much red into their false

No es bueno repetir lo que está dicho.
Después de haber hablado,
de haber vertido lágrimas,
silencio y sonreid:

nada es lo mismo.
Habrá palabras nuevas para la nueva historia
y es preciso encontrarlas antes de que sea tarde.

Entreacto

No acaba aquí la historia.
Esto es sólo
una pequeña pausa para que descansemos.
La tensión es tan grande,
la emoción que desprende la trama es tan
intensa,
que todos,
bailarines y actores, acróbatas
y distinguido público,
agradecemos
la convencional tregua del entreacto,
y comprobamos
alegremente que todo era mentira,
mientras los músicos afinan sus violines.
Hasta ahora hemos visto
varias escenas rápidas que preludiaban muerte,
conocemos el rostro de ciertos personajes
y sabemos
algo que incluso muchos de ellos ignoran:
el móvil
de la traición y el nombre
de quien la hizo.

Nada definitivo ocurrió todavía,
pero
la desesperación está nítidamente
dibujada, y los intérpretes
intentan evitar el rigor del destino
poniendo
demasiado calor en sus exuberantes

smiles, with which – it is plain – they are concealing their cowardice, the terror that governs their movements on the stage. Those ineffectual and tortuous dialogues concerning yesterday, a time past, complete, nevertheless, the broken vista that we have before us, and perhaps therefore explain many things, are the key that in the end justifies everything. Nor let us forget the words of love beside the pool, the changed expression, the violence with which someone said 'No', gazing at the sky, and the surprise that the stern gardener produces when he proclaims: 'It is raining, gentlemen, it is still raining.' But perhaps it is too soon to make conjectures: let us allow the stage machinery to be prepared, let those who are to die recover their breath, and let us think, when the play resumes and feigned grief becomes real in our hearts, that nothing can be done, that the conclusion we fear in advance is near, that without doubt the affair will and, as it must, end, as it is written, as it is inevitable that it should happen.

ademanes, demasiado carmín en sus sonrisas
falsas,
con lo que – es evidente – disimulan
su cobardía, el terror
que dirige
sus movimientos en el escenario.
Aquellos
ineficaces y tortuosos diálogos
refiriéndose a ayer, a un tiempo
ido,
completan, sin embargo,
el panorama roto que tenemos
ante nosotros, y acaso
expliquen luego muchas cosas, sean
la clave que al final lo justifique
todo.
No olvidemos tampoco
las palabras de amor junto al estanque,
el gesto demudado, la violencia
con que alguien dijo, «no», mirando al cielo,
y la sorpresa que produce
el torvo jardinero cuando anuncia:
«Llueve, señores,
llueve
todavía».
Pero tal vez sea pronto para hacer conjeturas:
dejemos
que la tramoya se prepare,
que los que han de morir recuperen su aliento,
y pensemos,
cuando el drama prosiga y el dolor
fingido
se vuelva verdadero en nuestros corazones,
que nada puede hacerse, que está próximo
el final que tememos de antemano,
que la aventura acabará, sin duda,
como debe acabar, como está escrito,
como es inevitable que suceda.

Over What I Love Most

OVER what I love most, over my affairs, your law and your power impose themselves. Years ago, years now distant, someone who is not I, offered you the most secret keys to my own dwelling. You kept them, they remain, and have still not been recovered.

. . . And flames of fear spring up within my heart on these cold nights. When you come stealthily, when you brutally bind me to you.

Other Nights

I HEAR these nights of rain on the window-panes, these nights of wind, and I cannot move.

The guard watches at the door of fear, a child prisoner, let him not cast his chains.

Other nights of heavy rain on the window-panes, other nights of wind, and again I ask questions.

Since it was all in vain, I have changed masters, at the door of sleep, the lady of light.

I Ask

MY father has died. His absence is echoed each day in the empty home.

I ask, and in addition to absence, in addition to losing the roads on this earth, what is death?

ALFONSO COSTAFREDA

Sobre lo que más quiero

SOBRE lo que más quiero, sobre las cosas mías,
tu ley y tu poder se imponen.
Años atrás, años ya en lejanía,
de mi propia morada alguien que yo no soy,
las llaves más secretas te ofrecía.
Tú las guardaste, quedan
sin ser recuperadas todavía.

. . . Y surgen llamas de pavor
dentro del corazón en estas noches
frías:
cuando tú vienes sigilosamente,
cuando tú brutalmente a ti me obligas.

Otras noches

A Maj-Britt

ESTAS noches de lluvia las oigo en los cristales,
estas noches de viento y no puedo moverme.

A la puerta del miedo vigila el celador,
prisionero infantil, no se desencadene.

Otras noches de lluvia profunda en los cristales,
otras noches de viento y vuelvo a interrogar.

Porque todo era inútil he cambiado de dueño,
a la puerta del sueño, dama de claridad.

Yo pregunto

HA muerto mi padre.
Se repite su ausencia cada día
en el hogar vacío.

Yo pregunto,
y además de la ausencia y además
de perder los caminos de esta tierra,
¿qué es la muerte?

I ask you, father, what is death? Have you found the peace you deserved? Have you found shelter in a new house, or are you wandering, and in the cold of the most severe winter, suffering from a total lack of love?

I ask you, father, if the dead are anything or if death is only a huge word that embraces all that does not exist.

The Dust Remains

FROM that thunder, from that terrible blaze that grew before my eyes, there has remained for ever, mingled with the air, a dust of hatred, a most sad ash that fell and fell on the earth, and goes on falling in my memory, in my breast, on the leaves of paper on which I write.

In Memory of Julia Gay

[his mother, killed in an Italian air-raid on Barcelona]

I HAVE spent half my days thinking of your return. You had to return.
In secret we denied your death, as one denies a god.

Yo te pregunto, padre, ¿qué es la muerte?
¿Has hallado la paz que merecías?
¿Encontraste cobijo en nueva casa
o vas errante, y sufres bajo el frío
del invierno más grande, del total
desamor?

Yo te pregunto, padre, si son algo
los muertos, o si la muerte es sólo
una inmensa palabra que comprende
todo lo que no existe.

JOSÉ AGUSTÍN GOYTISOLO

Queda el polvo

De aquel trueno, de aquella
terrible llamarada
que creció ante mis ojos,
para siempre ha quedado,
confundido en el aire,
un polvo de odio, una
tristísima ceniza
que caía y caía
sobre la tierra, y sigue
cayendo en mi memoria,
en mi pecho, en las hojas
del papel en que escribo.

A lo que fue Julia Gay

La mitad de los días se me fue
pensando en tu retorno.
Tenías que volver.

Nosotros, en secreto, negábamos tu muerte
como se niega un dios.

In a corner of the soul hope sounded with your sea name.

On the path, on the mountain, perhaps on street corners, as the blindfold fell at blind man's bluff, somewhere . . . You had to return.

I, beside the same river, awaited you in the water.

But No Further

BUT no further, I must not hurt you, I must not wound you more when with words of love I come near to your borders.

But I must not wound you . . . Sometimes when I come close to you, with so much love, I hide an asp in my depths, a poison, a sharp knife of which I did not know and which wounds love where it hurts most.

Sometimes I place this word, bread, on the table and it sounds like death, and I place the word friendship, and someone raises an armed arm to defend herself (or himself).

I think of love and something wounds your lips, I say *light*, and far away day moans; something that kills the heart is hiding, something that lies within love and may suddenly kill, or wound when I do not wish to.

En un rincón del alma
la esperanza sonaba con tu nombre de mar.

Por el sendero, por el monte, acaso,
por las esquinas, al caer la venda de la gallina ciega,
en algún sitio . . .
Tenías que volver.

Yo, junto al mismo río,
te esperaba en al agua.

JOSÉ ÁNGEL VALENTE

Pero no más allá

PERO no más allá, no debo herirte,
no debo herirte más cuando me acerco
con palabras de amor hasta los bordes.

Pero no debo herirte . . .
A veces cuando
me acerco a ti con tanto amor escondo
en lo profundo un áspid, un veneno,
un agudo cuchillo que ignoraba
y que hiere al amor donde más duele.

A veces pongo esta palabra: pan,
sobre la mesa y suena a muerte, pongo
la palabra amistad y alguien levanta
el brazo armado para defenderse.

Pienso en amor y algo tus labios hiere,
pronuncio luz y lejos gime el día:
algo que mata el corazón oculta,
algo que entre el amor yace y de pronto
puede matar, herir cuando no quiero.

How many times I have said Life, and how often was it perhaps death that was hiding unconsciously, how many times must I have blinded hope, how many times, in the belief that it was light have I cast words, stones, shadows, night and night against the sun that I so love.

Morning

NAKED morning, the purest dimond of day . . . It is better to awake. The merchants' caravans, fish slipping back into the sea. In very large carts, I see the poor in spirit and the poor in bread, the poor in words, and the poor in pomp passing.

But the morning is blue, and the mountains drink its clarity . . .

Who is calling me, who with a new born child's cry of hunger – the sun is high in the sky – has dared to weep? Farewells and returns, alike with handkerchiefs; the savour of salt, bitter as love. No one should weep.

Naked morning. Trees, high birds, winter, autumn . . . Peace.

The peasants bite the seeds that will multiply; they crowd their homes around their very fear. Oh, no one, no one must weep.

Cuántas veces he dicho vida y cuántas
tal vez muerte escondía sin saberlo,
cuántas habré cegado la esperanza,
cuántas, creyendo luz, habré arrojado
palabras, piedras, sombras, noche y noche
hacia el sol que amo tanto.

La mañana

LA mañana desnuda, el diamante
purísimo del día . . .
Vale más despertar.
Las caravanas de los mercaderes,
los pescados resbalando otra vez hacia el mar.
En larguísimos carros, cubiertos de deseos,
veo pasar
a los pobres de espíritu
y a los pobres de pan,
los pobres de palabra
y de solemnidad.

Pero la mañana es azul y las montañas
beben su claridad . . .

¿Quién me llama, quién
desde el vagido del hambre – el sol es alto arriba –
se ha atrevido a llorar?
Las despedidas y los regresos
con iguales pañuelos; sabor de la sal
como el amor amarga.
Nadie debe llorar.

La mañana desnuda: árboles, altos pájaros,
el invierno, el otoño . . . Paz.

Los campesinos muerden las semillas
que han de multiplicar;
alrededor del mismo miedo
aprietan el hogar.
Oh, nadie, nadie debe
llorar.

The light is high and pure for every breathing thing . . .

And beyond its beauty, and beyond, what is there? I give my children names, I build friendship. But my house is of time. What a bright awakening.

The Dying Man

THE dying man saw pass before his eyes mysterious signs, forgotten faces, birds of another country that had been his own (but in a strange sky).

Through the open window there entered the earthy colour of the storm. He heard the rustling of the olive-trees far off, in his remote childhood, wind-tossed now.

The air cracked with sharp reports. He saw the fields, the sun, the south, the years, the distance.

An opaque sky stretched over an alien land. And in a slow voice he assembled what was scattered, he collected gestures and names, the warmth of so many hands and shining days into a single sigh, huge and powerful as life.

La luz es alta y pura para cuanto respira . . .

Y más allá
de su belleza
y más allá ¿qué hay?

Pongo nombre a mis hijos,
edifico amistad.
Mas mi casa es de tiempo.
Qué claro despertar.

El moribundo

EL moribundo vio
pasar ante sus ojos signos
oscuros, rostros olvidados,
aves de otro país que fuera el suyo
(mas en un cielo extraño).

Por la ventana abierta entró el terrizo
color de la tormenta.
Oyó el rumor de los olivos
lejos, en su infancia remota,
azotados ahora.

Quebróse el aire en secos estallidos.
Vio los campos, el sol,
el sur, los años, la distancia.

Opaco cielo se extendía
sobre una tierra ajena.
Y con voz lenta
reunió lo disperso,
sumó gestos y nombres,
calor de tantas manos
y luminosos días
en un solo suspiro,
inmenso, poderoso,
como la vida.

Finally the rain broke the dark siege. Memory expanded . . .

May song bear witness for him who in the struggle achieved transcendence.

No Man's Land

THE city was becoming yellow and weary like a sad ox. The mist was slowly penetrating the long alleys. Wretched little city, remote, municipal, dark. We did not know what to do with life so as not always to return with nothing in our hands, like divers in the void. Unfinished words or impossible signs. Adolescents in the reverential order of families, and the solemn dead. Monday, Sunday, Monday. Rivers of loneliness. Long trains passed with no destination. And the mist came down, lapping the clearings, darkening the cold. Along the long alleys I had strayed from the enclosure of childhood, now bare, cut down, walled up by absence.

Rompió la lluvia al fin el cerco oscuro.
Dilatóse el recuerdo.
Pueda el canto
dar fe del que en la lucha
se había consumado.

Tierra de nadie

LA ciudad se ponía
amarilla y cansada
como un buey triste.
Entraba
la niebla lentamente
por los largos pasillos.
Pequeña ciudad sórdida, perdida,
municipal, oscura.
No sabíamos
a qué carta poner
la vida
para no volver siempre
sin nada entre las manos
como buceadores del vacío.
Palabras incompletas o imposibles
signos.
Adolescentes en el orden
reverencial de las familias.
Y los muertos solemnes.
Lunes,
domingo, lunes.
Ríos
de soledad.
Pasaban largos trenes
sin destino.
Y bajaba la niebla
lamiendo los desmontes
y oscureciendo el frío.
Por los largos pasillos me perdiera
del recinto infantil ahora desnudo,
cercenado, tapiado por la ausencia.

Poet in a Time of Wretchedness

HE spoke hastily. He spoke without hearing or seeing or speaking. He spoke like one in flight, suddenly ambushed among false leafages of affection and unreality.

He spoke without punctuation, without silences, interpolating in each pause gestures of rehearsed joy, in order, perhaps to avoid the furtive question, continuity with his past, his naked truth.

He spoke as if wishing to obliterate his life before an inconvenient witness, for which purpose he surrounded himself with secondary beings, who with their discarded scraps nourished a coarse vanity.

In this way he purchased silence at a high price, a stable position at a high price, the right to live at a high price, at a high price bread.

Noble metal perhaps that the hammer beat for a purer cause . . . A poet in a time of wretchedness, in a time of lies and of faithlessness.

A Witness

THE man who came from far away, that man whom the sisters were looking for, we do not know why, because he was in every way like the rest, except perhaps, we think, merely in the look in his eyes, but otherwise just the same, for we neighbours clustered beside the mud wall hardly knew which of them was going to direct the action; that man, I tell you, spoke a

Poeta en tiempo de miseria

HABLABA de prisa.
Hablaba sin oír ni ver ni hablar.
Hablaba como el que huye,
emboscado de pronto entre falsos follajes
de simpatía e irrealidad.

Hablaba sin puntuación y sin silencios,
intercalando en cada pausa gestos de ensayada alegría
para evitar acaso la furtiva pregunta,
la solidaridad con su pasado,
su desnuda verdad.

Hablaba como queriendo borrar su vida ante un testigo incómodo,
para lo cual se rodeaba de secundarios seres
que de sus desperdicios alimentaban
una grosera vanidad.

Compraba así el silencio a duro precio,
la posición estable a duro precio,
el derecho a la vida a duro precio,
a duro precio el pan.

Metal noble tal vez que el martillo batiera
para causa más pura.
Poeta en tiempo de miseria, en tiempo de mentira
y de infidelidad.

Un testigo

EL hombre que venía de lejos,
aquel a quien las hermanas anduvieran buscando,
no sabemos por qué, ya que era en todo
semejante a los otros,
salvo acaso, pensamos, en la sola mirada,
pero en el resto igual, pues casi no sabíamos
los vecinos apelotonados cerca del tapial
cuál de ellos iba a dirigir el acto;
aquél, digo, dijo unas palabras

few words that at once for us villagers made things clear as if he had just said: 'Lazarus, come out', and then we went back, when it was already evening, wearily chewing it over, saying to one another that this seemed unlike anything we had ever seen before, as if something else had occurred, something different or more secret, and we could only grasp the mere natural form of the event.

Hymn to Youth

WHAT have you come for now, youth, barefaced charm of life? What brings you to the beach? We grown-ups were peaceful and you come to wound us, reviving the most fearful, impossible dreams, you come to stir up our imagination.

Risen from the waves, all splendour, brilliance, pure sensation and undulations of a latent animal, you advance to the shore with small rosy breasts, with malicious buttocks like smiles, oh slim goddess with rounded ankles, and with the suggestiveness (so properly yours) of the belly, giving way to the birth of the thighs: delicate beauty, precise and indefinite, on

que luego para nosotros, la gente del lugar,
simplificaron
como si hubiese dicho sólo:
– «Lázaro, sal fuera» – ,
y nos volvimos luego, ya caída la tarde,
rumiando fatigados la saliva,
diciéndonos que nada parecía parecerse a lo visto,
como si otra cosa hubiera acontecido,
distinta o más secreta, y de ella no alcanzáramos
más que la sola forma natural del suceso.

JAIME GIL DE BIEDMA

Himno a la juventud

Heu! quantum per se candida forma valet!
PROPERCIO II, 29, 30

¿A QUÉ vienes ahora,
juventud,
encanto descarado de la vida?
¿Qué te trae a la playa?
Estábamos tranquilos los mayores
y tú vienes a herirnos, reviviendo
los más temibles sueños imposibles,
tú vienes para hurgarnos las imaginaciones.

De las ondas surgida,
toda brillos, fulgor, sensación pura
y ondulaciones de animal latente,
hacia la orilla avanzas
con sonrosados pechos diminutos,
con nalgas maliciosas lo mismo que sonrisas,
oh diosa esbelta de tobillos gruesos,
y con la insinuación
(tan propiamente tuya)
del vientre dando paso al nacimiento
de los muslos: belleza delicada,

which to rest a brow shedding tears.

And we see you come, the incarnation of a fabulous stretch of land along the river, with bulls, sea shells and dolphins, on the white sand, between sea and sky, still tremulous with water drops, dazzled with the sun and smiling.

You proclaim to us the kingdom of life, the dream of another life more intense and free, without desire inflamed like remorse, without desire for you, sophisticated and infantile little beast in whom the frank beauty of the starlet and the charming shyness of the prince coincide.

But suddenly you crease your brow, which is tormented by a moving and obtuse thought, and turning back to the sea your face on which shines amongst fair, wet locks the melancholy expression of Antinous, oh beautiful indifferent one, you walk along the beach, as if you did not know that men and hounds are following you, gods and angels and archangels, thrones, abominations . . .

After the Death of Jaime Gil de Biedma

IN the garden, reading, the shadow of the house darkens my pages, and the sudden cold of the end of August makes me think of you.

The garden and the nearby house, where the birds are twittering in the creepers, one August evening when it is beginning to grow dark, and the

precisa e indecisa,
donde posar la frente derramando lágrimas.

Y te vemos llegar, figuración
de un fabuloso espacio ribereño
con toros, caracolas y delfines,
sobre la arena blanda, entre la mar y el cielo,
aún trémula de gotas,
deslumbrada de sol y sonriendo.

Nos anuncias el reino de la vida,
el sueño de otra vida, más intensa y más libre,
sin deseo enconado como un remordimiento
– sin deseo de ti, sofisticada
bestezuela infantil, en quien coinciden
la directa belleza de la *starlet*
y la graciosa timidez del príncipe.

Pero de pronto frunces
la frente que atormenta un pensamiento
conmovedor y obtuso,
y volviendo hacia el mar tu rostro donde brilla
entre mojadas mechas rubias
la expresión melancólica de Antínoos,
oh bella indiferente,
por la playa caminas como si no supieses
que te siguen los hombres y los perros,
los dioses y los ángeles
y los arcángeles,
los tronos, las abominaciones . . .

Después de la muerte de Jaime Gil de Biedma

EN el jardín, leyendo,
la sombra de la casa me oscurece las páginas
y el frío repentino de final de agosto
hace que piense en ti.

El jardín y la casa cercana
donde pían los pájaros en las enredaderas,
una tarde de agosto, cuando va a oscurecer

book is still in my hand, were, I remember, your symbol of death. How I hope that in the hell of your last days this vision gave you a little sweetness, though I do not think so.

In peace, at last, with myself, I can now remember you, not in the hours of horror, but here, in the summer of last year, when in a throng – so many months expunged – the happy images return, brought back by your image of death . . . August in the garden in broad daylight.

Beside the swimming-pool glasses of white wine left on the grass, heat under the trees. And voices calling out names.

Ángel, Juan, María Rosa, Marcelino, Joaquina – Joaquina with little breasts like apples. You came back laughing from the telephone, announcing that more people were coming: I remember you running and the muffled impact of your body on the water.

And the nights too of complete freedom in the spacious house, all for ourselves, just like an abandoned convent, and the nostalgia of secret doors, that running through the rooms, searching in the wardrobes, and the amusement of alternate nudity and fancy dress, shaking the dust off smoking-jackets, high boots, breeches, charades, old erotic dreams of our adolescence, a solitary boy.

y se tiene aún el libro en la mano,
eran, me acuerdo, símbolo tuyo de la muerte.
Ojalá en el infierno
de tus últimos días te diera esta visión
un poco de dulzura, aunque no lo creo.

En paz al fin conmigo
puedo ya recordarte
no en las horas horribles, sino aquí
en el verano del año pasado,
cuando agolpadamente
– tantos meses borrados –
regresan las imágenes felices
traídas por tu imagen de la muerte . . .
Agosto en el jardín, a pleno día.

Cerca de la piscina
vasos de vino blanco dejados en la hierba,
calor bajo los árboles. Y voces
que gritan nombres.

Ángel,
Juan, María Rosa, Marcelino, Joaquina
– Joaquina de pechitos de manzana.
Tú volvías riendo del teléfono
anunciando más gente que venía:
te recuerdo correr,
la apagada explosión de tu cuerpo en el agua.

Y las noches también de libertad completa
en la casa espaciosa, toda para nosotros
lo mismo que un convento abandonado,
y la nostalgia de puertas secretas,
aquel correr por las habitaciones,
buscar en los armarios
y divertirse en la alternancia
de desnudo y disfraz, desempolvando
batines, botas altas y calzones,
arbitrarias escenas,
viejos sueños eróticos de nuestra adolescencia,
muchacho solitario.

Do you remember Carmina, fat Carmina climbing the stairs with her backside sticking out, carrying a candelabra in her hand?

It was a happy summer . . . *The last summer of our youth* you said to Juan in Barcelona when, nostalgically, we returned, and you were right. Soon came winter, the hell of month after month of agony, and the last night of pills and alcohol and vomiting on the carpet.

I saved myself by writing after the death of Jaime Gil de Biedma. Of the two it was you who wrote the better. Now I know to what degree the desire for illusion and irony were yours, the Romantic muted note that pulses in my poems that I like best, in *Pandemic* for instance. Sometimes I ask what my poetry will be like without you.

Although perhaps it was I who taught you. Who taught you to take vengeance on my dreams, out of cowardice, corrupting them.

¿Te acuerdas de Carmina,
de la gorda Carmina subiendo la escalera
con el culo en pompa
y llevando en la mano un candelabro?

Fue un verano feliz . . .
El último verano
de nuestra juventud dijiste a Juan
en Barcelona al regresar
nostálgicos,
y tenías razón. Luego vino el invierno,
el infierno de meses
y meses de agonía
y la noche final de pastillas y alcohol
y vomito en la alfombra.

Yo me salvé escribiendo
después de la muerte de Jaime Gil de Biedma.
De los dos, eras tú quien mejor escribía.
Ahora sé hasta qué punto tuyos eran
el deseo de ensueño y la ironía,
la sordina romántica que late en los poemas
míos que yo prefiero, por ejemplo en *Pandémica*.
A veces me pregunto
cómo será sin ti mi poesía.

Aunque acaso fui yo quien te enseñó.
Quien te enseñó a vengarte de mis sueños,
por cobardía, corrompiéndolos.

It is Not Night, It is Time

THE man, amongst the trees, passionately considers his memories. Deep shadows, dark, silent wings, and up above ancient stars surround him. He thinks that his life was light, that men and things were worthy to endure because their love was eternal. Jasmines reach him from the white walls of the garden, and the air leaves them scattered in the field. He looks at the lighthouse pulsing in the darkness, the sea is mute, he senses its constant movement. The light is now spent, and he knows that the things that endure live without him, and that men deny all the eagerness of the heart. Useless like the ancient star, like the far off faint lighthouse , but still alive.

A balcony of the house has lighted up, music reaches him from there. The orchard trembles beneath the shadows, withdraws into sleep. It is not night, it is time that reigns thus over the world. His eyes pierce it, and, brimming with tears, return from the mystery. With slow steps he takes the path to the house, he goes in sombre mood, feeling cold.

We Burned in the Wood

BUT how can one comprehend, without looking, the beauty of the wood, the greatness of the sea?

The wood was behind me, my ears knew it: the rustling of its leaves, its confused bird-song. Sounds that came from a remote place. And on the other

FRANCISCO BRINES

No es la noche, es el tiempo

El hombre, entre los árboles, medita
con pasión sus recuerdos. Le rodean
sombras profundas, silenciosas alas
oscuras, más arriba los viejísimos
astros. Piensa que fue su vida luz,
y que los hombres y las cosas eran
dignos de perdurar, porque era eterno
su amor. Llegan desde las blancas tapias
del jardín los jazmines, y en el campo
los deja el aire derramados. Mira
latir el faro en las tinieblas, muda
la mar está, presiente su constante
movimiento. La luz ya está gastada,
y sabe que las cosas que perduran
viven sin él, y que los hombres niegan
todo el afán del corazón. Inútil
como la estrella vieja, como el faro
lejano y débil, mas aún con vida.

Un balcón de la casa se ha encendido,
llega de allí una música. El huerto
tiembla bajo las sombras, se recoge
en el sueño. Quien reina así en el mundo
no es la noche, es el tiempo. Lo penetran
sus ojos, y arrasados por las lágrimas
regresan del misterio. Se encamina
con paso lento hacia la casa, va
con la mente sombría, siente frío.

Ardimos en el bosque

¿Pero cómo saber, sin la mirada,
la hermosura del bosque, la grandeza del mar?

El bosque estaba tras de mí; lo conocían
mis oídos: el rumor de sus hojas,
la confusión del canto de sus pájaros.

side the sea, striking the brow, without brushing it, covering it with drops. It was my skin that discovered its coolness, my somnolent sense of smell that let its harsh smell into my breast. But how can one know, without looking, the beauty of the wood, the greatness of the sea? For there was nothing more in the region of the breast but an extended shade.

(But what candescent cold burns my lids, what light makes me, what faint prolonged kiss reaches the very centre of the shade?)

Her face was young, her lips smiled, the restrained fire of her body was scorching light. We went into the sea, we broke the sky with our brows and, enveloped in the water, we gazed at the edge of the wood, its vast darkness. As we lay on the shore, I looked at her face: she was gazing at the clouds; the restrained fire of her body was a dark glow. We went into the wood, and at its edge halted our steps; we watched how the sea grew dark, lost, beyond the tree trunks. Her face was sad, and before it should grow old for ever, I pressed my lips to hers.

Sonidos que venían de un remoto lugar.
Y el mar del otro lado, golpeando
la frente, sin rozarla,
cubriéndola de gotas. Era mi piel
quien descubría su frescura,
mi soñoliento olfato quien entraba en el pecho
su duro olor.
¿Pero cómo saber, sin la mirada,
la hermosura del bosque, la grandeza del mar?
Porque no había más, en el lugar del pecho,
que una extendida sombra.

(¿Mas qué frío candente mis párpados abrasa,
qué luz me desvanece, qué prolongado beso
llega hasta el mismo centro de la sombra?)

Joven el rostro era,
sus labios sonreían,
y el retenido fuego de su cuerpo
era quemada luz.
Entramos en el mar, rompíamos
el cielo con la frente,
y envueltos en las aguas contemplamos
las orillas del bosque,
su extensa fosquedad.
Miré, tendidos en la playa, el rostro;
contemplaba las nubes;
y el retenido fuego de su cuerpo
era un sombrío resplandor.
Penetramos el bosque, y en las lindes
detuvimos los pasos;
perdido, tras los troncos, miramos cómo el mar
oscurecía.
Tenía triste el rostro,
y antes que para siempre envejeciera
puse mis labios en los suyos.

St Agatha's Dance

I SEE that you do not want to dance with me, and you are quite right. If till now I have only trodden on you, if till now I have not moved these lame feet to your air! You are always such a dancer, heart. Join the festivity; quickly, or you will be left without a partner! There is no school today. To the river, to wash oneself first, for one must be clean when the hour comes! Now they are here, now men come by rail, shining with hope, from all over the world! Now they begin to testify to their profession of happiness! Who was not looking forward to the fête? Who did not spend the days of the year taking care of his clothes for today? And now it has come. What cloaks, what white stockings, what flannel petticoats, what short breeches! Very gaily, as this girl wears her kerchief, wear your soul very gaily. Oh now I miss those times in which men joined together at their festivals like whey with cheese. Then indeed they gave their lives to the sun, their breath to the air, then indeed they were incarnated on earth. But why remember. I am in the midst of the festivities and now the early February night has almost closed in. And still not dancing, I alone! Come, dance with me for now I can clasp a waist tight, I can suit my steps to your lovely air! Saint Agatha, little Saint Agatha, tell

CLAUDIO RODRÍGUEZ

El baile de Aguedas

VEO que no queréis bailar conmigo
y hacéis muy bien. ¡Si hasta ahora
no hice más que pisaros, si hasta ahora
no moví al aire vuestro estos pies cojos!
Tú siempre tan bailón, corazón mío.
¡Métete en fiesta; pronto,
antes de que te quedes sin pareja!
¡Hoy no hay escuela! Al río
a lavarse primero,
que hay que estar limpio cuando llegue la hora!
¡Ya están ahí, ya vienen
por el raíl con sol de la esperanza
hombres de todo el mundo! ¡Ya se ponen
a dar fe de su empleo de alegría!
¿Quién no esperó la fiesta?
¿Quién los días del año
no los pasó guardando bien la ropa
para el día de hoy? Y ya ha llegado.
Cuánto manteo, cuánta media blanca,
cuánto refajo de lanilla, cuánto
corto calzón. ¡Bien a lo vivo, como
esa moza pone su pañuelo,
poned el alma así, bien a lo vivo!
Ah, echo de menos ahora
aquellos tiempos en los que a sus fiestas
se unía el hombre como el suero al queso.
Entonces sí que daban
su vida al sol, su aliento al aire, entonces
sí que eran encarnados en la tierra.
Para qué recordar. Estoy en medio
de la fiesta y ya casi
cuaja la noche pronta de febrero.
¡Y aún sin bailar: yo solo!
¡Venid, bailad conmigo, que ya puedo
arrimar la cintura bien, que puedo
mover los pasos a vuestro aire hermoso!
¡Aguedas, aguedicas,

them to let me dance with them, that I am a villager, another of the neighbours, tell everyone that I have waited for this day all my life. Listen. Listen to me, you who are now passing beside me and looking up for a moment without noticing, and there descends into your heart the eternal St Agatha's dance of the world, listen to me, you who know that the festival is ending and that you cannot keep it at home like a clean set of tools, and that it is escaping you, and now never . . . you who tread the earth and clasp your partner and dance, dance.

Snow in the Night

I WANT to see what wrinkles this damsel mask hides. What wretched scabs, what fierce plague the innocent face of each flake conceals. Scenes without vanity, they are covered with scaffolding, tremulous stucco, instant mouldings. It is the festival of lies: now it is mid-day in deepest night, and the earth's eternal open wound is healing over, and the houses shine with a new wash of lime that resurfaces their real, poor façades.

The snow, so loved in former times, blinds us, gives no light. Flake by flake,

decidles que me dejen
bailar con ellos, que yo soy del pueblo,
soy un vecino más, decid a todos
que he esperado este día
toda la vida! Oidlo.
Óyeme tú, que ahora
pasas al lado mío y un momento,
sin darte cuenta, miras a lo alto
y a tu corazón baja
el baile eterno de Aguedas del mundo,
óyeme tú, que sabes
que se acaba la fiesta y no la puedes
guardar en casa como un limpio apero,
y se te va, y ya nunca . . .
tú, que pisas la tierra
y aprietas tu pareja, y bailas, bailas.

Nieve en la noche

Yo quiero ver qué arrugas
oculta esta doncella
máscara. Qué ruin tiña,
qué feroz epidemia
cela el rostro inocente
de cada copo. Escenas
sin vanidad, se cubren
con andamiajes, trémulas
escayolas, molduras
de un instante. Es la feria
de la mentira: ahora
es mediodía en plena
noche, y se cicatriza
la eterna herida abierta
de la tierra, y las casas
lucen con la cal nueva
que revoca sus pobres
fachadas verdaderas.

La nieve, tan querida
otro tiempo, nos ciega,

like a thief, it falls, as if afraid. It falls tremulously, it falls hardly wounding itself on our everyday objects. So painless, its self-surrender is cruelty. It falls, it falls, hostile for sure, slow, well-tamed, nicely docile, as if held back by reins, that never dare to take over. It does not sprinkle water, but suffocates, smothers, giving not love, but patience.

It has blotted out the roads. And you say: 'Wake up, dawn is breaking.' (And it is night, deep night.) You say: 'Close the shutters, the sunlight is coming in.' And I do not want to lose again before this snowfall. No, I do not want to lie to you again. I must take off the mask from this hostile face that feigns a return of innocence for me at my door, and the foot that leaves a print.

Good-bye

ANYTHING would be worth as much as my life this evening. Any little thing, if any exists. The sound of your low shoe, without scruples, without return, is martyrdom to me. What victories does the lover seek? Why are these streets so straight? I do not look back, nor can I now lose sight of you. This is the land of punishment: even one's closest friends give false

no da luz. Copo a copo,
como ladrón, recela
al caer. Cae temblando,
cae sin herirse apenas
con nuestras cosas diarias.
Tan sin dolor, su entrega
es crueldad. Cae, cae,
hostil al canto, lenta,
bien domada, bien dócil,
como sujeta a riendas
que nunca se aventuran
a conquistar. No riega
sino sofoca, ahoga
dando no amor, paciencia.

Y borró los caminos.
Y tú dices: «despierta,
que amanece». (Y es noche
muy noche.) Dices: «cierra,
que entra sol». Y no quiero
perder de nuevo ante esta
nevada. No, no quiero
mentirte otra vez. Tengo
que alzarle la careta
a este rostro enemigo
que me finge a mi puerta
la inocencia que vuelve
y el pie que deja huella.

Adiós

CUALQUIER cosa valiera por mi vida
esta tarde. Cualquier cosa pequeña,
si alguna hay. Martirio me es el ruido
sereno, sin escrúpulos, sin vuelta,
de tu zapato bajo. ¿Qué victorias
busca el que ama? ¿Por qué son tan derechas
estas calles? Ni miro atrás ni puedo
perderte ya de vista. Esta es la tierra
del escarmiento: hasta los más amigos

information. My mouth kisses what is dying and accepts it. And the very skin of the lip is that of the wind. Good-bye. This event is useful, normal, so they say. You who can, stay with our things, for I shall go where the night wishes.

Sealed Night

IT was in infancy, on the roadside, in the vanished smoke of the departed ships. My heart would go off with them, on a course bound for eternity. And far beyond, where our gaze did not reach, being too small or too sad, something supported us. God, the grandfather of children, spreading the gulls over the limitless blue, was with us from sunrise to sunset, like the old workmen, and he rested his weary hand on our shoulders. Why think of sad things? My parents returned from work angry, we lived poorly at home, they were difficult and gloomy times. And nevertheless, I saw doves, I am certain, I was fond of my mother's busy hands, I knew life at first hand as something, more or less happy, that had no end. I always had a sailor's soul and great hope. From that child's point of view everything was clear and fresh as morning. I mean everything was false, pure deceit. You were not there, nor here, on the road's edge, nor in the vanished smoke of the ships. A boy was weeping before the cliff, beneath the hard standard of the night without God.

dan mala información. Mi boca besa
lo que muere, y lo acepta. Y la piel misma
del labio es la del viento. Adiós. Es útil,
normal este suceso, dicen. Queda
tú con las cosas nuestras, tú, que puedes,
que yo me iré donde la noche quiera.

CARLOS SAHAGÚN

Noche cerrada

FUE en la infancia, a la vera de los caminos, en el humo perdido
de los barcos que se alejaron.
Con ellos se marchaba mi corazón, con rumbo cierto
de eternidad. Y más allá, donde nuestra mirada no llegaba,
por pequeña o por triste, algo nos sostenía.
Dios, el abuelo de los niños, repartiendo
las gaviotas por el azul sin límites, estaba con nosotros
de sol a sol, como los viejos labradores,
y dejaba su mano cansada en nuestros hombros.
¿Por qué pensar en cosas tristes? Mis padres
volvían del trabajo con ira, se vivía mal en casa,
eran tiempos difíciles y oscuros.
Y, sin embargo, vi palomas, estoy cierto, tuve apego a las manos
atareadas de mi madre,
directamente conocí la vida
como algo, más o menos alegre, que no tenía final.
Yo siempre tuve un alma navegante
y una gran esperanza.
Desde el punto de vista de aquel niño
todo era claro y mañanero, quiero decir, todo era
mentira, puro engaño. Tú no estabas allí,
ni aquí, a la vera de los caminos, ni en el humo perdido
de los barcos. Un muchacho lloraba
frente al acantilado, bajo la dura enseña
de la noche sin Dios.

Knives in April

I HATE adolescents. It is easy to pity them. There is a carnation that freezes in their teeth, and how they look at us as they weep!

But I go much further. In their glance I make out a garden. The light spits on to the tiles the broken harp of instinct.

I am violently fenced in by this passion for solitude that cuts down young bodies and then burns them in a single bunch.

Have I to be, then, like these? (Life stops here.) A willow flames in the silence. It was worthwhile being happy.

Homage to Johann Sebastian Bach

IN the wood they are hunting Jesus and the elks with dark and sweet diamonds with lilies in their mouths silence the steps of autumn in the villages. Heaven like a name pronounced in a low voice Jesus Jesus the rifles sounding in Spring the belly of a naked girl on the sea petal and cloud the belly of a girl torn by mastiffs oh my God.

Lovers Wear a Rose on Their Breasts

LOVERS wear a rose on their breasts and usually kiss one another amidst the sound of sunflowers and propellers.

There are rose petals left by the wind in the corridors of clinics.

PEDRO GIMFERRER

Cuchillos en Abril

ODIO a los adolescentes.
Es fácil tenerles piedad.
Hay un clavel que se hiela en sus dientes
y cómo nos miran al llorar.

Pero yo voy mucho más lejos.
En su mirada un jardín distingo.
La luz escupe en los azulejos
el arpa rota del instinto.

Violentamente me acorrala
esta pasión de soledad
que los cuerpos jóvenes tala
y quema luego en un solo haz.

¿Habré de ser, pues, como éstos?
(La vida se detiene aquí)
Llamea un sauce en el silencio.
Valía la pena ser feliz.

Homenaje a Juan Sebastián Bach

EN el bosque dan caza a Jesús y a los alces
Con oscuros y dulces diamantes con lirios en la boca
El silencio los pasos del otoño en las aldeas
El cielo como un nombre que se pronuncia en voz baja
Jesús Jesús los rifles sonando en primavera
El vientre de una niña desnuda sobre el mar pétalo y nube
El vientre de una niña rasgado por mastines
oh Dios mío

Llevan una rosa en el pecho los enamorados

LLEVAN una rosa en el pecho los enamorados y suelen besarse entre un rumor de girasoles y hélices.

Hay pétalos de rosa abandonados por el viento en los pasillos de las clínicas.

The scholars sink their little pens between the nail and flesh and press gently until the blood begins to bubble up. Some appear dead under the last desks.

I shall be in love until death, and my hands will shake as they take your hands, and my voice will shake when you approach, and I shall look into your eyes as if I were weeping.

The waiters know these customers, who ask for a coin for the telephone at dawn and make futile calls, then hang up, ask for a gin, manage to smile, are thinking of their lives. At these hours night is a blue bird.

It is beginning to get cold, and the fair girls look at themselves trembling in the shop windows. A spouting of stars silently goes out.

Lights in a gleaming glass imitate the gloomy splendour of spring, its sombre blue blazes of fire, its sulphur and quicklime flowers, the cry of the ducks calling from the country of the dead.

Someone Stops in Front of the Flowers in a Cemetery

SHADY, twisting, paved, the road dropped through the valley, when on our way we were confronted by the violence of whitewash on a broad ancient wall with its mosses and nettles. And then, through the rusty railings, the splendour of flowers very blue on the dark grass. Precisely there, on that field

Los escolares hunden sus plumillas entre uña y carne y oprimen suavemente hasta que la sangre empieza a brotar. Algunos aparecen muertos bajo los últimos pupitres.

Estaré enamorado hasta la muerte y temblarán mis manos al coger tus manos y temblará mi voz cuando te acerques y te miraré a los ojos como si llorara.

Los camareros conocen a estos clientes que piden una ficha en la madrugada y hacen llamadas inútiles, cuelgan luego, piden una ginebra, procuran sonreír, están pensando en su vida. A estas horas la noche es un pájaro azul.

Empieza a hacer frío y las muchachas rubias se miran temblando en los escaparates. Un chorrear de estrellas silencioso se extingue.

Luces en un cristal espejeante copian el esplendor lóbrego de la primavera, sus sombrías llamaradas azules, sus flores de azufre y de cal viva, el grito de los ánades llamando desde el país de los muertos.

ANTONIO COLINAS

Alguien se detiene ante las flores de un cementerio

UMBRÍO, tortuoso, enlosado,
descendía el camino por el valle,
cuando nos salió al paso la violencia
de la cal en el ancho muro antiguo
con sus musgos y ortigas.
Y luego, entre las verjas oxidadas,
un resplandor de flores muy azules
en el césped oscuro.
Precisamente allí, en aquel prado

in which the light had imprisoned Death, you halted. But I did not make funereal deductions. You were simply drawn by what gives you vitality: the deep earth.

Head of the Goddess in my Hands

654 B.C.

DARK clay shapes your face that careful time preserves. To be man or to be god is the same today: only a little moistened earth which an ancient sun hardened, mortal beauty, a very mature light. But the time this fragile head has endured, which has contemplated for so many centuries the death of others, which lies in my hands, has become fleetingly eternal. On her brown face night falls, much sunset light falls on her two lips, and one day more of our life falls. It is a higher mystery, this of seeing how her body accumulates centuries while ours loses youth. The mystery of two clays that have been born from a single pit beneath a single fire. But only to one of them did Art give the virtue of being divine and, so, of never dying.

en que la luz tenía acorralada
a la Muerte,
detuviste tus pasos.
Mas no hice funestas deducciones.
Simplemente te atrajo
lo que te da la savia:
la honda tierra.

Cabeza de la diosa entre mis manos

654 a.C.

BARRO oscuro conforma tu figura
que mantiene el tiempo detenido.
Ser hombre o ser dios hoy es lo mismo:
sólo un poco de tierra humedecida
a la que un sol antiguo dio dureza,
hermosura mortal, luz muy madura.
Pero lo que ha durado esta cabeza
frágil que ha contemplado tantos siglos
la muerte de los otros, que en mis manos
descansa, se hace fugazmente eterno.
En su rostro moreno cae la noche,
cae mucha luz de ocaso en sus dos labios
y cae un día más de nuestra vida.
Misterio superior este de ver
cómo su cuerpo acumula siglos
mientras el nuestro pierde juventud.
Misterio de dos barros que han brotado
de un mismo pozo y bajo un mismo fuego.
Mas sólo a uno de ellos concedió
el Arte la virtud de ser divino
y, en consecuencia, no morir jamás.

November in England

I KNOW that now it is November over there in England, the nights are blue and copious with stars, a strange thing, for already the snow is falling on the mountains of Scotland, fire is voraciously consuming thorn branches, bare branches let through the sun, which the curtains filter sadly, and it leaves its old gold on the books of your libraries, one may still make out at the end of the frosty meadow, the lights of the greenhouses, this is the purest season, neither music, nor art, nor kisses, corrupt it, there is only something like an immense expectation without birds, a silence of very cold moons and of suns, that nevertheless tell the heart that is dreaming of other lands: listen, here the world ends, a sublime apotheosis of veneration and roses, do not go down to the sea which, dark and wet, harbours all death.

Giacomo Casanova Accepts the Office of Librarian Offered Him in Bohemia, by Count Waldstein

HEAR me, sir, my limbs are weary. My few friends are dying in the French Revolution. Look at me, I have travelled the countries of the world, the prisons of the world, the beds, the gardens, the seas, the convents, and I have seen that they do not accept my good will. I was an abbot within the walls of Rome, and it was fine to be a soldier in the burning nights of Corfu. Sometimes I have dreamed a little of the violin, and you know, sir, how Venice vibrates with music, and the islands and cupulas burn. Listen to me, sir, from Madrid to Moscow I have travelled in vain, the wolves of the Holy

Noviembre en Inglaterra

Happy is England
Yet do I sometimes feel a languishment
For skies Italian.

JOHN KEATS

YO sé que ahora es noviembre allá en Inglaterra,
son azules las noches y copiosas en astros,
cosa extraña pues ya la nieve va cayendo
en los montes de Escocia, voraz consume el fuego
las ramas del espino, cuelan desnudas ramas
el sol que filtran tristes las cortinas y deja
su oro viejo en los libros de vuestras bibliotecas,
aún se puede apreciar, en el fondo del prado
con escarcha, las luces de los invernaderos,
es ésta la estación más pura, ni la música,
ni el arte, ni los besos, la corrompen, sólo hay
como una expectativa inmensa sin los pájaros,
un silencio de lunas y de soles muy fríos
que sin embargo dicen al corazón que sueña
otras tierras: escúchate, aquí termina el mundo,
sublime apoteosis del respeto y las rosas,
no bajes hacia el mar que, tenebroso y húmedo,
alberga toda muerte

Giacomo Casanova acepta el cargo de bibliotecario que le ofrece, en Bohemia, el conde de Waldstein

ESCUCHADME, Señor, tengo los miembros tristes.
Con la Revolución Francesa van muriendo
mis escasos amigos. Miradme, he recorrido
los países del mundo, las cárceles del mundo,
los lechos, los jardines, los mares, los conventos,
y he visto que no aceptan mi buena voluntad.
Fui abad entre los muros de Roma y era hermoso
        ser soldado en las noches ardientes de Corfú.
A veces he soñado un poco el violín
y vos sabéis, Señor, cómo trema Venecia
con la música y arden las islas y las cúpulas.
Escuchadme, Señor, de Madrid a Moscú
he viajado en vano, me persiguen los lobos

Office pursue me, I drag a storm of tongues behind me, of poisonous tongues. And I only want to save my lucidity, to smile at the light of each new day, to show my steadfast horror of all that is dying. Sir, I stay here in your library, I translate Homer and write about my former days, I dream of the blue seraglios of Istanbul.

The City is Dead

The city is dead, is dead (S. Quasimodo)

DID you not find it enough to die once in the dead city, that you come back again within its cancerous walls, lit at times with putrefying greens? Are there still embers of dreams that burned in places, and on lips that you believed beautiful? Do you refuse to accept that here love was imagining birds, disinterring ruins?

It is raining, raining, and the music is black in these streets full of the walking crucified, of the dying at work, of unburied corpses that applaud and smile. Perhaps there may still remain in this space of broken dreams, of crushed dreams, another madman who is still dreaming and repeating: 'You have the light near you, the light is near.'

But now, as in past times, only a cold and empty silence answers you, although festal and blind turmoil may continue of the dead perfectly beautiful, of the dead perfectly wise, of the dead perfectly dead. All that can be heard is the sour and metallic fall of another night, like a huge, thick, black steel plate.

del Santo Oficio, llevo un huracán de lenguas
detrás de mí, de lenguas venenosas.
Y yo sólo deseo salvar mi claridad,
sonreír a la luz de cada nuevo día,
mostrar mi firme horror a todo lo que muere.
Señor, aquí me quedo en vuestra biblioteca,
traduzco a Homero, escribo de mis días de entonces,
sueño con los serrallos azules de Estambul.

La ciudad está muerta

La città è morta, è morta
S. QUASIMODO

¿NO tuviste bastante con morir una vez
en la muerta ciudad, que vuelves otra vez
entre sus cancerosos muros iluminados
a veces por verdores putrefactos?
¿Quedan aún las brasas de los sueños
ardidos en lugares y en labios que creíste hermosos?
¿Te niegas a aceptar que aquí estuvo el amor
imaginando pájaros, desenterrando ruinas?

Llueve, llueve, y la música es negra en estas calles
abarrotadas de crucificados que andan,
de agonizantes que laboran,
de insepultos cadáveres que aplauden y sonríen.
Acaso quede aún en este espacio
de sueños destrozados, de sueños machacados,
otro loco que aún sueñe y vaya repitiendo:
«Tenéis cerca la luz; está cerca la luz».

Pero, ya como en tiempos, sólo un frío y vacío
silencio os responde,
aunque siga festivo y ciego el ajetreo
de los muertos perfectamente pulcros,
de los muertos perfectamente sabios,
de los muertos perfectamente muertos.
Sólo se oye la agria y metálica caída de otra noche
como una inmensa, gruesa, negra chapa de acero.

Ineptitude of Orpheus and Praise of Alcestes

VIRTUE never suited the merchant who carries his misfortunes to the mirror, admires the purity of those secondary beings and classifies their diversity. Let the bliss cry out of the matron who loved in silence, was not afraid to die and, resurrected by Apollo, returned in mortal flesh to the old marriage bed: she gave up her innocence like a clever stroke of business. Not so the poet who loves his verses (Nature teaches us to fear death)* although he may gain possession retrospectively of his beloved through song; by not looking back however much he builds with his art, he only enjoys an outline of the dead woman.

Departure for Cythera

You will be as gods (Genesis III, 4)

TODAY when the sad ship is about to depart, with its spectacular monotone, I wish to stay on shore, see the colours converge in an ashen sea and, while the wind beats gently on the rigging and the manes of the gilded gryphons, hear far off in the darkness the oars, the riding lights, and be alone. Very often I have seen her leave from far off, her cannon and brocades and musical calls: the brilliant clamour of a ritual of secret graces and a learning as old as the world. I saw her take the open sea, light under a sweet cargo of dreams, dreams which do not debase and which power ransoms from the labyrinth of fantasy, and the painted faces of the masks, a happy and learned

* in Italian.

GUILLERMO CARNERO

Ineptitud de Orfeo y alabanza de Alceste

NUNCA cupo virtud al traficante
que traslada sus males al espejo
admira la pureza de esos seres segundos
y su diversidad taxonomiza.
Clame la beatitud de la matrona
que amó en silencio, no temió morir
y por Apolo resurrecta
volvió en carne mortal al viejo tálamo:
su inocencia rindió como un hábil negocio.
No así el poeta que sus versos ama
(Natura insegna a noi temer la morte)
aunque consiga en lo retrospectivo
posesión de su amada por el canto;
al no mirar atrás, cuanto en arte edifica
goza sólo dibujo de la muerta.

El embarco para Cyterea

Sicut dii eritis
– *Gen.*, III, 4 –

HOY que la triste nave está al partir,
con su espectacular monotonía,
quiero quedarme en la ribera, ver
confluir los colores en un mar de ceniza
y mientras tenuemente tañe el viento
las jarcias y las crines de los grifos dorados
oír lejanos en la oscuridad
los remos, los fanales, y estar solo.
Muchas veces la vi partir de lejos,
sus bronces y brocados y sus juegos de música:
el brillante clamor
de un ritual de gracias escondidas
y una sabiduría tan vieja como el mundo.
La vi tomar el largo
ligera bajo un dulce cargamento de sueños,
sueños que no envilecen y que el poder rescata
del laberinto de la fantasía,

luxury, not attributes of fear and oblivion. Also I have sometimes made the voyage with the intention of believing and being fortunate, and repeating to the stroke of the oars: 'Here ends the kingdom of death.' And I feel no resentment but an awkward desire that is not fulfilled by the acrobatics of the will, and a certain not very deep gratitude.

Tragedy of the Mad Horses

WITHIN my ears like machine-gun fire I hear horses at full gallop, stallions lost in the night. They raise dust and wind as their scorching hoofs strike the ground, as their tangled manes wound the air, as their fiery breath spreads out like sheets. Far off, very far off, not even death holds them back, they are desperate with fury plunging into the sea and crossing it like dolphins wounded with sadness. Stained with foam, they run with the sweat of

y las pintadas muecas de las máscaras
un lujo alegre y sabio,
no atributos del miedo y el olvido.
También alguna vez hice el viaje
intentando creer y ser dichoso
y repitiendo al golpe de los remos:
aquí termina el reino de la muerte.
Y no guardo rencor
sino un deseo inhábil que no colman
las acrobacias de la voluntad,
y cierta ingratitud no muy profunda.

JAIME SILES

Tragedia de los caballos locos

A Marcos Granell

DENTRO de los oídos,
ametralladamente,
escucho los tendidos galopes de caballos,
de almifores perdidos
en la noche.
Levantan polvo y viento,
al golpear el suelo
sus patas encendidas,
al herir el aire
sus crines despeinadas,
al tender como sábanas
sus alientos de fuego.
Lejanos, muy lejanos,
ni la muerte los cubre,
desesperan de furia
hundiéndose en el mar
y atravesándolo como delfines vulnerados de tristeza.
Van manchados de espuma
con sudores de sal enamorada,

rutting salt, covering distances, and reach the other shore, and immediately leave it again, when they have rolled on the ground, whinnying after ridding themselves of the foam, and covering themselves with sand. Suddenly they stop. Another passion surrounds them. Their step is gentle and nevertheless unquiet, their eyes glistening, foreseeing ambushes. Liquid sweat that covered them has suddenly turned to icy frost. As they pull up, their hoofs beat out an arpeggio on ground which disintegrates beneath them. Now, as always, they have met the mares who indeed are expecting them, and are gazing at them. Now the only fury and flame that exists is love, the delight of the blood, the rutting slaver, they snort as they mount their females. And then it is the quaking of fifes, the sound of bagpipes, the musical din that announces the coming of death. All fall silent. Teeth strike together and remain clenched.

It grows dark. Death swaddles them, they give themselves up and suddenly as though in an empty shell, in my ears I hear a collapse of furious hooves, a cloud of dust raised by manes, a cataclysm of bones that the night undertakes to send to oblivion.

ganando las distancias
y llegan a otra playa
y al punto ya la dejan,
luego de revolcarse, gimientes,
después de desnudarse las espumas
y vestirse con arena.
De pronto se detienen. Otra pasión los cerca.
El paso es sosegado
y no obstante inquieto,
los ojos coruscantes, previniendo emboscadas.
El líquido sudor que los cubría
se ha vuelto de repente escarcha gélida.
Arpegian sus cascos al frenar
el suelo que a su pie se desintegra.
Ahora han encontrado de siempre, sí, esperándoles las yeguas que los miran.
Ya no existe más furia, ni llama que el amor, la dicha de la sangre,
las burbujas amorosas que resoplan
al tiempo que montan a las hembras.
Y es entonces el trepidar de pífanos, el ruido de cornamusas, el musical estrépito
que anuncia de la muerte la llegada.
Todos callan. Los dientes se golpean quedándose
soldados.

Oscurece. La muerte los empaña, ellos se entregan y súbito
como en una caracola fenecida, en los oídos escucho
un desplomarse patas rabiosas, una nube de polvo levantado por crines,
un cataclismo de huesos que la noche se encarga de enviar hacia el olvido.

Hypnos and Thanatos

For Mario Hernández

Thanatos Through me silence breaks with sound, pulsings and skulls and human brows, bodies are transformed into marbled water, into a glazed permanence and a passing.

Hypnos You and silence are only a name, a word concealing nothing behind it, for what, whose, where has nothing been, and nothing has been of what, whose and where.

Thanatos And you have simply been the echo of a young voice one day, a dull desire that challenges the very being, a drugged yearning for what was not and might have existed once, perhaps in the memory.

Hypnos The darts rebound upon me from the rock, fly swiftly against me to become eternal. I feel your wings grow from you towards me, in everlasting movement and in time.

But also there exists another presence, another slow and secret whispering. If I was yours and you take me against my will, I slowly draw you towards me and against your will.

Sub Nocte

AND you leave me here facing Language, in just one same vastness of extensive blackness that blots me out, of a tattooed night that annuls me, for in you nothing sounds, piano-keys, touch, tattooing. Everything: correspondences extinguished far off, invisible script, zero of the nocturnal beginning and of the end.

Hypnos y Thanatos

Para Mario Hernández

Thanatos. – Por mí el silencio con sonido rompe
los latidos, los cráneos, las frentes
y en un agua de mármol los cuerpos se transforman
en permanencia vítrea y en tránsito.

Hypnos. – Tú y el silencio sólo sois un nombre,
una palabra que nada atrás encierra,
pues qué, de quién, en dónde ha sido nada
y nada ha sido de qué, de quién, en dónde.

Thanatos. – Y tú, sin más, eco de joven voz un día has sido,
torpe deseo que al mismo ser se enfrenta,
ebriedad que ansía lo que no fue y pudo
existir una vez, quizá, en la memoria.

Hypnos. – De la roca reviértenme los dardos
y contra mí, veloces, se eternizan.
Siento crecer de ti hasta mí las alas
que en movimiento duran
y en el tiempo.

Pero también existe otra presencia,
otro susurro lento y sigiloso.
Si fui de ti y contra mí me llevas,
contra ti y hacia mí, despacio yo
te traigo.

Sub nocte

Y ME dejas aquí, frente al Lenguaje,
en una sola y misma vastedad
de tinta extensa que me borra,
de tatuada noche que me anula,
porque nada en ti suena,
teclado, tacto, tatuaje. Todo:
correspondencias lejos apagadas,
letra invisible, cero
del principio nocturno
y del final.

Wandering Cleric

WALKING through the snow of Gothic scents, on the long roads of wide Europe, amidst cathedrals and towns of lengthened shadow, goes an ill-clothed man with a profound gaze. He has read Ovid, the Latins and bestiaries, perhaps drunk every wine on earth. Fornicated and loved in taverns and brothels with women without a history and with legendary ladies. He knows that life is only a strange thread of unconnected things, pleasures and pains, drunkenness and misery, books and gold. There is no end, or no one knows the end. Walking through the snow, happy and drunk, perhaps thrown out of some noble house, he mutters Latin verses, on the road to nowhere, the old Archpoet, a cleric of Cologne. *Man sees the face, but the heart lies open to Jove.* There is no end, or no one knows the end.

LUIS ANTONIO DE VILLENA

Clérigo vagante

ANDANDO por la nieve de góticos aromas,
por los largos caminos de la ancha Europa,
entre catedrales y villas de sombra alargada,
va un hombre, mal vestido, de mirada profunda.
Ha leído a Ovidio, latines y bestiarios,
bebido tal vez de todos los vinos de la tierra.
Fornicado y amado en tabernas y burdeles,
con mujeres sin historia y damas de leyenda.
Sabe que la vida es sólo un extraño
hilván de cosas inconexas, placeres y dolores,
ebriedad y miseria, libros y oro.
No hay final o el final nadie lo sabe.
Andando entre la nieve, feliz y beodo,
acaso echado fuera de alguna casa noble,
masca versos latinos, camino de ninguna parte,
el viejo Archipoeta, clérigo en Colonia.
Homo videt faciem, sed cor patet Iovi.
No hay final o el final nadie lo sabe.

De *El viaje a Bizancio*

INDEX OF FIRST LINES